WHEN THE

KISSING

HAD TO STOP

Also by John Leonard

Smoke and Mirrors: Violence, Television, and Other American Cultures

The Last Innocent White Man in America

Private Lives in the Imperial City

This Pen for Hire

Black Conceit

Crybaby of the Western World

Wyke Regis

The Naked Martini

WHEN THE KISSING HAD TO STOP

Cult Studs, Khmer Newts,
Langley Spooks, Techno-Geeks,
Video Drones, Author Gods,
Serial Killers, Vampire Media,
Alien Sperm-Suckers,
Satanic Therapists, and Those
of Us Who Hold a Left-Wing Grudge
in the Post Toasties New World Hip-Hop

JOHN LEONARD

THE NEW PRESS NEW YORK

Published in the United States by The New Press, New York, 1999
Paperback edition, 2000
Distributed by W. W. Norton & Company, Inc., New York

Versions of these essays appeared in earlier and shorter forms elsewhere, mostly in the *Nation* — and I continue to be grateful to Victor Navasky, Katrina vanden Heuvel, and Art Winslow for allowing me to educate myself in public — but also in the *New York Review of Books*, the *Yale Review, New York Newsday*, and on National Public Radio.

LIBRARY OF CONGRESS CATALOGING-IN-PUBLICATION DATA

Leonard, John, 1939 –
    When the kissing had to stop : cult studs, khmer newts, Langley
spooks, techno-Greeks, video drones . . . / by John Leonard.
      p.   cm.
    ISBN 1-56584-533-1 (hc.)
    ISBN 1-56584-643-5 (pbk.)
    I. Title.
PS3562.E56W48   1999
814'.54 — dc21   98-44584

The New Press was established in 1990 as a not-for-profit alternative to the large, commercial publishing houses currently dominating the book publishing industry. The New Press operates in the public interest rather than for private gain, and is committed to publishing, in innovative ways, works of educational, cultural, and community value that are often deemed insufficiently profitable.

The New Press
450 West 41st Street, 6th floor
New York, NY 10036

www.thenewpress.com

Printed in Canada

9 8 7 6 5 4 3 2 1

This book is for the two Ruths, who raised us right.

As for Venice and her people, merely born to bloom and drop,
Here on earth they bore their fruitage, mirth and folly were the
  crop:
What of soul was left, I wonder, when the kissing had to stop?

Robert Browning, A Toccata of Galuppi's

Contents

WHEN THE

KISSING

HAD TO STOP

Part One

Going Down
with Atlantis

Dreaming the Republic

You get off a boat and onto a mule, after which it's a thousand steep feet up from the black beach to the white bungalows, the blue Byzantine church, and a pink disco. You rent a cave in the pumice cliff overlooking the caldera, and the mind falls down like Icarus. This is Santoríni, the southernmost of the Cycladic islands. Thirty-five hundred years ago, it was Thera, a merchant-princely suburb of Minoan civilization. On its walls, Bronze Age artists painted bulls and birds, lilies and dolphins, bare-breasted women, brown boys boxing, and . . . blue monkeys. "Don't go too far," Don DeLillo warned us in *The Names*. "There's the Minotaur, the labyrinth. Darker things. Beneath the lilies and antelopes and blue monkeys." He's hinting at human sacrifice. But what does DeLillo know? He can't get from Linear A to Linear B any more than the rest of us who have puzzled the hieroglyphic Phaistos disk. Suppose we *need* to go too far? If there was ever an Atlantis—or any other lost city, golden age, republic of dreams, utopian community, subverted matriarchy, Eden, Arcadia, Mu or Macondo, Wonderland or Neverland—wouldn't it be nice to think that it consisted of this elegance and delicacy, this bygone playfulness? Blue monkeys!

When Sir Arthur Evans dug up Crete at the turn of the century, he found a blue monkey on a fragment of fresco in the palace of Knossos, although at first he mistook the figure for a "blue-skinned boy" gathering saffron. Then he rubbed some more and saw that the boy had a tail. Seven decades later, on Santoríni, no sooner had Spyridon Marinatos sunk his shovel into the ruins of Akroteri than he discovered an entire wall of blue monkeys cavorting like children in a progressive preschool. Also frescoed were griffins and a sphinx. But these blue monkeys weren't mythological. From the white bands on their foreheads, they were obviously long-tailed guenons, *Cercopithecus mitis*, probably brought back as pets from Africa to Knossos and Thera by sailors in the Minoan fleet. As much as lilies and dolphins, they seemed to embody a cheerful, inquisitive, gregarious race of dancers and acrobats whose language we still can't read but whose images speak of gardens and games. And then they vanished, like Minoan civilization itself, sometime between 1628 and 1480 B.C., in volcanic upchuck, seismic shock, killer tsunamis, poison gas, falling ash, and repressed memory.

Or did they? Richard Ellis, a marine artist and fluent scribbler of books on legends of the sea, prefers to believe in *Imagining Atlantis* that blue monkeys were still around in the Aegean as late as 430 B.C., and to blame for the Plague of Athens that knocked off Pericles, as their close relative, the vervet or green monkey, is responsible for the spread of the Ebola virus in Zaire and the Sudan. Ellis wants to believe this because, in seeking to debunk the whole wonderfully weird literature of Atlantology, before he can disenthrall us from the Thera-was-Atlantis thesis (all that bull-jumping monkey business, gone up in smoke or down in salty solutions), he must demystify the Platonic dialogues that got us fantasizing in the first place.

According to Plato, he heard about Atlantis from his maternal uncle, Critias the Younger, who got it from his father, Critias the Elder, who was told the story by a peripatetic Solon, who'd picked it up from a couple of priests in pharaonic Egypt. According to Ellis, Plato made the whole thing up. What he really felt bad about was the decline of his very own Athens, after the Persian wars, the Peloponnesian victory of the Spartans, and the dreadful plague. To add some color, Plato threw in a Temple of Poseidon that sounds an awful lot like the Temple of Artemis at Ephesus later described by Pliny, and the same sunken-city stuff that would show up subsequently in secondhand accounts by Strabo and Pausanias of the 373 B.C. earthquake that glubglubbed Helice in the Gulf of Corinth. Atlantis, for which Plato is the only extant source, never happened.

Oddly, this speculative argument comes at the end of a book at great pains to rebuke every author who claims to have located Atlantis anywhere in the world, from the Azores to Antarctica, from Scandinavia to the Sahara, from Ireland to Peru. They're all wrong, says Ellis, because they've twisted Plato to suit their own fixations, ignored his coordinates, and fiddled with his arithmetic. And so they have, like medieval Kabbalists. But if Plato was just allegorizing promiscuously, why should we care if later generations of Froot Loops like Edgar Cayce and Immanuel Velikovsky played fast and loose with the details of a *Critias* that's fictitious anyway? He made up his cave, too. And who'd want to live in Plato's own dreamy Republic, where a stand-up guy like Democritus would have been bent, folded, spindled, banned, and burned?

Nothing exists, except atoms and empty space. (Democritus)

I review Atlantis books once a decade, whether they need it or not. First up in 1978 was *The Secret of Atlantis* by Otto Muck, a German scientist predisposed to Spenglerian rinse cycles. Muck went up (working on the V-2 rocket) and Muck went down (inventing the U-boat snorkel). In between, he theorized an Atlantis on the Azores hump in the Atlantic Ridge, populated by seven-foot Cro-Magnons who spoke Basque and were kind to eels. It was destroyed by a giant asteroid that messed with the earth's axial rotation, punched holes in the ocean's floor, and sent up vapor clouds into a smog ball that lasted two thousand years. Its sudden sinking caused the Flood that made Noah famous, ended the Ice Age by allowing the Gulf Stream to lick the tenderloins of Europe, embarrassed many woolly mammoths, accounts for the migratory nuptial urge of eels to lay their atavistic eggs in the Sargasso Sea, and explains the heretofore mysterious Mayan calendar, said by Muck to mark the moment when Atlantis went down—at 8 P.M., on June 5, 8498 B.C. I told readers of *The New York Times*: "I believe every other word of it."

Paleontologist/astrobiologist Charles Pellegrino doesn't. In *Unearthing Atlantis* (1991) Pellegrino gave us the Big Picture, from weather reports in the Old Testament and classical literature to the latest chitchat on volcanology, glaciology, paleobotany, oceanography, and particle physics to deep readings of ice caps, acid layers, pottery clocks, carbon clouds, dinosaur teeth, clam bed fossils, Irish peat bogs, and California bristlecones. Instead of being hit on the Azores by an asteroid in 8498 B.C., Atlantis/Thera vanished in the fall of 1628 B.C. in a volcanic whoosh more powerful than a simultaneous explosion of 150 hydrogen bombs. Fifty cubic miles of rock became "as vapor in the heavens, death rolled into Turkey on the tongue of a tsunami," plagues came down on Egypt, and the Red Sea parted, after which the Minoan dancers disappeared, leaving behind an ornamental vase or two, rumors of bull worship, and not a single bone, until archaeologists began the disinterring of Akroteri that will take another three hundred years.

Actually, *Unearthing Atlantis* was supposed to come out in spring 1990, when I reviewed it from galleys. But difficulties between Pellegrino and the Greek government postponed publication for more than a year, a parenthesis in which I heard a lot from the excitable author. He will talk your head off anywhere, on top of the "smoking cathedral" of a volcano or underneath the sea where giant sandworms inhale sulphides and entire continents grind or drift from the pull of moon on bedrock. His is the view from Krakatoa, Pompeii, and Mount St. Helens, Stonehenge and *Glomar*, a Book of Numbers and a Book of the Dead. He sees a culture of genius in business for fifteen hundred years before the roof blew off: "In the Minoan world, every island had the Aegean for a moat. Competition was inevitable, universal control impossible." Thus the first navies and first condos; flush toilets and other technologies not recovered till the Islamic Middle Ages; brave men hunting bulls with ropes, beautiful women drinking the blood of those bulls from gold cups, and artists who painted monkeys instead of monarchs. Because of that explosion, vulgar Mycenaeans took over Club Med and Moses bunked from Egypt, after which, in Palestine, his People met these displaced Therans and Cretans, whom they called Philistines.

This is the Big Picture with a vengeance. In *Imagining Atlan-*

tis, amused by Muck, Ellis is almost furious at Pellegrino: *If Plato had been thinking about Thera, he would have mentioned a volcano!* Besides, Pellegrino should have credited James Mavor, who beat him to the Santoríni punch by a quarter of a century. Fair enough, except that Ellis and Pellegrino are equally in love with Minoan civilization. Both would rather write about labyrinths and courtesans, bulls' horns and octopus shields, striped dolphins, silver daggers, and a Goddess of Wild Goats than twenty pages of dead Greek. They'd even rather write about volcanoes and tsunamis. What Pellegrino does to fudge the flimsy evidence is go all the way back to the Big Bang. What Ellis does is make fun of Atlantologists. What neither acknowledges is that, from the beginning, we've finessed Plato's cautionary tale about a powerful and prosperous principality undone by corruption and arrogance because we'd rather use Atlantis to think about something else—to dream a republic in the impossibly nostalgic past or to imagine a utopia in the always radiant future, but in any case to posit an improvement on what we've got.

I'm not just talking about the oddball monomaniacs and their eccentric tangents that Ellis finds so entertaining, although they *are* suggestive: Atlantis and the Amazons (Diodorus Scilus); Atlantis as Tartessos (Rhys Carpenter, via Herodotus); a South Seas island (Francis Bacon) or between Casablanca and Agadir (Félix Berlioux), with a pet leopard named Hiram (Pierre Benoît); in Friesland (Albert Hermann), Yorubaland (Leo Frobenius), Andalusia (Ellen Mary Whitshaw), or Libya (Otto Silbermann); the Bahamas, the Crimea, the Yucatán, and the Bermuda Triangle, unless it's the Sahara (Count Byron Kuhn de Prorok), the Antarctic (Rand and Rose Flem-Ath), or Schleswig-Holstein (Jürgen Spanuth); as the Gardens both of Eden and the Hesperides, next door to the Elysian Fields, the Temple of Delphi, the Asgard of the Eddas and Mount Olympus (Ignatius Donnelly); Lemuria's sister city (Madame Blavatsky) and the "prehistory" and "collective unconscious" of mankind (an anthroposophical Rudolph Steiner). At one time or another, Atlantis has been associated with the cult of Osiris and the Popol Vuh, the Hurrian Song of Ullikummi and the Epic of Gilgamesh, the Toltecs and the Tao. And this is to scant novels by Bacon, Donnelly, Jules Verne, Arthur Conan Doyle, H. G. Wells, and Ursula Le Guin, and to forget entirely about such films as *Warlords of Atlantis*, in which Cyd Charisse starred as Atsil, Queen of an Atlantean master race who saucered in from Mars and would have evolved into Nazis if they hadn't been nibbled on by pre-Spielbergian velociraptors. But Atlantis as blue-monkey business has many more resonant meanings.

Sonia: "I don't believe in a perfect world, but I believe in a better one."
Zimmer: "My poor baby. You've become a liberal."
(Robert Stone, *Damascus Gate*)

We used to dream of utopian republics in both directions, past and future. An Atlantis frame of mind could be radical— dialectical materialism, Zionism, relativity; Blake's prophetic books, Godwin's *Enquiry Concerning Human Justice*, and Mary Wollstonecraft's *Vindication of the Rights of Woman*; Tolstoy's *What Then Must We Do?* and Gandhi's *Hind Swaraj*; Hildegard von Bingen's *Illuminations* and Paul Goodman's *Communitas*. Or reformist—Mennonites and Shakers, Oneida and Brook Farm, Fourier and Owen. Or moony—El Dorado and Prester John; Agapemone and Micomicon; Shangri-la and Camelot; Arden and Cockaigne; *Altneuland* or *Herland*; Brideshead or Bomarzo; black forests, sacred groves, Druidic roods, Yggdrasil, and Walden; morris dancing in Tannhäuser sandals. One thinks as well and almost at random of Erewhon, Télémaque, Christianopolis, *Looking Backward*, and pantisocratic Coleridge; Buckminster Fuller and Sabbatai Zevi; Ascona, Ticino, Los Alamos, and Aztlán; English garden cities, Israeli kibbutzim, Gary Snyder's Zen-Wobbly Kitkitdizze, Kurt Vonnegut's volunteer fire brigade, and Gene Kelly's Brigadoon.

To which I'd add personal favorites like Walter Raleigh's *The Discoverie*, Aby Warburg's *Mnemosyne*, Sigmund Freud's *Moses and Monotheism*, Italo Calvino's *Mr. Palomar*, Spinoza, Darwin, and the *I Ching*; the dreaming of astronomers in black holes and superstrings, of astrophysicists in heliopause, of Mandelbrot in fractals and of Mike Davis about Los Angeles. Dream republics of another sort can also be read in the fossil beds, ice caps, and carbon clouds of Baudelaire's Paris, Joyce's Dublin, Svevo's Trieste, Musil's Vienna, Döblin's Berlin, Konrad's Budapest, and Bely's St. Petersburg, as they are archaeologized in the Buenos Aires of Borges and Cortázar, the Havana of Cabrera Infante, and the Mexico City of Fuentes—the city as cinema, starring *change,* greed, riot, gossip, jazz, blur, quake, zoom, zap; dissolving into multitude, solitude, trajectory, and vertigo. About a benzene ring of urban ghosts—Joyce, Einstein, Lenin, and Trotsky—gathering at the Odeon in Zurich, Thomas Pynchon reminded us in *Gravity's Rainbow*:

> Whatever it was they all had in common: whatever they'd come to this vantage to score . . . perhaps it had to do with the people somehow, with pedestrian mortality, restless crisscrossing of needs and desperations in one fateful piece of street . . . dialectics, matrices, archetypes all need to connect, once in a while, back to some of that proletarian blood, to body odors and senseless screaming across a table, to cheating and last hopes, or else all is dusty Dracularity, the West's ancient curse.

Likewise Atlantological-utopian (and wistful thinking) was the millennia-long quest by theologians and philosophers for God in His own scattered Words—what Umberto Eco calls *The Search for the Perfect Language,* by which Eco does *not* mean glossalalias, xenoglossias, jargons, bricolage like pidgin, fictitious lingos like Rabelais's and Tolkien's, or the "oneiric" babble of the mystic and the loon, but *the* original or universal discourse, believed to have fled from us after the Tower of Babel swoon-song, somewhere anterior to Latin and Greek, on the other side of mother tongues like Hebrew, Egyptian, and Chinese, by whose fiery signs we read the world's grammar and the will of God. There isn't space to track through all of Eco's witty permutations, from Dante (proposing his vernacular as superior to Hebrew and himself as superior to Adam) to Nicholas of Cosa (insisting that the names by which the Greeks, Latins, Germans, and Turks designate divinity all derived from the same Hebrew tetragrammaton) to Guillaume Postel (who suggested that the second Messiah would be a woman, which may be why the Inquisition judged him "not guilty but insane"). But we skywrite on past Gessner, Kircher, Hobbes, Vico, Luther, and Leibniz unto Paracelsus, Pico della Mirandola, Giordano Bruno, Jakob Böhme, and the Rosicrucians—via ancient Persian, Aramaic, Sanskrit, Gaelic, Etruscan, Hungarian, Norse runes, Cyrano's birds, and the Celto-Scythian Hypothesis; through Orphic hymns, Chaldean oracles, hieroglyphs, glottogons, and astral magic; all the way to necromancy, steganography, alchemy, and theosophic or ecstatic Kabbala—till the philosophers decide in the eighteenth century that since they can't find the prototype or Original Stencil, they will have to invent an artificial substitute, a Sweet'n Low Panglossia to bind up (or, at least, to Christianize) the wounded world. Which clears the throat for international auxiliary languages like Volapuk, Tutonisch, Esperanto, BASIC, Pascal, and whining.

Much of this may sound ditzy—no wonder Atlantis crops up so often in their treatises—but the impulse was heroic, the mind-set utopian, and the thinkers every bit as smart as those of us who are so postmodern that we're paralyzed. When, frightened by the Thirty Years' War in the seventeenth century, Johann Valentin Andreae, Tommaso Campanella, and Guillaume Postel all took time off from looking for the perfect language to draw up projects for an ideal republic to ensure a universal peace, maybe their idealism had more to recommend it than the predatory behavior of our own trilateral commissioners and globocops, who long ago put to sleep such childish notions as a Greek polis, a Roman Republic, and a Christian charity. Or of our sullen plebescitic classes, who vote down government and taxes every chance they get. Or of the twerpy trillers of our literary vanguard—talk about your ecstatic Kabbala!—who have assured their graduate students that there's no such thing as causality, continuity, history, rational planning, standardized knowledge, coherent representation, or intelligent action, only semiotic showbiz. Human brain-stuff hasn't changed in five hundred years, or in fifteen thousand; it's culture that metastasizes. Even in the fevered present, parents and teachers try to raise children to ethical principle and purpose, Third World writers compose epics of emancipation, and entire peoples, many of them as dark and Asiatic as the Minoans, still engage in the Enlightenment project, quite as if they never got the bad news from the French front. It also seems to me that the artists of Thera—or Lascaux, or Altamira—could teach even Picasso a trick or two about *jouissance*.

Like Allen Ginsberg explaining "Eleanor Rigby" to a public-television audience, let *me* dream a couple of republics—one fictional and the other, gloriously, not.

> *Everything we want in a society is what we find brought out in the moment of insurrection. Spontaneity! Spontaneous hierarchy! Self-sacrifice! Staying awake all night! Working until we drop! Audacity! Camaraderie! The carnival behind the barricades—what it feels like when the police have just been kicked out of your quartier! Free eggs, free beer. . . . And don't forget what it feels like to throw open the gates of the prisons! What a great moment! This is the moment the true socialist worships and thinks will be incarnated in the society on the morning after.*

> (Norman Rush, *Mating*)

So much goes on in Rush's prodigal novel about true love, star-crossed anthropology, and rural development in southern Africa that we almost forget about the morning after. The morning after is Tsau—"something very avant-garde, supposedly very major and massive, a whole new village built from the ground up, in point of fact, somewhere in the north central Kalahari," an experimental matriarchal "New Jerusalem," "solar democracy," and "city of the sun." Tsau has been planned in the Botswana desert by the famously sardonic radical decentralist Nelson Denoon, an amalgam of Paulo Freire and Ivan Illich, after having acquired at previous projects an "entire sequence of truths . . . such as controlling the scale, working in the vernacular, cutting expatriate staff to near zero, locating yourself remotely enough to avoid premature disruption, balancing collective and individual incentives, basing your political economy on women instead of men—his theme song. Every female is a golden loom." And it's described in brilliant detail.

In the night, in the desert, first you hear the wind chimes and the blue-green glass bells suspended from chains in the crowns of albizias. Then you see, like flashing sequins of reflected light, the flanged cylinders in the windmills on the koppie; a pair of horns on the glazed ceramic water tank; the cistern fed by polyvinyl chloride tubes; spiral-channeled disks strung from torii-like crossbars ("a corridor of darling crepitation"); waist-high hedges and thatched rondavels; cloud trees, thorn trees, and goats. Later, in the blaze of daylight off of solar panels, you'll pick out the cement octagon and the plaza terrace; workshops, net houses, primary school, infirmary; mealie fields, kraals, and kilns; moccasins, pantaloons, and parasols; tracking mirrors for the solar ovens and turtleshell-shaped mud stoves for boiling water; dung carts pulled by children who earn credits for the delivering of messages and goods; plenaries, parlementes, carved lintels, spectrum-colored crockery; chess tournaments, ostrich farming, abacus lessons, menarche parties, kickball, Snake Women, death masks . . .

Never mind the Mother Committee and the Lamentations, the sunflower-oil economy and the deliberative judicial system. As Rousseau knew only too well, "The problem is to find a form of association which will defend with the whole common force the person and goods of each associate, and in which each, while uniting himself with all, may still obey himself." At Tsau, women are deeded their houses and plots; ownership entitles you to voting membership in the voluntary labor credit system; inheritance is restricted to female offspring and collaterals. At Tsau, there aren't supposed to be motorcars, guns, alcohol, abortions, witchcraft, or any other religion. But there are, of course, tensions. After eight years, isn't it time for bwana Denoon to cease promoting sauerkraut and croquet and get on with the rest of his life — maybe launch his long-promised crusade "to make bank secrecy illegal everywhere"? Anyway, "Who cared if he was willing to say of himself that he was wellknown to be gung ho for half measures and that if he had been in the October Revolution he would have been saying *some* power to the soviets?" You don't want to know what happens to Denoon. You may want to know what happens to Tsau but Rush isn't telling, except to hint that it will have to accommodate the slow subversions of booze (secret shebeens), prostitution (male, in a matriarchy), sectarianism and, alas, guns. The excuse for guns at Tsau is — surprise! — a sudden population explosion of vervet monkeys.

> *Gaviotas isn't a utopia. Utopia literally means "no place." In Greek, the prefix "u" signifies no. We call Gaviotas a topia, because it's real.*
>
> (Paolo Lugari)

When Paolo Lugari, whom Gabriel García Márquez has called the "inventor of the world," first visited the vastation of the llanos of eastern Colombia, sixteen hours by jeep from Bogotá, what he saw was something other than a steamed seething with malarial mosquitoes, a caramel-colored plain of muck as flat as a leaden sea and four times the size of Holland. "The only deserts are deserts of the imagination." He saw the future of civilization fashioned out of grass, sunlight, and water; Third World solutions to Third World problems; "a living laboratory" to which he would bring "pioneer-technicians" and "engineer-dreamers," chemists, botanists, geologists, anthropologists, mathematicians, architects, and astronomers; coffee and carnations; windmills and water buffalo; a musical-instrument factory and an enchanted forest made for singing.

That was almost thirty years ago; the community he huffed, puffed, and enticed into being thrives today astonishingly, in spite of the army, the death-squad paramilitaries, the narcotraffickers, and the guerrillas; in spite of the buying and selling of governments in Bogotá and the dumping of cheap grains and other foodstuffs from giant U.S. producers on Colombia's "free trade" market; in spite of the leached soil, the poisoned rivers, and the shortage of women. It is this story that Alan Weisman, on assignment with a team of journalists to produce a series for National Public Radio on the search for solutions to social and environmental problems, must have been delirious to discover. His splendid book, *Gaviotas: A Village to Reinvent the World*, has been mostly ignored by the mainstream press. And why not? It will only save our souls.

What the dreamers in the desert did, with a couple of grants from the United Nations and a workforce of Guahibo Indians, was to make fiberboard from grass and gaskets out of palm leaves; put up a nonpolluting tannery and pave roads and runways with their own Inca-like bricks; turn palm oil extraction residues into bovine feed supplements; build windmills and hydroponic nurseries and a "giant condom" irrigation system stitched together out of plastic garbage bags; invent solar motors, solar water heater panels, micro-hydro turbines, biogas generators, and every manner of water pump from a ram to a sleeve to a wheel mounted on a floating oil drum, not to mention solar grain and clothes dryers, a pedal-driven cassava grinder with a bicycle drive-train, a one-handed sugarcane press, a one-man manual cement mixer, a cork-screwing manual well digger and a rotating-drum peanut sheller — all of which they refused to patent.

They also put up a hospital you'd want to send your mother to, and when the government closed it down in a managed-health-care seizure, they turned the building into a research facility for medicinal plants. They contracted with the banks and the government to install solar heating for public housing projects in Bogotá and Medellín, and hired street urchins to make the collector panels, as they taught a squatters' colony in the capital city how to plant hydroponic farms on their rooftops — so successfully that soon a women's cooperative was supplying lettuce to a grocery chain. They created a community with no jails, judges, cops, crime, or locks, not much marriage and even less smoking. And it sits there, celebrating the Day of

the Bicycle and the Day of the Birds, in the middle of a comeback rain forest, much of it Caribbean pine whose bark fairly
oozes with a natural-gum resin Gaviotans sell to manufacturers
of paints, enamels, varnish, newsprint, soap, ink, and incense —
and to rosin the bows of violins, made right next door to their
factory for harps and cuatros. Not only is the forest good for the
ozone layer, but it has also brought back tanagers and oropen-
dolas, nightjars and lapwings, gray hawks and whistling herons,
butterflies and parrots. And the acoustics are perfect for concerts.

Enough. I'll end as sappy as a Caribbean pine. Imagine finding Atlantis in Colombia — as if the idea of a dream republic, like
the equally abused ideas of sanctuary and asylum, had been hiding out all along inside a magical realist novel, ready to contra-
dict every ugly Western idea of space — of golf courses and
theme parks, private beaches and company towns, restrictive
covenants and armed response, gated communities and strate-
gic hamlets, panopticons and bantustans — and I haven't even
mentioned my favorite Gaviotan invention, which is a sleeve
pump attached to a seesaw so that children playing at recess
might supply the water for their own school. Think of that. Plato
didn't, in his cave. Now, for those children on the seesaw, substitute blue monkeys.

Killing the Philosophers

Before we use a nifty novel, Philip Kerr's *A Philosophical Investigation*, as an excuse to talk about everything else under the fascistic sun, an overview of jurisprudence in the twenty-first century would be helpful, and Kerr supplies it with a straight face (sort of):

> The 1990s witnessed the discrediting of socially and economically fatalistic theories of why people commit violent crime. Attending only to the exterior causes of crime, any sense of personal responsibility was diminished. Today society no longer takes exclusive blame for how a person became a criminal any more than the individual himself: a combination of social and individual factors are seen as a better way to account for every kind of criminal behavior.
>
> Determinism is not considered to constitute a menace to freedom in the new century. A pragmatic assumption of order made for the sake of advancing scientific inquiry can hardly be questioned. This reverses an earlier trend in the social sciences which mistakenly sought to protect freedoms by confining determinism to the physical world, thus effectively "outlawing" all attempts at establishing "biological determinism."
>
> Modern social science does not consider predictability and generalization to be dangerous. Indeed, any advance in social science without first establishing certain notions about human behavior would not have been possible. To claim infinite adaptability for human behavior is no longer valid. Thus the concept that violent criminality has no real roots in us, being an external socially produced phenomenon, is now wholly discredited.

Now, then, just suppose that in London twenty years from now, having somehow to cope with an epidemic of "recreational murder," these hard-ass social scientists develop a test to determine which men in the general population are predisposed to serial sex-killing. Not preordained, but predisposed. By Proton Emission Tomography (a PET scan), "somatogenic determinants of violent crime" can be identified in snapshots of living brain cells. If you happen to be missing a Ventro Medial Nucleus

(VMN) to inhibit the Sexually Dimorphic Nucleus (SDN) in the reoptic (or aggressive response) area of your brain, you're invited in for counseling and drug therapy. Since you haven't yet done anything, your identity is protected, under a code name, in a computer program called, in one of Kerr's many witticisms, LOMBROSO (Localization of Medullar Brain Resonations Obliging Social Orthopraxy). In the same dreamy way that we name racehorses, sailboats, and slaves, so LOMBROSO codes "VMN-negatives" with handles like Aquinas, Dickens, Kierkegaard, Wordsworth, Hegel, and Hemingway. Unless you turn up anywhere near the scene of a violent crime, your secret is supposed to be safe with LOMBROSO.

Now suppose further that one such VMN-negative, appalled to learn what he's capable of, decides to indulge his predisposition in a socially redeeming manner. User-friendly himself, he cracks LOMBROSO's code, downloads a list of fellow potential serial killers, and proceeds—serially, of course—to kill them. We already have a philosophical problem on our hands, having to do with free will and genetic fate (or somatogenic determinism). The problem is complicated exponentially when the serial killer of would-be serial killers begins to identify with, behave like, and rationalize his actions in the language of the philosopher whose name the LOMBROSO computer assigned him: Ludwig Wittgenstein. *Naming confers meaning.*

Suppose, finally, that the New Scotland Yard inspector designated to track down this serial killer is "gynocide" detective "Jake" Jacowicz, just back from the Third Annual European Community Symposium on Techniques of Law Enforcement and Criminal Investigation at the Herbert Marcuse Center in Frankfurt, Greater German Reich. Jake is a "gynocide" instead of a homicide detective not only because serial killers generally kill women, but also because she's very much a woman herself, a specialist in "intuitive" reasoning. Once Jake figures out that "Wittgenstein" has confused himself with Wittgenstein, how will she proceed?

There is as much in this clever novel about language, grammar, and games, about nihilism and solipsism, about pure idealism, asserted propositions, conceptual error, and "the unknowableness of the empirical," as there is about genotypes and computer programs. It helps to know your Plato and Nietzsche, not to mention Kant, who is knocked off early on, and Descartes, who works for an advertising agency. Besides reading *Tractatus Logico-Philosophicus,* Jake sees her own "Neo-Existential" psychotherapist and consults a Cambridge philosophy don who has written a detective novel in which Plato, on a visit to Sicily in 388 B.C., solves the murder of a courier to King Dionysius of Syracuse, using Pythagorean mathematical principles. In due course, Jake will discover something important about her own sexuality, involving the smile she saw on her father's face, which is also the smile of Parmenides, who, you'll remember, invented logic.

Meanwhile—amid many references to Henry James, Salman Rushdie, William Blake, Karl Marx, Albert Camus, Oscar Wilde, T. S. Eliot, R. D. Laing, and J. R. R. Tolkien, and any number of sly jokes likely to send you scurrying back to Bertrand Russell's *History of Western Philosophy*—Darwin, Aquinas, Spinoza, Locke, *and* Bertie Russell are murdered before our very eyes by Ludwig Wittgenstein. And Socrates may be next. To reveal more of the plot is to kill joy instead of philosophers. But one important feature of the next century must be mentioned: "Punitive Coma." *PC* is what they do to bad guys instead of capital punishment. It's more cost-efficient than a life sentence. Behave too aggressively, and you face "an icy hypodermic full of limbo." This injection is called "hot milk." This novel is more like grenadine and hemlock.

Now we can dream in several directions: Do I really have to think about serial killers? Do I really have to think about sociobiology? Do I really have to think about Wittgenstein? What do I mean by "really"?

II. FROM JACK THE RIPPER TO JODIE FOSTER, VIA VIENNA, WEIMAR, AND THE SORBONNE

The serial killer is probably in more trouble than even Philip Kerr ever imagined, now that he no longer is simply the sensational subject of pulp fiction, tabloid journalism, local and federal law-enforcement agencies, and hack Hollywood copycats but has graduated into the lofty purview of cultural-studies monographs by free-floating and shrink-wrapped theorists of antisocial behavior, not to mention a chapter by John Updike and a whole novel by Joyce Carol Oates.

In *Bech at Bay* (1998), Updike undertakes the serial killing of every critic who has ever given Bech a bad review. (In one ingenious instance, the murder weapon is a Taoist poem by Seng Ts'an.) This is rather wittier than the Oates novel, *Zombie*, in which anti-hero Quentin, a thirty-one-year-old garbage sack of junk food and junk ideas, of Taco Bell beef burritos and dark matter in an expanding universe, is beyond not only parenting or social work, but even the flexible sympathies of Oates herself. He is Bret Easton Ellis's *American Psycho* without a platinum credit card. Except by abducting and lobotomizing young boys with an ice pick, he has no other way of creating someone who will love and obey him.

Serial murder used to have a better cultural pedigree, as Maria Tatar observes more than a little disapprovingly in *Lustmord*. About the way the tabloids of his time reported the murder of a prostitute by a carpenter, Robert Musil told readers of *The Man Without Qualities*: "They had expressed their abhorrence of it, but they did not leave off until they had counted thirty-five stabs in the abdomen, and described the long slash from the navel to the sacrum . . . while the throat showed the marks of throttling." Musil, of course, was feeling bad about Vienna on the eve of World War I. Tatar feels even worse about Weimar, after that war was lost, when everybody seemed to have tabloid tendencies. They were more than just morbidly curious about serial killers and sexual murder in Weimar. In high culture as well as low, in paintings by Otto Dix and Kurt Schwitters, novels by Alfred Döblin and Hermann Hesse, films by Fritz Lang, plays by Frank Wedekind, and graphics by George Grosz, they were pathologically obsessive. Dix painted himself as a "sex murderer" and smeared the canvas with red hand-prints. Grosz had himself photographed as Jack the Ripper amid mirrors, masks, and dolls. Wedekind allowed himself a star turn on stage as the Ripper and cast his wife as a victim. Lang gave us Peter Lorre as a child-murderer. Döblin somehow managed, in *Karl and Rosa,* to "sexualize" Rosa Luxemburg's assassination into a hysterical masochistic indulgence on *her* part, a self-invited and self-inflicted martyrdom through torture. And Hesse in *Steppenwolf* (1927) confided this epiphany:

> There, where the mark was, I plunged my knife in to the hilt. The blood welled out over her delicate white skin. . . . With a shudder I stared at the stony brow and the stark hair and the cool pale shimmer of the ear. The cold that streamed from them was deathly and yet it was beautiful, it rang, it vibrated. It was music! Hadn't I felt this shudder before and found it at the same time a joy? Hadn't I once caught this music before? Yes, with Mozart and the Immortals.

Tatar, a professor of German at Harvard and the author pre-viously of *Off with Their Heads! Fairy Tales and the Culture of Childhood,* explores this Weimar kinkiness in dense, elegant, persuasive case studies of Dix, Grosz, and Döblin; in sidelong glances at the pinball tilt to F. W. Murnau and Rudolf Schlichter; in historical sketches of the Vampire of Dusseldorf, the Silesian Bluebeard, nineteenth-century *Liebestod,* and "the extraordi-nary artistic investment in representing women" like Eve, Circe, Medusa, Judith, and Salome "as creatures of overpowering sexual evil"; with obligatory references to Otto Weininger and Klaus Theweleit, spicy quotes from Karl Marx, Susan Sontag, and Elisabeth Bronfen, and flash-forwards to the Boston Stran-gler, Son of Sam, *The Silence of the Lambs, Basic Instinct,* Nor-man Mailer's *An American Dream,* Patrick Süskind's *Perfume,*

Alfred Hitchcock, and Brian De Palma. (De Palma has explained: "I don't particularly want to chop up women but it seems to work." Not exactly Mozart and the Immortals.)

Lustmord then looks at Picasso's *Demoiselles d'Avignon* and Klee's *Dogmatic Composition* and worries about both "the gender politics of cultural production" and the "modernist project that aestheticizes violence and turns the mutilated female body into an object of fascination and dread." How come the artist so often seems to identify with the psychopath, and succeeds, after gaudy knife work, in casting *himself* as sacrificial victim and symbolic reborn phoenix? Bad boys! Dead girls! Chop-chop! Modernism!

As for Weimar as a momentary locus for an epidemic of such transgressive energies, imagine: Damaged men come back from war less than heroic. What do they find, besides the usual urban pathologies? Women happily whole, at work, and agitating about suffrage. The pathology of *Dolchstosslegende* ("stabbed-in-the-back stories") meets the fantasy of sexual revenge, as if women and Jews were one big vampire movie like *Nosferatu,* as if the corpse itself were a work of art. Not for the first time, fascism and modernism are conjoined; they correspond; they are letters from the same camp, with its weak male-ego boundaries and chimney smoke of human cinder.

I am reminded of another recent novel a whole lot better than Oates's *Zombie.* In Carol De Chellis Hill's *Henry James' Midnight Song,* we imagine ourselves, like Musil, in Vienna at the turn of the century. The dead body of a woman is discovered in the study of Dr. Freud. Although this body later disappears, the police stay put. All over Vienna, young women vanish from the streets, after which parts of them show up—detached toes, severed heads—at the bottom of garbage cans, in tops of trees, or iced in the Danube. The hysterically anti-Semitic Viennese accuse Jews, like Freud, of ritual murder. The worried emperor sends off to Paris for the Austrian-born Jewish detective Maurice LeBlanc, who is so smart he reads himself to sleep each night with Baudelaire.

Freud, and his dippy wife Martha, and his sister-in-law Minna, with whom he is having a secret affair, are suspects. So is Henry James, who thought he was consulting Freud on behalf of his sick sister Alice, but who's actually riddled with guilt because he strangled a cat. Suspect too is Edith Wharton, who travels with Henry, has her own secret affair with a London journalist, resents Freud's theory of childhood seduction because it probably happened to her, and actually burgles his office. And so is Carl Jung, whose unprofessional behavior with a female patient suggests that there must be an archetype for cad. We also meet the Zionist Herzl, back from the Dreyfus trial; the physicist Einstein, relativizing promiscuously; the playwright Schnitzler, a misanthrope; and the critic Kraus, who is worried that von Hofmannsthal will turn into another Heinrich Heine, "a Moses who strikes the rock of the German language with his rod and all that spurts forth is eau de cologne"; not to mention the symphonic composer Mahler, the Secessionist painter Klimt, and Wittgenstein's sister. All these people, when they aren't reading Baudelaire or Nietzsche, dream a lot—about horses and falcons, Jesus and Pascal, Hansel und Gretel. As well as blood, there is sex in the unconscious strudel, and a dead dog.

If I make *Henry James' Midnight Song* sound jaunty, to a surprising extent it is. What Hill doesn't know for a fact from the literature and scholarship she cheerfully makes up, with nerve and verve and mimetic genius—a slapstick of Great Minds, as seen through the eyes of a very Jamesian seventeen-year-old American girl, who might very well grow up to be Maria Tatar; whose sister wants instead to be either Isabel Archer or Anna Karenina; whose aunt is an Engels-reading suffragette; and whose cousin, a tiger-eyed Viennese countess, vamps our Parisian detective. But slapstick shifts to epiphany, in a set-piece Sunday in the Park with Edith and Siggi, and then, suddenly, to nightmare. Because history, Hill tells us in this oratorio and circus of a novel, is something more and other than an arty prop or even a transgressive text. These mushrooms are poisonous.

That blond head in the frozen Danube is not a Klimt. Under the statues of Goethe and Schiller, assassins fester. Opening its mouth to sing, Europe strangles. At the masked ball, in the labyrinth, there are anarchists and androgynes and misogynists and thugs. All these people, whether they know it or not, are full of *Lustmord* and dreaming of swastikas.

Mark Seltzer's mind scan / anal probe of the same fraught material, *Serial Killers: Death and Life in America's Wound Culture,* considers the acting-out VMN-negative not as a sociobiological predisposition but a sociopathologized "script," written at the juncture of "private desire and public fantasy" — a "radical entanglement between forms of eroticized violence and mass technologies of registration, identification, and reduplication . . . of copy-catting and simulation"; "the convergence of the life process and the machine process as collateral forms of information processing" and "reciprocal topographies of subject and context"; "the prosthetic environment of 'American nervousness,'" and "the strange permeability of bodies and landscapes . . . mapped onto the strange permeability of homelike and 'open' or public spheres." In mass transit to the usual contested site, Seltzer will footnote the usual *Jolly Roger* honor roll of Captain Hooks on the high seas of theory — Foucault, Lacan, Derrida, Baudrillard, Nietzsche, Adorno, Benjamin, Eve Kosofsky Sedgwick, Elias Canetti, Judith Butler, Frederic Jameson, Wendy Brown, Jürgen Habermas, and Cindy Sherman — before arriving at what he calls "the pathologized public sphere," which is an awful place to be, a *Cabaret* without the songs:

> shock and trauma; states of injury and victim status; the wound, the disease, the virus, and epidemics of violence; disaster, accident, catastrophe, and mass death; the abnormal normality of paranoia and psychosis; the pornography of mass-mediated desires and other forms of addiction and artificial life. The subject, on this model, can experience the social only as an intervention or invasion from without. . . . Along these lines, history and psychology, reality and fantasy, change places.

While Seltzer seems seldom to watch television—a patholo-gized public sphere if ever there was one, with three prime-time network series devoted entirely or in part to tracking down serial killers of the most flamboyant sort in the very season he pub-lished his book—he's gone to a lot of movies, which is where psychoanalysis hides out when it isn't doing cultural studies, and his reading is more various and downscale than Tatar's, in-cluding, for instance, novels by Zola, Bram Stoker, Jack Lon-don, William S. Burroughs, J. G. Ballard, Jim Thompson, Denis Johnson, William Gibson, and Patricia Cornwell ("psy-fi and sci-fi"), in addition to the memoirs, confessions, and media manifestoes of Ted Bundy, Charlie Starkweather, David Berkowitz, and the Unabomber. He even mentions Joyce Carol Oates, Philip Kerr, and Maria Tatar. And he is full of arresting facts—"the percentage of known black male serial killers is closely comparable to their proportion in the U.S. population as a whole" and "perhaps 10 to 15 percent of known American se-rial killers are women"—as well as vivid images:

> The fashion victim has . . . emerged as something of a model trauma victim. I am referring in part to the traumatized look of the fash-ion model on the runway: to the stylized model today on display, a beauty so generic it might have a bar code on it; bodies in motion with-out emotion, at once entrancing and self-entranced, self-absorbed and vacant, or self-evacuated; the superstars of a chameleon-like celebrity in anonymity.

This is heady stuff, with the signal virtue of blaming modern life instead of modern art for our "wound culture." But it tells us more about where the next monograph will be coming from than how to get on with either our jurisprudence or our citizenship. "Cultural psychoanalysis," Seltzer says, "gravitates toward paranoia and psychosis to provide its models of the historical and toward totalitarianism/fascism, or its preconditions, to pro-vide its models of the social." I have no doubt that cultural psy-choanalysis, feminist deconstruction, postcolonial studies, queer theory, and identity politics have enriched our appreciation of and skepticism about the face of the world and its secret subjunctives. But we still have to drip the coffee, raise the children, and wonder if we've behaved honorably before we go to bed at night or die. Agency is thrust upon us.

III. THE SOCIOBIOLOGY
OF I'M-ALL-RIGHT-JACK

You will have noticed that Philip Kerr's twenty-first century is sociobiological. It was all right when E. O. Wilson went on up at Harvard all about ants, but lately he's been sociobiologizing everything in sight, from xenophobia to adhesive-padded geckos. The sociobiologists are telling us that the whole world is pretty much the way it *should* be. That everything, from the Egyptian fruit bat to the status and role of women to the IQ test scores of black schoolchildren to the caste system in India, has been "epigenetically" pre-programmed. That there are little units of human behavior called "culturgens," thousands of them sitting there like the incest taboo in a positive feedback loop between gene and culture, dictating what societies can and can't do, obsessing in favor of patriarchy and against socialism. That if the people on top of this Chain of Being, in charge of this best of all possible worlds, are mostly male and mostly pale, talk to Darwin about it. We are *all* ants. Or maybe beetles.

This of course amazes. The world's all right because *I'm* all right, Jack. When some of us were unhappy at Harvard, back in the Oligocene epoch of geological Deep Time, the sociologist Talcott Parsons was an E. O. Wilson type. No matter how hard we pressed him in his "domain assumptions," he'd insist that the status quo was dandy, and so was Talcott Parsons, and this is a culturgen. Every day in every way, E. O. and Talcott get better and better, by staying just the same. Tenure at Harvard means that the social system can stop evolving. Natural selection!

Fortunately, Stephen Jay Gould is also up at Harvard, demystifying the E. O.'s. From Gould, we know evolution isn't a ladder; it's a bush with branches, a tree of life. Natural selection is messy. Environments aren't always favorable. Variations aren't always fortuitous. What we see around us, or in the mirror, is as much a consequence of chance, contingency, compromise, and opportunistic quirk as a product of necessity or design. Genes evolve, but so do organisms, and entire species, in fits and starts, on different plateaus. Some adaptations are swell, some are inefficient (consider the panda's bamboo problem), and a few have unpredictable surplus value. Look at our Big Brain. It didn't develop just to let us know that we must die, but how we think about death shapes our lives and dreams. Yes, biology constrains us, but there are blanks in our program; we are reasonably free to improvise new selves in a "dialectic" between the epigenetic template and all that disorderly space in the living world, the great surprise.

But you'll have noticed that sociobiologists like Wilson and biologist/geologists like Gould—not to mention industrial psychologists, cultural anthropologists, molecular physicists, Big Bang cosmologists, genetic engineers, biomystical Inner Children / Dolphin Symps, downloaded cyberpunks, the fish-eyed opinionizers in their Beltway blister packs on the TV yakshows, and the vampire bats of pomo in their campus Carlsbads—have usurped the discourse that used to be, prior to the modern age, the exclusive property of . . . *philosophers.* Who else now speaks to us of perfect knowledge in final things? When, say, the Chatwins, Ardreys, and Leakeys start arguing about such basic stuff as whether we all began on the African savannah as killers of our own kind, they don't consult the wisdom of the elders; they pick and choose among bickering and career-minded archaeologists, paleontologists, ethologists, and the rest of the desert-crazed, ant-eating, novelizing monomaniacs who dream our past on Ice Age toenails or a tooth.

Having ceded ultimate authority to the credentialed nitwits of the mini-sciences and the chirpy gauchos of the media pampas, how can we hope ever again to think through dilemmas of conscience? I blame this on the Wittgensteins who told us it's impossible to know for sure about anything important, and then, as if to prove their point, went away to be unhappy.

IV. THE UNHAPPINESS
OF THE WITTGENSTEINS

Kerr's "Wittgenstein," imagining he addresses the very same Society of Connoisseurs in Murder to which Thomas De Quincey in 1827 talked about killing off Descartes, Hobbes, Leibniz, Kant, and Spinoza, speaks from a passionate and hateful heart:

> Today it is even more obvious just how much good can result from the murder of one dusty, arid, old philosopher. Both Marx and Freud were murdered by Jaspers. Bertrand Russell and G. E. Moore should have been murdered by Wittgenstein, as Ramsey certainly was. Heidegger died very properly at the hands of A. J. Ayer. It can be argued that Quine may indeed have murdered Strawson; however, if he did, it could only have been with the assistance of Skinner. And Chomsky, well Chomsky may turn out to have killed nearly everyone he came into contact with.

Was the real Wittgenstein so bloody-minded? *Tractatus* argued, in seventy-five pages of poemlike "remarks," that language is a Great Mirror. A sentence, a proposition, is a "word-picture" of reality. But the Great Mirror is blinded by its own reflected radiance; it can't describe itself or what all propositions have in common: logical form. An essential form must *be* there, but we can't talk about what we can't see. Hence the dictum: "Whereof one cannot speak thereof one must be silent." This left a lot "unsayable"—God, for instance, and ethics—and Wittgenstein said none of it for the rest of his life. Nor did he care much for anything anybody else said, except maybe for the vagrant logical positivist. They should all shut up.

But in the posthumously published *Philosophical Investigations*, he repudiated *Tractatus*. As if by magic slate, there was no longer any such mystification as a "unifying essence." Instead, there were what he called "family resemblances" among beliefs; and also overlappings—"as in spinning a thread we twist fibre on fibre. And the strength of the thread does not reside in the fact that some one fibre runs through its whole length, but in the overlapping of many fibres." We are entitled to wonder what happened to Ludwig to make him change his mind, which is why so many books have been written about him, including at least one other novel besides Kerr's.

In 1987, a thirty-four-year-old American, Bruce Duffy, published *The World as I Found It,* a first novel—a kind of intellectual opera in which each abstraction got its own aria—so good that it has survived the rigorous standard set by the best biography, Ray Monk's *Ludwig Wittgenstein: The Duty of Genius* (1990). The philosopher of the "unsayable" leaves the capital of alienation, Vienna, for the hothouse of the Enlightenment, Cambridge, with a clarinet in a sock. The aspiring engineer was flying a kite when he first read Bertrand Russell. From 1911 through 1913, he worked with Russell on mathematics and logic, and met G. E. Moore, whose chair in philosophy at Cambridge he'd inherit in 1939. They found him brilliant, ferociously impatient, ill-mannered, and intimidating. He retired for a year to a Norwegian mountain cabin, there to chastise his impurities with scorpions. He fought during World War I for the Austro-Hungarian Empire, on the Russian front. He came back with *Tractatus* in his rucksack and for the next ten years shunned philosophy; gave away his personal fortune; taught grade school (and was, says Monk, physically abusive to the children); designed and built, in Vienna, a magnificent modern house for his sister Gretl, who was a patient of Freud's; read Otto Weininger's crazy book on the inferiority of Jews and women; listened to Mahler and felt bad, on the Ringstrasse . . .

Till his 1929 Cambridge comeback as a Trinity College fellow, where he hated High Table; whistled opera; shopped at Woolworth's; refused to knot a tie, wear glasses, or read Aristotle; was partial to Dostoyevsky, Blake, and American detective fiction; disliked Shakespeare and intellectual women; was hard on his colleagues ("Give up criticism, Leavis!") and brutal to his students, driving many away to factories and psycho wards. "Intolerable, intolerable," was his mantra. Asked if he thought Hitler was *sincere,* he replied: "Is a ballet dancer sincere?" And: "This running against the walls of our cage is perfectly, absolutely hopeless." Famously, for the record: "Of this I am certain, that we are not here to have a good time." And he certainly didn't. Gnomic, caustic, agoraphobic—yes, the philosopher of impasse and the cul-de-sac was afraid of open spaces—he died of stomach cancer in 1951, not at all sorry to see himself go.

Duffy doesn't reduce and "explain" Ludwig. That is, the "unsayable" doesn't arrive like a telegram from God after a particular trauma, the way, say, the Exclusion Principle occurred to Wolfgang Pauli while he watched the Folies-Bergère. Rather, the novelist braids him out of his many fibres, clustered associations, and animating metaphors: denied Jewishness, secret homosexuality, death wish, survivor guilt (those bullying dead brothers), the music he found purer than any philosophy, his difficult father's big house with seven pianos and thirty servants, the golem ghosts of the Prater, the new "key" of mass politics in anti-Semitic Vienna, Freud's forbidden fruit. "Language was the text," says Duffy, "but pain, it seems, was the subtext."

Monk's biography spends more time than Duffy's novel on Ludwig and religion. (Indeed, he succumbed to the metaphysical temptation. Wisdom, he said, is cold and gray, "but faith by contrast is what Kierkegaard calls a *passion.*" Father Zosima in *The Brothers Karamazov* was one of his heroes.) Monk also spends many pages on the gay question. (He's at pains to refute W. W. Bartley's *Wittgenstein,* with its imputations of rough trade.) Obviously, sex had as much to do with Ludwig's unhappiness as God did. But it's the astringent tannic-acid quality of the unhappiness that strikes us wherever we look for Ludwig. To know so much, and still to be so sad, after killing off so many fathers. . . . Susan Sontag might have said of him, as she said of Simone Weil:

No one who loves life would wish to imitate her dedication to martyrdom, or would wish it for his children or for anyone else he loves. Yet so far we as love seriousness, as well as life, we are moved by it. In the respect we pay to such lives, we acknowledge the presence of mystery in the world—and mystery is just what the possession of the truth, an objective truth, denies.

But I've begun to wonder, down among the philosophers, whether we oughtn't to be attending as much to their boo-hoo lives as to their gaudy texts. Now that we've mentioned her, what about Simone Weil, the philosopher/mystic who starved herself to death in wartime London in 1943? In his biography *Utopian Pessimist,* David McLellan calls her a "cross between Pascal and Orwell." She understood the evils of Stalinism as early as 1932, the evils of colonialism decades before Camus. She knew all about technological alienation from firsthand experience in the factories while the rest of them just talked about it in cafés. Her contemplation, says McLellan, "was not a means of stopping a nauseating world and getting off, but of seeing the world in a different and truer perspective, and, above all, of developing a sharp eye and ear for the traces of God in all human activity and experience." It was as if, because of her radical individualism, with her burning eye, she *saw through* everything, and on the other side was lucidity, which she called God. Or, to borrow her own image, Christ on the cross as a fulcrum, a point of rest between magnitudes, establishing balance and proportion.

And yet, for all the beauty that so stunned her, like Leonardo and Saint Francis of Assisi and Bach's Fourth Brandenburg Concerto, and all the brilliant style with which she wrote about it, like Stendhal—how *difficult* she was, how uncomfortable with herself: clumsy, homely, frail, repressed, an exasperation and a reproach. She would allow no one ever to touch her. Farmers for whom she worked didn't want her around because she never washed her hands or changed her clothes, and she was always talking about poverty, deportations, and the martyrdom of the Jews. When offered fine cream cheese, she declined, saying that the little Indochinese were hungry. In the thirty-four years she spent mortifying herself, she went from the Jewishness she denied to a flirtation with the Roman Catholic Church never to be consummated; from a politics that was a hodgepodge of Descartes and Marx to a theology that hodgepodged Plato, Pythagoras, and the Gnostics; from a pacifism that would have given Hitler whatever he wanted to the guilt that sent her stumbling to the front in the Spanish Civil War to a patriotism wanting to parachute itself down into occupied France. A year before she died, from refusing to eat enough to stay alive, she said: "Every time I think of the crucifixion of Christ, I commit the sin of envy." The coroner called it suicide. The priest who was supposed to be there at her funeral missed his train.

This wasn't *healthy*. I'm sorry. I know it's an article of left-wing faith that therapy is inauthentic and that those of us who go to twelve-step meetings and tell stories to get us through the night—about joblessness and paranoia, accidents and jail, child abuse and loony bins and AIDS, hallucinations and attempted suicide, waste and pain and disconnection and the end of love, in a black forest of bad chemicals—well, we just haven't figured out yet that all this is the fault of false consciousness, bad faith, the new technologies, and the International Monetary Fund. But when you feel as bad as Ludwig and Simone and don't do anything about it, you're a drag around the house, and not much better on the barricades.

Nietzsche's another. In his entertaining novel *When Nietzsche Wept*, Irvin D. Yalom, a professor of psychiatry at Stanford, imagines a meeting, in 1882, between the Tragic Muse himself and Dr. Josef Breuer, one of the founding fathers of psychoanalysis. While in Venice on vacation from Vienna, Breuer is approached by Lou Salomé, the Russian-born German novelist and cutiepie, a sort of nineteenth-century cross between Susans Sontag and Sarandon, who trifled in her time with the affections of Nietzsche, Freud, and Rainer Maria Rilke before marrying an Orientalist. In 1882, she's twenty-one years old and worried about Fred, who is thirty-eight, mad at her, and threatens suicide. Joe, at age forty a comfortable physician who makes house calls in a horse and buggy, is renowned for his "talking cure" of the pseudonymous Anna O. Lou asks Joe to undertake a similar cure of Fred, but secretly, because Fred's too proud to submit his mind for repairs to any mere mortal, and would also resent Lou's interference. Little does Lou know that Joe is extremely anxious about Anna O., whose real name is Bertha. Joe is a happily married man, but ever since his talking cure, all he thinks about are Bertha's breasts.

Never mind how Joe gets Fred into a Viennese hospital. It has something to do with Wagner and migraines. What's interesting here is that, while Joe thinks he is curing Fred of his despair, Fred is actually curing Joe of his midlife crisis. It will not perhaps surprise you to learn that Joe's mother's name was also Bertha. Meanwhile, there's this medical student to whom Joe is a mentor and who keeps popping in and out of the narrative with some odd notions about dreams. His name is Sigmund. Later, of course, Joe and Sig will coauthor *Studies in Hysteria,* and Fred will do *Zarathustra.* A whimsical Yalom suggests that if Nietzsche really had consulted Breuer, as he consulted so many doctors in those years, he might have invented psychoanalysis. Think of eternal recurrence as a return of the repressed. The very first couch potato!

We also get some zippy nihilistic sound bites from the Master: "That which does not kill me makes me stronger." And: "To love women is to hate life." You'll remember all over again why Nietzsche seemed so important when you were sixteen years old. If you were a boy. Even then girls were healthier. Reading thigh-slappers like "Man shall be trained for war and women for the recreation of the warrior," girls were less amused. The point is that after he didn't meet Breuer in Vienna, after eternal recurrence, the will to power, self-transcendence through self-denial, and the ever-popular abyss, Nietzsche still dragged himself alone off to Italy, where he couldn't afford a room with a window on the warming South, to feel bad (about Lou) and go mad (babbling of popes and pariahs). He was not a guy you'd call up when you got the blues. None of them has been, not since Spinoza. Certainly not Michel Foucault, the famous sexologist. What *are* we to think about Foucault, for whom Nietzsche was such an inspiration? It isn't his fault that Berkeley students in the early 1980s misconstrued him as a sort of metaphysical Eraserhead. But the inability of the French philosopher to stay out of San Francisco's leather bars and bathhouses, though he may have known he was dying of AIDS, does raise lurid questions about ethics, denial, philosophy, and the French, all of which are asked in *The Passion of Michel Foucault* by James Miller, who looks for the answers in a close reading of the secret life and evasive texts in which Foucault hid himself, like a minotaur in a labyrinth.

What Miller finds is an "unrelenting, deeply ambiguous and profoundly problematic preoccupation with death, which [Foucault] explored not only in the exoteric form of his writing, but also, and I believe critically, in the esoteric form of sadomasochistic eroticism." The texts are "an allegory of endless domination, from the hangman torturing the murderer to the doctor locking up the deviant." They argue that every institution (asylums, prisons, schools, professions) is in the "corrective technologies" business of beating down the individual, to "neutralize his dangerous states" and create "docile bodies and obedient souls." How to escape these "numbing codes of discipline"? By deconstructing the body as if it were a text; by seeking what Foucault called the "limit-experience" in art, dreams, drugs, madness, and S/M. Through such "limit-experiences," we find our "demonic aspect," "secret being," and "singular fate." Through passion and delirium, by risking "fatal vertigo" in "revolutionary discontinuity," "erotic transgression," "secret self-ravishment" and "absolute sacrifice," we might achieve an "insurrection of unsubjugated knowledges" — what Heidegger called the "ontology of unthought." Rapture, and perhaps transcendence. But also, and not unwittingly, death.

The mentors who brought Foucault to this pass included other philosophers, like Nietzsche, Heidegger, Kant, the Stoic Seneca, and the Cynic Diogenes; writers like Sade, Beckett, Hermann Broch, Raymond Roussel, and Georges Bataille (who was into Aztec sacrifice); painters like Goya, Bosch, Brueghel, Dürer, and van Gogh (with his black crows); composers like Barraque, with whom he had an affair, and Stockhausen, to whom he listened while tripping out on LSD; playwrights like Artaud and buddies like Althusser. With such cohorts, no wonder he would end up insisting that modern doctrines of moral responsibility are a form of "terrorism."

Finally, there is Michel himself, who hated his surgeon father and who attempted suicide in grade school with a razor and a rope; who quit analysis when his therapist went on vacation; who trafficked with structuralists, Maoists, and hashish; whose clever mind was blown in California—in Death Valley, by acid; in San Francisco, by handcuffs, blindfolds, and riding crops, by hot wax dripped on alligator clips, by a dungeon and a crucifix—with his shaved head, wire-rimmed glasses, and leather chaps. "The bald savant," says Miller, "as a postmodernist sphinx."

Troubled as he is by what he tells us, Miller is also almost painfully sympathetic. I'm less so. Never mind the damage Foucault might have done in San Francisco. Consider a larger suicidal trendiness. As anxious as all these postwar French intellectuals were to get rid of their imaginary father, Jean-Paul Sartre, they killed off socialism, humanism, and the Enlightenment in the process. They were so busy strangling their wives, like Althusser, or dying of alcoholic poisoning like Barraque, or overdosing on drugs like Roussel, or going crazy like Artaud that they left behind them nothing but squeaky pips like Bernard-Henri Levy. It was as if they murdered reason. Why should we be surprised? After all, Heidegger's "ontology of unthought" led him to the "limit-experience" of the Nazis, to Hitler's hot-wax carnival of death.

V. BAD CHARACTERS
IN THE PHILOSOPHICAL NOVEL

Heraclitus was a warmonger, besides thinking Homer "should be turned out of the lists and whipped." Empedocles was so full of delusions of godhood that he jumped into a volcanic crater. (About which there is a poem: "Great Empedocles, that ardent soul, / Leapt into Etna, and was roasted whole.") Anaxagoras believed in moon men. Pythagoras hated beans. Plato, besides hating poetry and music, wanted to burn every book ever written by Democritus. Socrates has to take the rap for the tyrant Critias, and Aristotle for Alexander the Despotic Great, and both thought slavery was swell and women weren't. Diogenes was in favor of incest and cannibalism. Lucretius, often insane, killed himself. Zeno advised us not to feel bad if our wives or children died; it in no way compromised *our* virtue. Seneca lent a lot of money, at exorbitant interest, to the Britons, causing their revolt. Marcus Aurelius was a lousy father. Are we having fun yet?

Plotinus, the founder of Neoplatonism, managed to ignore all the war and pestilence tearing the empire apart, just like the church fathers in the Dark Ages. Ecclesiastes was hard on women ("From garments cometh a moth, and from women wickedness") and harder on slaves ("Fodder, a wand, and burdens, are for the ass; and bread, correction, and work, for a servant. . . . Set him to work, as is fit for him: if he be not obedient, put on more heavy fetters"). Origen did a terrible thing to himself. Saint Augustine abandoned not only his wife but two mistresses; still, it was the pear tree he went on about. Saint Cyril, patriarch of Alexandria, specialized in pogroms, and belongs in Dante's Inferno for what he did to Hypatia.

Hypatia! Ever since Gibbon, some of us have had such a crush on her—in *Mason & Dixon*, Thomas Pynchon even imagines a missing Shakespeare play, *The Tragedy of Hypatia*—that we were reluctant to read Maria Dzielska's revisionist account of what really led up to the events of 415 A.D. Gibbon was furious about it: "On that fatal day, in the holy season of Lent, Hypatia was torn from her chariot, stripped naked, dragged to the church, and inhumanly butchered by the hands of Peter the reader and a troop of savage and merciless fanatics: her flesh was scraped from her bones with oyster-shells, and her quivering limbs were delivered to the flames."

Hypatia—the fourth-century Neoplatonist, astronomer, and mathematician, about whom either Palladius or Panolbios is supposed to have written a reverential ode; the "immaculate star of wise learning" and the virgin-scientist who invented an astrolabe to calculate the zodiac's ascendant sign and a hydroscope to measure the weight of liquids; "the last of the Hellenes," whose gruesome demise is said by Martin Bernal to have marked "the end of Egypto-Paganism and the beginning of the Christian Dark Ages"—has gotten good press since at least 1720, when the zealous English Protestant John Toland published his inflammatory *Hypatia or, the History of a Most Beautiful, Most Virtuous, Most Learned and in Every Way Accomplished Lady; Who Was Torn to Pieces by the Clergy of Alexandria, to Gratify the Pride, Emulation, and Cruelty of the Archbishop, Commonly but Undeservedly Titled St. Cyril.* After which Voltaire himself couldn't shut up about the "bestial murder . . . by Cyril's tonsured hounds, with a fanatical gang at their heels," of such a young and lovely paragon of pre-Enlightenment rational thought.

She shows up in a Henry Fielding novel, as "a young lady of greatest beauty and merit" done in by "those dogs, the Christians," and in one of the last fevered dreams of the Symbolist Gérard de Nerval before he hanged himself from a lamppost. Charles Leconte de Lisle and Contessa Diodata Roero de Saluzzo wrote poems about her; Maurice Barres, a short story; and the clergyman-novelist Charles Kingsley, a long polemic. In our own century, there have been plays by Mario Luzi; historical novels by André Feretti, Jean Marcel, and Arnulf Zitelmann; and a prose-poem portrait by Ursule Molinaro. British and American positivists like J. W. Draper claim her as a heroine of science. Feminists in Athens and in Indiana have taken her name for their scholarly journals. And Judy Chicago has invited her to dinner. All that's missing is an opera, a miniseries, and a sneaker commercial. Like Cleopatra, Mary Magdalene, Joan of Arc, and your pick of the litter of Madonnas, Hypatia has been retailored to suit the psychic needs of anybody retrospecting her, rational or romantic or nostalgic. Usually she's young and beautiful; mostly a virgin, though on occasion married off to the philosopher Isidore; always a pagan ganged up on by the beastly Christians; invariably, as Bertrand Russell put it, "lynched."

What Maria Dzielska, a scholar on the cultural life of the Roman Empire at Kraków's Jagiellonian University, has done to this pretty picture is what Lucy Hughes-Hallet did to the Queen of the Nile in *Cleopatra: Histories, Dreams and Distortions.* When Hughes-Hallet was done with Cleo, we knew that she wasn't Egyptian but Greek; that the asp that bit her was really a cobra, and bit her on an arm instead of a breast; that she was otherwise fully clothed, in royal robes as befits a working queen who spoke nine languages, wrote some books, and cut a deal with the Nabateans for oil rights in the Dead Sea. So Dzielska demystifies Hypatia, sifting patiently through the original sources, from the *Suda* lexicon to the correspondence of Synesius of Cyrene.

Dzielska finds that Hypatia was sixty years old when she died, "certainly not endowed with an enticing, pleasing or sympathetic personality," and disliked by the local rabble for her elitist airs. That what she knew about hydroscopes and astrolabes she probably got from her father, Theon, who got it from Ptolemy, and what they used them for, anyway, was fortunetelling. That she was less an Enlightenment philosophe than a transcendentalist-astrologer, and while she may have trifled with Chaldean, Orphic, and Hermetic texts, and was doubtless a Pythagorean mystic, she was no more devoted to Thoth the baboon-headed god than, say, John Updike. That her circle of aristocratic young men included more Christians than pagans, and there wasn't a peep out of any of them when goons attacked the Serapeum in 391 and shattered the Bryaxis statue with an ax. That her quarrel with Cyril, the newly invested bishop of St. Mark's so busy expelling Novatians and Jews from the city, was party-political rather than religious. Hypatia backed the prefect Orestes (also a Christian). Thus her martyrdom was "murder for a political purpose"—a kind of power-grab: "They killed a person who was the mainstay of the opposition against [the patriarch], who through her authority and political connections provided support for the representative of state authority in Alexandria contending against Cyril."

But she did die a virgin. She found the body repugnant. According to Damascius, one of her regular students fell in love with her. "Unable to control his feelings, the young man confessed his love. Hypatia resolved to punish him, and she found an effective method of chasing him away. As a symbol of the female body's physicality, she showed him her sanitary napkin, remonstrating: 'This is what you really love, my young man, but you do not love beauty for its own sake.'"

There's much, much more in Dzielska. And one supposes we need to know most of it. But it seems somehow sort of . . . tacky. Anyway—

Nice as he was, Saint Francis of Assisi left us an Order that enjoyed itself far too much during the Inquisition. Erasmus lacked the courage of a Thomas More, Machiavelli pandered to Lorenzo, and Luther and Calvin and Loyola you already know about. Because Avicenna, Roger Bacon, and Spinoza had a thing about rainbows, I like all three of them. Hume was a nice guy, too, though he hurt us in our inductive reasoning. Descartes got up at a very cold five o'clock each dawn to talk to Queen Christina of Sweden, because she let him play with a sword, which was more fun than a pineal gland. Leibniz, that "windowless monad," stole from and then lied about Spinoza, and so deserved exactly what he got, as Dr. Pangloss in Voltaire's *Candide*. Rousseau dumped all five of his children by Thérèse at a founding hospital. I'd rather recall Kant being traumatized by *Emile* than Schopenhauer's finding in the Upanishads a consolation he didn't deserve after throwing a seamstress down a flight of stairs for which he had to pay her off for the next twenty years.

Get a letter from Marx (Engels got most of them) and all he does is wheedle. Always he's broke (he spent his inheritance on guns for the radical Brussels workers in 1848), usually sick (pleurisy, bronchitis, asthma, carbuncles, inflammations, malfunctions of the eyes, liver, and spleen), invariably abusive ("toads," "fungus," "canaille," "trashy democratic rabble," "sewer-aesthetes"), and appallingly anti-Semitic. On the other hand, Engels spent more in one month for the upkeep of a private stable for his horse than Marx made in any month even when on the payroll of the *Herald-Trib.* A. J. Ayer claims that "Teddy" Wiesengrund-Adorno, the mustard-cutter of the Frankfurt School, was a victim of "student unrest, suffering a heart attack when some of his female pupils uncovered their breasts and danced around in mockery of him." And Hannah Arendt carried on a love affair with Martin Heidegger, before and after the death camps.

Not for the first time, nor for the last, I mourn the passing of Jean-Paul Sartre, philosophizing novelist, pamphleteering playwright, "pope of existentialism," tireless ambassador of the French Left to the Third World, ugly duckling superstar and celebrity intellectual—a one-eyed chain-smoking piano-playing boozehound, pillhead, and womanizer who wrote an average of twenty pages a day every day of his hectic life, in hotels, at cafés, on barricades, in jail, losing more manuscript than most writers publish: "We are alone without excuses. This is what I mean when I say that man is condemned to be free." It's instructive that for his writing of fiction and of *The Words,* his splendid invention of his childhood, he was craftily sober. For philosophies and polemics he was stoned, usually on corydrane, a compound of aspirin and amphetamines. He doped himself up to kill God. To the end, he kept the activist faith, risking himself on Algeria, hitting the streets with Maoists and anarchists, as if to rub up some warmth from their contradictions and even their stupidities, marching until his other eye went out. He talked himself into commitment and stayed there, even at the price of relinquishing his claim on us as a great imaginative writer. He gave away his millions without stint or grudge, and died propertyless and almost penniless, still ferocious about freedom and choice, without excuses, looking in his old fake-leather jacket once again to the indignant young, a Chaplin-like "small old tramp," says one of his biographers, "carelessly wandering from the Closerie des Lilas to La Coupole, with 'nothing in his hands, nothing in his pockets . . .'"

Why do I think of Kierkegaard? While Sartre can be found in almost any Parisian café, you have to work hard to locate Kierkegaard in the city where he lived and died, of fear and trembling at age forty-two. There's a single room devoted to his memory (letters, snapshots, book jackets, pipe), upstairs at the Köbenhavns Bymuseum. Whereas they'll haul you by air-conditioned bus all over Copenhagen on a daylong tour of the habitats and artifacts of Kierkegaard's contemporary, Hans Christian Andersen, ending with a visit to the statue of the Little Mermaid. At the statue you will be told that Hans was his own imaginary mermaid, as well as an Ugly Duckling. In 1964, vandals decapitated the Little Mermaid. Its severed head is still missing. Maybe some Søren cult did the dirty deed, disgusted with a feel-good Denmark of blond heads drinking blond beer and licking blond ice cream cones. Or maybe, if you don't think blond thoughts, they cut off your head.

But this isn't what I mean. What I mean is, the opposite of "mean" need not be "nice." The opposite of "mean" could be "generous," like Sartre, whom his buddy Giacometti once compared to another melancholy Dane: "You're beautiful," said Giaco to Jean-Paul. "You're like Hamlet. Yes. You always think Hamlet was a tall thin guy, and so on, eh? No, me, I'm sure he was a little fellow who drank beer, eh? A little fat man with hair like yours and eyes like yours."

Spooking the Horses
of the Apocalypse

So I am watching William Colby, on camera, on television, disagree with Richard Helms about how intelligence agencies are supposed to behave, both in the field and in front of oversight committees. This is midway through *CIA: America's Secret Warriors*, a three-hour gimlet-eyed 1997 Discovery Channel miniseries on the song-and-dance of shadowy Whiffenpoofs from "Wild Bill" Donovan to Aldrich Ames. And Colby, the agency director from 1973 to 1976, is sounding reasonable. It was Colby who told Congress in the wake of Watergate that the CIA had for years tapped telephones, opened personal mail, and spied on thousands of Americans, as well as plotting to assassinate foreign leaders and performing LSD experiments on human guinea pigs. For giving away the "family jewels," he was reviled by colleagues like Helms (so proud of himself as The Man Who Kept the Secrets). James Jesus Angleton, the paranoid counterspy who gets his own half hour in the miniseries and who terrorized the agency for decades until his forced retirement in 1974, even suspected Colby of being that much-sought "super mole" in the very cerebellum of Spook Central. And in recent years Colby had campaigned for an end to the nuclear arms race, going so far as to call for a 50 percent cut in the Pentagon budget, the money saved to be spent instead on domestic social programs.

But a month after talking to the producers of *America's Secret Warriors*, Colby was dead. He had vanished in the spring of 1996 from his summerhouse in Rock Point, Maryland. In the kitchen, they found a glass of wine, a sink full of clamshells, a loud radio, and a warm computer. On the banks of a Potomac tributary not far from Cobb Island, they found an abandoned canoe. He was, everyone agreed, an expert seaman and a fine swimmer and had been cracking jokes Thursday night before he disappeared. After his body washed up, almost everyone also agreed to blame the high winds and choppy waves of a sudden squall. The exceptions are those of us as paranoid as Angleton, only in reverse. Why let hate radio have all the fun?

With consultants like Tom Powers, the unauthorized biographer of Helms, *America's Secret Warriors* is no kinder to its subject than Bill Moyers was in *High Crimes and Misdemeanors* on PBS. But even entertainment television, at least since *Miami Vice* and including *The Equalizer,* has had its florid doubts about these cowboys of the clandestine. G. Gordon Liddy, E. Howard Hunt, Sam Giancana, Oliver North, and the Golden Triangle will do that to purveyors of popular culture, as well as to elite novelists like Don DeLillo and Joan Didion. How much of an *X-Files* stretch is it, really, after research projects in psychic phenomena and mind control, to imagine Angleton as a druid priest, an Alamut assassin or a kundalini serpent? As Umberto Eco has explained in *Foucault's Pendulum,* "There exists a secret society with branches throughout the world, and its plot is to spread the rumor that a universal plot exists."

Part One, "Brotherhood," is a historical overview, from Ivy League Eagle Scout recruitment during World War II for the OSS to how Allen Dulles learned to love the Cold War to the 1989 Velvet Revolutions and crumbling of the Berlin Wall. Along the way, we hear about Iran (deposing Mossadegh for Anglo-American Oil), Guatemala (deposing Arbenz for United Fruit), the Bay of Pigs (infuriating JFK), Laos (where the agency's coddling of drug lords and trafficking in poppy seeds established a precedent), Vietnam (where the Phoenix "pacification" program sanctioned torture, assassination, and severed ears), Chile (deposing Allende for Dr. Kissinger), Nicaragua (mining harbors and funding contras), and Afghanistan (Stingers for those Mujahideen who later brought us the World Trade Center bombing). Omitted are civil war in Greece, Farouk in Egypt, Huks in the Philippines, Sukarno in Indonesia, and the Kurds, as well as the suborning of college professors, labor leaders, and journalists.

Part Two, "Betrayal," spends time with the counterintelligent Angleton, who had been so traumatized by the treason of his buddy Kim Philby that he saw "doubles," "screens," "deep covers," and disinformation wherever he looked, and whose baroque suspicions ruined the careers of any hapless agent who even vaguely resembled the shadowy image of the "mole" in the tales spun by his pet KGB defector. *America's Secret Warriors* seems to be saying that Aldrich Ames, who started selling out his country a decade after Angleton got the boot, escaped detection for so long because an agency so demoralized by Angleton's paranoia was also distracted by congressional investigations into its "dirty tricks." Ames himself gets a surprising amount of face on camera, most of it grinning as if pleasantly mystified by his own corrupt behaviors and alcoholic grandiosity. I'll think out loud about him in a minute.

Part Three, "Blowback," is exceedingly gloomy about the "unintended consequences" and "boomerang" effect of clandestine agency actions. Deposing Mossadegh and installing the Shah of Iran on his Peacock Throne led to the Ayatollah and a hostage crisis. Backing Saddam against these Iranians led to an invasion of Kuwait and the Gulf War. We seem to have trained the Mujahideen, after they got rid of the Russians, to terrorize the West as well as to harvest opium. Terrorism, drugs, and the CIA are all fingers on the same hand in the same black glove in Afghanistan, Latin America, and Southeast Asia. Is it any wonder that South Central LA is suspicious of a CIA plot to finance the contras by selling cocaine in the ghetto?

No one program, not even a miniseries in which all these cowboys look like advertising account executives, can do everything. Watergate deserves more attention, and even the agency's critics concentrate in *America's Secret Warriors* only on "operations"—the sexy, secret stuff. One misses some analysis of the "intelligence" they gathered, or, more to the point, failed to. In this, the miniseries is as deficient as a spate of recent books on the spooky subject. In *From the Shadows,* Robert M. Gates tells us he wasn't such a Dr. Strangelove after all, even if, after decades of hand-to-hand combat with the Evil Empire, he just happened to miss the biggest story in the agency's history, the collapse of the Soviet Union. In *Secret and Sanctioned,* Stephen Knott tells us that covert operations against Chile, Libya, and Castro are an old American story. George Washington had his own spooks, and contemplated kidnapping the King of England; Thomas Jefferson wanted to burn down Saint Paul's Cathedral in London. In *Wild Bill and Intrepid,* Thomas F. Troy retells the origin myth of the CIA, from the point of view of the OSS and MI-5. ("Wild Bill" Donovan, he assures us, was *not* a British spy.) And in the posthumously published *Reflections of a Cold Warrior,* Richard Bissell seems pretty pleased with himself, after Groton, Yale, Guatemala, and the Congo, although the Bay of Pigs wasn't quite so peachy-keen. (Bissell, of course, is lucky he's dead. A long-suppressed 150-page "Survey of the Cuban Operation," in which CIA Inspector General Lyman Kirkpatrick investigated the 1961 disaster and blamed it on the arrogance, ignorance, incompetence, and "pathetic illusions" of his own agency—imagine mounting a counterrevolution in the Caribbean with operatives who can't even speak Spanish—would finally surface in February 1998. The single extant copy of this 37-year-old report, which Bissell seems not to have consulted in writing his memoir, was discovered locked in the director's safe.)

Not by accident, two of these books were published by Yale.

The tigers of wrath are wiser than the horses of instruction.

(William Blake)

From such straws and scraps as the eager beavers of the dailies brought up in their teeth, we will build a dream house; even a memory palace. At *last,* the Mole. Not that Aldrich ("Rick") Hazen Ames is exactly who Angleton had in mind when he went Chiquita Bananas after too much staring into what his old buddy T. S. Eliot called the "wilderness of mirrors." Angleton, the Poet/Counterspy of Langley, needed a nemesis at least the size of a Sir Richard Francis Burton, dutifully reporting back to Charles Napier on the nights he spent in the male brothels of

Karachi. Or the great Mogul emperor Akbar who ordained in the sixteenth century a spy corps with four thousand officers, most of them Untouchables. Or maybe even the philosopher of war, Sun Tzu, who probably invented espionage more than 2,500 years ago in Wu, deceiving his own spooks so that when they were captured, before they were killed, they would disinform the enemy. For an Angleton to wake up and smell the orchids, he needs someone of . . . *substance.*

Instead we have our Rick, a lazy, bibulous, bespectacled, fifty-two-year-old, $69,843-a-year second-generation, mid-level operations officer, on counternarcotics watch for drug traffic in the Black Sea, who couldn't even spell "accommodate" and who sold out Nathan Hale for a Jaguar and a Jacuzzi. Not to mention condos in Bogotá and in Cartagena, the dacha and the ranch and the two-story house on Randolph Road in Arlington, Virginia, for which he plunked down $540,000 in cash. In a backyard, beside the Jacuzzi, a gym for five-year-old Paul. In the garage, beside the $65,000 Jaguar, a $19,500 Honda. In various local, Swiss, and Italian bank accounts, at least $300,000. On the credit cards, from 1985 to 1993, charges of $450,000. All this, and all Rick had to do was tell the Russians all he knew about our agents in their country, maybe ten covers blown—including that of his own mirror-image "Prologue" in the KGB Counterintelligence Directorate—and perhaps as many firing squads. Signal sites! Dead drops! Caracas!

Rick, not exactly a genius, got away with seven years of conspicuous consumption because there were so many others like him lolling about the Langley campus—gentlemen spies whose aristocratic wives were reputed to be wealthy. Besides, like the thirty-eight double agents for Fidel Castro whom the agency hired just in time for the Bay of Pigs, he passed his polygraph test. As wonderfully impersonated by Timothy Hutton in a cable-television movie in the fall of 1998, he could talk himself at the bottom of a shot glass into believing almost anything—that he had been passed over for promotion because of his superior intelligence; that spooking itself had degenerated from a chess match worthy of grandmasters to a vulgar game of checkers; that fetching up transparent baggies of cold cash in Rock Creek Park was somehow clever. From booze, his ego boundaries dissolved in a fog of low cunning, moist resentment, and rationalizing spin-rinse.

I guess they needed the Honda so Maria could go shopping, which she did a lot of at the local Bloomingdale's; and to school, at Georgetown, where she sought a Ph.D. and was writing a thesis, according to a neighbor, on "Heidegger or some other philosopher." Maria del Rosario Casas Dupuy Ames, forty-two years old, is more interesting than her husband—a bookworm Angleton could have *talked* to. Born upper-middle-class, on the stylish north side of Bogotá, she went to all the right schools, including Princeton for a semester, before graduating summa cum laude from the University of the Andes, where she taught Greek, *literary theory,* and contemporary culture while brooding about "Esthetic Problems in Hegel with Respect to Literature," before she was spirited away to Mexico City, in 1982, as the cultural attaché in the Colombian Embassy, where she was making $1,000 a month when Rick met her. Things hadn't worked out for Rick—in Ankara, or Langley, or New York, where his first marriage fell apart. But in Mexico City, he recruited his first agent, and paid her, before he married her, to inform on her own country.

Or so we're told. Who recruited whom? Let's play Angleton for a minute. Maria's father, Pablo Casas Santofimio, was a mathematician turned politician; a governor, a senator, a university rector. Maria's mother, rather more vividly, had a reputation in Bogotá bohemian circles for bringing home hard-luck salsa musicians. But there's this cousin, Alberto Santofimio, who is said by *The New York Times* "to have close ties to members of the Medellín cartel, principally the late Pablo Escobar." Well. And Rick's been transferred at Langley from counterintelligence to counternarcotics. Suggestive? To which tease we add the tidbit that Rick's defense attorney, Plato Cacheris, had previously represented not only Sheik Kamal Adham, the Saudi intelligence chief up to his burnoose in the B.C.C.I. scandal, but also . . . *Fawn Hall,* Ollie North's centerfold shredder during Iranamok. And would graduate to . . . *Monica Lewinsky,* in the Oval Orifice. I am the last Wobbly. I believe in one big union and one big conspiracy, most of which we'll never know for sure about because they shredded Bill Casey's brain.

When time has ceased to be anything other than velocity, instantaneousness and simultaneity, and time as history has vanished from the lives of all peoples . . . then, yes, then, through all this turmoil a question still haunts us like a specter. What for? Whither? What then?

(Martin Heidegger)

But, of course, the agency never asked me in. Almost alone among my peers in the fifties and sixties, I went unapproached by the CIA. It was a lot like, well, not belonging to a final club at Harvard, an eating club at Princeton, or a secret society at Yale. It was in fact *exactly* like not belonging to a secret society at Yale. The first American spy was a Yale grad, Nathan Hale, and it's not surprising that identical statues of him stood for so long on the Old Campus in New Haven and on the lawn in front of Langley. But as Robin Winks explains in *Cloak and Gown,* Yale really got up to its elbow patches in the spy biz during World War II. Professors of history and literature and economics, not to mention the crew coach, went undercover themselves or recruited their students to derring-do for the OSS. At spy parties in wartime London, even the British joined in singing "The Whiffenpoof Song." At war's end, some of the Old Blue derring-doers went back to school, but more stayed on to start and staff the CIA. Most of them were at worst what Winks calls "sentimental imperialists," determined to bring the American message to a messy world by whatever means necessary—which meant bribery, forgery, fraud, and blackmail. (By stopping short in 1961, Winks manages not to have to think about political assassination.)

But a few were very odd ducks indeed, and none odder than James Jesus Angleton. Before he left Yale for counterintelligence he had been a serious poet. He published *Furioso,* a first-rate literary magazine full of difficult modernists like Ezra Pound, whose enthusiasm for Mussolini was apparently contagious and whom Angleton some years later would spring from the loony bin. Besides T. S. Eliot, Thomas Mann also came to lunch. At Langley, where he was known variously as Mother, Orchid, the Gray Ghost, Trimsky (for his Trotsky-like salt-and-pepper mustache), Gobby (For "God's old beast"), the Poet, and the Fisherman, Angleton was so obsessed with the notion that a "mole" had penetrated our Hypertext that he saw "doubles," counterfeit identities, masks of the inimical Other wherever he looked, except in the smiling face of Kim Philby. If *he* could imagine it, *they* must be doing it. (Compare this to KGB defector Victor Sheymov's inside account in *Tower of Secrets* of life at Dzerzhinsky Square: "For security was paramount for the KGB. Defense was the key to offense. The worst case was assumed in virtually every situation. Absolutely no one was to be trusted. . . . For Victor this was by now a natural mindset— quite as important as the existence of any real or imagined intruders.") Angleton's paranoia was more than just demoralizing to counterintelligence. It led him to ignore Soviet defectors who had genuinely important information to retail. It also led him to ruin with suspicion the careers of many agents. Pushed out, perhaps by Kissinger, in 1974, he left behind not "Gerontion" but a *Waste Land.*

Where our Rick, with not very much on the ball, would subsequently thrive.

But this is to anticipate. Imagine, back when the agency was riding high in the popularity polls, before the Church committee and the Rockefeller commission found out about its violations of its own charter—the 7,200 files with the 300,000 names of American citizens; the assassination plots against not only Castro in Cuba but also Patrice Lumumba in the Congo, Abdul Kassem in Iraq, Rafael Trujillo Molina in the Dominican Republic, and Ngo Dinh Diem in Vietnam—back when rah-rah Elis and other Ivy Leaguers had already graduated from using the Yale Library as a front for an Istanbul scam to subverting departments of anthropology and political science at colleges all over the nation; then newspapers, foundations, and labor unions; the National Student Association, the Congress for Cultural Freedom, and *Encounter* magazine. When a noisome counterculture attacked the universities in the 1960s, those universities could hardly pretend to be ivory towers. Like so many other American institutions, they'd long before been compromised, starting at Yale, in the library, among the poets.

What a swashing of the buckles and the Bissells! It was so easy to take out King Farouk in Egypt in 1952, in favor of a Nasser. And Mossadegh in Iran in 1953, after he nationalized the holdings of Anglo-Iranian Oil. And Arbenz in Guatemala in 1954, after he nationalized 400,000 acres of idle United Fruit Company banana plantation. Why let Sukarno get away with whatever he wanted in Indonesia, when we could make blue movies about him, and had these feisty colonels on Sumatra? Why shouldn't Cuba, in 1961, be as much of a duck shoot as the Philippines had been in 1950, when they made sure Magsaysay stomped the Huk guerrillas? What could possibly be wrong with spending $2.6 million to make sure Eduardo Frei knocked off Salvador Allende in the Chilean elections of 1964, then another $8 million to prevent Allende's confirmation as President in 1970? (One of the sentences the CIA censored in the first edition of Victor Marchetti's *The CIA and the Cult of Intelligence* was from Dr. Kissinger, who said of Chile at a 40 Committee meeting in June 1970: "I don't see why we need to stand by and watch a country go Communist due to the irresponsibility of its own people.") Just look how much good it did us in the Middle East to fork over $12 million to King Hussein's mother in Jordan, $40 million to King Saud of Saudi Arabia, and who knows how much to Saud's brother, Prince Faisal? Such space cadets we were, Lonesome Rangers prepared at hideouts like the School of the Americas to advise and train secret police in Third World countries everywhere, even troops for the Dalai Lama's guerrilla incursions into Tibet, to whom we were ultimately as faithless as we'd later be to the "Red Sox / Red Cao" covert-action emigré insurgents of Hungary, Poland, Romania, and Czechoslovakia, the Meos in Laos, the Montagnards in Vietnam, and the Kurds in Iraq and Turkey.

Meanwhile, at counterintelligence in Langley, when he wasn't wiretapping inconvenient journalists, Angleton busied himself with a "theme analysis" of the *Ramparts* magazine table of contents. Elsewhere on campus, they were looking into thought control, artificial intelligence, paranormal psychology, ESP, UFOs, life on other planets, and astrology. Did you know that none of Yale's secret society buildings has any windows? Neither, of course, does Stonehenge, or the Dome of the Rock, or Machu Picchu, or Moscow Center in Dzerzhinsky Square. What do you suppose their secret is? Doesn't it sound like a novel by an Italian semiotician? *Indiana Umberto and the Templars of Doom?* For seven hundred years, the Templars have plotted to seize control of the earth's magnetic poles, the "telluric" tides and currents. Now, at Yale, they've not only got the CIA. They've also got literary criticism: the "linguistic predicaments" of Paul de Man.

From Skull and Bones—and Druids and Rosicrucians and Deconstructionists—we might have expected something like Operation Mongoose, by which Castro's subscription was to be canceled with botulin toxin in his cigars, hypodermic needles in his fountain pen and scuba suit, thallium salts in his shoes (to make his beard fall off), a second coming of Jesus Christ in some night-sky fireworks, and the Mafia. Or something like Watergate and the black-bag job on Dan Ellsberg's psychiatrist. Or Iran/contra, with the Bible and the cake and the funny money from the Sultan of Brunei. Such a boys' club it must have seemed, such a *safe* house and happy hunting ground of hoplites, berserkers, and samurai, storm-cloud Maruts and Taoist warrior-sages—Gilgamesh, Achilles, Arjuna, Crazy Horse—with secret books, sacred seals, and trendy computer graphics. How almost Kabbalistic! I mean, they had castles on the Rhone, châteaux in the Loire Valley, temples in Kyoto. Why not great

Bealim with glowing bellies, nail-hearted Nuremberg Maidens, and a banyan hung with horns of Tug? Or, on an altar of sacrifice to Yaldaboath, a menhir, a tesseract, an orgone box, a Swedenborg death mask, a black Celtic virgin, and the foreskin of Hermes Trismegistus?

Meanwhile, our crack intelligence agency—what ho, smiling strangeness!—will end up rudely surprised by North Korea's invasion of the South; the British-French-Israeli invasion of the Sinai and Suez; the launching of Sputnik; missiles in Cuba; the Yom Kippur War; an Ayatollah Khomeini; the collapse of the nonprofit police states of Eastern Europe; Aldrich Hazen Ames; and the Hindu hydrogen bomb. I'm not saying the KGB, with a lot more blood on its hands, wasn't equally surprised by the fall of the Shah of Iran. Nor that other intelligence agencies haven't made themselves just as obnoxious in the Cold War era: The Royal Canadian Mounties, for many years the secret service of Canada, likewise got caught breaking and entering, opening mail, wiretapping illegally, in their frenzy to subdue Quebec separatism. Among multiple indecencies, the East German Stasi managed to compromise the reputation of Christa Wolf. The French to this day are not sufficiently embarrassed at having blown up the Rainbow Warrior sailboat in New Zealand's Auckland harbor, killing a Portuguese photographer, to keep Greenpeace from bothering their South Pacific nuclear test zone. (Nor did they inform Mitterand before botching a plot to overthrow Qaddafi. And their behavior during the Algerian War was contemptible.) Israel's Mossad in the notorious Lavon Affair in the fifties sought to undermine U.S. confidence in Nasser by launching terrorist attacks on British and American properties in Egypt, and blaming the Egyptians. (In *By Way of Deception*, Victor Ostrovsky suggests Mossad knew in advance about the Mercedes truck bomb that destroyed our Beirut Marine barracks in October 1983, and didn't tell the CIA. He also goes on about kangaroo courts and assassin hit lists.) Italy's intelligence agency has so many bizarre links with the Mafia, P2 Masonic lodges, and the Mussolini fringe, it's amazing they ever heard of the Red Brigades. A right-wing nut faction at MI-5 sought to save Kenya for the Empire with a disease that attacked the sacred baobab tree, hoping thus to frighten Kikuyus into thinking that the tree gods were anti–Mau Mau. Think of Libya with Billy Carter on its payroll, and Bulgaria on Waterloo Bridge with a poisoned umbrella. Boys just wanna have fun.

I hear the ruin of all space, shattered glass and toppled masonry, and time one livid final flame. (James Joyce)

Yes, I know, it's all supposed to be spy satellites and computer cryptanalysis these days. But it isn't, is it? Iran/contra comes and goes, and so does the Walsh Report, and we still don't know what Robert M. Gates or Clair St. George knew, and neither does DCI Woolsey. Moreover, it's getting harder to work up an indignant sweat at the freshest scandal. After all, guys like Rick and Edwin "Johnny" Walker were just in it for the money. Money isn't interesting enough to whip up the old spy hysteria, after which it was always necessary to fire some teachers.

Remember the good old days of the Woodstock typewriter, the Bokhara rugs, the bad teeth, the old Ford, and the pumpkin? I had lunch, in the late fifties, with Whittaker Chambers. It was like having lunch with the Brothers Karamazov. We talked about his favorite poets (Rilke and García Lorca), his favorite city (Venice), and the Beat generation (he liked Ginsberg). All I could see was his sitting there, outside a federal grand jury room, reading Dante. And Ethel Rosenberg, rooting for the Brooklyn Dodgers in the deathhouse. And Col. Rudolf Abel, not a bad artist, painting Christmas cards and sending them, from Leavenworth, to his CIA pen pals. They had style, like Christopher Marlowe, who was probably murdered for fingering Catholics. Or Daniel Defoe mopping up Jacobites between *Robinson Crusoe* and *Moll Flanders*. Or Prussia's William Steiber, who invented the agent provocateur just in time for the revolutions of 1848. Or the Boy Scout Baden-Powell pretending to be an entomologist in order to infiltrate a Dalmatian fortress. I was almost rendered nostalgic by the FBI arrest, in October

1997, of Pentagon lawyer Terry Squillacote, her union-leader husband Kurt Stand, and their private-eye best friend Jim Clark, on charges of continuing to spy for East Germany years after there no longer happened to be any East Germany. Imagine a foreign intelligence service calling itself *Hauptverwaltung Aufklärung* ("Enlightenment Headquarters") and sending out coded messages from the "Holy Father" asking hapless agents to listen to the "Voice of God" (short-wave radio), before undertaking "missionary work" on a "pilgrimage tour" with "holy relics" (miniature cameras). Imagine American parents actually naming a son Karl and a daughter Rosa, after Karl Liebknecht and Rosa Luxemburg. Never mind the ethics of espionage. Whatever happened to the esthetics?

In the March 7, 1994, *Time* magazine, there was a rundown of the new mercenaries and their varied price tags: Ronald Pelton, $35,000; Jonathan Pollard, $50,000; Richard Miller, $65,000; Edward L. Howard, $150,000; Larry Wu-Tai Chin, $180,000; Jerry Whitworth, $332,000; and John Walker, $1 million. This omits William Kampiles, who sold a whole surveillance satellite system to a Soviet agent in Vienna for only $3,000. And David H. Barnett, who shopped thirty CIA officers and their agents in Jakarta for $92,000. And Army Sgt. Clyde Conrad, worth a cool million after selling, to Hungary, U.S. missile and NATO tank secrets. Plus of course our Rick, tops so far at $2.7 million and still counting. "We take this very seriously," said White House press secretary DeeDee Myers. "We don't like it one bit." But *New York Newsday*, in one of the oddest editorials I've ever seen, had a different point of view: "It's heartening in a way to know that Ames, like recent American traitors, apparently was motivated by money, not out of disillusionment with his country. That at least implies the failure is his own."

Goodness—as if overweening greed weren't as all-American as lynching bees. What *are* we thinking? The same thing, I suppose, as Graham Greene was thinking back in 1989, when the novelist returned to London from a Moscow visit with Kim Philby, to tell the *Sunday Telegraph* that he "forgave" Philby his treason because, after all, Philby had been "fighting for a cause he believed in. He wasn't doing it for the money."

I see. As if by now it shouldn't be axiomatic that means corrupt ends, what ideologues can't wish away with a wave of a rhetorical or a millennial wand, designer therapists will excuse with their good news of a sanctioning self-love. Against my avarice, it is possible to object. But don't you dare reproach my feelings of empowerment. And yet: The teeth of the police grinning in the windows of our midnights are sincere, so are the hooded hangmen, and so is the terrorist, that burning bush, and the pink-cheeked bomber of abortion clinics. About their sincerity, there is the glisten and gloss, the electricity, of a baby eel. They are Shining Path, as in Peru. They run amok, like the long knives of Suharto, after which there were 500,000 dead Indonesians. Torquemada believed in a cause, and so did Robespierre, and so did Goebbels. Say hi to Pol Pot. It's amazing how much damage can be done by people who aren't doing it for the money.

> *The Enlightenment is dead, Marxism is dead, the working class move-*
> *ment is dead . . . and the author does not feel very well either.*
>   (Neil Smith)

Once upon a time I dreamed that perhaps Langley itself was a hieratic monument, like the temples and pyramids of Egypt. From a helicopter, it even looked like Karnak, on three axes, as if in a fusion of art, science, and religion to configure such esoteric knowledge as the location of the ductless glands, the Chinese acupuncture points, and dualities of light and dark, of Horus and Set, yin and yang, gravity and levity, Ormazd and Ahriman, Quetzalcoatl and Tezcatlipoca. This led to bootless meditations on Pythagorean numerology; bird, bull, and scarab symbolism; and the Secret Science of the Pharaohs. But then they read my mail.

I decided for a while that every intelligence agency is its own Balkan country, a geography of impasse, capable of believing anything, full of historical grudges against Turkey and its own siblings, playing deadly Cold War games, dangerous to civilization. But so too is every terrorist sect both a Balkan country and a secret service, self-referential and self-infatuated. The blood-intimate relationship between the agent and the terrorist is our time's special kinkiness.

After too many Don DeLillo novels—remember that, like Maria del Rosario Casas Dupuy Ames, one of the ex-wives of the Professor of Hitler Studies in *White Noise* was also a part-time spook: "She reviewed fiction for the CIA, mainly long serious novels with coded structures"—and, naturally, Norman Mailer's *Harlot's Ghost,* I concluded that government intelligence itself is a modernist construct, a paranoid text, a furious unstitching of the magic carpet for a figure or a pattern, so many Secret Sharers and Underground Men and forged identity papers. At Yale, of course, John Hollander was so struck, while reading Sir John Masterman's long-suppressed memoir of World War II scientific spooking *The Double-Cross System* (Yale University Press!), by such code names as Mutt and Jeff, Brutus and Bronx, Zigzag and Tricycle, Lipstick, Peppermint, Garbo, and Weasel, that he wrote a book-length poem about them, *Reflections on Espionage,* reimagining writers like Pound, W. H. Auden, and Robert Lowell as spies, "living a hidden life in the actual world." But in another way, Nabokov had already done the same job in *Pale Fire,* and so had Angleton, in the "chill delirium" of his orchids. Zembla!

However: Everybody knows that modernism's dead. And so is the Soviet Union. So where are the binary oppositions? All those codes and ciphers look in vain for a cult message. We are guarding the secrets we've stolen from *them* against the secrets they're stolen from *us,* and all we do is listen to each other, and all we hear are scrambled language games. Instead of coherent representation, "palimpsests of traces," *sous rature,* paranomasia, collage/montage/pastiche. In *Tower of Secrets,* Sheymov recalls his KGB school days: "The instructor gave an example of one of the earliest techniques used for concealing a message. First, the sender had to write the message on the freshly shaved head of the messenger. Then, after his hair grew long enough to cover the message, the messenger was dispatched to his destination. Having arrived, his head was shaven again, chopped off for extra security, and delivered to the addressee on a silver platter." These are the headless horsemen of the apocalypse—of what deconstructionists call an *aporia,* a terminal impasse. Listen to David Lehman, who's in the middle of *Signs of the Times* but might as well be at Yale or Langley, hallucinating:

> In a Marxist model of knowledge, the superstructure—the tangible products of culture—camouflages and reinforces the hidden reality of class warfare. In a Freudian model, the manifest content of a dream is a cover or disguise for its latent meaning. In a deconstructive model, the text that is the world is similarly a camouflage. Like the Marxist's superstructure and the Freudian's manifest content, it is something to be seen through. The difference is that here, in contrast to the Marxist or Freudian schemes, there is no ultimate meaning to which one can penetrate. There is only the constant deferral of meaning, the infinite play of signification, and finally, the equilibrist's wire across the linguistic abyss.

So here we be, interrogating the text of the postmodern world like a mad Derrida, finding that everything we read has been "problematized," all the "hierarchies" and "hegemonies" are bankrupt, there are no discriminations possible between presence and absence, center and margin, sign and signified. Spycraft, like criticism, is *atolelic*: It requires no other object of study, nothing outside itself. To spook is to deconstruct without *jouissance.* Texts, Roland Barthes told us before they got him in Paris with a laundry truck, speak not of the world but of other texts. Instead of meaning, there are mirrored infinities. Paul de Man, another Yalie with lots to hide, insisted "the bases for historical knowledge are not empirical facts but written texts, even if these texts masquerade in the guise of wars or revolutions." Moreover, why read at all? "Language is unreliable"; "sign and meaning can never coincide"; "considerations of the actual and historical existence of writers are a waste of time from a critical viewpoint." Which leads us, famously, to schizoid nowhere: "Death is a displaced name for a linguistic predicament."

Do you believe this? Do you believe anything? What a mandate, for the next Angleton, the next Sheymov, a yuppie Ames. There is no meaning, so behavior doesn't count. There is no death, no shame, no scruple, not a hope, only coded discourse, linguistic predicament, and incantation. With its gaudy false-bottomed narratives and its dreamy disinformations, spooking has been postmodern long before there ever was a Jaguar, a Jacuzzi, or a Sorbonne. Counterintelligent!

Lolita Lights Our Fire

Beyond the seas where I have lost a sceptre,
I hear the neighing of my dappled nouns.

His family called him "Poops." The St. Petersburg dreams of the young Nabokov in his sailor suit were not of umbrellas or balloons; he dreamed instead of himself as a moth, with a pin stuck through his thorax. Chased out of Russia by Lenin and out of Germany by Hitler, mourning his martyred father (a diplomat and editor) and his gun-toting mother (a Christian Science convert), deaf to music, dubious of politics, opposed to the very idea of a future ("the obsolete in reverse"), this chain-smoking lepidopterist insomniac, amateur boxer, semipro tennis bum, and would-be Pushkin, with his jigsaw puzzles, chessboards, magic kits, and symbolist booklets, passed forever into exile. He would take with him, however, a kingdom of consciousness. If you can't go home again but happen to be brilliant, you create "intangible property" and "unreal estate," whose meanings and patterns, harmonies and anagrams, sunsets and stained glass are as splendid to behold as the Byzantine imagery of the Orthodox church you disdain, as you disdain Dostoyevsky, Marx, Freud, and homosexuals. But you'll also dream in your novels of insanity and suicide, of artist-criminals and artist-madmen, of strangled wives and slaughtered sons and debauched nymphets. You will seethe for Zembla, or Antiterra, or some other insect world.

It happens that *Lolita* was the first book I ever reviewed, in August 1958, for my college newspaper. I picked it up hoping it was as dirty as they said it was; found it to be funnier than *Catcher in the Rye*; understood it to belong to a long and flashy line of American nomad novels that had begun on a raft with Huck Finn and would eventually include Kerouac's *On the Road*, Updike's *Rabbit, Run*, Bellow's *Adventures of Augie March*, Clancy Sigal's *Going Away*, Anne Tyler's *Earthly Pos-*

sessions, and various Didions/DeLillos; got most of the references to Poe, Melville, T. S. Eliot, Louisa May Alcott, and Eugene O'Neill, as well as Hansel and Gretel, Sleeping Beauty, the Little Mermaid, Dick Tracy, and Bluebeard—and some of them to Shakespeare, Swift, Blake, Joyce, and Robert Louis Stevenson, plus Baudelaire, Sherlock Holmes, *The Blue Angel* and *The Rubaiyat,* Cervantes and Kafka, but not Gogol. I definitely missed references to Goethe and Pushkin; Flaubert, Ronsard, and Proust; Marat and Romain Rolland; Petrarch, Horace, Propertius, and Catullus; Maeterlinck and *Melmoth the Wanderer.* And so on, unto Hegel, Schlegel, and *The Perfumed Garden of Cheikh Nefzaoui.* As much as obsession, *Lolita* was "about" American space, the English language, Lewis Carroll's Alice, Prosper Mérimée's Carmen, and Jekyll-and-Hyde doppelgängers.

Not until Alfred Appel's *The Annotated Lolita* (1970) and volume two of Brian Boyd's biography (1990) did I learn about N's stalking of little girls on buses to eavesdrop on the vernacular and his consulting of tabloid crime stories and teen magazines, jukebox songs and Girl Scout manuals, gun catalogs and articles on barbiturates. I picture him now, in Telluride or Yellowstone or Portal, writing the Great American Motel Novel when it was too wet to butterfly. Once, dismayed by noisy honeymooners in the next cabin, he sat outside in the middle of the night in the backseat of his own car, imagining *Lolita* on index cards. Love's a bitch, and so is art. But Nabokov had translated *Alice in Wonderland* into Russian, as Whittaker Chambers had translated *Bambi* into English; and so *Lolita,* like *Witness,* was doubtless a sendup of fairy tales, not to mention a satire on various myths of romantic love. Besides being unreliable, the narrator was obviously crazy. Even so, as always with literature that matters, the language transfigured.

It's probably not worth mentioning here that when I reviewed Nabokov's *Ada* for the daily *New York Times* in 1969, Alfred Appel reviewed it in the Sunday *New York Times Book Review.* I noted—and Appel didn't—the existence of a fussbudget character named "Ronald Orange," who was annotating the philosopher Van's treatise on time. This earned me a rebuke from the Master himself, indignant in Montreux, claiming he'd never have done such a thing to his good friend Alfred. Of course not. On the other hand, hadn't he booby-trapped his Pushkin translation with a "sapajou" joke just to bomb his buddy Edmund Wilson? . . . But back to our story.

Long before Adrian Lyne's *Lolita* was rejected by Hollywood, Nabokov's *Lolita* had been rejected by Viking, Simon & Schuster, New Directions, and Farrar, Straus. Even after a naughty Maurice published it in Paris in 1955, Doubleday would bail out on an American edition because greedhead Girodias held the rights for ransom. But by the time Walter Minton cut a Putnam deal with all the parties, the way to intellectual respectability had been paved with a ninety-page excerpt in *Anchor Review,* a mash note to the novelist in *Partisan Review,* a book-club selection already in hand, and blurbs lined up from Graham Greene, William Styron, and Lionel Trilling. Scandal and Swifty Lazar did the rest: 100,000 copies sold in three weeks; $100,000 for paperback rights; $150,000 for film rights; Laurence Olivier, Marlon Brando, and David Niven all wanting to play Humbert; cocktails with John Wayne, Gina Lollobrigida, and Marilyn Monroe; television jokes by Steve Allen, Dean Martin, and Milton Berle; and an Alan Jay Lerner musical that never made it from Boston to Broadway.

Actually, a Sondheim sort of musical may have been the way to go, taking all the literature Nabokov made fun of and dressing it up in period costume for fantasy song-and-dance routines. . . .

If his popular literature course at Cornell "was eclipsed in student numbers only by Pete Seeger's folk-song class," he had nevertheless written all those Russian novels nobody yet knew about, not even devoted undergraduates like Richard Farina, Joanna Russ, and Thomas Pynchon. Why should they believe him when he told them that Balzac, Stendhal, Faulkner, Mann, and even Henry James ("that pale porpoise and his plush vulgarities") were a waste of optic nerve; that "sick," "morbid," "loathsome," "gloating," "despicable" Dostoyevsky stank of "topical politics and sweat"; that Freud, too, was humbug ("Let the credulous and the vulgar continue to believe that all mental woes can be cured by a daily application of old Greek myths to their private parts")? After all, *The New Yorker* hadn't believed him about Lenin—which may explain his friendship with the campus FBI agent, his conviction that the scholar Roman Jakobson was a Soviet agent, his lifelong complimentary subscription to *National Review,* and his sympathetic identification with Joe McCarthy (like Elvis and Nixon). After *Lolita,* none of this mattered. He never again had to teach another Pynchon.

None of us—in Cambridge, in Ithaca, in Berkeley—knew that there was a Kinbote in our obsolete future, more menacing than Quilty. That in *Pale Fire* Poops would write a college novel so savage it made Mary McCarthy and Randall Jarrell look downright cuddly till William Gass came along with *The Tunnel* to top all three (which Poops and Gass go oddly unmentioned in the recent *Lingua Franca* takeout on the genre that also manages to omit college novels by Malamud, Bellow, Roth, Alison Lurie, Richard Stern, and DeLillo.) That, in *Ada,* he would sleight-of-hand the century with an anthropological description of an alternative world, Antiterra, apprehended only by philosophers, lunatics, and sci-fi novelists; a theory of time as a sort of icebox of freeze-dried images ever-ready for a quick thaw in the imagination's microwave; a parody of *Anna Karenina* in particular, Russian novels in general, and the notion of novels period; and a love story that started out with a twelve-year-old girl and ended up incestuous. Until nine years after his death, we didn't even know that he had written an earlier, nastier first draft on nymphetomania, *The Enchanter,* in Russian and without *Lolita*'s boundless vistas of the "lovely, trustful, dreamy, enormous country" that Humbert "defiled with a sinuous trail of slime."

While it's hard to like a man who didn't like Turgenev, it's even harder to imagine that *Lolita,* the novel or the movie, inspired anyone to predatory pedophilia.

I've put off reading Lolita *for six years, till she's eighteen.*

(Groucho Marx)

How much more convenient it would have been if the new $60-million *Lolita* were just a lousy movie—and not at all surprising to anyone who sat through any of director Adrian Lyne's previous glitterdome gaudies, from *Flashdance* and *9-½ Weeks* to *Fatal Attraction* and *Indecent Proposal.* Like Alan Parker and Ridley Scott, Lyne graduated to feature films from the floating signifiers of British television advertising and can be counted on for cultural productions as slick as fashion spreads, as glossy as car commercials, and as shallow as cyberspace. We are also properly skeptical of actors as self-righteous as Jeremy Irons (who played Claus von Bülow in *Reversal of Fortune* as if he were Andy Warhol at a slumber party of Scientologists) when they send up black balloons of indignation about Hollywood and "political correctness" at press conferences in sunny Spain. At the San Sebastian Film Festival in September 1996, Lyne and Irons were furious because they hadn't found an American distributor for their movie, in spite of six weeks of postproduction liposucks to rid the screen of anything that might possibly offend the 1996 Child Pornography Protection Act—which draconian statute, scribbled in haste by cowardly legislators in a burning Capitol rotunda, forbids "any visual depiction, including any photograph, film, video image or picture [that] is or appears to be of a minor engaging in sexually explicit conduct." Understand that they weren't talking about just *any* distributor, but about a major studio prepared to spend another $25 million to fire up and fossil-fuel the PR smoke machines. Many studios had already seen at least an hour of the new *Lolita,* and their not-for-attribution cover story had been that it wasn't worth the risk capital.

"Stunned" is how Adrian Lyne described himself as feeling about Hollywood's rejection. In Spain, however, he'd admitted to being "not altogether surprised." The atmosphere in America has become very moralistic in the last three years," as it had been in the fifties when *Lolita* was first published. "It is a country where six-year-olds are sent home from school for kissing their classmates, where in Oklahoma, police raided video stores, seizing copies of *The Tin Drum.*"

But now we've seen all 137 minutes, on Showtime cable, and while Lyne's *Lolita* isn't as wonderful as the *New York Times* and the *Wall Street Journal* say it is—the warmer the month, the hotter the hyperbole—it's better than we had any right to expect. A nervously perspiring director may be looking over his shoulder at a curmudgeonly novelist, as Volker Schlöndorff worried about Günter Grass in his reverential rendition of *The Tin Drum,* but Irons as Humbert is at least less *likable* than James Mason was in Stanley Kubrick's 1962 *Lolita*; you wouldn't want him anywhere near your kids. Dominique Swain, the fourteen-year-old Malibu beach bunny who plays the twelve-year-old nymphet ("light of my life, fire of my loins"), is a lot less Baby Doll sluttish than Sue Lyon, with the added ingredient of talent. Frank Langella as Quilty, Humbert's nemesis and doppelgänger, is a lot more sinister than Peter Sellers, whom Kubrick licensed to mainline on burlesque. (His is the only nudity in the film, full-frontal and unaroused, in a classic Western player-piano shootout; otherwise, in this peekaboo production, nary a nipple.) And, though some of us are of the opinion that Shelley Winters *can't* be improved on, an astonishingly svelte Melanie Griffith doesn't embarrass herself as Lolita's awful needy mother.

Moreover, Lyne's *Lolita* is more expansive than Kubrick's. According to Alfred Appel's annotations, there were 342 motels mentioned in the novel—342 being, not coincidentally, the address of Charlotte's house on Lawn Street and the number of the fateful room at the Enchanted Hunters hotel. Kubrick, filming in genteel England, left out all of them, as he omitted the vertigo of westward landscapes and their suturing superhighways. Whereas Lyne hits the American road; sings out the long vertebral lines of telephone poles; pulls in at gas stations and rest stops for pints of ice cream and beds that vibrate; gobbles up desert and horizons. There's a *lostness* about his *Lolita*. And within this lostness, the fetish thrives—the underwear ribbon from Humbert's bygone Annabel; pigtails and pj's; toenail-clipping and bug-zapping; typewriters, weathervanes, bubble-gum; even, alas, lipstick and a banana. It's pretty much the entrapment in pathetic sorcery that a deracinated Humbert deserves.

So why the fuss? Because America is as crazy as Humbert.

You can always count on a murderer for a fancy prose style.

As if Günter Grass didn't have enough trouble, being treated like a Turk in his very own country, Oklahoma City decided in the summer of 1997 that the 1979 movie version of his best-known novel, *The Tin Drum,* violated a state "decency" law forbidding any suggestion of sex that involves anybody under age eighteen, or even actors pretending to be underage. This is the usual story of a gospel radio station saying the movie was "kiddie porn," and fundamentalists calling themselves "Oklahomans for Children and Families" picking up the hairy ball and taking it to the cops, who took it to a district judge, who said he had no choice but to deem it obscene because of a minute or two of what might be oral sex involving Oskar, who, you'll remember, refused to grow up as a protest against adult fascism; and already, before we can even get to the chief county prosecutor who felt that anyone in possession of the film could face felony charges, there are too many ironies in the fire. But the Oklahoma City police decided to use that fire to toast various Amendments to the Constitution—descending on video rental outlets to confiscate copies of *The Tin Drum* and demand the names and addresses of customers who had rented the movie; then descending on those customers, in their own homes at night, to seize the guilty cassettes. One customer they happened to descend on also just happened to be an official of the American Civil Liberties Union.

Maybe Lyne and Irons are right. On the other hand, nearby
Tulsa chose not to imitate Oklahoma City's night of the long
scissors. And everybody seems to be suing everybody else—
even the Oklahoma City cops are being sued, for violation of the
Video Privacy Act—while in a federal appeals court in San
Francisco papers have been filed challenging the constitutional-
ity of the Child Pornography Protection Act itself. So *Romeo
and Juliet* is probably safe for now, along with underage sex in
the Bible, not to mention all those TV programs that alerted us
in the first place to the sexual abuse of children, including a dra-
matization by Anjelica Huston of Dorothy Allison's *Bastard out
of Carolina* that so dismayed Ted Turner he bumped it from
TNT, and thus it had to blush unseen on the same Showtime
that dared as well to narrowcast *Lolita*.

But we neglect the crucial point, which has nothing to do
with novels by Nabokov, Günter Grass, or Dorothy Allison, and
the films inadequate to their magic acts of language. Statutes like
Oklahoma's and the Child Pornography Protection Act are our
homegrown fairy tales, ghostly adumbrations of the hysteria that
swept over us in the 1980s. We know perfectly well that children
are most at risk at home, from their own families and adult
friends. Yet we bought into scenarios as lurid and preposterous
as teenage witches conspiring against Salem in 1692 and goat-
faced Bolsheviks against Stalin in the thirties. What a low decade, the eighties—of so much giddy greed and anxious
tremors. On the one hand, in court and on TV: battered-child
syndrome, rape-trauma syndrome, child sexual abuse syndrome, and post-traumatic stress disorder. On the other, in pre-
schools and day-care centers across the country, from Malden to
Manhattan Beach, from West Point to Miami: kiddie porn sex
rings and pedophile cults; sodomy, rape, group sex, and satan-
ism; forks, spoons, screwdrivers, Lego blocks, black candles,
and monster masks; blood-drinking, corpse-dumping, baby-
eating, and the sacrifice of animals, especially bunny rabbits,
which were to ritual-abuse scenarios in the eighties what black
whirlybirds are to militia wet dreams in the nineties. And the

unlikeliest bedfellows seemed to have found in these premillennial jitters the oddest common cause—as if a splinter faction of feminists had an investment in the ubiquity of incest, and fundamentalist Christians in the ubiquity of devil worship, and hypnotherapists in our abduction by aliens from Microsoft.

From Ofra Bikel on public television's *Frontline,* we got the appalling particularities of a single case in Edenton, North Carolina. From Debbie Nathan and Michael Snedeker in *Satan's Silence,* we got the day-care witch hunt. While Frederick Crews, an emeritus professor of English at Berkeley, had his own ox to gore—he had been equally scornful of Freudian, Marxist, feminist, poststructuralist, and any other form of criticism that looks at literary texts only to find them guilty of something—his two articles in the *New York Review of Books* in 1994, attacking the whole idea of "repression," helped alter the intellectual climate. Bikel herself took time out in 1995 for four more *Frontline* hours interviewing adults who claimed to have "recovered" traumatic childhood memories after decades of denial; their stunned families; therapists who accepted at face value or actively encouraged nightmare confabulations of abuse in *previous lives*; and the lawyers who were suing everyone—even, to their indignant surprise, the therapists themselves.

No one rational is saying there isn't any child abuse. Nor that there isn't any child sexuality. Nor that we don't in self-defense occasionally repress a painful memory, except perhaps in upfront Berkeley. But if not from our own observation, then surely from Ofra Bikel, we also know there is child *fantasy,* which is manipulated by advertisers of products and merchandisers of entertainment as much as by satanic therapists. Moreover, there is *adult* fantasy. We are so insecure and negligent in our parenthood and in our citizenship, caught between a public sphere (officialdom) that feels hollow and a private sphere (family) that feels besieged, that we seem to project onto the body of an imaginary child—"innocent," "missing," "inner," coveted, abused, eroticized, abandoned, homeless, emblematic, and commodified—all our fear and rage. Caretakers become scapegoats. And novels, and movies, and television, and Calvin Klein.

About Lolita, Humbert told us that she was "the ideal consumer, the subject and object of every foul poster," to whom all advertising was ultimately directed—and she would, of course, consume herself. In one of those peculiar reversals of the very terms of hyperreality in which Nabokov specialized, as if caught "in the lining of time," all our children are nymphets, our adults are Humberts and Quiltys and Kinbotes, the culture we dream in our sailor suits is an insect Zembla, and the face on the milk carton at the supermarket is our own mug.

Knee-Deep in the Alien Corn

Forget *Seinfeld*—a cheese doodle of urban fecklessness in which, to every penis joke, the white-bread slackers wore a prophylactic smirk. The truly momentous occasion on pop culture's 1998 social calendar was the June 19 opening of the big-screen *X-Files* movie. The paranormals who started lining up the morning after the last episode of the fifth season of the Sunday-night Fox TV series were as worried about Agent Mulder as Agent Scully was. Scully, the red-haired forensic pathologist, used to doubt Mulder's theories of alien abduction, which is why they were paired by the FBI in the first place. But that was before Scully herself was raptured up to a mother ship, hickeyed with biochips, and maybe even diddled in her Irish Catholic DNA. While Mulder had begun to wonder, in the fifth season, if his sister's body-snatching could have been a false memory implanted in him by a shadowy multinati/syndicate cabal of chain-smoking Cancer Men, Scully just barely escaped torching on a suspension bridge by orifice-impaired golems who may or may not have been "rebel" aliens opposed to the colonizing of planet Earth by shape-shifters, viral-like oil slicks, and killer bees.

If you don't know what I'm talking about, you haven't been paying attention. "THE TRUTH IS OUT THERE," *The X-Files* explains as it scrolls its credits. And that truth, from Roswell to the Grassy Knoll to the Christic institute, is paranoid—a serial embodiment of DeLillo's intuition in *Underworld* of "some deeper meaning that existed solely to keep him from knowing what it was." Personally I've always enjoyed those episodes of *The X-Files* devoted to a self-contained Rod Serling woo-woo more than those elaborating the eschatology of UFO invasion—for instance, the one about the serial-killing translator of medieval Italian poetry who met lonely women in chat rooms on the Internet, parked with them in big American cars in bereft municipal spaces, secreted a membrane of gastric juice that smothered even better than a baggie, then fed on their fatty tissue: Vampire liposuction! On the other hand, I was also abducted by Calista Flockhart.

But so alert has *The X-Files* been to every fitful conniption of a petit mal culture that it is now received wisdom, or at least Established Lore—with its own websites, a product line of mugs, caps, T-shirts, comic books, prosthetic limbs and gels, and a ten-city "*X*-Po" road show in hangars like the Javits Center in Manhattan. It even makes jokes, not only about what Mulder calls "the military-industrial-entertainment complex," but about itself as well: How, it has wondered out loud, could the same bungling government that gave us the Susan B. Anthony dollar and Amtrak possibly sustain a conspiracy to suppress evidence of an invasion by saucer-borne polliwogs who have been sucking our sperm and snatching our eggs ever since the Pyramids? ("GOVERNMENT DENIES KNOWLEDGE" is another of the program's bumper stickers.)

By now you probably know that in the movie—after glimpses of a conspiracy that ranges from Dallas to Washington to London to Tunisia to Antarctica, and its murderous cover-up by the Federal Emergency Management Agency; after Blythe Danner, Martin Landau, sand dunes, ice caps, the terror-bombing of a federal building, and a mad dash through the alien corn pursued by black helicopters and cybernetic bees—Mulder finally sees an alien ship, approximately the size of San Francisco, while awful *gooey* things are happening to Scully. Before I explain what any of this portends, first be advised of some ground rules and flimflam. I call *The X-Files* and likeminded cinemas "paranoirs." Those regressive hypnotherapists who buy into alien abduction, as they buy into satanic-ritual abuse, I call "psyclops." And those academics who insist on publishing monographs about such phenomena, I call "Cult Studs"—for their piratical boarding, under the black flags of Foucault and Lacan, of pleasure craft on the pop seas; their swashbuckling style and their slaughter of the innocents. You may ignore these terms. Years ago nobody paid any attention either when I sought to characterize a new species of lit crit—so fixated on the dirty little secrets of genital organization in dead writers that it neglected to notice the language with which they transformed their experience—as "Bed Pan."

Now, then: Celtic-cross crop circles! Cattle mutilations! Anal probes! Mind scans! (How come these aliens are so seldom interested in stealing our *brain* cells?)

> *I have described something I myself witnessed, and I have reported something which I was told by someone else, but someone I believed as thoroughly as if I had witnessed the scene myself. I will now add something which I have read about.* (Saint Augustine, *The City of God*)

Sometime in June or July 1947, a flying disc crash-landed near Roswell, New Mexico, littering the scorpion-riddled landscape with hairless, earless, four-fingered ETs whose dead bodies were whirlybirded by black helicopters to "Area 51," a secret military compound in the Nevada desert, where they've been covered up ever since, except on the Fox network, the Sci-Fi, A & E, and Showtime cable channels, in dozens of movies, an equal number of itchy websites, thousands of magazine and supermarket tabloid articles, and almost as many books, including *The Complete Roswell UFO Encyclopedia* from the folks who'd earlier brought us *The Official X-Files Magazine,* just in the nick of a *Time* magazine cover story on Roswell's own fiftieth-anniversary celebration, "Encounter '97," which included a flying-saucer soapbox derby, a UFO belly dancer, and a speech by Erich von Daniken.

On the Tuesday before Encounter '97, the Air Force held a televised press conference, not to discuss Agent Orange in Vietnam or uranium bullets or smarty-pants bombs in the Gulf War, but to release a 231-page report on all things Roswellian. According to the A.F., those weren't aliens; they were weather balloons and crash-test dummies from parachute drops. About Area 51 it had no comment. This inspired the funniest column Maureen Dowd has yet written for the *New York Times,* suggesting that Dick Gephart and Janet Reno *must* be aliens, and that

Bob Bennett, Dick Armey, and Brian Lamb had obviously been saucerized and fiddled with.

Oddly, the Air Force probably told a partial truth. Phil Patton explains in *Dreamland: A Personal Journey through the Secret World of Roswell and Area 51* that the real Roswell story indeed involved military balloon projects like Moby Dick and Mogul, spying on Soviets instead of the weather. It can't be accidental that the 509th Bomb Group, the special unit that vaporized Hiroshima and the only unit capable in 1947 of using atomic weapons, was in charge at Roswell. And we know for sure that Area 51 is the top-secret military reservation where Lockheed Skunk Works developed its U-2; the CIA its SR-71 Blackbird drone; and the Pentagon its F-117 Stealth fighter, which—along with other "black" aircraft like the robotic Aurora, the titanium-alloy Orient Express, the batlike Black Manta, and the whale-shaped Flying Shamu, plus the usual red darters, orange orbs, and green magnesium flares dropped by test pilots to decoy heat-seeking missiles and the usual MIG Ferrets picked up at an Israeli swap meet—are likely to be what ufologists actually see in the desert night sky, when they aren't just stoned on crystal meth. But I'm getting ahead of myself, and therefore missing most of the fun.

According to Jodi Dean in *Aliens in America: Conspiracy Culture from Outerspace to Cyberspace*, 27 percent of Americans told Gallup they believe aliens have visited; 17 percent told *Time*/CNN they believe in alien abduction, 65 percent that a UFO crashed in Roswell, and 80 percent that the feds are covering up what they know; and another 2 percent told Roper they had been abducted themselves, which translates into 3,700,000 adults—and since many claim multiple kidnappings, we're talking about an air-traffic-control nightmare. I'd like to know more about these people. Are they mostly male/female; whiter than black, Asian, Latino; Catholic, Protestant, Jewish, Muslim; likelier to have graduated from high school or college; watchers of paranoirs; left-handed gun-owning pro-life Perot voters; previously therapized; lactose-intolerant? Dean claims the UFO community "combines a reasonable replication of the demographics of the United States (tilted toward the white middle class)," but the footnote to which she directs us concedes: "At present I can't provide solid evidence for this statement." She also asserts that "a common (though mistaken, classist, and elitist) view is that people who believe in UFOs are poor, uneducated, white, and usually American. Poll data suggests otherwise." But for this assertion there isn't even a footnote, much less poll data.

Never you mind. Dean is a Cult Stud at Hobart and William Smith Colleges who has gone to waterbed with a scrum of psyclops and seen in the flickering light "apocalyptic modes of truth." At least she's up-front in choosing to credit what "abductees" actually say about those missing minutes, the "absence that itself marks an alien encounter," the tracking devices and the sex crimes. Cult Studs usually hide their cards behind their patter, as if what they really believed about the phenomena they massage were less important than the flashdance of their minds at play among riotous signifiers. This was Carl Jung's game when quizzed on flying saucers in 1958. He wrote a little book, *Mythus: Von Dingen, die am Himmel gesehen werden,* in which it mattered not at all to Carl if the "archetypal circles in the sky" were real or "symbolical rumors"; he just maundered on about "the shape of the center," icons as "weightless as thought," mandalas, rotundums, "lenticular" galactic shapes, and the eyeball of a watching God. The man was his own cave, inside of which it is impossible to distinguish the Swiss cuckoo from the fascist tom-tom.

Still, Dean tricks up belief with obligatory buzz: "Advocating these alien experiences as worthy of serious attention is effected by appropriating the discourse of therapy. . . . [Therapists] access the production of these feelings and experiences, pointing to a truth beyond the witness." This truth is, naturally, postmodern and "consensual," based on "the intensity and authenticity of the emotions a person expresses while hypnotized and the consistency of the person's memory with those of other abductees." It stands in principled opposition not only to the "government-juridical discourse" and "the dominant rationality" of "elite, official 'arbiters of reality,'" but also to what John Mack at Harvard calls "the Western scientific paradigm." Moreover, since "various Marxists, feminists, and multiculturalists have stressed the importance of knowledge gained at the margins; the importance of the oppressed as epistemologically superior to the falsely disembodied, disconnected view from nowhere," the very stigma attached to a belief in UFOs "enables the alien to function as an icon for some difficult social problems"—like illegal aliens (from, of course, Third Worlds), alienated labor, AIDS, NASA, the New World Order, anxieties about breeding, miscegenation, and hybridity, repressed sexualities, silenced subjectivities, boundary breakdowns and border transgressions associated with "end-of-the-century culture" and "end-time strangeness."

Perhaps I'm falsely disembodied, but the view from my nowhere is that real oppression is a lot heavier than not being believed when you go on *Ricki Lake,* while still selling thousands of copies of your book about what they did to your Bermuda Triangle in the Teilhardian noosphere. Even if the S/M script the hypnotherapists write for the "abductees" does less damage to our neighborhood than the Black Mass fairy tales they sanction about bloody bunnies and tortured tots at the local day-care center—and, of course, the psyclops stuck on child molestation insist that alien abduction is a "screen" memory for incest, while the psyclops stuck on sperm-sucking see the screen the other way around—I still wonder which films these fantasts go to, which comic books they lip-read, and if it's ever occurred to them that "the intensity and authenticity" of an emotion no more warrants our respect than liking hip-hop and hating breakfast; says even less about why we get up in the morning; and says *nothing* about whether the individual experiencing this emotion is exalted, confused, or bonkers—headed to an altar, a support group, an agriglyph or, in Nike sneakers, to Heaven's Gate.

There is an old bon mot, sometimes ascribed to Sir Hamilton A. R. Gibb of Oxford . . . , that every Arab word has its primary meaning, then its opposite meaning, then something to do with a camel, and lastly something obscene. Similarly, it was said at Harvard, when I was there in the '6os, that every Sanskrit word means itself, its opposite, a name of God, and a position in sexual intercourse.

(Wendy Doniger, *The Implied Spider*)

Why saucers? That's easy. Patton reports in *Dreamland* that on June 24, 1947, a pilot near Mount Rainier in Washington saw nine objects "as shiny as mirrors" flying at tremendous speed in a "boomerang" formation and later told an Oregon newspaper columnist that they "flew like a saucer would if you skipped it across the water." The Associated Press picked up the story, and in the AP version the objects changed from flying like a saucer into "saucer-like" objects, and then into "flying saucers."

Why polliwogs? Whence this recent consensus that the long-distance Other is, to quote Dean, a "hairless chalky-colored creature with large black eyes," looking like a froggy preborn fetus? It is certainly the dominant trope of the paranoir, as well as TV commercials for air fresheners, skateboard accessories, Volkswagens, Diet Coke, Kodak film, AT&T cell phones, Milky Way candy bars, Rice Krispies, and Stove Top stuffing. Dean links this Fetal Chic less to obsessiveness about abortion or Spielberg's 1977 flying-harmonica movie *Close Encounters of the Third Kind* than to "anxieties around reproduction, mothering, and the capacity to protect one's children," as well as to Christa McAuliffe's death in the 1986 Challenger explosion, which "opened cultural imaginings of space to the sacrifice and victimization of women." In fact, as Tom Disch tells us in *The Dreams Our Stuff Is Made Of: How Science Fiction Conquered the World,* the hairless androgyne is as old as Poe's "Mesmeric Revelations" ("You will have a distinct idea of the ultimate body by conceiving of it to be entire brain") and later elaborated by H. G. Wells, whose Martians in *The War of the Worlds* were "heads, merely heads. Entrails they had none." Pure neocortex had naturally selected to shuck itself of unsightly body hair and body parts.

Reverse this evolutionary torque, and what you get swimming up the phylogenetic ladder is at first fishy, then froggy, and finally Frankenstein. Factor in punk rock and skinheads, not to mention Sinead O'Connor doing her Vatican rag. (I won't get into the needy mother in Sigourney Weaver's *Alien* movies or the missing father and the lost child in Steven Spielberg.) Aliens in TV paranoirs are either white and bald, or black and buggy, unless they're angels. I read Tom Disch because he traces the origins of Whitley Streiber's best-selling "nonfiction" traumatic seizures—the latest of which, *Confirmation,* is full of hard evidence of Whitleys among us, all of them on remote control from alien implants in their head-holes (and a diet rich in Streibers)—back to remarkable prefigurations in his earlier vampire fictions that happen hardly to have sold at all, much as another second-rate sci-fi novelist, L. Ron Hubbard, would only make a bundle when he started a religion. While Disch's real business is a witty and cranky ramble through the pulp form—sex, drugs, rock 'n' role and J. G. Ballard—with digressions on right-wing politics, an overindulgence of Heinlein, a back-of-the-hand to Ursula Le Guin and a once-over-far-too-lightly for Frank Herbert and cyperpunk (no Pat Cadigan, no Neal Stephenson), he is briskly dismissive of Roswell as the Atlantis, Mu, and Oz of UFO believers. He also reminds us just how banal the aliens are we meet in abduction scenarios, compared to those in sci-fi. This accords with my own instinct that visitors from, say, Sirius the Dog Star wouldn't look like anything we're capable of imagining; that we'll *know* they are alien because they'll *look* unknowable—not even insecticidal or reptilian, but maybe enzymes, crystals, or bacteria; a Trekkie Borg-like Hive, a Netscape bot, a waste-product virus, or a few hummed bars of dodecahedral music.

Why abduction, and so much hanky-panky with eggs and sperm? "All that is solid melts into air," Marx explained in the *Manifesto*. The truth is out there, in the unbearable lightness of

American being. We are no longer safe on the tribal streets; equally weightless, in orbit and cyberspace; balloonlike, in exile or migration; tiddlywinks on the credit grid; fled abroad, like jobs and capital; disappeared, like Latin American journalists; missing, like runaway children; bugged, tapped, videotaped, downsized, hijacked, organ-donored, gene-spliced, lite-beered, vacuum-sealed, overdrawn, nonrefundable, void where prohibited, and *stealthed*. Not to mention those problematic dislocations caused by sleep paralysis, temporal lobe lesions, overmedication, bad-trip designer drugs, frequent flying, seasonal affective disorder, bad workspace ergonomics, and the blue meanies.

We are also warming up for the Apocalypse. We have got the millennial jeebies. Not only from Daniel in the Old Testament, and Revelation in the New, but from The Second Book of Esdras, the Syriac Apocalypse of Baruch, the Dead Sea War Scroll, and the William poems of Blake and Butler Yeats—we dread unsealed books, Judgment Day, and Lakes of Fire. Each troubled age embodies its own worst fears—in devil worship or demonic possession, succubi and incubi; in Lilith, Grendel and Caliban; in Gog, Moloch, and Minotaur; in cannibals, vampires, furies, gorgons, hellhounds, Norns, and Hydras; in the dragon, the mermaid, and the Sphinx. The difference in the past was that the image of this dread was propagated in the temple, the cave, or the asylum instead of mass-merchandised by the hypnotherapeutic media.

There used to be faeries, goblins, trolls, pooks, gnomes, snow maidens, munchkins, sylphs, and hobbits who seized and transported us to other dimensions where time got funny. (Decades and sometimes centuries passed in a single night for Irish peasants, German monks, Japanese fishermen, and ripped Van Winkles, of which they remembered wild hunts and mad jigs in ghost forests with black hounds or wet Nuggies.) There used to be saints, Christian or Sufi, playing hide-and-seek with God in the soul's dark night, undergoing "evaporations of personality," variously possessed by Clouds of Unknowing, Uncreated Light, ecstasy, and automatic writing. (For instance, Saint Theresa, thrown "into a great fear . . . when I saw my body thus lifted up from earth," or ravished by a Spear of Gold, causing Trans-verbation. And Saint John of the Cross: "They sometimes see the forms and figures of those of another life, saints or angels, good and evil, or certain extraordinary lights and brightness. They hear strange words, sometimes seeing those who utter them and sometimes not. They have a sensible perception at times of most sweet odours, without knowing whence they pro-ceed.") There have always been freaks—wild men and missing links, wolf boys and zombies, witches and geeks. ("Erotic con-traband," says Leslie Fiedler. Or, as Diane Arbus explained: "There's a quality of legend about freaks. Like a person in a fairy tale who stops you and demands that you answer a riddle. Most people go through life dreading they'll have a traumatic experi-ence. Freaks were born with their traumas. They're aristocrats." See the dwarf in the art of Raphael, Mantegna, Velázquez, Car-reño de Miranda, Carpaccio, Van Dyck, Veronese, and Goya.) Lamps, Mirrors, Doors, Stairs, Stigmata! Toads, bats, spiders, red fiends with black freckles, angelic or amphibian incarna-tions of "trespass and grace"! Manticores, unicorns, hippo-griffs, and the seven-breasted Black Diana of Ephesus! Epilepsy helps, as in Saint Paul and Mohammed. And you needn't be a Steven Marcus to have noticed that repressed Victorian sexual-ity caused lots of ghost stories. When the 509th Bomb Group dropped Little Boy on Hiroshima, we got Godzilla, the first ra-diation mutant—after which a Cold War's worth of bad-seed aliens, of Triffids, Pods, Blobs, and Body Snatchers, of man-eating dandelions, meteoric slimeballs, bloodsucking carrots, and collectivized Bolshevik killer ants. Why not, just in time for the Second Coming, a spectral regiment of the Unborn—a Casper the Hermaphroditic Ghost?

Fearing (and desiring, too) to be possessed, we conjure the Other we think we need, and get the Dracula we deserve.

> *Leopards break into the temple and drink to the dregs what is in the*
> *sacrificial pitchers; this is repeated over and over again; finally it can be*
> *calculated in advance and it becomes a part of the ceremony.*
> (Franz Kafka, "Leopards in the Temple")

What Phil Patton brings to this groaning board is a brilliant book in which nothing is as it seems, while everything has a rational explanation, and yet, even so, the "rational" is its own sort of Dracula. "You know," he is told by a droll acquaintance, "trailer camps cause tornadoes. It's a scientific fact." To which Patton replies: "And maybe deserts cause UFOs?" But it is the military bases and secret research facilities located in those deserts — "the presence of all that strange and frightening weaponry" — that disposes people to see discs and lights.

His dreamland, although an episode of *The X-Files* removed it to Utah, is in the Emigrant Valley of southern Nevada, "the Shangri-La, the Forbidden Temple of black, or secret aircraft," set inside 4,742 square miles of restricted airspace "and four million acres of bomb range — a space as big as a Benelux nation. It would come to be called by many names: Groom Lake, Watertown, Paradise Ranch, Home Base, Area 51." He also calls it "Pentagonia, a junction of the twin ideologies of nuclear power and air power." This "invisible culture" casts "a great shadow," which is the reciprocating "culture of ufology — the anti-matter of the matter."

At its perimeter — from Bald Mountain or Freedom Ridge — both sides are looking at each other through nightscopes and scanners. Inside are the military and their black engineers. Outside, uneasily complicit, are the "youfers" (the saucer-heads) and the "stealthies" (hoping for a glimpse of the latest "silver bullet" that will render America invincible to its many enemies).

For a youfer, Dreamland is Area 51, Hangar 18, and Level 5; gravity waves and Zeta Reticuli; secret bases on the moon and Mars; "omnibeams," "etherians," "genetic interventions," and Ashtar; igloo-shaped ships and spacewomen with names like Lyra; the planet Clarion, the voice of A-lan, the lost continent of Lemuria and beautiful Venusians mating with apes; gray robots in serfdom to praying mantises, hybrids incubated for their vital enzymes, surveillance orbs the size of basketballs, "Dream Police," and the manufacture of time-warp saucers by escaped Nazi scientists in league with the alien "Serpent People" at the center of a hollow earth.

For a stealthie, this "secret city" is where all the spy planes come from; only as alien as our government is to its citizens; no more peculiar, really, than sister installations in an archipelago of Pentagonias, of nuclear labs, ballistic-missile ranges, spy-satellite consoles, and radar test stations from White Sands and Los Alamos to China Lake and El Mirage, from Tikaboo and Tonopath to the Blue Cube of Sunnyvale; a "black-budget" world of ramjet engines and nuclear cannons, waste spills and weapons accidents, fallout and cancerous white spots the size of silver dollars on dead deer; walking tanks, robot planes, laser light, Darkstar, Black Yak, Teal Rain, Have Blue, Project Grudge—and no more singular, either, considering the existence abroad of similar warrior mindscapes like Machrihanish, Kapstan Yar, Yuratum, and Lop Nor.

Patton, of course, is a stealthie. He likes some of the youfers, but he grew up a childhood nut about airplanes, and knows what he sees in the night sky, and never met an angel or an alien (that "huge fetus or hungry child, with big Keene kid eyes . . . an echo of Munch's *Scream*—the very face of modern angst!"), nor bought into the eighties craze for abduction (with "its sexual and personal obsessions—I was taken because I was special, I was abused—tied in with the talk-show psychology"). And even though his well-furnished mind is more at home with the poems of Wallace Stevens and the Edo prints of Hiroshige than joysticking with the Stealth pilots as they practice-bomb America in the dark (Minnesota boat docks, Denver high-rises), what really riles this wonderful writer and civilized man—and what all of us, including Agent Mulder, ought to be worried about instead of ET—is the kidnap of democracy by black budgeteers in a shadow republic, who spend $40 billion a year on secret weapons for a stealthy Star Wars wet dream.

After the Gulf War, you'll be happy to know, the Air Force let Annie Leibovitz snap a shot of a Stealth for *Vanity Fair.* And in the twilight zone of Area 51, where citizens are not allowed, the desert tortoise has made a comeback, and the snowy plover and long-billed curlew, the kit fox and the mountain lion, four species of bat and six kinds of rattlesnake.

Tropic of Cancer
(A Post Toasties Postscript)

*It is only in lighting this cigarette that I discover my concrete possibility
or, if one prefers, my desire to smoke.*

(Jean-Paul Sartre, *Being and Nothingness*)

No more than it was any accident that the 509th Bomb
Group was in charge at Roswell is it merely coincidental
that the principal villain in the *X-Files* series is a chain-
smoker, who may or may not have done terrible things to Mulder's mother.

How does one qualify for a Cult Stud monograph? I understand that categories of the stigmatized, victimized, and oppressed such as women, blacks, gays, the downsized, and the
immune-deficient are too obvious, too old-fashioned, and too
Old Left. But why alien abductees, serial killers, and drag
queens and *not*, say, sanitation engineers, computer illiterates,
or nuns? Why, among so many sample groups of oddballs and
outsiders, do the first-born get so much attention, and the
adopted, and even evil twins, but *not* surfer bums, vegans, or
mimes? How many times have we paddled our guitars like kay-
aks upstream on the pissy waters of rock music into realms of
swamp gas where Fats Domino and "Blueberry Hill" are subversive; where Elvis ended the Ike Snooze; where Jim Morrison,
running to fat and demons in the mind-blown desert, embodied
not only the satanic Nietzsche flipside of *La Bamba* but also a
Lizard King in leather pants; where Janis and/or Jimi died for
our sins, the Sex Pistols killed the Kennedys, Ice Cube doesn't
like Koreans, and Bruce Springsteen is a border intellectual?
Why not lavish such ingenuity on the designated pariah of the
last two decades—the American *smoker*?

See the unseemly scramble, as if for African colonies, of vote-
grubbing city councils in half the nation's toxic dump sites to
shut down mild-mannered restaurants, even bars, where once

upon a time our Bogies and Bacalls gazed at one another through a pall of mall. And this is not even to talk about the fright wig who sat down yesterday right next to me in an otherwise empty *smoking* section at the local coffee shop, wearing the pelt of a dead marsupial and smelling like the guts of a sperm whale, to complain immediately about the cigarette I'd already stubbed out because I've been browbeaten into feeling ashamed of my pariah self in a shameless republic of moralizing busybody bullies, professional crybabies, post-therapeutic vegetarian hysterics, and Rogaine-abusing Health Nazi joggers.

This is not a brief for the Merchants of Death. They wouldn't read it, anyway, so busy are they suppressing research papers on the behavior of nicotine-addicted dope-fiend rodents. This is a brief for the dope-fiend rodents. From *Essential Substances,* Richard Rudgley's "cultural history of intoxicants," we know that, to feel better about the world, Siberian shamans from the Stone Age on partook of the fly-agaric mushroom. Nor would the rock paintings of San bushmen of the Kalahari and Shoshonean Coso of the California Greater Basin have looked the same without some sort of hallucinogen. We know from the Bat Caves of southern Spain, as from the tomb art and Breton megaliths of neolithic France, that poppies were about, as there had been in the Late Minoan III period of ornamental vases. Hemp abounded on the Pontic Steppes and all over the Carpathian basin, in "pipe cups" from the Caucasian Early Bronze Age and in grave chambers at the Hochdorf Hallstatt near Stuttgart. Among Scythians, an ecstatic vapor bath was as much of a favorite way back then as it is now among Arctic peoples. In the Indian *Rig Veda* and the Iranian *Avesta* there is an awful lot of *soma* mentioned, and no other way to account for the geometries of Persian carpet design. The *mang* consumed to secure the visions of that third-century classic of Zoroastrian literature the *Book of Arda Wiraz* probably contained some of the same chemicals found in the Amazonian jungle vine, *Banisteripsis* (or *vaje*), used by Amerindians for the clairvoyant detection of criminal activities as well as spotting jaguars. Bird-bone snuffing tubes!

Spatulas! Cactus! To initiate themselves in the secrets of male identity, the Mountain Ok people in New Guinea first use ginger, then tobacco, and finally mushrooms. Tukano Indians boil bark for *ayahuasca*. In Peru, Ecuador, and Bolivia, they chew coca; in Yemen, Ethiopia, Somalia, and Kenya, qat; in West Africa, kola nuts; and to meet their minimum daily requirement of apomorphine, Mayans used to smoke water lilies.

And I stick burning leaves in my foodhole. So, as a matter of fact, do Kurt Vonnegut, Molly Ivins, Susan Brownmiller, Vaclav Havel, and Lech Walesa. So did Pablo Picasso, Mary McCarthy, FDR, and George Sand. Charles Kuralt couldn't get to LA from New York without flying first to Antwerp or to Mexico City, which may be why he quit CBS instead of cigarettes. One of the pleasures of going to Sweden a while ago for the Nobel Prizes was firing up late at night with Toni Morrison, Fran Lebowitz, and Sonny Mehta. *In Stockholm, they've got ashtrays in the elevators.* We are undercover everywhere, like moles at Langley. And from the opprobrium, you'd think we were gay, or Jewish, or maybe even Violence on Television. And some of us probably are. But whatever happened to Live and Let Hack?

We have *always* known tobacco's bad for us. For the Iroquois of New York and the Mayans of the Yucatán, to whom the leaf was god, maybe lung cancer and emphysema were a payback to Europe for user-friendlies like smallpox and syphilis. Consult the witty social history in Richard Klein's *Cigarettes Are Sublime* and you find that, as early as 1604, King James I warned his subjects that "the habit of smoking is disgusting to sight, repulsive to smell, dangerous to the brain, noxious to the lung" — although James was also out to get Sir Walter Raleigh, who is said to have puffed away in the Tower of London. An alarmed Parlement of Paris, in 1631, outlawed smoking in prisons. The equally alarmed city fathers of Colmar, in 1659, prohibited the bourgeoisie from partaking. By our own 1890s, twenty-six states had banned cigarettes, till World War I overnight made puffing patriotic. Anti-tobacco hysteria rises and falls according to phases of a social moon with its own ulterior agendas, the way the Inquisition, when it got to Mexico in 1571, tried to stamp out peyote among the Toltecs and Chichimecas.

Exceptions will always be made in the middle of the moralizing. At the very moment Joseph Califano, Jimmy Carter's Secretary of Health, Education and Welfare, launched a $50-million campaign against smoking, his president was swearing before a group of North Carolina tobacco growers, with tears in his eyes, that he'd never sanction cutting their subsidies. On the same day that Louis W. Sullivan, George Bush's Secretary of Health and Human Services, declared war on the Merchants of Death, the White House chief of staff was cutting a deal with the majority leader of the Senate to gut the Clean Air Bill. Nor is any administration about to mess with yearly exports of $4 billion worth of American tobacco abroad; we close our eyes and think instead of the balance of payments. You will perhaps have noticed that on the very day Bill Clinton's Secretary of Labor, Robert Reich, called for banning all smoke in every workplace, the United States was the only Western nation at the Geneva meetings of the Organization for Economic Cooperation and Development to vote against banning the export of toxic industrial wastes to Russia, Eastern Europe, and the Third World.

But Klein, a Cornell professor of French and the editor of *Diacritics,* engages us on another level. He quit cigarettes himself upon finishing a book that was then rejected by twenty-five healthier-than-thou publishers before they loved it on Tobacco Road, where Duke University has a press equally friendly to Frederic Jameson and carcinomas. *Cigarettes Are Sublime* is literary criticism, political harangue, "an ode to cigarettes," an exercise in hyperbole—"the rhetorical figure that raises its objects up, excessively, way above their actual merit . . . not to deceive by exaggeration . . . but to allow the true value, the truth of what is insufficiently valued, to appear"—and also an act of mourning. In the secret history, peculiar physiology, depth psychology, and symbolic culture of smoking, he finds "a crucial integer of our modernity."

As if they were linked rings of smoke, we are asked to contemplate Molière and Baudelaire; Mallarmé, Pierre Louÿs, Jules Laforgue, and Jean-Paul Sartre; Mérimée's *Carmen* and also Bizet's (she worked, of course, in a cigarette factory in Seville); Svevo's great novel about smoking and psychoanalysis, *The Confessions of Zeno*; war fictions by Hemingway, Mailer, Styron, and Erich Maria Remarque; movies like *Casablanca*, in which everybody smoked incessantly and symbolically *except* Ingrid Bergman; the dandy, the prostitute, the Goya, the Casanova, and Immanuel Kant on the concept of the sublime; the iconography of Gauloises (the Soldier) and of Gitanes (the Gypsy); the humble weed as a source of esthetic satisfaction, an aid to reflective consciousness, a variety of religious and/or artistic expression, a tool for managing anxiety, a symbol of sexual and political freedom, minor god, lyric muse, mystic joy, consolation, sacred and erotic object, parenthesis, prayer, and "principle of camaraderie."

Now listen up. Hitler, who hated smoking, especially hated seeing women do it; there were signs saying so all over the Reich. A European Community health survey indicates that women are much more likely to smoke in countries like Holland, where they are most liberated from traditional places and roles, than in countries like, say, Portugal. "A woman who smokes in public," Klein says, "offends those who think that women are supposed to be veiled." This suggests to me that *the anti-smoking hysteria is misogynistic.* Then there is smoking "not only as a physical act, but a discursive one," "a wordless but eloquent form of expression," "a fully coded, rhetorically complex, narratively articulated discourse with a vast repertoire of well understood conventions that are implicated, intertextually, in the whole literary, philosophical, cultural history of smoking. . . . In the present climate, the discursive performance of smoking has become a form of obscenity, just as obscenity has become an issue of public health." This suggests to me that *prohibition is censorship.* Finally, there is "the popular ethic of democratic generosity associated with tobacco in general, and with cigarettes in particular." As cats can look at kings, beggars can bum from Bourbons. "If Prometheus had stolen fire from Heaven in order to light his cigarette," wrote Mme. de Giradin in 1844, "they would have let him do it." This suggests to me that *smoking is a form of socialism.*

Never mind that they won't let me smoke anymore even at the AA meetings to which I have dutifully reported for the last decade. These days when bums ask for a light, we burn them alive in our parks. Years ago, injured in my camaraderie, I left No-Smoking Berkeley on the last jumbo to New York before tobacco was banned on domestic flights, as if on the last American chopper out of Saigon. I'd spent three days in the Third World capital of Flower Power and my youth, unable anywhere to light up, and having everywhere to listen to assistant professors of Yup and Jog complain about the homeless and the derelict on Telegraph Avenue while eating at Chez Panisse and shopping at Andronico's with its thirteen varieties of shrimp and twenty-seven different sauces. Since then, they've even banned stink-weed smoke in Synge-along Irish bars like the Starry Plough: Shining Path can pass the hat, but Joe Camel has to go outside and hump himself on Prince Street. Isn't it kind of stuck-up, wanting to live forever?

Toni Morrison tells the story, perhaps apocryphal, of a European intellectual making her first visit to Manhattan since the late fifties. (I imagine a second coming of Simone de Beauvoir.) The two are in a cab cruising down Fifth Avenue early in the evening. The visiting intellectual studies the sidewalks through the window. "I hadn't realized," she says at last, "how many prostitutes there are in New York." A perplexed Morrison looks out, too. Then, finally, our Nobel Laureate is able to explain: "Those aren't *prostitutes.* Those are *smokers.*"

Part Two

FALLING OFF
THE PACIFIC RIM

DeLillo's American Jitters

It's about time Don DeLillo came up with a miracle, even if what this miracle amounts to is an airborne optical illusion—a conjoining, in the spangled sky above the Bronx, of billboard, commuter train, sunset, orange juice, and the Angel Esmeralda. The poster boy of postmodernism is a secret Holy Roller. Like Simone Weil, he would parachute to God. As much as his ten previous novels have been droll about movies and television, about supermarkets and advertising, about football and rock music, about science fiction and the stock exchange, about organized crime and the CIA, they are also full of dense light, black bees, deserts, caves, and cults—of prophecy and pilgrims. These pilgrims, as hungry for meaning as Greek goats, are forever chewing through gaudy packaging, surface chatter, coded circuits, and layered film, past number, alphabet and ideation to "the fallen wonder of the world." It's just that till now their topographies have been as godforsaken as Kafka's or Beckett's. But Sister Edgar, the nun in *Underworld* who lines her room with Reynolds Wrap to ward off nuclear fallout, will not only see an angel and die ecstatic; she is promptly whisked for purging into cyberspace. And on the World Wide Web, after this Moloch of a novel has devoured in its brilliant passage everything from baseball to the Cold War and everybody from J. Edgar Hoover to Lenny Bruce, DeLillo declares virtual peace.

While the novel's magnificent, the blessing's mixed. We receive it up to our dentures in garbage dumps of nuclear waste. We have been tracking through five decades the baseball Ralph Branca pitched to Bobby Thomson at the Polo Grounds on October 3, 1951, hit by Thomson for a pennant-winning home run on the same day the Soviet Union exploded an atomic bomb. J. Edgar Hoover was at that game, in a box seat with Jackie Gleason, who vomited all over Frank Sinatra's shoes. Hearing the crowd's roar, feeling "the sun's own heat that swallows cities," looking at a *Life* magazine color reproduction of

Bruegel's *The Triumph of Death,* this other Edgar is imagined by DeLillo to have thought: "For every atmospheric blast, every glimpse we get of the bared force of nature, that weird peeled eyeball exploding over the desert—for every one of these he reckons a hundred plots go underground, to spawn and skein."

And we will follow all of them, these mushroom clouds in the American head, backward as if a reverse trajectory, with the arc of the ball returning from the future to Thomson's bat and Branca's hand—like a countdown to critical mass and chain reaction, to a fission and fusion of the glossolalias of art and science, politics and religion, cities and deserts and fathers and sons. Or upside down, as if we climbed rung by rung out of Dante's Inferno through circles of treason, hypocrisy, tyranny, and blasphemy past heresy, sloth, avarice, and incontinence to a modern Limbo like Eliot's Waste Land, with Homer and Virgil in the home-team dugout. I'm not just being fancy. "The word plutonium," DeLillo explains, "comes from Pluto, god of the dead and ruler of the underworld." So semi-seriously I suggest that the home-run ball is both a Holy Grail *and* the Golden Bough—which sacred sprig, you'll remember, is what Aeneas took with him after the fall of Troy, a peace offering to Proserpina and a talisman against terror, upon his descent into the Land of the Dead to seek from his expired father a preview of Roman history's coming attractions. *Underworld* spends most of its wasteful Cold War also looking for a lost father.

But there are many underworlds in *Underworld*: bomb shelters, subway tunnels, commodity pits, and Mafias; underground art, underground testing, and the underclass of the inner city; burial mounds, pyramids, and condominiums of garbage; denial, repression, and the fossil fuels of childhood memory; secret governments, secret histories, and secret technologies; black markets in drugs, sex toys, and sports memorabilia; a lost-and-found Eisenstein movie called *Underwelt* and a village of deformed children not on any map of Kazakhstan; catacombs and cul-de-sacs. DeLillo, speaking in tongues like

Lenny Bruce, articulates the lowlife lot of them—the American bombhead jitters.

The war was on television every night but we all went to the movies.

(Americana)

When Nick Shay's Italian father, a low-rent bookie, walks out one night for a pack of Lucky Strikes and vanishes forever from the Bronx, Nick is sure he was wasted by the mob—dumped somewhere wet. So Jimmy Costanza's son grows up juvenile delinquent, stealing cars, shooting pool, and sleeping with Klara Sax, the artist wife of the high school science teacher, Albert Bronzini; even, for no other reason than the gun in his hand, killing a drug dealer in a storage room in the rat warrens under an apartment house; after which he will do time in an upstate prison, a Minnesota Jesuit college, and a canary cage in corporate speechwriting before he finally finds, in a Sunbelt skyscraper, "a faith to embrace."

> My firm was involved in waste. We were waste handlers, waste traders, cosmologists of waste. I traveled to the coastal lowlands of Texas and watched men in moon suits bury drums of dangerous waste in subterranean salt beds many millions of years old, dried-out remnants of a Mesozoic ocean. It was a religious conviction in our business that these deposits of rock salt would not leak radiation. Waste is a religious thing. We entomb contaminated waste with a sense of reverence and dread. It is necessary to respect what we discard.

Whereas Nick's younger brother Matt, who just assumes his father ran away, will grow up wonky—taught to play competitive chess by the cuckold Bronzini; abandoning that "hostile" game to become a graduate student of fission's trigger principles, a Spec 5 army intelligence analyst who translates dots on aerial reconnaissance photos "into letters, numbers, coordinates, grids and entire systems of knowledge" for the next Vietnam bombing mission, and, in a secret desert installation, a weapons worker "of the soft-core type" who figures out "the lurid mathematics of a nuclear accident or limited exchange": "Go to the desert or tundra and wait for the visionary flash of light, the critical mass that will call down the Hindu heavens, Kali and Shiva and all the grimacing lesser gods."

Matt eventually flees his underworld of endgames for a do-gooder job in a tank for thinkers. But Nick is one of DeLillo's hollow drums on whom the century beats its dread. He amplifies, he resonates, he even emulsifies, but somebody else took the picture and made the music. For Nick, it's Branca's ball, not Thomson's: "It's about the mystery of bad luck, the mystery of loss." Baseball and fathers! On the one hand, Nick thinks he's immune to history; it isn't *his* head "on someone else's body in the photograph that's introduced as evidence." On the other, seven hundred pages later, he longs for "the days of disorder . . . the days when I was alive on the earth, rippling in the quick of my skin, heedless and real. . . . This is what I long for, the breach of peace, the days of disarray when I walked real streets and did things slap-bang and felt angry and ready all the time, a danger to others and a distant mystery to myself."

Meanwhile, Klara has abandoned Bronzini and the Bronx to become a famous conceptual artist. (Think Georgia O'Keeffe, but also Louise Nevelson.) She escorts us to the best Manhattan art world parties, gallery openings, poetry readings, and camp-outs of film buffs for Eisenstein and Zapruder — even to Truman Capote's masked ball, at which J. Edgar shows up costumed as a butch biker "riding into town to take over leadership of the sadists and necrophiles." Through her eyes, we see the rooftop gardens and stricken medieval streets, "with strange draped women, scarfed like Tuaregs, living in junked cars . . . the ones with their own radio programs that you didn't need a radio to listen to because they followed you down the street in the endless inspired catastrophe of New York," and the intimacy between art and death. And she, too, will end up in the atomic desert, sandblasting and redecorating a scrapheap of abandoned B-52 bombers:

> We're painting, hand-painting in some cases, putting our puny hands
> to great weapons systems, to systems that came out of the factories and

assembly halls as near alike as possible, millions of components stamped out, repeated endlessly, and we're trying to unrepeat, to find an element of felt life, and maybe there's a sort of survival instinct here, a graffiti instinct—to trespass and declare ourselves, show who we are. The way the nose artists did, the guys who painted pinups on the fuselage.

Then again, maybe not. Felt life, "the past that never stops happening," has been left behind in the immigrant Bronx where DeLillo himself grew up but hasn't before written about except passingly in *Ratner's Star*—where Bronzini persists in his saintly rounds from barber to butcher, so wonderfully aware that he desires to stop a little girl in mid-hopscotch, to "stop everything for half a second, atomic clocks, body clocks, the microworld in which physicists search for time—and then run it backwards, unjump the girl, rewind the life, give us all a chance to do it over again." Where the Cold War nun Sister Edgar continues to distribute food to the homeless and destitute despite nightmares of "a cosmic cloud of slushed fetuses floating in the rings of Saturn." Where the runaway Esmeralda, before she is raped, murdered and tossed like garbage from a rooftop, hides in "a junkworld sculpture park" of cannibalized cars. And where Ismael Munoz, a k a Moonman 157, an AIDS-infected graffiti artist beyond Klara's wildest conceptualizing, leads an urban insurgency that's almost semiotic:

> You have to stand on a platform and see it coming or you can't know the feeling a writer gets, how the number 5 train comes roaring down the rat alleys and slams out of the tunnel, going whop-pop onto the high tracks, and suddenly there it is, Moonman riding the sky in the heart of the Bronx, over the whole burnt and rusted country, and this is the art of the backstreets talking, all the way from Bird, and you can't *not* see us anymore, you can't *not* know who we are, we got total notoriety now, Momzo Tops and Rimester and me, we're getting fame, we ain't ashame, and the train go rattling over the garbagy streets and past the dead-eye windows of all those empty tenements that have people living there even if you don't see them, but you have to see our tags and cartoon figures and bright and rhyming poems, this is the art that can't stand still, it climbs across your eyeballs night and day, the flickery

jumping art of the slums and dumpsters, flashing those colors in your face—like I'm your movie, motherfucker.

Everything, and everybody, is connected, all the jitterbugs who pass around the baseball, from the truant black teen who first grabs it to his wastrel father who auctions it off to an ad exec, who gives it to *his* son, who will pilot one of those B-52 bombers that Matt plots Vietnam missions for and Klara ends up painting in the desert—and so on, unto a memorabilia collector who appreciates "the revenge of popular culture on those who take it too seriously," a "garbage guerrilla" from the tambourine sixties, a Blackstone Ranger pop-tart feminist, and the Texas Highway Serial Killer. Even Lenny Bruce connects, channeling Cuban missiles to an audience of graybeard Beats who don't even need this crisis to hate the bomb: "The bomb was their handiest reference to the moral squalor of America, the guilty place of smokestacks and robot corporations, *Time*-magazined and J. Edgar Hoovered, where people sat hunched over cups of coffee in a thousand rainswept truck stops on the jazz prairie, secret Trotskyites and sad nymphomaniacs with Buddhist pussies."

Obviously, DeLillo's ear has lost none of its perfect parodic pitch, nor his sentences a cubit of their shadow cunning. As ever in his novels, each a far-flung language system where the gravity is variable, the films foreign, the expressionism abstract and the Joyce jazzy, he seems to grin and dervish. We are made of words; we seek periods to stop thinking; we pratfall upon alibi, code and cant; lapse into dependent dangles and the humming of the pixels. Or he sets a gnomic charge like Semtex. Or, as choral as he's cinematic, he will sing cantatas of the damned. And then nail us to a cross:

> She sees the flash, the thermal pulse. She hears the rumble building, the great gathering force rolling off the 16-bit soundboard. She stands in the flash and feels the power. She sees the spray plume. She sees the fireball climbing, the superheated sphere of burning gas that can blind a person with its beauty, its dripping christblood colors, solar golds and reds. She sees the shock wave and hears the high winds and feels

the power of false faith, the faith of paranoia, and then the mushroom cloud spreads around her, the pulverized mass of radioactive debris, eight miles high, ten miles, twenty, with skirted stem and smoking platinum cap.

The jewels roll out of her eyes and she sees God.

We're presently assembling evidence about the French Revolution indicating that a dissident faction of the sans-culottes used to assemble secretly under cover of dark for the sole purpose of wearing culottes.

(Great Jones Street)

As if they sought like redneck Dickeys to deliver him from middlebrowsing, pomo critics have taken DeLillo into the woods and done funny things to him. In this debauching, until now, he would appear to have acquiesced. Cryptic and reclusive, for more than a quarter-century he has issued bulletins from zones of dread on the unbearable lightness of American being and "the claustrophobia of vast spaces"; on motels, miniature golf, serial killers, "abandoned meanings," and "crisis sociology"; on paper money with pretty pictures, the candy colors of consumer products, the siren songs of advertising, and the incantatory power of cliché; on Speed Wash, Alpo, astrology, "popcorn and killer drugs." "BREATHE! GLEAM! VERBALIZE! DIE!" we are told in *Ratner's Star.* In the parentheticals between sign and signifier, names are named: Tegrin, *White Noise* whispers to us; Denorex and Selsun Blue; Random Access Memory, Acquired Immune Deficiency Syndrome, and Mutual Assured Destruction—"void where prohibited."

So many movies: David Bell is making one in *Americana.* In *Great Jones Street,* a character explains: "The whole concept of movies is so fundamentally Egyptian. Movies are dreams. Pyramids. Great rivers of sleep." Lyle, in *Players,* "found himself bored, often, at the theater (though never at movies), even when he knew, could see and hear, that the play was exceptional, deserving of total attention. This kind of torpor was generated by three-dimensional bodies, real space as opposed to the manipulated depth of film." The whole frantic project in *Running Dog* was to acquire a pornographic movie filmed in Hitler's bunker.

Volterra in *The Names* seeks to capture on camera the alphabet killer cult in the very act of snuff: "Film is more than the twentieth-century art. It's another part of the twentieth-century mind. It's the world seen from inside." Murray, in *White Noise*, is asked to teach a course in the cinema of car crashes. One of *Libra*'s co-conspirators, Wayne, dreams himself inside *The Seven Samurai*. And in *Underworld*, there's Eisenstein.

But even more television: *Ratner's Star* imagines an afternoon TV game show: "Abort That Fetus!" *Players* ends in a motel room with "serial grief" on the screen. *Libra* begins with Lee Harvey Oswald and his mother watching "blue heads," *Racket Squad*, and *Dragnet* in the Bronx—after which it's the Warren Commission. Karen, *Mao II*'s ex-Moonie, can't get enough of TV news, of exercise programs, riots, disasters, and "the terror that came blowing through the fog": "She was thin-boundaried. She took it all in, she believed it all, pain, ecstasy, dog food, all the seraphic matter, the baby bliss that falls from the air." In *White Noise*, a tiresome Murray tells his students:

> TV offers incredible amounts of psychic data. It opens ancient memories of world birth, it welcomes us into the grid, the network of little buzzing dots that make up the picture pattern. There is light, there is sound. . . . Look at the wealth of data concealed in the grid, in the bright packaging, the jingles, the slice-of-life commercials, the products hurtling out of the darkness, the coded messages and endless repetitions, like chants, like mantras. '*Coke is it, Coke is it, Coke is it.*' The medium practically overflows with sacred formulas.

From so much seraphic lint, it's easy enough to infer a postmodern project of decentered self, mediascape pastiche, nostalgia, camp, and kitsch. From the dirty kids' books Fenig writes in *Great Jones Street*, the L. Ron Hubbard caricature in *Ratner's Star*, the misspelled novel Tap is writing in *The Names*, the "long serious novels with coded structures" Dana reviews for the CIA in *White Noise*, the novel that Bill can't finish in *Mao II*, the Oswald scripts they counterfeit in *Libra*, and the lonesome-dovey mash notes the serial killer posts to a cable-newscast prom queen in *Underworld*, cyberpunk professors are entitled to conclude that DeLillo has problematized the very idea of a master narrative, if not tinkled on it. And from his rock lyrics, football slanguage, brain fade and graffiti, his bat caves and Chinese mirror-making, his Elvis and his Hitler, border intellectuals are confirmed in their suspicion that everything in the data drizzle and magnetic flash is equally weightless or equally trivial, that all books, films, ads, TV shows, baseball cards, music videos, and fathers are socially constructed compost heaps of previous texts, at best unwilling stooges and at worst bad-faith purveyors of the dominant discourse—that all of us, Chicken Littles and Tiny Tims, are likewise each the helpless vector of forces we can't even locate, much less modify.

Where were you when James Dean died? I was writing a monograph on the boomerang in *Ratner's Star.* Except that Don DeLillo is as thin-boundaried as his Moonie Karen. The terror blowing through his fog is *real*; it has landscape, temperature, humidity, the time of day, and a scorched skin. You might even say it's *unbalanced.* Always seeking value, he is preternaturally alert to its absence or corruption. Drive-by consumerism is the least of his apprehensions. Hiroshima and the Holocaust showed up early, stayed late, and decided to squat. Deathward is the culture's motion, like the falling of all matter in the universe and the terminus of every plot. And even so, there's levitation, like the hot-air balloon in *Underworld,* looking down on Klara's bombers; or, in *Ratner's Star,* those box kites with their paper lanterns "resembling a class of mythical invertebrates determined to burn themselves away rather than return to porous earth, where they'd earlier shed the silk of transfiguration."

Who hit the road in *Americana*? "Sons of the chemistry sets in the five-walled city," running from Indochina. And where will they end up? In Dealey Plaza, in death-dealing Dallas.

Bloomberg in *End Zone* is "unjewing myself" because he's tired of "historical guilt," and Myna wears a mushroom cloud, and Major Staley was a crew member on the Nagasaki mission. Lucky Strike! In this Texas desert, we are meant to wonder:

Perhaps there is no silence. Or maybe it's just that time is too compact to allow for silence to be felt. But in some form of void, freed from consciousness, the mind remakes itself. What we must know must be learned from blacked-out pages. To begin to reword the overflowing world. To subtract and disjoin. To re-recite the alphabet. . . . To call something by its name and need no other word.

In *Great Jones Street,* Buckey knows he would be better off if only he could "love the age . . . Float on its clotted oil." But: "It was an evil thing to consider, allying myself with the barest parts of the mass awareness, land policed by the king's linguists, by technicians in death-system control, corporate disease consultants, profiteers of the fetus industry." Till they come for him with the trope-killing hypodermic syringe, he will instead lay tracks like "VC Sweetheart," "Cold War Lover," and "Protestant Work Ethic Blues." In *Ratner's Star,* what they discover in Field Experiment Number One is that the signal they thought they'd picked up from outer space is a boomerang from our deepest past, which achieved its own chain reaction and so had to start all over again in a cave. In *Players,* Kinnear thinks that the government has become, perhaps, *too* interesting, acting out its massive fantasies: "We thought they bombed villages, killed children, for the sake of technology, so it could shake itself out, and for certain abstractions. We didn't give them credit for the rest of it." Why, in *The Names,* are so many Americans abroad? "Bank loans, arms credits, goods, technology. Technicians are the infiltrators of ancient societies. They speak a secret language. They bring new kinds of death." (Which also helps explain Owen's fascination with "the language of the mathematics of war, nuclear game theory, that bone country of tech data and little clicking words.") If, in *White Noise,* some people are larger than life whereas "Hitler is larger than death," perhaps what we need is "The Stanford Linear Accelerator 3-Day Particle-Smashing Diet." Kennedy really and truly dies all over again in *Libra,* and so does Oswald, like a premodern in the black noise. As much as *Mao II* was about television and silk-screen Warhols and novelists as would-be terrorists, it was also about Beirut.

Weapons and waste throng this fiction, and burial mounds of guilty evidence—like the "true underground" of generals, bankers, and presidents in *Great Jones Street*, "far beneath the speed freaks and cutters of smack"; the temple cave of the Great Hole in *Ratner's Star* where Shazar Lazarus, in a biomembrane, worries about alphabets and sperm demons; the ghost engines and teams of behaviorists in the sewerworld of *Players*; the supermarkets, chemical mists, moon dust, and gene pools of *White Noise*; a fireproof cubicle in *Libra* full of "theories that gleam like jade idols"; shaft graves, vaulted cisterns, subway tunnels, salt domes, imaginary Chinas. . . . Not even lovely ancient Crete is safe. "Beneath the lilies and antelopes and blue monkeys," *The Names* reminds us, are "darker things"—the labyrinth, the Minotaur, and the sign of a double ax on a 3,700-year-old pillar crypt, insinuating human sacrifice.

> *He sensed the connections being made around him, all the objects and shaped silhouettes and levels of knowledge—not knowledge exactly but insidious intent. But not that either—some deeper meaning that existed solely to keep him from knowing what it was.* (Underworld)

Here is where I ought to trace a thread of "christblood colors" through all eleven novels—from Dymphna, the Nervous Breakdown Saint in *Americana*, to Saint Vincent, who won't even answer the telephone at his own hospital in *Great Jones Street*, to the nun in *White Noise*, who only pretends to believe in heaven and hell because "somebody has to," to Sister Edgar, bride of the *Underworld* bombheads; the two-tiered Gothic windows, armor-clad icons, silent Luthers, revivalists speaking in tongues and playing with snakes, Baptists on picnics and Calvinists with bagpipes and more Jesuit priests than DeLillo could ever possibly have met in his college years at Fordham. And to snatch as well at passing spores of "hyperatavistic" blood cults, like the Happy Valley Renegade Faction or Ta Onomata. To look for the sacred on stray obelisks and on pavements mosaics and in the eyes of hermaphroditic Indian doll-gods. To back-channel in the band waves of Taoism, animism, and Pythagoras; of

Vedanta, Kabbala, and Zen. But trust me: these books are saturated. Owen in *The Names* is emblematic, noting first that "if Greek or Latin characters are paving stones, Arabic is rain"; then wondering, "Was religion the point of language?"; and finally getting the message, in Aramaic: "The river of language is God."

In *Underworld*, we have lost our Father. Imagine, as in *End Zone*, competing liturgies of play-action, pass-run option, sprint-out, aerial game, and blitz on the one hand—or, on the other, selective ordnance, collateral destruction, circular error probability, post-attack environment, thermal hurricane, stark deterrence, megatonnage, and overkill—Titans, Spartans, and Poseidons. "When the Old God goes," *Mao II* told us, "they pray to flies and bottlecaps." Or television, garbage, the market, and a mushroom cloud. "It's like the lying and cheating General Motors does," says a character in *Americana* about the Catholic Church: "You still need cars."

It seems to have been Don DeLillo's project from the beginning to see through signs to the sacred—to invade the Day-Glo glitterdome that pretends to "custom-cater" to our "silky and intimate" desires, even as "the force of converging markets produces an instantaneous capital that shoots across horizons at the speed of light, making for a certain furtive sameness, a planing away of particulars that affects everything from architecture to leisure time to the way people eat and sleep and dream"; to pick up and then tune out its every acoustic inflection, all the clattering sharps, flats, crackles, and pops of a Big Bang soft-sell military/consumer culture; to listen for a deeper chord.

But down in the fear there's only silence. What's a great novelist to do? In *Ratner's Star* he took on not only "avant-garde" mathematics but science itself: structure, system, symmetry, and coherence in our picturing of deployed matter; order in nature, essence in number, beauty in reason, and proof in the abstract pudding—and what we got for all our trouble was a "noncognate celestial anomaly." As happens surprisingly often in DeLillo, we also ended up in India, where a sadhu gave us the word:

> You see our right entanglement in all around us, the press to measure and delve. There, see, in the annotated ivory tools, lengths of notched wood, in the wave-guide manipulation of light and our nosings into the choreography of protons, we implicate ourselves in endless uncertainty. This is the ethic you've rejected. Inside your desolation, however, you come upon the reinforcing grid of works and minds that extend themselves against whatever lonely spaces account for our hollow moods, the woe incoming. Why are you here? To unsnarl us from our delimiting senses? To offer protective cladding against our cruelty and fear? The pain, the life-cry speak our most candid wonders. To outpremise these, by whatever tekite whirl you've mastered, would be to make us hypothetical, a creature of our own pretending, as you are.

And in *The Names,* he turned from the language of science to utterance itself: the secret syllables of blood recollection, the shared past of alphabets that spelled the name of God, the evolution of meaningful letters out of "terrible holy gibberish" — from geographies of gesture and pictographs of a house, a camel, an ox, a fish, the palm of your hand, or the praying-man shape of the Sinai — to mallet-and-chisel mysteries, scriptural rage, a "frenzy of knowing," and the adductive force of sweet whispers in the booming dark before we see, above the Sanskrit pavilions, white vultures scribbling on bruised sky. After which our anti-hero, mortified to learn that all along he had been really working for the CIA, is ready at last to visit the Acropolis:

> This is what I found, deeper than the art and mathematics embodied in the structure, the optical exactitudes. I found a cry for pity. This is what remains to the mauled stones in their blue surround, this open cry, this voice we know as our own. . . . I move past the scaffolding and walk down the steps, hearing one language after another, rich, harsh, mysterious, strong. This is what we bring to the temple, not prayer or chant or slaughtered rams. Our offering is language.

So is DeLillo's. *Underworld* ends with a transcendent and redemptive act of grace. While this astonishing novel may have earned it, America certainly hasn't. But it is in the nature of grace to be gratuitous, to bless us in spite of ourselves, as if we didn't know from mustard seeds; to unjump, unrepeat, rewind, do over. In *End Zone,* after his mother is shot to death by a lunatic, Bloomberg goes into the desert and paints a flat stone black. A friend will later find this stone and think it miraculous. From his black stones, in the latitudes of our vastation, DeLillo, too, has made a miracle. Having mourned the fallen wonder of the world, like one of those Author-Gods who are supposed to be extinct, he creates his own basilica and sacrament, calling it the Bronx.

Revenge of the Poisoned Twinkies

When Bret Easton Ellis's *Less Than Zero* was published back in 1985, William F. Buckley Jr. called to ask if I'd chat about it on *Firing Line*. I had a broken arm and a broken mind, and saw no reason to bestir myself from my bed of pain to talk on television about a black popsicle of a novel in which a guy named Clay comes home to Los Angeles from Camden, a Bennington sort of eastern college, to spend Christmas vacation with his well-heeled zombie support group watching MTV, blowing lots of coke, cruising in sporty cars to noisy clubs, plugging each other in like electric guitars, and finding themselves still so bored that they gang-rape a young woman, cut off her breasts, and stick candles in her wounds. Thus I missed my first chance as an Old Fart to disdain the Way-Cool New and Totally Grody.

By the time of the next Ellis, *The Rules of Attraction* (1987), instead of a puppy-novelist, we confronted an epicycle of the Ptolemaic system of hype, according to which the heavens move in eccentric orbits around a vacuous editorial need for gas. Thus the Brat Pack, a cohort of New York literary teenyboppers with names like Bret, Jill, Jay, Meg, David, and Tama, some of whom had gone to Bennington, most of whom festered in nests like Nell's, and all of whom showed up in one another's books and blurbs, for which they got more than their fair share of buzz. Well, the Old Fart thought, young writers always herd together, moving like thick-skinned ungulates over the inky savannahs, dodging potshots from great white hunters at self-important periodicals. It was the same in Paris before the French Revolution, when everybody wrote pornography, and after World War II, when everybody was Absurd. It happened in nineteenth-century St. Petersburg, when Belinksy got mad at Gogol, for which Dostoyevsky was almost shot. And in turn-of-the-century Kent and Sussex, where Joseph Conrad, Henry James, H. G. Wells, and Ford Madox Ford combed each other's thinning hair. And in China not much later, with Kang Youwei, Lu Xun, and Ding Ling. Not to mention Bloomsbury, about which we have heard too much already. Plus: the Algonquin Round Table, the French Riviera, the *Partisan Review*, the North Beach Beats, and all those Cold Warriors of the Congress for Cultural Freedom bought and paid for by the CIA.

What you do is wait around to see if any of these ungulates turns into a unicorn. Bret, Jill, Jay, Meg, Tama, and David would either grow up to be more interesting than their immune systems and their urine samples or they wouldn't. Meanwhile, was it really necessary to review a novel in which Ellis went back to Bennington—excuse me, Camden—to set up shop in the big holes in the tiny heads of Sean, Paul, Lauren, and Victor, none of whom ever went to class, read a book, mustered a fierce feeling, or surprised a coherent idea because they were all too busy doing drugs or committing suicide? Stoned, horny, ungrateful, uncomprehending, nobody in *The Rules of Attraction* seemed capable of love, art, politics, unselfishness, or even enthusiasm. It's taken most of us most of our lives, and several momentous occasions, ever to feel as bad for fifteen minutes as these kids had apparently felt since Pampers.

Of course, upon the occasion of *American Psycho* (1992), dropped by Simon & Schuster, picked up by Vintage, picketed by NOW, it was impossible not to express an opinion. Meet Sean's older brother Patrick, a twenty-seven-year-old Wall Street broker who went to Exeter and Harvard instead of Hollywood High and Camden. When Patrick in his Ralph Lauren silk pajamas isn't listening to Whitney Houston or *Les Misérables* on his Sansui stereo system with the six-foot Duntech Sovereign 2001 speakers in Brazilian rosewood, or eating quail sashimi and chocolate-chip sorbet at a minimalist bistro, or snorting cocaine at the latest downtown armpit, or buying, on his way to a masseuse or the tanning salon, magazines like *Esquire* and *Lesbian Vibrator Bitches* . . . what this Patrick does is torture dogs, pop the eyes out of homeless beggars, and dismember Yuppies.

There is no reason this couldn't have been funny: if not Swiftian, at least a sort of *Bonfire of the Vanities* meets *The Texas Chainsaw Massacre*. And, for the first two hundred pages, some of it actually is. Ellis has an ear for the homophobic and misogynistic fatuities of his social set, and an eye for their A. Testoni loafers, their Oliver Peoples nonprescription glasses, and their minoxidil. Since everybody looks alike, they're always mistaking each other for somebody else. I like the scene at the Chinese laundry, where they can't wash the blood out of Patrick's clothes. The TV talk show he watches each morning also amuses: "Deformed People," "Dwarf-Tossing," "Teenage Girls Who Trade Sex for Crack," and "Has Patrick Swayze Become Cynical or Not?"

Satire means never having to say you're sorry. Besides, isn't Ellis also Political? When Patrick tells people that he's "into murders and executions," what they hear him say is "mergers and acquisitions." And when he makes obscene telephone calls to Dalton girls, what he whispers to them is, "I'm a corporate raider. I orchestrate hostile takeovers. What do you think of that?" To which one of the girls, unfazed, replies: "Dad, is that you?" In other words, when *American Psycho* then goes on at lipsmacking length about the rape of an Aspen waitress with a can of hair spray, the nailing of Bethany's fingers to a hardwood floor, and the sodomizing of a severed head, it is really a critique of the Fetishism of Commodities. And I am really Antonio Gramsci.

But, or so I thought, pop culture has a way of compensating for its overmuch with something equally, reciprocally, excessive. Less than a year after *Psycho*, Bret Easton Ellis would be compensated for, and exceeded by, Lorena Bobbitt—a Valerie Solanas for the nineties. As Camille Paglia, the Lawrence Welk of postfeminist soundbiters, was quick to pontificate: "It's a kind of wake-up call. It has to send a chill through every man in the world."

In one word, you reproach us with intending to do away with your property. Precisely so; that is just what we intend. (Karl Marx)

Tina Brown chose not to publish in *The New Yorker* an article she commissioned from Gay Talese on John Wayne Bobbitt's wayward penis. I cannot imagine a better magazine assignment, in the impish spirit of William Shawn, unless the *New York Review of Books* should have decided to send Philip Roth to Manassas, Virginia, for the trial of Lorena Bobbitt on charges of having on June 23, 1993, cut off her husband's offending member with an eight-inch red-handled kitchen carving knife. Surely the penis is to Gay Talese and Philip Roth what Hiroshima was to John Hersey and Jonathan Schell. There has been more than enough mystical chitchat about symbolic sets of male sex organs like the Triangle of Pythagoras and the Trinity of Christ and the Triad of the Hegelian Dialectic. It's time we struck some deep scrotumnal bass notes.

And surely after its adventures in the world, John Wayne's refugee penis deserves a name of its own. Call it Ishmael. Or Columbus. Or Roto-Rooter. Or the Flying Dutchman. Or Bret.

Anyway, as his trial (for marital sexual assault) and hers (for "malicious wounding") began that November, we didn't have Talese to read in *The New Yorker* and so had to make do with Kim Masters, who profiled Lorena Leonor Bobbitt in the November *Vanity Fair,* and Lawrence K. Altman, M.D., whose article in the *New York Times* retold, *Dragnet*-style, the heroic story of a team of surgeons who spent nine-and-a-half hours reattaching Ishmael to the host-body of the twenty-six-year-old bouncer at the go-go Legends Bar, some eight hours after he was maliciously wounded. Dr. James T. Sehn, the urologist on call at Prince William Hospital, is quoted by Altman as saying that "there was no damage to the nerves in the stump."

We won't even discuss the account in the *Washingtonian,* called "Cutting Edge Journalism," of the way the press reported this story. Nor the joke, attributed to a Virginia law enforcement official, about "a special dog" enlisted to track down the wayward penis: "a cocker spaniel." And, no, I can't tell you whether the Legends Bar has severance pay.

Briefly, Lorena, a twenty-four-year-old, five-foot-two-inch, ninety-five-pound Venezuelan immigrant, says that she was sexually abused and raped by her husband, who forced her to have an abortion and, incidentally, never waited for her to come to orgasm: "I just wanted him to disappear." Through his attorney, John Wayne, an ex-Marine whose Quantico dress blues first attracted Lorena's eye in 1988, denied everything. But the texture is in the details. Of *course*, a marine base is notorious for testosterone poisoning, but did his name *have* to be John Wayne? Must he have come from Niagara Falls with both a learning disability and an attention-deficit disorder? When Lorena made her escape at 4 A.M., with the organ and the knife, in a 1991 Mercury Capri, was it some weird form of mourning for her unborn child that made her toss Columbus out the window and onto the lawn of the Patty-Cake Daycare Center? When volunteer fireman Howard Michael Perry found Roto-Rooter, did he really have to stick it in a Ziploc bag? Was it altogether necessary that Lorena work in a nail salon, even if she embezzled $7,200 from her employer and even though that employer, Janna Bisutti, nevertheless stood by her? And if, indeed, she already had a media advisor for book and movie rights, where was he when Lorena sat down for a steak dinner, with Kim Masters of *Vanity Fair*, and asked for another knife because the Bret was too tough? And I haven't even mentioned the tape recorder, the satellite dish, the plastic Christmas tree, the Kentucky Fried Chicken, the spandex shorts, or the wedding breakfast at Bob's Big Boy.

None of this would happen at the Royalton, where Condé-Nasties dish. But out there in the Trash Culture, Lorena Bobbitt is more like Mary Beth Whitehead in the Baby "M" case, from the wrong side of the social tracks, than she in any way resembles Kali, the Black Mother of the Indian subcontinent, with her girdle of fingers and necklace of skulls. Or Aramaic Atargatis, Fish Mother of the Syrians, who insisted on castration as a prerequisite for priesthood. Or Darago the Volcano Goddess of the Philippines, demanding once a year a manly sacrifice, like a magazine subscription renewal. Or Cybele, the Great Mother of the old Near East, who did permanent damage to her lover/grandson Attis. Or the Gaia who fashioned from "gray adamant" the sawtoothed sickle with which Cronos hacked off his father's sex.

Waif-thin Keene-eyed Lorena, in fact, lacks even the pluck and perk of those TV heroines, from Farrah Fawcett in 1984 to Melissa Gilbert twice a season ever since, who've made Abuse-of-the-Month movies a redress-of-grievance network genre. As if dreaming instead of Caracas, she did the deed in some sort of fugue state, while John Wayne Bobbitt tossed in his dress-blue sleep. Lorena looks more like Luot-Hozjit, the kindly virgin of the Russian Lapps, covered with reindeer fur. Although we may have hoped that the Virginia courts would be as easy on her as the German courts were on Günter Parche, who used *his* knife on someone, Monica Seles, clearly better at her job than John Wayne was at his—still, Lorena hasn't done matriarchy any favors.

One also thinks of Tz'u-hsi, the Dowager Empress of China from 1861 until 1908, whose Forbidden City eunuchs, Marina Warner tells us, were required to carry their testicles around in labeled jars, available for court inspection. And of the eighteenth-century *skoptsy,* in prerevolutionary Russia, whose sectarian leader Selivanov, after a hard day of ecstatic flagellation, decided to castrate himself and talked everybody else into following suit. On the evidence of the activities of Russian *skoptsy,* Chinese and Byzantine eunuchs, and Ottoman janissaries, it's hard to see why Texas ever thought that castrating rapist Steve Allen Butler would turn him into the Pillsbury Doughboy—as if a missing sperm count would render our Steves (or our Patricks) *cute*; as if by state-sanctioned butcher-boy behavior, any of *us* become more manly.

Then there's the curious case of Napoleon, whose missing penis got so much ink a couple of years ago in the *Times Book Review*, involving novelists like Peter Doyle, Angela Carter, and Thomas Flanagan and institutions as august as Christie's and Columbia. Even curiouser, Donald Richie, in *Geisha, Gangster,*

Neighbor, Nun, reports visiting a postwar Tokyo working-class pub, the Star Chrysanthemum Water, where every night at ten the men would cover their private parts and start to giggle as Sada Abe in flaming kimono began her indignant descent, "like a basilisk," down spiral stairs to the grilled squid and the pickled radish. In 1936, this same Sada Abe had accidentally strangled her lover, then cut off his penis and carried it around for days. She went from prison to performance art. Oshima later made a movie about her, *In the Realm of the Senses,* which critics compared unfavorably to Marco Ferreri's *The Last Woman,* released the same year, in which a sad young Gerard Depardieu emasculates himself with an electric carving knife. Neither movie has the vulgar kick of the American B-minus classic *I Spit on Your Grave,* in which a gang-rape victim does it to a garage mechanic in a bloody bubble bath.

Merely months before Lorena, in perhaps the worst novel he'll ever write, *Cape of Storms,* the South African André Brink reimagined Adamastor as a Titan of black Africa whose enormous sexual organ, which he must wrap like a rope around his waist, gets in the way of his lech for a white European nymph, and we're led to believe that civilization means castration. On the other hand, in her most recent novel, *Possessing the Secret of Joy,* Alice Walker explained that worse things go on all the time—except to women. But about clitordectomies, *Vanity Fair* is so far silent.

I wish I had a better Marxist angle. Marx, after all, deplored "the status of women as mere instruments of production." But, dialectically speaking, is the penis a fetishized commodity? Or is it capital (bankable sperm)? Something else may be going on in the accessorizing culture that we need the fashion-conscious media to construe for us. For instance:

(1) *A Tip of the Hat with Severed Hands*: On the same day in July 1987 that an anonymous Belgian bought Rene Magritte's black bowler at a London auction for $26,000 and then disappeared without a word, Buenos Aires grave robbers disinterred

the corpse of Juan Peron, lopped off his hands, and held them for $8 million in ransom. They vanished, too.

(2) *Bring Me the Head of Saul Kent's Mother.* In February 1988, Dora Kent, age eighty-three, was decapitated at the request of her son Saul, age forty-eight. Saul's mother's severed head was stashed in liquid nitrogen by a cryonic outfit called Alcor Life Extension until such time as medical science found her a new body. Unfortunately Dora seems not to have signed the requisite consent forms. And she may not have been legally dead when beheaded. And when the Riverside County, California, coroner paid a visit to the freezer, none of the six heads he found there was hers.

(3) *The High Price of Semen*: In July 1975, a California man who stored a sample of his semen at a sperm bank and then had a vasectomy, on learning that his sperm deposit had been accidentally destroyed despite two fail-safe monitoring systems, sued the Chartered International Cryo-Bank at Cathedral Medical Center for $5 million.

(4) *The Sperm Turns*: On March 4, 1992, Dr. Cecil Jacobson, an Alexandria, Virginia, "fertility specialist," was convicted by a federal jury of fifty-two counts of fraud and perjury after inseminating maybe seventy-five patients with his own semen. "It's a shock," said Super-Donor Jacobson, "to be found guilty of trying to help people."

Before the Bobbitts, I took these cold-front bulletins as a sort of template of the late-century Bret Easton Ellis American male, who dreamily imagines his immortality as: MOM AND SPERM ON ICE. Or: YOUR IRON JOHN IS IN GOOD HANDS WITH JUAN PERON. Now I suppose Doris Kent is shaking her head, wherever it is. Something else is going on, something like the reassembly of the body of Osiris by his sister Isis after its dismembering by Set, during which, unable to find his penis, she made do with a golden dildo (which precious metal phallus served Osiris well enough for him to sire upon his sister a sun god, Horus). Or, as in the demented Balkan theologies so thoroughly ventilated by Milorad Pavic in his *Dictionary of the Khazars,* perhaps a search for all the pieces of the broken body of the original Adam (Cadmon or Ruhani), whose angel-making reassembly, by glossaries and alphabeticons, will unriddle the Universe. Either way, it's a social project worthy of postmodern flimflam: Adam or Orisis, we shall only see him in the mirrors of the media.

Which means, since we couldn't have Talese, that the Court TV cable channel should have engaged Jerry Seinfeld. After all his masturbation and circumcision jokes, he'd have been the ideal anchor for live coverage of Lorena's trial. A TV *movie* will be trickier. It should be shot from the point of view of the penis, as a parable of dispossession. This penis that nobody envied is not only the decentered self, but also the postmodern subject. There is, moreover, only one man to play the part. *Not* Woody Allen, but another comic who makes penis jokes; who, beeping like a microwave, speaks to us as if picking up signals from Andromeda via a plate in his head; whose jokes seem to fly in our faces like fruit bats or toothpaste or hand grenades; whose brilliant mind unmade of equal parts of politics and paranoia, of music video and psychotherapy, is a garbage disposal of high cultures and of low; a scrambled egghead; a Jack-in-a-Pandora's box . . . Robin Williams as the Flying Dutchman, wearing Magritte's black bowler.

> *One has only to listen to children aged between two and five playing, alone or together, to know that the pulling off of the head and the ripping open of the belly are themes that occur spontaneously to their imagination, and that this is corroborated by the experience of the doll torn to pieces.* (Jacques Lacan)

So there was Antonio Gramsci on a summer morning in Jerusalem in 1994, on the balcony outside my King David Hotel room, waiting for Shoemaker-Levy 3 to interface with the sixteenth-century ramparts of the luminous Old City, picking up galley proofs of *The Informers,* as if Lorena had never happened, as if Camille Paglia had actually been wrong, as if, like dragon's teeth, chill-proof Brets grow photocopies of their tumescent selves. *Nothing has changed because of Manasass.* I know you don't care where I was when I resorted to the new Ellis, but I mimic his situational esthetics. Each of the dozen or so of the Living Dead, the Eviscerati, who speak to us in *The Informers* will insist on explaining his or her exact whereabouts in Wasteland Los Angeles in the Go-Go-to-Nowhere 1980s.

Mostly young, invariably tan, they all wear Wayfarers sunglasses and talk a sort of lobotomized Hemingway, flat and affectless, like box scores or stock quotations, which makes it hard to distinguish one yeast infection from another, especially when everybody drinks Absolut, Stoli, apricot-apple juice and Tab; and everybody smokes either Benson and Hedges or clove cigarettes, when they aren't tripping out on pot, coke, Librium, Valium, Darvocet, quaaludes, nitrous oxide, and animal tranquilizers; and everybody who isn't eating at Spago, Chasen's, the Polo Lounge, or Canter's Deli drives a BMW, a Mercedes, a Porsche, or a Jaguar down Sunset to Malibu, Encino, Studio City, or a place on Melrose where you can see Janet Leigh get stabbed over and over again in the torn-curtain scene from *Psycho*; and everybody listens to Madonna, Boy George, Fun Boy 3, the Beach Boys, the Go-Go's, the Cars, and Oingo Boingo; and everybody reads *Vanity Fair* or *Vogue* or *Penthouse* or the Calendar section of the LA *Times,* but mostly *GQ.* Nevertheless:

Graham deals dope, before and after his father dies. Christie sleeps mostly with Graham, but sometimes with Martin. Martin makes music videos and keeps a bayonet beneath his bed. Bruce writes for *Miami Vice* and goes to zoos. Cheryl is a TV newscaster whose favorite movie is *Flashdance.* Peter murders a kidnapped little boy in a trailer-park bathtub. Tim's really pissed off because a waiter put garbanzo beans in his salad after being told specifically not to. Tim's father listens to Stephen Sondheim. Bryan, the rocker, hurts groupies, but only in Tokyo, so maybe it doesn't count. Sean's not in LA, either; he's back east at Camden, where he doesn't answer any of Ann's letters, maybe because he's wondering what happened to Patrick. Jamie and Dirk are vampires.

Vampires? Yes: A bowl of Anne Rice Krispies, just add Tab. I mean, Graham and Christie are a fun couple, and so are Graham and Martin. And *The Informers* is full of scintillating chitchat. For instance: "I don't go out to Palm Springs anymore because whenever I'm there I feel very wasted and it's a drag." And: "You never grasp anything, Tim. You look okay, but nothing works." And: "I know what the word gone means. I know what the word dead means. You deal with it, you mellow out, you head back to town." Or (my personal favorite): "You were on edge last week. I couldn't deal with you just sitting in a chair saying nothing and holding that giant avocado." But Jamie and Dirk are the Rosencrantz and Guildenstern of this *Piglet*. I was about to suggest you close your eyes and hold your nose while I quote a passage of the sort that gets Ellis in trouble with everybody except Norman Mailer. But now I see from a comparison of the galleys with a finished copy of *The Informers* that this very same passage seems to have gotten Ellis into trouble with his editor as well. It's a day at the office for Jamie. According to the galleys:

> . . . and then I scream and jump on her and rip her throat out and then I fuck her and then I play with her blood and then I rip her entire pussy out, actually detach the entire thing from the body, intact, and I suck her stomach, ropes of intestines, from the giant red-black cavity I created, wiping mounds of flesh all over myself, using it as a lubricant to jack myself off with and then after that basically everything's okay.

Whereas, according to the bound book:

> . . . and then I scream and jump on her and rip her throat out and then I fuck her and then I play with her blood and after that basically everything's okay.

I am, of course, scandalized. All the famously feckless, hardbody, postmodern, creepshow, nihilistic slice-and-dice has been . . . wished away. Readers of the finished copy will never know the cheap thrill of Eros in a Cuisinart. Those ropes! That lubricant! How Dostoyevsky!

Anyway—cool, like, uh, Dracula. A Gramsci would pounce:

"Vampire Capitalism!" Plus, maybe: "Money makes you dumb!" But Gramsci never saw one of Martin's music videos; his cell wasn't wired for cable. What Ellis has digitized, instead of a novel, is a video. He channel-surfs—from bloody bathroom to bloodier bedroom; from herpes to anorexia; from dead rats in the swimming-pool drain to black ants carrying sections of someone's intestine back to their queen to Egyptian lizards who eat poisoned cockroaches and die all over a $5,000 Betamax— and we're back again at our own boredom, on Michael Landon's yacht. Jacking off by remote control! No wonder Kurt Cobain checked out.

On the other hand, I suppose Ellis could be saying that LA sucks.

I read this stuff so you don't have to. Having done so, the Old Fart has three thoughts:

• Poor Bennington. First Ellis. Then Jill Eisenstadt, whose own Bennington novel, *From Rockaway,* was better than *The Rules of Attraction* because it spent more of its time in blue-collar Brooklyn than in white-shoe Vermont, even though Ellis appeared as a character, as Eisenstadt would likewise show up in Ellis, reciprocity being cute. And finally Donna Tartt, who, in *The Secret History,* calls Bennington Hampden instead of Camden, but where we also catch a glimpse of a student dope dealer with mob connections who will remind you of Ellis, who must have been more interesting on campus than he is in novels. At least in Tartt, during the first third of her 524 pages, we actually spend time in the classroom listening to a professor, and students even discuss books as if there were a point to college, and abstract ideas about beauty and terror and ancient Greeks are entertained as though there were something else to do with a mind besides blow it. But then *The Secret History* descends from its hothouse Dionysian revels to incest and murder and hyperventilation, none of which seemed necessary back when Mary McCarthy and Randall Jarrell were writing *their* novels about Bard.

• Poor LA. First Charlie Manson. Then those pretty-boy

voids, the Menendez brothers. Then a summer movie like *Speed,* which, however entertaining, has a secret subtext: *They'll do anything to discourage public transportation in Los Angeles.* And finally an August novel like *The Informers,* the return of the Bloodsucker Preppies. Joseph Wambaugh, James Ellroy, and Walter Mosley write brilliantly about LA. But none dropped out of Bennington. Between them, Mike Davis in the pages of his *City of Quartz* and Anna Deavere Smith on stage with *Twilight: Los Angeles* have given us entire operas of a Pacific Rim multiculture. But they've never been to Nell's. Such children of Hollywood as Jill Robinson, Nora Ephron, Brooke Hayward, and the late Johanna Davis managed somehow, after the abyss winked at them, to sky-dive. But they've trafficked with no vampires. Once upon a time, back when she imagined Maria in *Play It as it Lays,* Joan Didion felt as bad about Southern California as Ellis does. All of us did who grew up there, flunking volleyball and puberty rite. It's like the Pop Art you find not only at the major studios but also at the Temporary Contemporary, past the kosher burrito stand before you get to the *Los Angeles Times*: so many spiders, somehow Jelly Belly bloody, in the cinnamon-colored sand. But Didion moved on, from the Third World of women to such Third Worlds as El Salvador, Cuban Miami, and the burning walls and broken tile of geopolitics. Nor is she a cannibal.

• Poor me. On my very own Christmas visit to the piñata of my childhood, I got annoyed with a West Side folksinger who'd come along for the ride. She wanted to sing "Little Boxes," the Malvina Reynolds ditty. Seeger sings it; they all do, making fun of the "ticky-tacky" houses of California — "a green one and a pink one and a blue one and a yellow one . . . and they all look just the same." Why is a California tract house more laughable or contemptible than a Minnesota farm, a Tennessee shack, a SoHo studio, or a barge in the Florida Keys? We only got to ours my junior year of high school, with pigeons and a basketball hoop and the monastic cell in which I read all night and listened to Chuck Berry and Little Richard and wrote my poems against the hydrogen bomb. The children of ticky-tack end up in libraries and asylums just like everybody else.

Now my children are grown up to their own discrepancies. They went to college when Ellis did. The friends they bring home and sometimes marry are the age of his characters. Some are brilliant, some beautiful, some crazy, some gay, and even a few morose. But they've all gone into the wide world without a remote control. None deals dope or kills serially. You won't find them in Ellis's novels, which downers seem dreamed up instead by fearful middle age, hating the very idea of youth, *ordaining* the young to be joyless and mindless. I've a suggestion for Clay, Sean, Lauren, Patrick, Graham, Christie, Martin, Jamie, Dirk, and the rest of these poisoned Twinkies: Have you considered career counseling? If not therapy, why not e-mail or Tibet? Perhaps Amnesty, the Peace Corps, or a kibbutz. For a truly refreshing change of pace, become a nun.

California Screaming

The sky is falling and so's the yen. For the City of Angels it's a Slim-Fast diet and a deep-pore cleansing of fire and flood, earthquakes and drought, tornadoes and tsunamis. Not to mention man-eating mountain lions, plague-ridden squirrels, killer bees, locusts, gridlock, and the goat-sucking vampire Chupacabra. Plus—since *Ecology of Fear: Los Angeles and the Imagination of Disaster* is a Mike Davis book—robber barons, master builders, snowmelt stealers, real-estate swindlers, offshore funny money, class war, race hate, labor violence, immigrant hordes, psychotic cops, color-coded gangs, and death-wish cults. *Chinatown* meets *Blade Runner* and *Volcano* at the corner of Hollywood and Watts. So dismayed is Davis by the "uniquely explosive mixture of natural hazards and social contradictions" in this "Walden Pond on LSD" that he resorts to chaos theory and the prophet Amos. If his magnificent *City of Quartz* (1990) was a cyberpunk vision in a postmodern desert, *Fear* is the return of the repressed as a Big Bang.

Let's begin where he ends—up in the air, in a polar-orbiting multisensor satellite on a normal pass over the Pacific coast on a late April afternoon in 1992, snapping "hot spots" with its AVHRR (Advanced Very High Resolution Radiometer). These infrared images of "heat islands" are received in San Diego, transmitted to the Satellite Oceanography Laboratory at the University of Hawaii, and analyzed down to their subpixels by geophysicists, who discover "an exceptionally large thermal anomaly, extending over more than eighty-five square kilometers." What the geophysicists are looking at is South Central, where three new fires were started every minute in the several hours before the images were recorded. The radiometer "has taken the temperature of a social explosion" roughly the size of the volcanic eruption of Mount Pinatubo in the Philippines. This "thermal anomaly" is the Rodney King insurrection.

That some such thermal anomaly would afflict LA was a

given in *City of Quartz*. As was the fact that banks, corporations, and upscale downtown merchants would be better prepared for it than they'd been in 1965, even if the cops weren't. Among many other things, *Quartz* was an account of "the militarization of city life" after Watts—the "architectural policing of social boundaries" and "the totalitarian semiotics of ramparts and battlements"; the embodiment of a "Fortress LA" in surveillance towers and corporate citadels, elevated pedways and subterranean concourses, "tourist-bubble" theme parks and panopticonic shopping malls, residential enclaves like hardened missile silos and libraries like dry-docked dreadnoughts. All of which dovetailed nicely with the pacification of the poor—a "human landfill"—in strategic-hamlet housing projects, urban Bantustans and Bedouin encampments, on barricaded streets in ghetto neighborhoods bereft of public toilets ("crime scenes") and zoned against cell phones and whistling, with barrel-shaped bus benches to make sure nobody could sleep on them, caged cash registers in the convenience stores, bulletproof acrylic turnstiles in the fast-food joints, metal detectors in the hospitals, lockdowns in the schools and curfews that outlaw groups of more than two juveniles from "associating in public view," even in their own front yards.

"In the erstwhile world capital of teenagers," Davis told us, "where millions overseas still imagine Gidget at a late-night surf party, the beaches are now closed after dark, patrolled by helicopter gunships and police dune buggies." In San Marino, they shut down the parks on weekends to keep out Asians and Latinos.

How well this "Brinks Aesthetic" worked is clear from *Fear*. No sooner had Simi Valley acquitted the cops who rioted all over Rodney, than "sentient" buildings with mainframe brains went into Bunker Hill Prevent Mode. Steel gates rolled down over entrances to the great bank towers, escalators froze, electronic locks sealed off pedestrian passages, and a financial district safe from sansculottes could go on happily recycling Japan's trade surplus into Southland turf-and-surf. Too bad about the Koreans. Someone should have told them that a "postmodern bread riot" was preordained after a 30 percent decline in light-manufacturing jobs in a single decade, combined with 1990 cutbacks in defense spending and the super-yen's seppuku, followed by a two-year tripling of unemployment among immigrants, plus simultaneous slashes in AFDC and Medical benefits, had plunged the economy into its worst recession since 1938.

But the ferocious argument of *Fear* is that no thermal is really anomalous, not in LA. As polymathic as his city's polyethnic, Davis has consulted earth scientists, environmental historians, deep ecologists, and structural engineers. He has synthesized the research and the dreadful intuitions of geographers, geologists, archaeologists, seismologists, and paleoclimatologists. He has mastered nomenclatures of basal zones, microbiota, ungulate eruptions, blind thrust faults, thermoluminescence, "moment deficit paradox," and "nonlinear resonance." Besides class divisions, there is another kind of grinding under our numb feet. The worst is yet to come:

> geodetic surveys [and] paleoseismic studies of active faults suggest an earthquake frequency in the Los Angeles region over the past several millennia that is dramatically higher than the record of the past two centuries. There have, in other words, been too few quakes to relieve the accumulation of stress generated by plate tectonic motion as Los Angeles hitchhikes northward on the Pacific Plate.

Southern California, a midlatitude littoral like ancient Crete, central Chile, South Australia, and the Cape Province of South Africa, is *overdue*. The modern period—"one of the most unusual episodes of climatic and seismic benignity" since the Holocene—is "the fourth wettest of the past 4,000 years" with "one of the lowest rates for extreme events within the last 600 years." (The recent six-year drought, from 1987 to 1992, was chickenfeed compared to two epics in the Middle Ages, from 890 to 1100 and from 1210 to 1350.) There hasn't been a truly catastrophic quake in 210 years, when there should have been a dozen or more. But "a growing scientific consensus" suggests that the LA basin "is awakening from its long seismic siesta, and that the Northridge disaster—God help us—was little more than a yawn." And Northridge was the costliest natural disaster in American history.

Notice that I haven't even mentioned global warming or El Niño.

Meanwhile, by turning deserts into parking lots, historic wildfire corridors into housing tracts, wetland liquefaction zones into marinas, and floodplains into industrial squats and slurbs, market-driven developer greed and real-estate bingo have ensured that human malfeasance will compound natural catastrophe. Besides the usual stucco death traps, slapdash construction and shoddy materials have also gone into the sort of precast concrete "Supercubes" that collapsed all over Armenia; killer department stores, public schools, and mini-malls; freeways that buckle, dams that crack, and downtown tenements that go up like kindling because retrofitting ordinances are ignored by slumlords and fire inspectors. Having purchased seashores, foothills, and canyons for its villas and "ranchitos," for its golf, beach, and yacht clubs, rich white privilege expects a "socialized disaster relief" paid for by spending cuts in social programs for the Technicolored poor. And while entire ecosystems (like salt marshes, grasslands, oak savannahs, and vernal pools) have been lost in the last century and a half, a new "pet-and-garbage ecology of the suburbs" has attracted from the permeable margins of the remaining wild a motley of opportunistic scavengers and carnivores—lawn-eating deer, junk-food raccoons, ravens swooping down on roadkill, and coyotes howling in Hollywood Bowl. Lurking in this Black Forest of the *noir* imagination are not only carjackers, paramilitaries, toxic dumpers, and tribes of feral youth but bears partial to hot tubs and cougars who've acquired a taste "for slow, soft animals in spandex."

Typical of LA's mindset is that wildfires are always blamed on some "incendiary other"—Indians, hoboes, Wobblies, itinerant farmworkers, Axis saboteurs, satanic child molesters, Muslim terrorists, and the Sierra Club—rather than the negligence of Southern California Edison or the gastric ulcers of Mother Nature. And that wild dogs, black bears, and mountain lions are "criminalized" as "gangbangers" and "serial killers," while the urban underclass is "bestialized" as "predators" and "wolf packs." Coming and going, white fright, white flight, and white noise have always been the Southland's storyboard.

Egypt one knows without visiting it, and China the same; but Los Angeles is unique in its bright horror. (Gore Vidal, *Messiah*)

Davis himself is an arsonist, igniting combustible ideas. And an exorcist, as if to suck the venom from the wound. And a mythographer, scotching all those mind-maps in which LA plays "the double role of utopia *and* dystopia for advanced capitalism." And a New Left Fontana tough guy, arriving at the contested site of urban studies not in the River City guise of Robert Preston with trombones but as Springsteen with a Clarence Clemmons sax. Or—I pile it on and whip the cream in imitation of his own wild style—a beach-boy Babel (the red cavalry), a MacArthur Park Gramsci (detective novels, Grand Guignol, superstructured subjectivity), and a biker Zapata (come down from the Santa Monicas to scourge Malibu). David Rieff, who barely had time to read *City of Quartz* before hustling his own manuscript, *Los Angeles: Capital of the Third World,* off to the printer, called it a "glum book." And it certainly wasn't a singing telegram. But it was as full of jumping beans as of internal contradictions. Its facets slapped us into sentience.

By "us," perhaps I mean those children of the Southland desert (an "abstraction of dirt and dollar signs") who, moving from one suburb to the next to a third ("little pastel pods of Chardonnay lifestyle, air-conditioned and over-watered, with scented brand-names"), had to take the same course in potted California history half a dozen times, in none of which were we ever told that Father Junipero Serra's missions were a system of forced labor. That, what with lynchings, brothels, and a murder every night in the 1870s, "Anglo-ruled Los Angeles [was] the most violent town in the West," as it would be "the most nativist and fundamentalist of big cities" in the first two thirds of the twentieth century. That, in order to sell "the promised land of a millennarian Anglo-Saxon racial odyssey" to "the restless babbitry of the Middle West," Col. Harrison Gray Otis, his son-in-law Harry Chandler, their open-shop LA *Times,* and a syndicate of developers, bankers, and transportation magnates locked out unions, outlawed picketing, and terrorized dissidents. That, even where there *were* unions, black people couldn't join them, any more than they would be admitted into county nursing schools till 1948. And that, long before they got around to Rodney King, LA cops had a German border-guard tradition of beating up left-wingers in Pershing Square on May Day and zoot-suiters in East LA any old time.

Quartz not only recovered from the memory hole this secret history of the sunshine boys and their will to white dominion — their theft of water, bulldozing of Joshua trees, and dogma of "absolute property" — but also celebrated a residue of oppositional shadow cultures about which we've been equally amnesiac: Job Harriman, for example, the socialist almost elected mayor in 1911; Llano del Rio, a "ragtime utopia" and "brave red kibbutz" in the Mojave desert; Upton Sinclair's 1934 campaign to "End Poverty in California"; social critics like Louis Adamic on class violence and Carey McWilliams on "exceptionalism"; artists like Boris Deutsch, Edward Kienholz, Craig Kauffman, and Ed Ruscha; jazz musicians like Ornette Coleman, Eric Dolphy, and Don Cherry; and, of course, noir novelists like James M. Cain, Horace McCoy, Nathanael West, Raymond Chandler, Budd Schulberg, Chester Himes, Joan Didion, Ross MacDonald, John Gregory Dunne, John Rechy, and James Ellroy, not to mention Thomas Pynchon, whose *Vineland* was also a recovery of the lost history of a progressive left coast.

In fact, so entertaining and opinionated was the *Quartz* "scanscape" of LA's intellectual scene that the temptation was to rush through subsequent chapters — on the changing structure of a surprisingly porous power elite; a manual working class of Latinos, a "rentier stratum of Asian investors," and Chinese, Korean, Armenian, Israeli, and Iranian ethnic family capitalisms; the "disaggregated nimbyism" and "residential anarcho-syndicalism" of white-flight home owners, culiminating in the "Bonapartism" of Howard Jarvis and Prop 13; and a topography of gangland, of Crips and bloods and "the crypto-Keynesian youth employment program operated by the cocaine cartels." As lively as this stuff was, how could it compete with a film noir defined as equal parts American hard-boiled novel, German expressionist cinema, psychoanalysis, and Orson Welles? Or with capsule descriptions of "exiles" like Adorno and Horkheimer, fresh from Frankfurt, ignoring wartime turmoil in the local aircraft plants, and Brecht, missing all the fun in Boyle Heights dance halls, Central Avenue nightclubs, and Wilmington honkytonks. Or of the "sorcerers" at Cal Tech, "hub of a vast wheel of public-private research and development" that led not only to Hughes Aircraft, Aerojet General, a Jet Propulsion Laboratory, and a Rand Institute but to Scientology as well. And of the "mercenaries," cashing in on a boom in cultural investment by international real-estate capital—"Houston architects, London painters, New York critics, Tokyo designers, Boston composers, Oxford historians, and Parisian fakirs." Stick it in your tricorn, Derrida and Baudrillard!

> Back in Los Angeles, we missed Los Angeles.
> (Randall Jarrell, "Thinking of the Lost World")

There is a lot of the same sort of smart-bombing of the germ factories in *Fear*, including a whole section devoted to "The Literary Destruction of Los Angeles"—in dystopian novels by Octavia Butler, Gore Vidal, Carolyn See, J. G. Ballard, Kim Stanley Robinson, Steve Erickson, and Cynthia Kadohata and in movies from *Them!* (mutant ants), *The Slime People* (toxic juicebugs), and *Slithis* (yuppie-eating "ecocrud") to more recent releases like *Escape from L.A., The Crow: City of Angels, Independence Day,* and *Volcano*—by nukes, quakes, hordes, monsters, pollution, gangs, terrorists, floods, plagues, comets, tsunamis, cults, volcanoes, firestorms, mudslides, droughts, freeways, fogs, global warming, Bermuda grass, and the devil. This leads into wonderful digressions on the modern fascination with dead cities, the cult of catastrophe, and our growing obsession in the alien eighties "with a clandestine and eroticized extraterrestrial presence. . . . In the shadowlands of white anxiety, the distinction between the images of the space alien and illegal alien was subjected to repeated elision. Immigration and invasion, in a paranoid register, became synonyms." Thus: black holes, hijacked bodies, zombies, clones, androids, and the angels of the apocalypse.

Which drops Davis by bathysphere into the communal fantasies in the pulp sediment of the mass mind. And what he finds there, from B movies to soft-core porn to religious rants, from Buck Rogers to Philip Wylie to Larry Niven to *The Turner Diaries*, is just plain scary—Aryan warriors and Yellow Peril . . . mongrelization and ethnic cleansing . . . Vietnamese assassins, Zulu KGB agents, South Central cannibals, degenerate Latinos addicted to hallucinogenic moth grubs that turn them into spiders, and "ACLU maggots and sleazeballs." You will believe him:

> The abiding hysteria of Los Angeles disaster fiction, and perhaps of all disaster fiction—the urge to strike out and destroy, to wipe out an entire city and untold thousands of its inhabitants—is rooted in racial anxiety. From the earliest nineteenth-century examples of the literary destruction of London and New York to the latest survivalist fantasies about Los Angeles, white fear of the dark races lies at the heart of such visions (with the sardonic critique of cults and fringe culture coming in a distant second). And it is this obsession, far more than anxieties about earthquakes or nuclear weapons, that leads us back to the real Los Angeles as well as to the deepest animating fears of our culture.

But Davis has earned his right to these standard issue cultural studies generalizations by connecting the ecological to the political. He pronounces them only after we have seen, in such chapters as "The Case for Letting Malibu Burn," that the rush to rebuild on the site of a disaster waiting to happen—a site where disaster has *always* happened, a site that should decades ago have been "hazard zoned" against development in the first place—is paid for out of the public's pocket, in the form of federal relief, insurance breaks, and low-interest loans at the direct expense of low-income housing, environmental protection, rural health grants, urban parks and recreation programs, and funds for youth employment. This was precisely the deal struck by House Speaker Newt Gingrich with a craven White House after the Republican Congress in 1995 kidnapped the $6.6-billion disaster relief bill and held it hostage until Democrats agreed to cut $16.3 billion from already budgeted domestic spending. Westlake slums, only twenty-two miles from Malibu, burn down at least as often, and Northridge also caused extensive damage to the African-American Crenshaw district, although the media ignored it. But "the politics of disaster relief" have become "the moral equivalent of class warfare. The first casualty of the temblor was any residual interest in economic recovery efforts and job creation in the neighborhoods traumatized by the 1992 riots. Rebuilding the valley supplanted 'Rebuild LA.'" Nor, in a tax-slashing Southern California, are there any significant local resources left to pay for new programs. And in Sacramento, "underfunded campuses battle overcrowded prisons for the last scraps from the governor's table."

Prison! Also, of course, a gated community. Since 1980, while California's colleges and universities were downsized by eight thousand jobs, California's prisons have hired another 26,000 new guards for another 112,000 new inmates. In 1980, there were 22,500 prisoners on these bad-behavior campuses. By 2005, the Department of Corrections estimates an inmate population of 341,420. While white men commit at least 60 percent of rapes, robberies, and assaults, young black men from LA are twice as likely to end up in prison as in college, where it would cost half as much to keep them. And so, to the infamous University of Chicago dartboard model of big-city "human ecology"—of "concentric urban zones" organized according to "biological" forces of "invasion, competition, succession and symbiosis" — to such social Darwinian determinants as income, land value, class, and race, Davis adds an iron curtain of fear and trembling.

Here's a pretty picture of another thermal anomaly:

> The crisis also tested Malibu's strange, bespoke morality. When the firestorm temporarily cut off the highway as an escape route, trapped residents had to make some tough choices. The *Malibu Times* celebrated the case of two intrepid housewives from the Big Rock area who loaded their jewels and dogs into kayaks and took to the sea where they were eventually rescued by blond hunks from Baywatch Redondo. Only the fine print revealed that, in saving their pets, they had left their Latina maids behind.
>
> *Horses caught fire and were shot on the beach, birds exploded in the air.*
> (Joan Didion, *The White Album*)

Sorry to get personal, but from this brilliant book I realize that I grew up in Los Angeles during exactly those two decades, from 1940 to 1961, that were the mildest even in the benign modern period. Of course, just as the tectonic plates were gnashing their teeth beneath my sneakers, so must the class war and the immigrant-bashing have gone on around me, off the freeway somewhere, on surface streets to which a right-wing LA *Times* seldom ventured. It wasn't that I was entirely apolitical. From my mother's Stevensonian liberalism, the militant nostalgia of a UAW area rep recalling the CIO's left-wing purge, the thrilling harangues of a refugee Wobbly on the Pike in Long Beach, and the novels of John Dos Passos, I had romantic inklings of a larger burning world, also off-ramp somewhere. *The Nation* arrived weekly in a plain brown wrapper. For mimeographing an off-campus newspaper in my garage, I earned an FBI dossier, just as my high-school principal promised me I would. And I even went downtown to the newsstand where you could buy a copy of *People's World*; to the Pathfinder bookstore—burned down during the Rodney riots—to check out Trotsky; to ludicrous rallies of Gerald L. K. Smith's anti-Semitic Christian Nationalists; to the Masonic lodge where Charles Coburn railed against an income tax; to the pitched tents of the evangelicals where they gave you a stick to beat off Satan even as they were scooting some other sucker, with *his* stick, through an opposite flap into the same sinful darkness.

Besides which, couldn't some of us hush-puppies be counted on to go the Greek Theatre every time Harry Belafonte came to town?

But it never occurred to me to question the ownership of the hillsides and the oceanfront, nor in this speed-bump suburban reverie to wonder at my own pale privilege. I was too busy being the pampered beneficiary of an affirmative-action program designed for all those just like me—blue-eyed, blond-haired, boyish, and goyish—who had been cut like keys to fit in the locks that opened the doors to upward mobility. GI housing, tidelands oil money to pay for tracking in the schools, the avuncular indulgence of chemistry teachers and deputy sheriffs, Odd Fellows essay contests, Lions Club and Kiwanis college scholarships, Boys State and Boys Nation and Ivy League "geographical distribution" quotas, all conspired at a being so light I was guaranteed to levitate, a bright balloon that bounced from mentor to mentor into surly middle age, from which, looking back, I find myself most admiring of those who have renounced their privilege—as if we ever really can, as if it isn't who we are.

And till now I never bothered to imagine what those clandestine and eroticized aliens will think when they arrive at last to poke and probe at our tree rings and pollen cores and bone lesions. Will they wonder if the surfboard was as sacred to our culture as bulls and dolphins had been to ancient Crete—whether we'd ever deserved our sunshine or honorably earned our death?

One last thermal anomaly. When her own house burned down in the Oakland fires, and all her manuscripts with it, Maxine Hong Kingston told a reporter: "Did you know that when paper burns, it's very beautiful? It's just amazing to look at a burned book. It looks like feathers, the thin pages, and it's still book-shaped, and you touch it, and it disintegrates. It makes you realize that it's all air. It's inspiration, and air, and it's just returned to that."

Frankly, Maxine is too good for us. Mike Davis is more like what we so richly deserve—a Captain Midnight; an auto-da-fé.

Didion Does NAFTA

As if she had fever, her skin burned and crackled with a pinpoint sensitivity. She could feel smoke against her skin. She could feel voice waves. She was beginning to feel color, light intensities. . . . All that day she felt the power surging through her own body. All day she was faint with vertigo, sunk in a world where great power grids converged, throbbing lines plunged finally into the shallow canyon below the dam's face, elevators like coffins dropped into the bowels of the earth itself.

(Play It as It Lays)

In a 1997 appreciation, almost a CAT scan, of Joan Didion's novels and essays in the *New York Review of Books,* Elizabeth Hardwick speaks of "a carefully designed frieze of the fracture and splinter in her characters' comprehension of the world," "a structure for the fadings and erasures of experience," and, to accommodate "the extreme fluidity of the fictional landscape," a narrative method of "peculiar restlessness and unease." She cites bereaved mothers and damaged daughters; "percussive dialogue" and "sleepwalking players"; a martyred "facticity" and revelations "of incapacity, doubt, irresolution, and inattention"; "a sort of cocoon of melancholy," "a sort of computer lyricism," and "a sort of a muscular assurance and confidence"; a "witchery" of "uncompromising imagination" and "an obsessive attraction to the disjunctive and paradoxical in American national policy and to the somnolent, careless decisions made in private life."

All of which is true, but doesn't explain why I read Didion like a Peeping Tom or industrial spy, through binoculars or a green-goggled nightscope, from a bungalow on the other side of the moat—as if I'd steamed her mail, tapped her phone, or bugged her bed; as if she were microdotting postage stamps with all our guilty secrets. About Doris Lessing, she once wrote: "For more than twenty years now she has been registering, in a torrent of fiction that increasingly seems conceived in a stubborn rage against the very idea of fiction, every tremor along her emo-

tional fault system, every slippage in her self-education." Except
for "torrent," she could have said the same about herself, at least
until the 1980s.

As it happens, Didion said these things about Lessing in an
article I asked her to write in 1972 for the *New York Times Book
Review*, a critique of *Briefing for a Descent into Hell*. As it also
happens, we had been California kids together in Manhattan in
the late fifties, published in the unlikely pages of William F.
Buckley Jr.'s *National Review* alongside such equally unlikely
beginning writers as Garry Wills, Renata Adler, and Arlene
Croce, back when Buckley hired the unknown young just because he liked our zippy prose styles and figured he could take
care of our politics with the charismatic science of his own personality. Later, ruefully, he'd call us "the apostates." We are
probably to blame for George Will. (In *Slouching Towards Bethlehem*, remarkably foreshadowing entire books by Janet Malcolm, Didion explained: "My only advantage as a reporter is that
I am so physically small, so temperamentally unobtrusive, and
so neurotically inarticulate that people tend to forget that my
presence runs counter to their best interests. And it always
does. . . . *Writers are always selling somebody out*.") Naturally, I've read every word of hers ever since, for clues on who
we had been and what we had become, for how and why.

Even so, she would have seemed perhaps the least likely of
her generation to have turned into a disenchanted legionnaire
on the far-flung borders of the American imperium, an appalled
witness, like Don DeLillo, Norman Rush, and Robert Stone, of
ripple effects the size of tsunamis. These are the writers we
count on to compensate for the confabulations of Kmart samurai
like Tom Clancy, Nibelung trolls like Elliott Abrams, and the
counterintelligent agencies, especially since commercial television no longer seems to care. No irony intended: the hugger-
muggers of the secret government used to be a prime-time
staple. Back in the glory days of *Miami Vice*, that gaudy amalgam
of cop show, music video, and car commercial, even if only seen
in fitful sneeze through filters of psychedelic lollipop in surreal

sandwiches of rearview mirror, revolving door, and hubcap, cued to songs by Phil Collins, Cyndi Lauper, Ted Nugent, the Fat Boys, the Pointer Sisters, and the Stones, while Little Richard, Roberto Duran, and G. Gordon Liddy lounged around in retina-cooling pastels at pomo-arty murder scenes, there was feverish substance. In *Miami Vice,* we couldn't help noticing that Latin America had taken over from Southeast Asia as the pulp imagination's preeminent Third World hell-on-wheels, with druglords as Vietcong and the Andes as one big nose cone.

While there might also have been episodes on arms dealers peddling stolen Stinger missiles and Nationalist Chinese generals moving opium out of the Golden Triangle with the help of elephants and spooks, not a month of *Vice* went by without some mention of conspiracies of right-wing businessmen, loony paramilitaries, coke-squeezed rugmunchers, freak-patrol cartels, and National Security Agency gonzo renegade ex-Marines, with an increasingly baroque filigree of CIA/DEA connivance, to smuggle cocaine to pay for arms for Frito Bandito freedom fighters who specialized in raping and killing radical nuns. Versions of this same plot, involving drugs, death squads, and clandestine agency cover-ups, surfaced as well in half a dozen television movies in the eighties, and in series as various as *Lou Grant, Cagney & Lacey, The Equalizer, Shannon's Deal,* and *Law & Order,* as if every executive producer in Burbank had been on the mailing list of the Christic Institute. In retrospect, it's amazing that Iran/contra surprised *anybody.*

Who cares now, except the *San Jose Mercury News* and the Joan Didion who discovered in El Salvador in 1982, between embassy lunches and body dumps and midnight video screenings of *Apocalypse Now* and *Bananas,* that Gabriel García Márquez was actually "a social realist"?

Somewhere in the nod we were dropping cargo. Somewhere in the nod we were losing infrastructure, losing redundant systems, losing specific gravity. Weightlessness seemed at the time the safer mode. Weightlessness seemed at the time the mode in which we could beat both the clock and affect itself, but I see now that it was not. (The Last Thing He Wanted)

Late in *The Last Thing He Wanted,* either Didion or a "not quite omniscient author" so much like her as to make no difference asks us to imagine Ted Sorensen swimming with the dolphins. Sorensen, Robert McNamara, Arthur Schlesinger Jr., Douglas Dillon, George Ball, and their wives really did gather at a pink hotel in the Florida Keys for an anniversary reunion, a sort of group-grope of wheeze-kid new frontiersmen, at which they congratulated themselves on their tough-love handling of the Cuban missile crisis. Didion wishes there could be some similar reunion of the characters in her novel responsible for what happened in 1984 on another Caribbean island, an incident that "should not have occurred by any quantitative measurement." Then, perhaps, when her troubleshooting "ambassador without portfolio," Treat Morrison, is done swimming with dolphins, he will climb the stairs in the pink hotel and find Elena McMahon waiting for him on the balcony in her nightgown. "Oh yes," Didion insists: "This is a romance after all." And: "I want those two to have been together all their lives."

Elena's husband in Hollywood makes business deals; her father in Miami makes arms deals; her government in Washington makes covert deals. Unable "to fake this anymore," Elena leaves her marriage, her newspaper job on the campaign trail, her father dying on the eve of his biggest deal, and a country that no longer makes any sense to her, first for Costa Rica and then for the sort of island we only know from hurricane maps on the Weather Channel, where, eating a chocolate parfait and bacon, reading an Italian grammar and a textbook on infectious diseases, she meets Treat, "a mover, a shaker, a can-do guy" who can call up the Oval Office if he wants to. Elena's there to collect on her father's deal. Treat's there to figure out what the other movers and shakers are up to. Neither realizes they're in the middle of an assassination plot and covert sideshow to divert attention from Iran/contra onto a phony Sandinista arms transaction.

The wonder of this sinewy novel, written as if by laser beam in gnomic haikus, is that the reader wants these two troubled people "to have been together all their lives" as much as Didion does—some other ending; erasures and revisions; maybe even a hug. Of course, from the Didion who wore a bikini and a migraine to every volcanic eruption of the postwar culture—the Didion of whom we could say what Randall Jarrell said about T. S. Eliot, that he'd have written *The Waste Land* about the Garden of Eden—we don't expect hugs. But then we'd never expect an essayist who in *Slouching Towards Bethlehem* liked Howard Hughes and John Wayne more than Joan Baez or the flower children, who in *The White Album* found more fault with Doris Lessing, Hollywood liberals, and feminism than she did with mall culture and Manson groupie Linda Kasabian, to end up in *Salvador, Miami,* and *After Henry* so savagely disdainful of Ronald Reagan and the "dreamwork" of American imperialism. Nor would we expect a novelist who started out with *Play It as It Lays,* her brilliant but solipsistic account of moviemaking, abortion, substance abuse, freeways, suicide, and sadomasochism, to leave town for Boca Grande *(A Book of Common Prayer),* Costa Rica *(The Last Thing He Wanted),* and other "tropic[s] of morbidity and paranoia," to grow up from Nathanael West and Raymond Chandler to V. S. Naipaul and Graham Greene.

It's not just that the *momentum* she worries so much about has taken Didion in surprisingly leftward directions, as well as south, but that she has been surprising all along, while we were beguiled by the ice-pick prose and the sibylline icon—that desert lioness, that tawny sphinx crouched on the faultlines of the culture, alert and weeping at every shiver of tectonic plates. As early as *Bethlehem,* for every fatidic syllable on frazzled nerves or love gone wrong, rattlesnakes and mesquite, there was also a reporter's curiosity about Alcatraz, Newport, and body bags from Vietnam. She was even moved to try to hum, from a North Vietnamese songbook, "When the Party Needs Us Our Hearts Are Filled with Hatred." *The White Album,* a hornbook of the nameless blue-eyed willies, of the unbearable lightness of California being, of discrepancies sent up like kites to catch some lightning and bloody butter on a crust of dread, had nonetheless a lot to say about the storage of nerve gas in an Oregon army arsenal, Huey Newton and the Panthers, Bogotá and Hoover Dam. In *After Henry,* on a December morning in 1979, she will visit "the Caritas transit camp for Vietnamese refugees near Kai Tak airport, Kowloon, Hong Kong, [where] a woman of indeterminate age was crouched on the pavement near the washing pumps bleeding out a live chicken." Or she just happens to stop in on a Berkeley nuclear reactor, flashing her back to fifties grammar school days of atom-bomb drills and fifties nightmares of white light meaning death, all the while chatting up the engineer while she inspects the core, the radiation around the fuel rods, the blue shimmer under twenty feet of clear water, the fishing rod, and a rubber duck. She thinks of Henry Adams at the 1900 Great Exposition in Paris, learning "to feel the forty-foot dynamos as a moral force, much as the early Christians felt the Cross." Then, astonishingly, this:

> It had been, at the time I saw the TRIGA Mark III reactor in the basement of Etcheverry Hall, seventy-nine years since Henry Adams went to Paris to study Science as he had studied Mont-Saint-Michel and Chartres. It had been thirty-four years since Robert Oppenheimer saw the white light at Alamorgordo. The "nuclear issue," as we called it, suggesting that the course of the world since the Industrial Revolution were provisional, open to revision, up for a vote, had been under discussion all those years, and yet something about the fact of the reactor still resisted interpretation: the intense blue in the pool water, the Cerenkov radiation around the fuel rods, the blue past all blue, the blue like light itself, the blue that is actually a shock wave in the water and is the exact blue of the glass at Chartres . . .

Beyond metaphor, this is that figure in the carpet she is always complaining she can't find. Or maybe the watermark on a page from *The Book of Kells.*

So about that hug. Would she allow herself? Didion is a declared agnostic about history and narrative and "reasons why." She is a devout disbeliever in promises, barricades, social action, moral imperatives, the past as prologue, the production ethic, the relevance of personality, the primacy of personal conscience, abstract thought, magical explanations, and American exemptions. But her nights are full of beasts she *does* believe in: "tropism[s] towards disorder"; punishment and Original Sin; dislocation, dread, and dreams. (To her diary Elena confides: *"The most terrifying verse I know: merrily merrily merrily life is but a dream."*) Nevertheless, "We tell ourselves stories in order to live. The princess is caged in the consulate. The man with the candy will lead the children into the sea." The stories she tells to get her through the night are of "extreme and doomed commitments," all about wounded women making strange choices in hot places with calamitous consequences. This, let's face it, is romantic, even if hushed up like a Hemingway: "Maybe she looked at him and saw the fog off the Farallons, maybe he looked at her and saw the hot desert twilight. Maybe they looked at each other and knew that nothing they could do would matter as much as the slightest tremor of the earth, the blind trembling of the Pacific in its bowl, the heavy snows closing the mountain passes, the rattlers in the dry grass, the sharks cruising the deep cold waters through the Golden Gate."

Or Ted Sorensen swimming with the dolphins.

Some real things have been happening lately.

(The Last Thing He Wanted)

There was, from the beginning and never entirely abandoned, the neurasthenic self: bad sexual conduct, unpardonable sins, punishments swift and personal, something unnameable; the person, the female, who endures "the usual intimations of erratic cell multiplication, dust and dry wind, sexual dyaesthesia, sloth, flatulence, root canal"; who has discovered "that not all of the promises would be kept, that some things are in fact irrevocable and that it had counted after all, every evasion and every procrastination, every mistake, every word, all of it"; who drinks bourbon to cure herself of "bad attitudes, unpleasant tempers, wrongthink"; who has misplaced "whatever slight faith she ever had in the social contract, in the meliorative principle, in the whole grand pattern of human endeavor"; who believes that human behavior is "essentially circumstantial"; who knows that "sad is different from overwrought"; who is conserving energy, "as if attention were a fossil fuel"; who puts her head in a paper bag to keep from crying; who lacks "all temperament for paradise"; who has not been the witness she wanted to be; who got married instead of seeing a psychiatrist; whose Guatemalan domestic will steal her diaphragm; whose nights are troubled by peacocks screaming in the olive trees—an Alcestis back from the tunnel and half in love with death. *You know me, or think you do.*

As we were told in *A Book of Common Prayer*:

> Fear of the dark can be synthesized in the laboratory. Fear of the dark is an arrangement of fifteen amino acids. Fear of the dark is a protein.

And always there was California—"love and death in the golden land." About Los Angeles: "a city not only largely conceived as a series of real estate promotions but largely supported by a series of confidence games, a city currently afloat on motion pictures and junk bonds and the B-2 Stealth bomber." About Hollywood: "as in all cultures in which gambling is the central activity, a lowered sexual energy, an inability to devote more than token attention to the preoccupations of the society outside. The action is everything, more consuming than sex, more immediate than politics; more important always than the acquisition of money, which is never, for the gambler, the true point of the exercise." About everywhere else: lemon groves and eucalyptus breaks and Dial-a-Devotions; Taco Bells, Thriftimarts, and poker parlors; flowering plums and cyclotrons; tumbleweeds and cactus; capri pants and Double Indemnity; Big Sur and the Getty; Death Valley and the Pacific, "turned ominously glossy during a Santa Ana period"; Scientologists, Maharishis, and baby-sitters who see death in your aura; that "place in which a boom mentality and a sense of Chekhovian loss meet in uneasy suspension; in which the mind is troubled by some buried but ineradicable suspicion that things had better work here, because here, beneath that immense bleached sky, is where we ran out of continent" —*horses caught fire and were shot on the beach, birds exploded in the air.* As we were told in *The White Album*:

> Quite often during the past several years I have felt myself a sleep-walker, moving through the world unconscious of the moment's high issues, oblivious to its data, alert only to the stuff of bad dreams, the children burning in the locked car in the supermarket parking lot, the bike boys stripping down stolen cars on the captive cripple's ranch, the freeway sniper who feels "real bad" about picking off the family of five, the hustlers, the insane, the cunning Okie faces that turn up in military investigations, the sullen lurking in doorways, the lost children, all the ignorant armies jostling in the night.

But as early as 1965, too much rained upon in Los Angeles, instead of going to Hawaii to read Orwell on a beach, she found herself driving south into Mexico, to Guaymas in the Sonoran desert: "The point is to become disoriented, shriven, by the heat and the deceptive perspectives and the oppressive sense of carrion. . . . Graham Greene might have written it: a shadowy square with a filigree pergola for the Sunday band, a racket of birds, a cathedral in bad repair with a robin's-egg-blue tile dome, a turkey buzzard on the cross." After which she will drown south, as Robert Penn Warren in *All the King's Men* drowned westward—to Yucatán and Bogotá; white skies, idle casinos, and a salt mine; shawls, parrots, copra, macramé, anaconda skins; termites in the presidential palace and rust in the Oldsmobile; "obscurely sexual misunderstandings and bewilderment" among mineral geologists and CIA men "traveling on one or another incorporeal AID mission"; banana palms, tanks, kidnappings—and, all of a sudden, "I no longer know where the real points are." She's become the anthropologist in *A Book of Common Prayer* who lost faith in her own method, who stopped believing "that observable activity defined anthropos":

> I studied under Kroeber at California and worked with Lévi-Strauss at Sao Paulo, classified several societies, catalogued their rites and attitudes on occasions of birth, copulation, initiation and death; did extensive and well-regarded studies on the rearing of female children in

the Mato Grosso and along certain tributaries of the Rio Xingu, and still I did not know why any one of these female children did or did not do anything at all.

Let me go further.

I did not now why I did or did not do anything at all.

El Salvador is Conrad's heart of darkness: "Exterminate all the brutes!" Ghost resorts on empty Pacific beaches; underfed cattle, mongrel dogs, armored vehicles, bulletproof Plexiglas, "a prolonged amnesiac fugue." In El Salvador, "one learns that vultures go first for the soft tissue, for the eyes, the exposed genitalia, the open mouth. One learns that an open mouth can be used to make a specific point, can be stuffed with something emblematic; stuffed, say, with a penis, or, if the point has to do with land title, stuffed with some of the dirt in question." Roberto D'Aubuisson, Roque Dalton García, Archbishop Romero, ARENA, El Mozote, students, nuns. . . . At an embassy lunch, crystal glasses for chilled wine and, for the fish, porcelain plates with American eagles. . . . "In this vast brutalist space that was the cathedral, the unlit altar seemed to offer a single ineluctable message: at this time and in this space the light of the world could be construed as out, off, extinguished." She seeks Halazone tablets for drinking water in "Central America's Largest Shopping Mall," where, past the weapons check, Muzak plays "I Left My Heart in San Francisco" and "American Pie," and pâté de foie gras is on sale to matrons in tight Sergio Valente jeans, along with Bloomingdale's beach towels and bottles of Stolichnaya vodka:

> This was a shopping center that embodied the future for which El Salvador was presumably being saved, and I wrote it down dutifully, this being the kind of "color" I knew how to interpret, the kind of inductive irony, the detail that was supposed to illuminate the story. As I wrote it down I realized that I was no longer much interested in this kind of irony, that this was a story that would not be illuminated by such details, that this was a story that would perhaps not be illuminated at all, that this was perhaps even less a "story" than a true *noche obscura*. As I waited to cross back over the Boulevard de los Heroes to the Camino Real I noticed soldiers herding a young civilian into a van,

their guns at the boy's back, and I walked straight ahead, not wanting to see anything at all.

But of course she will go on to see everything in all these wasted latitudes: Managua and Santiago, Haiti and Rawalpindi, Jakarta and Saigon, Taipei and Penang, Tunis and Phnom Penh, Dakar and Surabaya, Jedda and Dhahran. And meet everybody: embassy drivers, airline stewardesses, assistant professors of English traveling on Fulbright fellowships, tropical agronomists traveling under the auspices of the Rockefeller Foundation, journalists with paperback copies of *Homage to Catalonia,* desk clerks, bar girls, air couriers, wild cards, salesmen of coco dryers and rice converters, dealers in information and weapons-grade uranium, in cash transfers and end-user certificates, black flights and tiger ops, assets and extractions, "lurid phantasmagorias" and "chiffonades of hemotoxins" — *drop fuel, jettison cargo, eject crew, lose track.*

Later on in Miami there will be a trial involving wigs, glue, Samsonsite attaché cases full of cheesecloth Handi Wipe rags and .38 caliber revolvers, timers and firecracker fuses, an Eveready Energizer alkaline battery and an Uzi. But where we'll really end up, after drowning south, is more like Kuala Lumpur:

> We were sitting in a swamp forest on the edge of Asia in a city that had barely existed a century before and existed now only as the flotsam of some territorial imperative and a woman who had once thought of living in the White House was flicking termites from her teacup and telling me about landing on a series of coral atolls in a seven-passenger plane with a man in a body bag.

And somewhere in the same psychological vicinity is where Elena McMahon lands in *The Last Thing He Wanted:*

> I see her standing in the wet grass of the runway, her arms bare, her sunglasses pushed up into her loose hair, her black silk shift wrinkled from the flight, and wonder what made her think a black silk shift bought off a sale rack at Bergdorf Goodman during the New York primary was the appropriate thing to wear on an unscheduled flight at

one-thirty in the morning out of Fort Lauderdale–Hollywood International Airport, destination San Jose, Costa Rica, but not quite.

Nothing, in fact, is appropriate to wear, because none of us should be there.

When we talk about the process then, we are talking, increasingly, not about "the democratic process," or the general mechanism affording citizens of a state a voice in its affairs, but the reverse: a mechanism seen as so specialized that access to it is correctly limited to its own professionals, to those who manage policy and those who report on it, to those who run the polls and those who quote them, to those who ask and those who answer the questions on the Sunday shows, to the media consultants, to the columnists, to the issues advisers, to those who give the off-the-record breakfasts and to those who attend them; to that handful of insiders who invent, year in and year out, the narrative of public life. (Joan Didion)

This is what Didion learned from years of political reporting, on and off the campaign trail, and passes on to Elena in her latest political novel. And that's what Didion has been up to since *A Book of Common Prayer,* writing political novels that are also Latin, postcolonial, or maybe even NAFTA novels, embodying her extraordinary range of intuitions and anxieties into a narrative of private life confounded out there "on the far frontiers of the Monroe Doctrine," in the can-do arena of "buzz"—from, in *Play It as It Lays,* the sardine cans and vermouth bottles in Maria's sink, the visitations of hummingbirds, the FBI, and I Ching; from, in *A Book of Common Prayer,* Charlotte's nightmares of sexual surrender and infant death, a pet cobra that drinks Wild Turkey and the lizard in the crèche; from, in *Democracy,* the shadow on the scan that was Inez, her sibling gestalt and aversion therapy, the light at dawn during the Pacific atom bomb tests, the disposable needles and glassine envelopes in a Snoopy wastebasket, and the cost of a visa to leave Cambodia before they closed Phnom Penh; out of all the bush and oil fires in her essays, the earthquakes, tidal waves, mudslides, and volcanoes, the vandals, bikers, and gang-rape; the four-year-olds in the burning cars and abandoned refrigerators, and the rattlesnakes in playpens. Against the "hydraulic imagery" of this arena, with its conduits and pipelines and diversions, she opposes a gravitational imagery of black holes and weightlessness. Against dummy corporations, phantom payrolls, pacification, Soviet AK-47s, hijackings and Tupamaros, she opposes wild orchids washed by the rain into milky ditches of waste. Half of *The Last Thing He Wanted* is depositions, cable traffic, brokered accounts, classified secrets, rocket launchers, and fragmentation mines. The other half is jasmine, jacaranda petals, twilight, vertigo, dread, and dreams.

Evita meets Malraux.

Cyberpunk Rocks

Can we talk? I mean, meat to meat, without goggles or gloves or Microsoft brain sockets?

Tired of hauling itself around, meat dreams of flying, like a fax. Gravity sucks. Slugabed in the romper room, tethered to an all-news war porn channel, flatlined by the adman / music video consumer grid, home shopping for friendship in the beer commercials, reading a heavy metal comic, "sampling" on the CD carousel a customized sequence of Sonic Youth, Pussy Galore, and Tom Petty's *Jamming Me,* even crouched in front of our very own software as if it were a harpsichord, online and downlinked to all the other ghosts in the machine, jacked in instead of jacking off—we imagine, through the looking glass, *inside where the information is,* a weightless fourth dimension, some sort of Surf's Up, maybe a raft for Huck and Jim. We long for and *intuit* a digitized Xanadu: Lucy in the Sky with Diamonds.

> *I'm the local stringer for Ceres Datacom network. I hold citizenship in it, though legally speaking it's sometimes more convenient to be treated as wholly owned depreciable hardware. Our life is information—even money is information. Our money and our life are one and the same.*
> (Bruce Sterling, *Schismatrix*)

This is cyberspace. It was cartographed for the first time by William Gibson in his novel *Neuromancer* (1984) and elaborated thereafter in *Count Zero* (1986) and *Mona Lisa Overdrive* (1988). It is an *elsewhere* dream of meat emancipated—into a "consensual hallucination" of the glowing cores and burning grids and neon clouds and crystal nerves and singing spheres of a universe of information; pyramids and shopping malls of data; the havens of the matrix. All of Gibson's heroes are computer hackers who project their "disembodied consciousness" into this 3-D chessboard "nonspace of the mind." Usually they are thieves doing mercenary work "for other, wealthier thieves, employers who provided the exotic software required to penetrate the bright walls of corporate systems, opening windows into rich fields of data. " But what they find beyond the "green cubes" of Mitsubishi banks and the logarithmic "spiral arms" of the military intelligence agencies, in the middle of their "fluid neon origami trick" of levitation, is the *rush* of warp velocity. These thrill-seeking cowboy cybernauts, biker buttonheads, "new age mutant ninja hackers," all of them, are speed freaks. With no place to stand, suggests Istvan Csicsery-Ronay Jr., co-editor of *Science-Fiction Studies,* they "must move, always move."

Understand that this is all imaginary. Other science-fiction writers, before, during, and after Gibson's trilogy, also dreamed their way into what they called the Grid, Net, Web, or Matrix, but none so lyrically. It's no longer possible to imagine computer space at all, *embodied* data, except on Gibson's terms. And his buddies hardly bother. Except for Pat Cadigan, they're a tight bunch of Wild Boys, anyway—Bruce Sterling, Larry Mc-Caffery, John Shirley, Lewis Shiner, Marc Laidlaw, Randy Rucker—so white and middle-class that maybe hacking is a form of suburban flight. As like-minded young writers always have, they slum together, moving like herds of nervous and neurotic zebras from Texas to the coasts and back again, celebrating one another in interviews, anthologies, and blurbs. If, on the evidence of their most recent novels, Gibson's *Virtual Light* and Sterling's *Islands in the Net,* a few have wearied of the repetition compulsion, this is what they get for having made the cover of *Time,* for having inspired an Oliver Stone TV miniseries, for having rippled the equanimity of the Net.

> *First you see video. Then you wear video. Then you eat video. Then you be video.* (Pat Cadigan, "Pretty Boy Crossover")

Cyberspace itself has become a commodity bought and sold on the concept exchange of sci-fi, hackerdom, pomo academe, and crash clubs. From it derives the whole idea of *cyberpunk.* As Herb Caen in the fifties, in the San Francisco *Chronicle,* coined "beatnik" to trivialize the Kerouacs and Ginsbergs, so in the eighties a columnist for the Washington *Post* coined "cyberpunk" to giggle at the neuromantics. But this stuck, too: hard science and pop culture; reality hacking and new-wave rock; blown minds and blown fuses; alienation, confrontation, and chaos theory. Cyberpunk is an outlaw culture: against late capitalism and its marketing of our commodified emotions, the Grace of Hip. (From now on, let the *machines* be subjective.) And it's a fashion statement: black leather jackets, mirror shades, nose studs, nipple rings, tattoos. (After such mutilation, the meat might as well be left behind while a decentered self goes digital, in there where we never know what we look like, anyway.)

So besides sci-fi, cyperpunk is a style of and a take on meat/machine interface: the kiss of a killer cyborg. It's video games, performance art, trash culture, leather bars, designer drugs, hip-hop, film noir, John Cage, Max Headroom, crystal meth, and gangster chic; Sex Pistols and Robocops, Yamaha TX81Z FM tone generators and RX5 digital rhythm programmers, fractals and Mandelbrot. It is Mike Saenz's "adult" computer adventure named "Virtual Valerie" and Pepe Moreno's Batman computer comic "Digital Justice"; the photoscan sequence in Ridley Scott's *Blade Runner* and the vector graphics in Disney's *Tron*; the industrial noise of SPK and Skinny Puppy, Kraftwerk's "cyberpop" roborock, and Steve Wilson's Buffalo River Grain Elevators; Mark Pauline's ram cars and robot scorpions and David Therrien's Crucifixion and fetal-cage crash machines. It is also, as we shall see, ineluctably postmodern.

Understand, too, that cyberspace isn't virtual reality. Not exactly. As an idea, VR's been around a long time in sci-fi, only called something else, from Aldous Huxley's "feelies" to Robert Heinlein's "waldoes." Philip K. Dick had an "empathy box," James Morrow some "dreambeans," John Varley his "memory cube," and Ray Bradbury fiddled variously with a happiness machine, an interactive soap, and the crystal walls of "The Veldt," wherein he was eaten by an imaginary lion. You can check out these and other retro visions in Karie Jacobson's anthology *Simulations.* But as a practicality, with eyephones, datagloves, bodysuits, and feedback loops, entering a world of computer-generated simulations of everything from a "smart" bomber to a protein molecule, from cadavers (virtual surgery) to solar systems (virtual astronomy), VR is still at a clumsy holographic stage, with here and there some "telepresence" (seeing things from a robot's point of view), but yet to cross the "vibrotactile" threshold, not even up to the primitive standards of Gibson's "simstims," and nowhere near the dirty-dancing dream of "teledildonics" (virtual sex).

> *In the dark space of virtual reality, in this universe of organs without bodies, the human body floats like a chemical afterimage, with no purpose (the body is a terminal function), no final destiny, and no (evolutionary) role beyond that of a predator flipped into parasite. Perhaps the last function of the body is to be sequenced as data.*
>
> (Arthur Kroker, *Spasm*)

Nevertheless, VR participates in the known world. What is generated is a *model,* based on something real (or at least agreed upon, like Euclidean geometry). Whereas cyberspace, while likewise a representation of computer graphics, is modeled on nothing more than Gibson's imagination, or Bruce Sterling's, or Pat Cadigan's, or, in the Technicolored Panasonic Metaverse of *Snow Crash,* Neal Stephenson's. Cyberspace is a trope. Reading about this trope, we can't help noticing that what goes on at ground zero is at least as interesting as what happens in the inner spaciness (*Tarzan and the Androids*). Cyberlit's twenty-first century, like the postapocalyptic landscapes of Mad Max on the road or in the Thunderdrome, is one big blasted heath. The whole world is a Third World. And its divine beings, before the advent of artificial intelligence, are the multinationals and gangster cartels, writing their own program in a spiderspeak of green decimals. Case, *Neuromancer's* cowboy, sees these multinationals, "arcologies," *zaibatsus,* and yakuzas as having "attained a kind of immortality," having evolved in their hives of cybernetic memory like "vast single organisms, their DNA coded in silicon."

Throughout his cyberspace trilogy, Gibson is obsessed with yakuza and everything else Japanese. But except for Chiba City, with its "bent medicals" and "black clinics," Tokyo sounds like everywhere in the twenty-first century in the "Sprawl"; like Istanbul and Mexico City, New Delhi or Singapore. It's one big Third World refugee black market fire sale—of seafood briquettes, *shuriken* daggar-stars, eyes, genitals, information, viruses, and narcotics like "wiz," Tennessee opium, endorphin analogs, Memphis Black, and Blue Nine. For the poor, there is no escape to cyberspace; there are only simstim serial soaps . . . and the streets, which belong to the gangs (Gothicks, Kasuals, Dusters, and Lobes) or to the cults (mostly obsessing about image addiction) or to the terrorists (like the "nihilistic technofetishists" who strike at "the media gestalt"). In cyberlit, the class war, like everything else, *implodes*.

No wonder Case leaves town with Molly, the "razor girl" with mirror eyes, as Turner will with Angie, who can actually dream in cyberspace without a neural jack. But of course they take their dread and paranoia with them. If brain death from the black ice of the *zaibatsus* doesn't get them, voodoo horsemen like Baron Samedi, Lord of Graveyards, might. (Yes, voodoo. Having ascribed to digital technology some kind of consciousness, Gibson then seeds it with animisms.) And if not Baron Samedi, then maybe an artificial intelligence like Wintermute, who would sell out anybody for a soul of his own. Cyberlit *loves* AI: machine dreams. In *Count Zero* the only artist left in the universe is an AI who makes sad songs and Joseph Cornell–like boxes out of found "objects" like memory and waste. In *Mona Lisa Overdrive*, no sooner has the matrix gotten to know itself than it discovers the other: *our* cyber meets *their* space.

Maybe there is a machine that will take us away, take us completely, suck us out through the electrodes out of the skull into the machine and live there forever with all the other souls it's got stored there. . . . Each will have his personal rocket. Stored in its target-seeker will be the heretic's EEG, the spikes and susurrations of heartbeat, the ghost blossomings of personal infra red, each rocket will know its intended and hunt him.

(Thomas Pynchon, *Gravity's Rainbow*)

Sadly, most of this gestalt's missing from *Virtual Light,* Gibson's first mainstream best-seller, as most of Bruce Sterling's weirdest cyborg-diplomat stuff in *Schismatrix* was omitted from *Islands in the Net*—though not, in either case, the multinationals and the criminal cartels. *Virtual Light* is a chase-movie script about a pair of stolen glasses, through which you see the "data feed" on what it is you're looking at. Whatever the matrix knows will be downloaded and fed directly into your optic nerve. And what the reader sees is very bad news for San Francisco, till Rydell, a rent-a-cop, and Chevette, a bicycle messenger, and Yamazaki, an anthropologist, and Sublett, a refugee from a trailer-park video sect that finds the face of God in old movies on TV, join forces with an underground gaggle of computer hackers calling themselves the Republic of Desire to declare virtual war on both a Japanese yakuza conglomerate called "Sunflower" and a Southern California law-enforcement satellite called "Death Star."

Once you've met the god-eating rock-dream chimeras of the Republic of Desire, you will realize that the godfather of cyberpunk has developed some doubts about hackers. But the future according to Gibson is still one big Third World, like the dystopian Los Angeles in Mike Davis's *City of Quartz.* All the sympathetic people in Gibson's novel seem to live, after equally devastating earthquakes and AIDS epidemics, on the Oakland Bay Bridge, literally "in the suspension," in a barrio/shantytown of steel bones, severed tendons, pawnbrokers, herbalists, dropouts, tattoo parlors, sushi bars, and a dive called Cognitive Dissidents. Not for any of *them* a Costa Rican "data haven" or Korean robot cleaning bug. Nor are they about to leave the hovel without packing a respirator and a fractal knife, because either the Sword of the Pig is waiting for them or the South Island Front, wolfmen or death cookies. Yamazaki the anthropologist speaks for the author: "We are come not only past the century's closing . . . the millennium's turning, but to the end of something else. Era? Paradigm? Everywhere the signs of closure. Modernity was ending. Here, on the bridge, it long since had."

Chevette the messenger girl is someone new in Gibson, not a gun moll, or Tonto to the Lone Cybernaut. She may have been inspired by Y.T., a jailbait skateboard Kourier in Neal Stephenson's *Snow Crash* (1992), as Stephenson's "Metaverse" was clearly inspired by Gibson's cyberspace. *Snow Crash* is the most intellectually rambunctious cyberpunk novel since *Neuromancer.* In Stephenson's future, there is no law at all. A nightmare Los Angeles is divided into war zones: "Burbclaves," where the solid citizens hide out, behind private security guards, from a gridlocked cruise-missile spree-killing America; "Franchulates" (Franchise-Organized Quasi National Entities) like Uncle Enzo's Mafia, Mr. Lee's Greater Hong Kong, and Narcolombia; "Sacrifice Zones" abandoned because their cleanup costs exceeded their total future economic value; and "Shantytowns" full of hard-core Third World unemployables breathing amino acids. The only way out of this LA, if you are rich enough, is to "goggle" your way into the boundless inner VR world of Metaverse, where your phantasmal "avatar" can play with everybody else's.

Alas, someone's messing with this Metaverse. Not only has a giant raft appeared along the California coast—a boat people biomass of tens of thousands of refugees all speaking in tongues—but a new drug, Snow Crash, blows the minds of the Macintosh-programming "technomedia" priesthood. In hacker lingo, "snow crash" is a systems virus that explodes the gridwork of your pixels. Here it also means *an attack on the deep neurolinguistic structures of the hacker brain!* Who'd do such a thing? Someone sounding like an amalgam of H. Ross Perot and L. Ron Hubbard, with the help of the Russian Orthodox Church and an Aleut whale-killer with his own H-bomb.

I'm nowhere near the matrix of a plot also involving ancient Sumer, the cult prostitutes of Asherah, the Epic of Gilgamesh,

Sargon II, Noam Chomsky, and George Steiner. Our only hope for a binary universe resides in a half-black half-Korean samurai-mafia pizza deliveryman and freelance computer geek named Hiro Protagonist, and his fifteen-year-old blond Lolita-like cohort Y.T., who skateboards from one burbclave to another by harpooning passing traffic. Not only do these two board the raft; they also descend into the netherworld of "Flatland," which, with a nod to Edward Abbott's classic of the genre, is both the electronic text of metaverse and the hypercard of our DNA, where the prophet Jeremiah will be drowned out by Vitaly Chernobyl's heavier-than-metal nuclear fuzz grunge band.

Religion as a virus? Actually, Scientology shows up a lot in cyberpunk. There are passing references in Gibson and Cadigan, and the Bruce Wagner virtual reality comic strip for *Details* that inspired the *Wild Palms* miniseries may also have had Hubbard, Scientology, and Dianetics in mind in its portrayal of Tony Kreutzer, the wealthy industrialist and former sci-fi writer who has his own TV network with VR sitcoms; his own religion, a Church of Synthiotics; his own cult parishioners, "The New Realists," and his own fascistic paramilitaries, known as "The Fathers" because they kidnap the children of their many enemies. All this, plus a rhinoceros.

Much as *Snow Crash* blizzards my pixels, it still fits neatly into Csicsery-Ronay's gleeful put-down of the whole genre of shape-shifting crash-body outriders on the digital frontier:

> [How] many formulaic tales can one wade through in which a self-destructive but sensitive young protagonist with an (implant / prosthesis / telechtronic talent) that makes the evil (megacorporation / police state / criminal underworld) pursue him through (wasted urban landscapes / elite luxury enclaves / eccentric space stations) full of grotesque (haircuts / clothes / self-mutilations / rock music / sexual hobbies / designer drugs / telechtronic gadgets / nasty new weapons / exteriorized hallucinations) representing the (mores / fashions) of modern civilization in terminal decline, ultimately hooks up with rebellious and tough-talking (youth / artificial intelligence / rock cults) who offer the alternative, not of (community / socialism / traditional values / transcendental vision), but of supreme, life-affirming hipness,

going with the flow which now flows in the machine, against the spectre of a world-subverting (artificial intelligence / multinational corporate web / evil genius)?

Ahem. Well, Pat Cadigan's better than *that*. In *Synners* (1991), Cadigan takes VR the next chilling step: from flatscreen to headmount to brain-socket. Boreholes into the limbic system! Manipulation of the parietal lobes! Taproots to the visual and auditory cortices! *Coming soon to a brain near you.* "Post-Millennarist Fundamentalists Claim Sockets Facilitate Demonic Possession via Rock Music," reads one protest against the technologized Pleasure Principle. Another says: "Lobby for Decency Declares Brain an Erogenous Zone, Demands Mandatory Hatting." But the real problem with sockets is that they cause brain hemorrhage. And since almost everyone in *Synners* is plugged in somewhere or other to the Net, a sort of viral stroke goes *online,* and all systems look to crash. While several characters confront this possibility with a very punk shrug of the black leather shoulders — "If you can't fuck it and it doesn't dance, eat it or throw it away" — others behave a whole lot more like readers of progressive periodicals.

Hiding out in yet another postapocalyptic sprawl called the Mimosa are the usual band of hackers, calling themselves "synners" because what they do is synthesize; they're in a constant state of hallucination. Fez and Keeley are male. Gator, a tattoo artist, and Sam, who gives new meaning to "laptop," and Gina, who makes music videos, are very much female. Gina, a terrific character, has lost her boyfriend Mark, not only to the sockets but also to the Net. Mark never liked his body — "Meat . . . had to expend so much energy and attention just dragging itself around that it tended to miss a lot" — but if the system crashes, so will he, because he's *all* system now. (Naturally, in a female cyberfiction, there are *relationships,* including father-daughter, unrequited love, and a romantic triangle that solves itself by cloning.) Meanwhile, waiting for every nonbody in the agitated Net is Dr. Artie Fish, the obligatory Artificial Intelligence, who has come to know itself because so much data overload from so many hackings *woke up the matrix!* Artie needs help from the meat, and gets it after many references to Schrödinger and Heisenberg, plus some Bob Dylan and a "deja-voodoo" joke clearly aimed at William Gibson. *Synners* is delicious.

> *Images — millions of images — That's what I eat — Cyclotron shit —*
> *Ever try kicking the habit with apomorphine? — Now I got all the images*
> *of sex acts and torture ever took place anywhere and I can just blast it out*
> *and control you gooks right down to the molecule — I got orgasms — I got*
> *screams — I got all the images any hick poet ever shit out — My power's*
> *coming. . . . My power's coming. . . . And I got millions of images*
> *of Me, Me, meee.* (William Burroughs)

But now we must be less so. While you can probably imagine how the assistant professors of problematizing the ontologies in Lacanian fugue states felt when they first saw cyberpunk, I went and read Scott Bukatman's *Terminal Identity: The Virtual Subject in Postmodern Science Fiction* anyway, as well as Larry McCaffery's thick anthology of snippets and critical scrim, *Storming the Reality Studio.* Such a rattle of signifying chains, it makes you worry about abysses of nonmeaning. Phenomenologically speaking, the constitution of being as an activity of interface! Surrealism without the unconscious! Esthetics of immersion! Inscripted bodies! Disciplinary technologies! Objective mirage! Machine subjectivity! Mediascape pastiche! Neologic excess! Deathmetal technomutant morphing unto paradigm shift! No more texture, no more depth; no more town, history, paternity, morality, public sphere, or tonal system; no more memory and no more meat, merely surfaces, speed, and what Frederic Jameson calls "a peculiar kind of euphoria." How nice to be able to pretend to your disgruntled students that you're a swinger. (According to Bruce McHale: "We can think of science fiction as postmodernism's noncanonized or 'low art' double, its sister-genre in the same sense that the popular detective thriller is modernist fiction's sister-genre.") And, without ever leaving the campus, to bamboozle left-wing friends into thinking you're still on the barricades. (*Computers and Corporate Crime:* "Tactics of the Byte in Vampire Capitalism.") And, without ever risking originality by engaging artifacts of genius, to persuade the tenure committee that you wear with flair a Heidegger safari jacket, Foucault platform heels, Lacan epaulets, and a Walter Benjamin boutonniere. The wild boys in the matrix should be grateful that someone seems to take them seriously. Hell, maybe they even believe it.

Every time I hear another mention of Bataille's "paradigmatic tropes of sacrificial excess and bodily affirmation," I reach for my harmonica.

> *On his way to Diego's, Jeffrey discovers a woman harmed by information excess. All the symptoms are present: bleeding from the nose and ears, vomiting, deliriously disconnected speech, apparent disorientation, and the desire to touch everything.* (Ted Mooney)

It was one thing when these french fries and frankfurters found out that novels programmed on computers, open-ended and interactive, are the perfect children, fertilized in vitro, of every deconstructionist theory that ever opened in New Haven. George P. Landow explains all this in *Hypertext.* Barthes on "ideal textuality" in a "galaxy of signifiers," Derrida on "multivocality" and "metatext," Baudrillard on a shift from "tactile" to "digital," Foucault on "bottomless networks" and so on, all might as well have been preparing an instruction manual for the nonlinear, anti-hierarchical, centerless, and marginless fictions we might each of us hack in the metaverse, and of the sort that Landow, dismayingly, quotes. But we don't have to read any hypertext fiction; Robert Coover did it for us (twice!) in the *Times Book Review.* Cyberpunk's another antimatter, and just look what they've done to our song.

Jameson, having been traumatized into a pomo frame of mind by the Bonaventure Hotel in Los Angeles, sees in "the waning of affect" an end to bourgeois ego, social class, art, ideology, and style; a snapping of Lacan's signifying chain; a substitution of "intensities" for "feelings"; and a dominating of our daily life,

our psychic experience, and our cultural languages "by categories of space rather than by categories of time." Guy Debord
goes on about "the society of spectacle," as if he'd never heard of
Octavio Paz on the baroque, or ever seen a cathedral or a pyra-
mid, or read Simon Schama on hot-air ballooning before the
French Revolution, or thought about spectacular symbols like
the crescent and the cross, the swastika and the dollar sign, the
hammer or the sickle. From Baudrillard, orbital and gravitational metaphors in weightlessness. From Merleau-Ponty, "a
layer of invisibility in the strict sense," made "present as a certain absence." From Paul de Man, "vertiginous possibilities of
the referential aberration." From Jean-Louis Lyotard, "incredu-
lity." From Heidegger, never mind. From Bukatman himself,
along with many "imbrications" and "diagetics," a "decentered
self" and a "virtual subject" in "disembodied space," also a treatise on how SF, with its heightened rhetoricity and relentless
neologizing, "defamiliarizes" the startled reader, making possible a characteristically pomo queasiness about ontology.

*Except where it is adopted as a necessary means of secret communica-
tion, the use of a special slang in any employment is probably to be accepted as evidence that the occupation in question is substantially make-
believe.* (Thorstein Veblen)

It's swell to hear in passing of some "slipstream" novelists who
have variously interfaced with cyberpunk, like Pynchon, At-
wood, DeLillo, Hoban, Wittig, and of course Burroughs, that
cutup, though one wonders exactly what happened to Doris
Lessing and Kobo Abe, Italo Calvino and Stanislaw Lem,
Borges and Nabokov, not to mention constructivists in Russia
and futurists in Italy and a host of others who have sailed these
seas of signs, shopped in these emporiums of styles, consulted
the encyclopedias of the fleeting and the fragmentary, wandered
so nomadically through the old quarters of these ruined imperial
cities, buzzed at the honeycombs of playful and schizoid networks of commerce and commodities, irreverent pastiche and
contrived depthlessness, brutal aesthetics and shock spectacle.

Nor are the roots of punk in traditional and new wave SF neglected, with even a nod to Bernard Wolfe's underrated *Limbo,* although one does miss *Dune.* Feminist critics like Vivian Sobchack, Donna Haraway, Veronica Hollinger, Barbara Creed, and Claudia Springer, with another tale to tell about "inscripted bodies," actually have more fun in both *Storming the Reality Studio* and *Terminal Identity* than pomo guys doing pomo guy things. For masculine laughter on the virtual subject we must look to Arthur Kroker's "theory-fiction" *Spasm,* with its inspired rants about Biosphere 2, Michael Jackson, latex sex, Madonna, and the dead Elvis; the "dryware of sado-masochism lite" and the *"recline of Western civilization,"* though even Canadian wildman Kroker buys into AI machine dreams against all evidence that the genetic engineers are lots farther along, custom-compounding organic mutants, than the cyberneticists are anywhere near an artificial hand or eye, much less consciousness.

But the real story here is that pomo, having killed off all of its fathers (a Marx, a Freud, a Sartre), having murdered every "metanarrative" it could get its claws on (scientific progress, the class struggle), now proposes its metafigural self as the metanarrative not only of science fiction but of everything else in the Post Toasties world. Who else cohabits so comfortably with the neologistic and defamiliarizing, with a rhetoricity half as heightened, as these odor-eaters in pump-up Nikes? Virtual criticism—as if pomo had invented our agnosticism about reality itself; as if we hadn't before been lied to; as if the shamans of the great religions hadn't long ago experienced "out-of-body" ecstasies every bit as thrilling as cyberspace or designer drugs; as if we'd never before in our fossil subtext been lost, antsy, uncertain, improbable, and downright *pastiched* during the epochal "decenterings" of Mongols, plagues, Copernicus, and Darwin; as if before postmodernism there had never been the blues.

"Into the code": space-pad, send-key, readout, blink rate, arbitrary input, navigation error. . . . Information isn't knowledge, and information *density* isn't wisdom. It makes you wonder. When was this meeting where they voted out existential humanism and voted in pomo? Why wasn't I invited? Isn't pomo really one big cover-up for the failure of the French to write a truly interesting novel ever since a sports car ate Albert Camus? Without gravity, can there be any grace? Instead of sitting around being *valorized* by pomo, why aren't the punks out there doing something about the ownership of the modes of production by Bell Atlantic, Liberty Media, Walt Disney, Rupert Murdoch, Bill Gates, Si Newhouse, Viacom, and Time Warner? Have any of these people, pomo or punk, during downtime ever read *Beloved* or *Midnight's Children* or *One Hundred Years of Solitude*; spent a night as a volunteer in a homeless shelter, worked with AIDS patients, saved whales, stopped a troop train or a lynching, sought to walk in the virtual shoes of schoolteachers, migrant workers, and physical therapists, *engaged* what's really out there among the "end users," beyond the "abstracted interface," the "database protocol," the "test-bed methodology," and the "parallel processing," instead of posturing in front of it, striking attitudes like matches? Are Shining Path and Khmer Rouge punk? Postmodern? Is virtual reality the same as phone sex? What if technology, having been pixeled into sentience, proves to be just as full of *false consciousness* as all the rest of us? Is it really true that ten minutes of a Mozart piano sonata enhances abstract brain activity? Don't you, too, hope that when the last soft machine in cyberspace is about to disappear into the ultimate black-rabbit-hole of death-metal digits adding up to NULL case, what it will whistle in the dark is something like a *Magic Flute*?

Pynchon's Crazy Age of Reason

More than seven hundred pages later, when this splendid eighteenth-century beast of a book seems to have hunkered down for a dying fall of grace notes—after the melancholy Gothic-depressive Charles Manson and the sporty manic danger junkie Jeremiah Dixon have sailed rough seas to Cape Town, St. Helena, and Delaware Bay; after an excess of salt, pitch, pipe smoke, bagpipes, sheep fat, caffeine abuse, darkling beetles, apparitions, and mirages; after slave colonies, opium dens, spirit villages, Stonehenge, and the gallows; after Hottentots, Malays, Presbyterians, Dutch Calvinists, Jesuit priests, Mohawk Indians, Jenkins' Ear, and Rebekah's ghost; after Ben Franklin, George Washington, Tom Jefferson, Captain Volcanoe, a French chef, a Chinese geomancer, a Viking spy, a giant cheese, a giant beet, a giant worm, talking dogs, electric eels, mechanical ducks, and an American golem; after a Transit of Venus, a Vector of Desire, a Purity of Azimuth, Realms of Velocity and Spleen, many Enigmata of the Invisible World and an Epsilonicks of Damnation—our stargazing heroes are reunited back in England, some the wiser and gone fishing. Mason tells Dixon about Ulster, where there were faery lights in the infernal bog and coffins disguised as claviers. Dixon tells Mason about the Arctic, from which aliens abducted him.

Well, more like elves, trolls, or gnomes. Go with the floe. Under the North Pole's ice cap, inside Earth as we think we know it, is another, hollow world—a *terra concava* where the lakes are ceilings secured by centrifugal force, in whose inner void the Little People hang upside down like bats. They have been sending messages by magnetic compass and other telluric mediations. They are curious: How can Dixon bear to live topside, so exposed to the terrible Lights and Outer Darkness? Hasn't he noticed that in his convexity he's always leaning *away* from everybody else, while these insiders are forever, in fellowship, pointed *toward* one another? But they are also fearful—

especially of Masons and Dixons: "Once the solar parallax is known . . . once the necessary Degrees are measur'd, and the size and weight and shape of the Earth are calculated inescapably at last, all this will vanish. We will have to seek another Space."

This is the Thomas Pynchon who just can't stop himself, who ups antes and lowers booms. Like his mechanical duck, if he keeps flying, we won't see and can't catch him. I should be telling you that *Mason & Dixon* is shapely and coherent. That you'll care about a baffled astronomer and a horny surveyor in the grip of forces they can't even locate, much less modify. That, for the first time in a Pynchon, we get extended families (difficult fathers and lonely children), magnanimity instead of mockery, closure instead of dissolution. But already, to prove myself worthy of a masterwork, I'm haring down absurdist wormholes.

Underground! In *V*, there were channels, tunnels, sewers, trollfolk, a besieged Malta, and a Borgesian Vheissu hiding out at the *other* Pole. In *The Crying of Lot 49*, as if in the midsixties he had already imagined e-mail and Microsofties, there was Tristero, that subterranean signal system of the dispossessed in a "separate, silent, unsuspected world." In *Gravity's Rainbow*, there was Dora, the prison camp and underground Mittelwerke city of rockets and salt; and white lunar latitudes where "*there is always the danger of falling*"; and "the invisible kingdom" of the crematoria on "the other side" of Pokler's vacuums and labyrinths; and *Schwarzkommandos* who believed the souls of their dead waited in the Arctic; and the last V-2, launched with its Aryan payload at that very same pole. In *Vineland* there were Thanatoids and the dolphinlike *woge* who hid beneath the ocean to see what we did with their world—as well as Frenesi's dream of a Flood and phantom divers who would bring back up whatever had been taken, whatever had been lost.

"Signs and symptoms," said Pointsman the Pavlovian in *Gravity's Rainbow*: "Could Outside and Inside be part of the same field?" Follow the bouncing ball . . .

From historical odds and ends and the field journal they left behind, Pynchon reimagines Mason and Dixon before, during, and after the four-plus years, 1763 to 1767, they took to draw their 2144-mile-long line through the American wilderness, dividing the proprietorships of the Penns of Pennsylvania and the Calverts of Maryland, ordaining our North and South. From his omnivorous reading, with his diabolical genius for mimicry, he also re-creates their tumultuous era, an Age of Reason crazy with divine kingship, chartered monopolies, and the trading in human flesh; French Encyclopedists, Royal Society astronomers, genocidal colonizers, and seething religious sects; pornography and revolution. And from the depths of his jaunty disenchantment, he calls into brilliant question the very ways we measure, map, and misconstrue history, landscape, time, space, stars, and selves—as if by pin, needle, pencil, lens, plummet, clock, pendulum, and compass we will ever settle on an Angle of genuine Repose, or achieve orbit, or abstract anything important about women and comets, or see the sailing shapes of love and death and wind and light.

"Geometry and slaughter!" says Squire Haligast in *Mason & Dixon,* on being advised of the Prussian victory at the Battle of Leuthen in 1757: "The future of war, yet ancient as the mindless Exactitudes of Alexander's Phalanx."

To do all this Pynchon has written his *own* eighteenth-century novel, as though by a Jonathan Swift gone elsewhere than Lilliput and Brobdingnag, or a Dr. Johnson improving greatly upon *Rasselas* by shifting it from Abyssinia. (Sam will even show up at the end of *Mason & Dixon* to call Mason a lunatic.) There is a Henry Fielding stream-of-consciousness, a lot of tacking toward the Laurence Sterne and, unless I'm mistaken, also some borrowings from the Noble Savage woo-woo of Chateaubriand's *Atala*. (You will recall the heavy-breathing Vicomte had a hard time finding a Northwest Passage because nobody'd told him there were Rocky Mountains.) The Mary Wollstonecrafts, mother and daughter, seem to have been consulted, along with their husband and father William Godwin and his *Adventures of Caleb Williams*. Nor would familiarity with Cotton Mather come as a surprise. Or the John Williams who wrote *The Redeemed Captive Returning to Zion*, the Joel Barlow who wrote *The Hasty-Pudding*, and the Charles Brockden Brown who wrote *Wieland, Osmond*, and a terrific essay on somnambulism (and was, like Dixon, a radical Quaker). And this is not to mention everything Pynchon had to know about Aristarchus, Laplace, Kepler, Newton, and celestial mechanics; Clive of India, Baron Münchhausen, and the Danse Macabre; Matteo Ricci (Jesuits in China), Anton Mesmer (who used Ben Franklin's glass harmonia to stupefy the ladies), hyperthrenia ("excess of mourning"), comparative religion (including Mithraic cults), revolutionary politics (Franco-American), Dutch sadomasochism (with its odd emphasis on the Black Hole of Calcutta), baking bread (Mason's father), mining coal (Dixon's father), class, race, Freemasons, Illuminati, Feng Shui and the Kabbala, astrolabes and spices, Paul Bunyan and Johnny Appleseed, balloons, automata, and sorcery.

Anyway, as in the *Peregrinations of Dr. Diocletian Blobb,* a text he imagined for *The Crying of Lot 49* (along with a seventeenth-century Jacobean revenge play in which characters perished of "every mode of violent death available to Renaissance man including a lye pit, land mines [and] a trained falcon with envenom'd talons"), *Mason & Dixon* is "full of words ending in e's, s's that looked like f's, capitalized nouns, y's where i's should've been" and many, many comma/dash/space splices, — as, for instance, —

Does Britannia, when she sleeps, dream? Is America her dream? — in which all that cannot pass in the metropolitan Wakefulness is allow'd Expression away on the restless Slumber of these Provinces, and on Westward, wherever 'tis not yet mapp'd, nor written down, nor ever, by the majority of Mankind, seen, — serving as a very Rubbish-Tip for subjunctive Hopes, for all that may yet be true. — Earthly Paradise, Fountain of Youth, Realms of Prester John, Christ's Kingdom, ever behind the sunset, safe till the next Territory to the West be seen and recorded, measur'd and tied in, back into the Network of Points already known, that slowly triangulates its Way into the Continent,

changing all from subjunctive to declarative, reducing Possibilities to
Simplicities that serve the ends of Governments, — winning away from
the Realm of the Sacred, its Borderlands one by one, and assuming
them unto the bare mortal world that is our home, and our Despair.

But Pynchon is also very much a modern who not only knows
from narratology but has always obliged with blind trails for
pomo burrowers into the palimpsests. Thus, on a snowy Philadelphia Christmas in 1786, after Mason and Dixon are both
dead, their story is told Joseph Conrad–style by the Rev. Wicks
Cherrycoke, who was with them in Cape Town and then again
on the Mall they made of America, though he skipped St. Helena. (There's a Cherrycoke in *Rainbow* too. Does it matter? Not
as much as several appearances of "Fender-Belly" Bodine in
M & D: the template of Pig.) While Cherrycoke was seen to take
lots of notes, his young listeners are aware that some of this stuff
he couldn't possibly know. These lines get tangled when a character from a 1786 pulp serial, on the lam from a Jesuit brothel in
Quebec, shows up and stays put in the Ur-Novel twenty years
before her fictitious time. (If Pynchon has fun with the *Ghastly
Fop,* he even more enjoys playing Timothy Tox, a Rudyard
Kipling of colonial PA, a producer of doggerel by the pound.
Besides the usual dogs, there are the usual puns—e.g., "Dutch
Ado about nothing.")

If I stop to explain the Jesuit brothel in Quebec; or what Mason did during the eleven days the Georgians stole from the
Julians in England in 1752; or how Dixon happened to learn to
fly at The Cudgel and Throck; or the difference between "The
Daughters of the End of the World" and the Girls on Call in the
Black Hole of Calcutta at the Cape Town Lodge; or how come
George Washington has a black Jewish slave who makes kasha
varnishkes and sings "Havah Nagilah"; or why Zsuzsa Szabo
wears the dress uniform of the Nadasdy Hussars; or whether it is
possible for anybody *else* to read Aristotle on comedy, Shakespeare's *The Tragedy of Hypatia,* and "all the good bits Thomas
left out from the Infancy Gospel"; or whatever possessed
Jacques de Vaucanson's Mechanickal Duck to flap away to a

New World of "savage Women, giant Vegetables [and] Buffalo herds the size of Paris"; or how to date The Third Sex, who are Dead; or the first British pizza, the Surinam Torpedo, runic Ogham and Dark Hepsie, the Pythoness of the Point—there won't be space left over to answer the question Mason on his deathbed asks Ben Franklin ("What Phantom Shape, implicit in the Figures?"), nor to explain why M and D, at the conclusion of their Iliadic *Wandervogel* "into Futurity," should wind up feeling like "a Peppercorn in the Stuffata, stirr'd and push'd about by any Fool who walks by with a Spoon."

Somebody else is pulling their strings, that's why. Certainly the Royal Society, to which neither will be elected because of their lower-class origins, has an investment of prestige in stargazing and "lunar Obs" to devise "a reliable way to find the true Longitude at sea." (This problem, eventually solved instead by John Harrison's chronometer, has been the excuse for two recent books, Dava Sobel's resonant cultural history *Longitude* and Umberto Eco's self-indulgent novel *The Island of the Day Before*.) But for whom is the fixing of marine longitudes such an urgent issue? The British Navy, for one. The British East India Company, for another. The whole colonial enterprise, for a third. Which means the French, the Dutch, and even the Levantines are suspicious. To whom we must add a conspiracy of what Ben Franklin calls "the two most powerful sources of Brain-Power on Earth,"

> the one as closely harness'd to its Disciplin'd Rage for Jesus, as the other to that Escape into the Void, which is the very Asian Mystery. Together, they make up a small Army of Dark Engineers who could run the World. The Sino-Jesuit conjunction may prove a greater threat to Christendom than ever the Mongols or the Moors.

Such puppetmasters jerk and scatter our hapless hirelings, who are more like Hansel and Gretel than Addison and Steele, in "an Herodotic Web" of Enigmatic Tangents—to Cape Town, where they'll set up "Snouts" to track the eclipse of a Transit of Venus; to St. Helena where they traffick with convicts, madmen, slaves, and chartered company "Perpetuals" while also enduring "the spookish fug of Maskelyne's Sermons upon the Unknown"; and to America, "when the World was yet feudal," to hew by ax a "Visto" through the heart of the darkness eight yards wide and due west, in a *Decameron* of misfits who might as well have time-traveled to enlist after the last V-2 obliterated Vheissu—Children of the Rainbow as mad and motley as the clairvoyants, telekinetics, lobotomizers, Behaviorists, midgets, and vaudevillians in the White Visitation, pioneer Slothrops on a lonesome and perilous range. If *V* was Henry Adams and Ludwig Wittgenstein shooting alligators in New York City sewers, and *Rainbow* a conjoining of Spengler, Freud, Rilke, Céline, and S. J. Perelman, and *Vineland* a lysergic-acid Icelandic saga, *Mason & Dixon* is a "Westward Ho!" to the Culture of Death, with Joseph de Maistre and Frantz Fanon and their Merry Pranksters in a Day-Glo Conestoga wagon. "Was there a mistake in the Plan of the Day?" Mason wonders. "Did we get a piece of someone else's history?"

And what do they find in their perpetual motion of departure and return, at the margins? On the one hand, everywhere: commerce, covetousness, and imperialism's greedy profit-taking— "Something richer than many a Nation," explains mad Maskelyne, "yet with no Boundaries,— which, tho' never part of any Coalition, yet maintains its own great Army and Navy,— able to pay for the last War, as the next, with no more bother than finding a Key to a certain Iron Box,— yet which allows the Britannick Governance that gave it Charter, to sink beneath oceanick Waves of Ink Incarnadine." On another hand, also everywhere, depressing Mason, enraging Dixon: slavery, oppression, and a geometry of violence "more permissive than Euclid"—markets in half-breed babies; nightmares of reprisal; smallpoxed Indians. As Maskelyne also explains: "for Commerce without Slavery is unthinkable, whilst Slavery must ever include as an essential Term, the Gallows,— Slavery without the Gallows being as hollow and Waste a Proceeding, as a Crusade without the Cross." On the third hand, all over the globe, lunacy—in great winds, blown sands, seas of blood, and unsealed coffins; a Jenkins' Ear to hear confessions and the Wolf of Jesus in a hot-air balloon; "Suicide-Banks," "Madness-Pools," and magic pearls from the brains of cobras.

Finally, these four hands count ghosts: shadowland shapes of the shamefully martyred, silently repressed, and nameless dead; borders transgressed, cries unheard. Against such a spectral teem—Invisible Hands of another kind of Market, Dreambodies, Ghost-fish, Guardians, Black Dogs, Indian Glow, Werewolves, and Gnostic remnants; Prophecies, Fetches, and Deep Creatures with a Stare; hallucinatory passages down forbidden trails through darkness primeval into burial mounds and Radiance; the capital, dividends, trust funds, and charged terrain of *Magic*—all the profane states of Europe with their "Machines, Powders, Rays, Elixirs," their leagues of philosophers and their crazy reasonings, must quail in fear. "Invisible yet possessing Mass, and Velocity, able not only to rattle Chains but to break them as well," Mason will think in Cape Town. And, after returning from an America that should have been innocent:

> Mason has seen in the Glass, unexpectedly, something beyond simply reflection, — outside of the world, — a procession of luminous Phantoms, carrying bowls, bones, incense, drums, their Attention directed to nothing he may imagine, belonging to unknown purposes, flowing by thick as Eels, pauselessly, for how long before or after his interception, he could never know.

Imaginary space! Sacred borderlands! Rapture & Vertigo! So, in the eighteenth-century world according to Pynchon, instead of waiting for Godot, Vladimir and Estragon hit the road. And Rosencrantz and Guildenstern find themselves in *Gulliver's Travels* instead of Stoppard's Hamlet. Yet bless Tom, for he has Magick'd. Haunted by the ghost of his dead wife, Mason starts a second family and bequeaths his own sons to the New World, though it was Dixon who had wanted to stay in America. And Dixon, "the unwavering Lark of the Sanguine," gone nymphing by moonlight for sea trout in a stream of English consciousness, will see through his pride into the minds of the secret sharers of the Earth. What a pity he dies before Romantic poetry, grand opera, psychoanalysis, or Hollywood movies. In Wagner he might have been a bassoon. The pair of them, pointing *toward* each other in a *terra concava,* are better at buddy bonding than Gilgamesh and Enkidu. And *Mason & Dixon*— like *Huckleberry Finn,* like *Ulysses*—is one of the great novels about male friendship in anybody's literature.

Let's Hear It for the Luddites

Imagine Mor Greave: hand-loom weaver, village schoolmaster, secret scribbler of notes on nature and politics; acquainted in the Yorkshire hills with "ceremonies of moving light"; experiencing, in a moonlit courtyard rubble of classical carvings, suspended lintels, collapsed floors, stone troughs, and star wheels, some sort of ecstatic seizure—"Although exhausted, he was also illuminated. He was glowing like a hot coal"—fleeing Lady Well across the moors with a violin on his back and a magic egg-shaped stone in his pocket.

Now imagine Mary the Scar, a prostitute Mor meets among disorderly soldiers in a pub, in her blue cloak, with painted cheeks and dyed red hair, a woman of hard times and easy virtue who taught herself to read from tombstones, the Bible, and pornography; who has heard some Mozart on the harpsichord but who is also on the run from a blind child buried in a wishing well whose hungry mouth she stopped with dirt. "You with your fiddle," says Mary to Mor, "and me with my own instrument for playing . . . we'll get by." But they are not allowed to.

Besides Mary and Mor, there's Mor's son Edwin, who draws maps of Africa and Greece; who rises before dawn to work barefoot in Paradise Mills; who, for disobedience in the factory, will be crucified upon a crossbeam above the needles of a spinning frame. And motherless Margaret, brought to Lady Well in a tumbrel, dressed up in pauper's blue, submitted to rapeseed oil and leather belting, driveshafts and tobacco spittle, prayer books and dirty candle stubs. Edwin and Margaret will steal away in the smoke for Manchester and sailing ships and some other childhood. They aren't allowed to get by, either.

Meanwhile, from the master's attic, a mad syphilitic face grins down. In pubs they speak of Cicero and the Roman republics. Informers fester and spies are pestilential. An artist's easel looks like a gibbet. A comet is a sign of revolution. See colliers with picks on their shoulder, fishmongers with knives, masons with hammers, weavers with sickles, carpenters with steel yardsticks, and "flurries of white as bands of women passed. It was snowing aprons. The women were carrying heavy rolling pins." In the yard of the Eagle, out of sacks stuffed with straw, a six-foot figure is mounted on a donkey cart:

> The innkeeper provided the straw, his wife gave a giant turnip for its head, and an old weaver who lived in bachelor retirement at the inn, haunting the taproom with memories of France during the Revolution, contributed a pair of his white corduroy trousers and his most precious possession, his blue liberty cap.

Say hi to King Ludd.

The Rape of the Rose is a very Grimm fairy tale about the Luddite rebellion in 1812. The Luddites have come down to us in our high-school history texts as mindless vandals, nineteenth-century smashers of machines as the Iconoclasts were ninth-century smashers of images. From 1811 to 1812, disaffected artisans and redundants destroyed a thousand mills in the Nottingham area alone — as if, by breaking a spinning jenny, a shearing frame, or a power loom, they could stop "progress" in its technological tracks. From the point of view of the Industrial Revolution, Luddites were reactionary and obstructionist. From their own point of view, the perspective of the workshop, factory floor, and village green, something had gone terribly wrong in a depressed and war-weary England of bad harvests, rising prices, redoubled population, rack-renting, food shortages, landlessness, and mass unemployment.

But we seldom hear it from a Luddite point of view. In Gertrude Himmelfarb's *The Idea of Poverty: England in the Early Industrial Age,* they don't even rate a mention in the index. Not that they left a lot to work with: In 1812, unions themselves were illegal — not until 1825 were they allowed to negotiate on wages and working hours; not till 1871 could they strike — and machine-smashing was a capital offense. To put anything down on paper was suicidal. And it was almost as dangerous, later on, to reminisce. No firsthand account of Luddite activity has survived for historians to construe, no periodicals, minute books, or memoirs. "Luddism," as E. P. Thompson reminds us, "ended on the scaffold."

But it's payback time. Glyn Hughes, a poet and a playwright as well as a novelist, lays on intricate metaphors—William Blake's "bed of crimson joy"; the fierce light of a mill furnace like "a savage idol dancing in the flames"; the Wars of the Roses (white for Yorkshire, red for Lancashire); the war against Napoleon in Spain ("they paint the 'ouses white down there, and the blood was splashed red as roses on the walls"); Mary's hoof-shaped crimson birthmark ("the two horns reaching to the corner of her mouth and eyes"); Mor's erotic dreams of a woman with "a dark red flower"; and motherless Margaret's ravaging ("My rose! My perfect angel!" says a mill owner, the odious Horsfall, for whom the workhouse is also a brothel).

In Mor Greave though, whom Mary calls "More Grief," machine smashers get their scribe, a Tom Paine for the underground lodges, the "charity clubs," and "burial societies." At the very moment Jane Austen is writing *Mansfield Park*, "More Grief" is writing his *Beggar's Complaint*. For the likes of a Mor and a Mary, writing and reading are themselves subversive acts:

> It reminded her of rows of black trees on a distant horizon, or of the shapes of hedgerows racing across the landscape. . . . She watched the quill entering the bottle, leaving it, and touching the paper. The people whom she had seen writing had been mostly magistrates, clerks, clergymen and majors, who made a quiet display of it and who were mostly copying formulas. A hand-loom weaver—school-master—author was a new phenomenon. . . . "You should be careful of bottles of ink. They're like gunpowder."

Through these black trees and racing hedgerows we see the cottage Mor left behind in Lady Well, with its smoke and human staleness, machine oil and rising damp, a tin scoop for oatmeal, a brown jug for drinking water, a windowsill geranium . . . the candlelit cave of a mill to which Mor sold his children, where, among steel rods and bobbin racks, from shearing machine to dye vat, those children are beaten to keep them awake . . . a workhouse, a whorehouse, a madhouse, a Methodist church, a squatter farm . . . a blacksmith who when he isn't busy making bobbin racks will fashion a mantrap for poachers; Mad Dick, the army deserter, who will apostrophize the lash; Gartside, the pariah pederast, who reads Ecclesiastes in the wilderness; Joanna Southcott, the brain-diseased and virginally pregnant enthusiast of a Second Coming; "King Tom Maitland," come to put down insurrection, as if from the pages of Edward Said, "full of surprises":

> After the French Revolution, 'e led a secret expedition for the Royalists that somehow ended up in America and the West Indies. He was in Santo Domingo and surrendered Port-au-Prince to the black slave leader, Toussaint-L'ouverture. . . . Served on both sides of the world 'as King Tom. Calcutta and Madras, Commander of Ceylon, then in the West Indies.

Besides Maitland, other actual historical figures include Luddite heroes like George Mellor and John Booth; Horsfall, who fired his cannon at the workers and who will be assassinated after this novel's finished; Cartwright at his Rawfolds barricade of spiked rollers and tubs of vitriol; Burton, whose house burns down. It was an unmerry England, we're reminded, where the first owner of the first machine-driven spinning mill was also the first to enslave children, from age five, on fourteen-hour shifts six days a week. (If you "held back" one of your children you were "ineligible" for famine relief.) Where a man could be hanged for poaching a rabbit and a woman for stealing a shilling's worth of shoes. (Not by accident did prosecution of the Game Laws intensify just as the landed classes developed their leisurely rituals of hunting and shooting.) Where, in the 1830s, of the 680,000 families of agricultural laborers, 300,000 were on poor-relief. (For union activity among such laborers, in Dorsetshire in 1834, the "Tolpuddle Martyrs" got seven years in a penal colony.) Where, in one direction out of Manchester, delinquents and dissidents got themselves "transported" to Australia; in another, troublemakers were conscripted as cannon fodder for the Napoleonic wars; and, in a third, slave ships sailed for America.

No wonder Mor identifies with a wounded eagle at the end of a rope, fed an occasional mouse, "crumpled into an undignified bundle of feathers, like a burst pillowcase in the snow." Some of this we got in passing in the nineteenth-century novel: from Harriet Martineau's *A Manchester Strike* and Frances Trollope's *Michael Armstrong: The Factory Boy;* from Dickens on Coketown, Kingsley in *Alton Lake* on tailoring sweatshops, Disraeli in *Conningsby* and *Sybil,* Elizabeth Gaskell in *Mary Barton* (so contemptuous of and terrified by Chartists under her bed), and Charlotte Brontë in *Shirley* (a fictionalized account of Cartwright's Rawfolds, sympathetic to the mill owner, appalled by the dirty lowlife drinkers, "down-draughts," and "bankrupts" who besieged him). There is a wonderful passage in George Eliot's *The Mill on the Floss*:

> But good society, floated on gossamer wings of light irony, is of very expensive production; requiring nothing less than a wide and arduous national life condensed in unfragrant, deafening factories, cramping itself in mines, sweating at furnaces, grinding, hammering, weaving under more or less oppression of carbonic acid — or else, spread over sheepwalks, and scattered in lonely houses and huts on the clayey or chalky corn-lands, where the rainy days look dreary. This wide national life is based entirely on emphasis — the emphasis of want, which urges it into all the activities necessary for the maintenance of good society and light irony . . .

But *The Rape of the Rose* as much resembles these nineteenth-century English "industrial novels" as Faulkner and Flannery O'Connor resemble network television movies in their Social Worker mode. As in a TV movie, so in the industrial novel, everything is made to come out right by goodwill, coincidence, and pluck. (In his late-twentieth-century novel *Nice Work,* David Lodge has his Marxist-feminist college instructor, Robyn, explain that the Industrial Novelists were incapable of resolving the ideological contradictions inherent in their own social position, because the very idea of revolution was unthinkable. So they took care of the problems of their characters by a fortuitous marriage, a miraculous inheritance, a sudden death, or emigration to Australia. *Nice Work*, by the way, concludes with a legacy *and* a marriage proposal *and* emigration.) Closer analogues are Thomas Flanagan's *The Year of the French* and John Berger's *Pig Earth*. In *The Rape of the Rose*, as in the dye vat in one of its satanic mills, we are saturated in brutish fact and vivid metaphor; as fast as the colors, so are the dooms. Strait is the jacket that history weaves, on such a power loom, for "More Grief."

Or is it? For the Luddites, Glyn Hughes reclaims a radical consciousness, since squandered or repressed. Mor Greave's hardly a mindless vandal, an aspect of mob mind and *ressentiment*, one of the great Fearful ("The brigands are coming!"), not even a Pugachev. He is, in fact, a lot more sophisticated than any of Eric Hobsbawm's "primitive rebels" or "social bandits"— cowboys, cossacks, *cangaceiros*, vaqueros, *haiduks*; Robin Hood, Zapata, and Macheath; Rob Roy, Dick Turpin, and Opportune Rain Sung Chiang—even if Mary the Scar perhaps anticipates the prostitutes of the Paris Commune. Although Himmelfarb tells us that if such men were reading, what they read were probably Gothics and Newgates, the "yellowbacks" and "silver forks" and penny dreadfuls, Mor Greave has read Plato, Plutarch, Shakespeare, and Rousseau. With him he carries a copy of Paine's *Common Sense*. From so many "old Jacks" (Jacobins) in the vicinity, he recognizes a liberty cap; he's heard of the Bastille. To his journal he confides: "The sufferings of the poor are not the effects of divine dispensation, but the offspring of wicked men and bad systems."

From Raymond Williams in *The Country and the City*, we know that dispossession started in England long before the spinning frame and power loom. The process of "enclosure," getting rid of open-field villages and common rights, began in the thirteenth century and reached the first of its peaks in the fifteenth and sixteenth, a "long process of conquest and seizure . . . land gained by killing, by repression, by political bargains." By the eighteenth century nearly half of all cultivated land was owned by five thousand families; in a population of perhaps eight million, four hundred families owned a quarter of the cultivated land. Instead of a peasantry, then: the tenant farmer, the wage laborer, agrarian capitalism, squirearchy, child abuse.

From Hobsbawm in *The Age of Revolution* (and from Hobsbawm and George Rude in *Captain Swing*), we know that the paternalism of this squirearchy breathed its last with the notorious Speenhamland system of 1785, whereby the social order of the villages would be preserved in its dependency by subsidizing low wages out of rates, on a scale calculated by the price of bread and the number of children. After which: an industrial capitalism red in tooth and claw, and the punitive Poor Laws of the 1830s. Those small farms surviving the Napoleonic wars failed by the thousands in the postwar depression. For England, besides Luddites, this meant what Hobsbawm calls "a form of collective bargaining by riot": the Pentridge and Grange Moor uprisings; the "Bread or Blood" demonstrations in East Anglia in 1816; the Ely riots, the Laborers' Revolt, and the "Captain Swing" campaigns of 1830; rick burnings and forced-food levies; suspension of Habeas Corpus and the imposition of martial law. Across the channel Émile de Giradin was warning readers of the *Journal des Debats*:

> Every manufacturer lives in his factory like the colonial planters in the midst of their slaves, one against a hundred, and the subversion of Lyons is a sort of insurrection of San Domingo. . . . The barbarians who menace society are neither in the Caucasus nor in the steppes of Tartary; they are in the suburbs of our industrial cities.

Mor Greave, before he hits the road, has a different point of view:

> Across the warp, his shuttle threaded the colors of a sunrise—a broad band of saffron yellow that faded into red. The market called for somber cloths, but he was symbolizing revolution. True to his symbol, everything around it was dark and shadowy: both the room and the

country beyond, out of the roots and stems of which is rose-and-yellow, unsaleable tints had been distilled., . . . He sat all day like a crow perched in a forest of strings and bits of wood.

From E. P. Thompson in *The Making of the English Working Class,* we hear for the first time that Luddism, far from "blind protest," was *"a quasi-insurrectionary movement,* which continually trembled on the edge of ulterior revolutionary objectives." Steeped in a long "industrial tradition," protected from informers by the support of their communities and "a working-class culture so opaque that it resisted all penetration," croppers, stockingers, and weavers undertook the finances and correspondence of a complex entity, communicated with the West Country, and sent delegates as far away as Ireland. Like Mor Greave, they'd read their Plato and their Paine; a few had even read Adam Smith. Beginning late in 1811, having pledged a dreadful oath, small bands of masked men attended by sentinels and couriers embarked upon a series of organized strikes against selected industrial targets, in the service of an agenda almost Chartist: a legal minimum wage, control of the "sweating" of women and children, arbitration, engagement by the "masters" to find work for skilled men made redundant by machinery, the prohibition of shoddy work, a right to open trade union combinations. At stake was more than the degradation of labor and the cheapening of product. Thompson explains:

> At issue was the "freedom" of the capitalist to destroy the customs of the trade, whether by new machinery, by the factory-system, or by unrestricted competition, beating-down wages, undercutting his rivals, and undermining standards of craftsmanship. . . . It requires an effort of imagination to understand that the "free" factory-owner or large hosier or cotton manufacturer, who built his fortune by these means, was regarded not only with jealousy but as a man engaging in immoral and illegal practices. The tradition of the just price and the fair wage lived longer among "the lower orders" than is sometimes supposed. They saw *laissez-faire,* not as freedom, but as "foul imposition." They could see no "natural law" by which one man, or a few men, could engage in practices which brought manifest injury to their fellows.

The midnight men who attacked Cartwright's mill at Raw-folds may have looked back to the guilds and forward to Chartism, but what they saw in both directions, says Thompson, was "an alternative political economy and morality to that of *laissez-faire.*"

Isn't this paleoromantic? Manual labor: left-nostalgia. It's easy enough to see why folks in Silicon Valley, on Route 128, at Boeing or General Dynamics, down home in the New South of robotized Toyota hatcheries, busy turning Poland into another Bolivia like the rest of their graduating class at Harvard Biz, your basic greedhead commodities trader and your basic Sanskrit-quoting nuclear physicist, would want to hide under the Barcalounger: The *Luddites* are coming! "They did not sow, neither did they reap," wrote Barbara Ehrenreich of the go-go 1980s, "but rather sat around pushing money through their modems in games known as 'corporate takeover' and 'international currency speculation.' " But how long has it been since any of us pushed anything more compelling through our modems than essays for *The Nation,* in games called "criticism"? From strawberry-picking stoop labor in my Southern California boyhood; a residuum stripper at an oil refinery; the tearing down of trees for a one-horse lumber mill in the San Bernardino mountains, the sawing of them into boards, the stacking of them to sweat out pitch, the hellhole to which we descended to burn up scraps, a strike for a better wage than seventy-five cents an hour; afflicting with a forklift the cronelike fairy-tale apple trees on a frosty New Hampshire morning where migrant pickers refused to let themselves be organized—from all this I ran away to college so that ever after *my hands are clean.* Nor am I alone in this fastidiousness.

How come those Webbed ducks of Fabian socialism, Sidney and Beatrice, never noticed that Luddites were the godfathers of the British Labour Party and the T.U.C.? How come John Booth and George Mellor never got the time of day from Marx and/or Engels? For Owenites, the steam engine was so thrilling they practically whistled it. Italian Futurism! Russian Constructivism! American Cyberpunk! Let them eat Babbage! Such a thralldom to the latest gizmos and their magical accessories, especially on the part of critics who can't change a tire and left-wing Five-Year-Planners, ought to give us pause and perplexity. Maybe because of guilt, I find in my files a copy of the radical sixties journal *democracy,* with an article in it by M.I.T. historian David F. Noble, called "Present Tense Technology," which can only be described as anguished.

According to Noble, Luddites "were perhaps the last people in the West to perceive technology in the present tense, and to act upon that perception." Actually on the battlefield of innovation, best situated at the point of production to grasp what it meant for their dignity and livelihoods, unencumbered "by any alien and paralyzing notion of technological progress," bothered less by gig mills and spinning jennies than by "the efforts of capital to restructure social relations and the patterns of production at their expense," seeing "not some inevitable unfolding of destiny but rather the political creation of a system of domination that entailed their undoing," well, they said no thanks. Ever since, insists Noble, "the idea of technology has lost its essential concreteness, and thus all reference to particulars of place and purpose, tactics and terrain":

> And without moorings in space, the disembodied idea has wandered adrift in time as well. Technological development has come to be viewed as an autonomous thing, beyond politics and society, with a destiny of its own which must become our destiny too. From the perspective of here and now, technological development has become the blind weight of the past on one hand, and the perpetual promise of the future on the other. Technological determinism—the domination of the present by the past—and technological progress—the domination of the present by the future—have combined in our minds to annihilate the technological present.

Pouget made the same anarcho-syndicalist point in 1900: "The worker will only respect machinery *on the day* when it becomes his friend, shortening his work, rather than as *today,* his enemy, taking away jobs, killing workers. . . . Workers have no systematic will to destroy apart from the aim of such destruction. If workers attack machinery it is not for fear or because they have nothing better to do, but because they are driven by imperious necessity." But of course, after 1938 in Spain, there weren't any more anarcho-syndicalists.

More Grief! Where are the Luddites when we need them? They're certainly not to be found among journalists who phone in their copy in order to cross a picket line in an invisible frame of mind. Nor among academics for whom the class struggle is a campus speech code. Nor among hackers who may blizzard our computer pixels with a cyberpunk fiction unremittingly dystopic but who are so goggled into future tripping in Virtual Reality that they're not about to mess with anybody's motherboard. I suppose the closest thing we've got these days to a Luddite is the ecoterrorist.

But I like to think of Mor in the present tense with someone like Jean Gump, the grandmother who went to prison for eight years for defacing a nuclear missile. From jail, Gump told Studs Terkel: "As inmates, we're property. We belong to Mr. Meese, we belong to the Bureau of Prisons. A month ago, a young woman had come here from another federal institution. She had been locked up for fourteen months, without seeing the light of day. On arriving here, she was so happy to be out in the sunlight, she lay down and got herself a sunburn. They wrote a shot— that's an incident report. The shot read: Destruction of government property." *This property was her skin, which she had burned.*

Using Mor Greave's sunrise colors, maybe it's time that more of us worked on our tans.

Part Three

MIXED MEDIA

All the News That Gives Me Fits

Actually, I still own *New York Times* stock—nonvoting, of course—having exercised my option to buy when I quit the paper in 1982, and having failed to dump the shares when I should have, before Black October 1987. I was interviewed by Ed Diamond for his book on the newspaper, *Behind The Times*, and he quotes me accurately, and he gets most of the things I know about mostly right, so I mostly trust him when he tells me something new. I am, in these pages, neither valorized nor vilified. When Diamond mentions my name to John Rothman, the Keeper of the *Times* Archives, Rothman sniffs: "Some people just aren't good *Times*men." And then he promptly edits himself: "Some people aren't good *organizational* men." I can live with that.

But more about my "brilliant, erratic" career as a "California hipster" and "Vietnam-era provocateur," my "depression and alcoholism," some other time. I'd rather jump on Diamond's book as though it were a trampoline. Eating! Nesting! Styles! Did you know that with the eager approval of his editors, Bryan Miller, the twice-weekly *Times* reviewer of restaurants, ran up American Express and Visa bills of $125,000 a year, not counting taxis?

There won't be a completely persuasive account of the *Times* until William Gaddis writes a novel about it in the form of a Joycean elephantiasis of an Editor's Note from A. M. Rosenthal or Max Frankel. Something like Norman Rush's *Mating* might also do—as if West Forty-third Street were Botswana and each new Executive Editor ordained in the no-smoking newsroom a utopian Tsau with windmills, rondavels, boomslangs, dung carts, abacus lessons, ceramic death masks, Anti-Imperialist Lamentations, "militant nostalgia," a Mother Committee, and an ostrich farm.

So far, Gay Talese has come closest, in *The Kingdom and the*

Power (1969), like Carlyle on the French Revolution. In the concluding pages of Talese, as the Southern gentlemen are tumbreled off to retirement or the guillotine, what rough beast do we see slouching? Abe Rossenthal, of course. But also "Punch" Sulzberger—greatness thrust upon him by the death of his father. Harrison Salisbury, as we might expect, is a lot more Russian in *Without Fear or Favor* (1980), full of black bread, white snow, silver domes, and firebirds: Rosenthal rampant, like a double-headed eagle, wondering behind his heraldic shield, "Why do people hate me so?" Joe Goulden, in *Fit to Print* (1988), is the Kitty Kelley and Rush Limbaugh of *Times* notaries, obsessed with sex and booze and leftist conspiracies, and flagrantly wrong on everything I know about. But for Goulden too, Rosenthal's most of the story, a Robespierre and a Rasputin and "the little boy on the center of the stage shouting for attention." Even Nan Robertson in *The Girls in the Balcony* (1992)—a history of women at the *Times* (and their class-action suit) about which I don't pretend to be impartial because it portrays me as behaving with more principle than I can remember or than is seemly—can't stop thinking about Abe, who was her friend, who did her wrong.

Ed Diamond would like to remind us that, while editors get most of the publicity, they are still hired help. Publishers run newspapers, because they like to and own them. It was Punch during the Abe era who made the important decisions, not only on the business side, selling off a corporate stake in cable TV for Sunbelt newspapers and special interest magazines and fleeing the city for suburbia and satellite editions of a national *Times*, but also on the editorial end, deciding after market research on a more user-friendly broadsheet and coming down hard, against his own editorial board, to endorse Daniel "Pat" Moynihan instead of Bella Abzug for the Senate in New York's 1976 Democratic primary—and it has been Punch's son, Arthur Ochs Sulzberger Jr., who made those decisions in the Max interregnum and the Lelyveld succession. Publishers propose and dispose of an Abe, a Max, a Scotty, and a Clifton. And the

Sulzbergers have fixed it so that the *Times* stays in the family at least through the middle of the twenty-first century.

But even Diamond can't keep his adjectives off Rosenthal—and not only because Abe gave him access to his archival papers when nobody else would. A Dostoyevsky novel needs its Crime and Punishment; a Father Zosima, a Grand Inquisitor, and an Underground Man; an Idiot and the Possessed. Max is too much a gentleman, waving his pipe instead of a sword. The Sulzbergers just aren't lurid enough for Restoration melodrama or even one of those prime-time TV soaps in which the dynastic rich are punished for their money by bad luck and bad sex. It's not, after all, as if they were Model "T" Fords, with the second Henry out to avenge his father, a hapless Edsel, at the expense of his grandfather, Henry I, the anti-Semitic crackpot, soybean fetishist, and hater of jazz and golf, while everyone else in the family descends into sex, sottishness, landgrab, megalomania, and Eurotrash. The Sulzbergers are, thank God, less thrilling.

This leaves Abe: a creature of passionate excess. Compared to the muddles of the Max Era—Patricia Bowman's "little wild streak" and her seventeen Palm Beach traffic tickets; Nancy Reagan, Maureen Dowd, and Frank Sinatra in bed together one Sunday morning on the front page—what Rosenthal did to Richard Eder, the drama critic, Ray Bonner, the Mozote reporter, Sydney Schanberg, the cityside columnist, and Richard Severo, the Elephant Man, not to mention Ada Louise Huxtable and A. H. Raskin, plus what he *didn't* do for women, blacks, and gays, is positively grand operatic. Once upon a time, he sang the Third Floor into Being like a Bruce Chatwin Aborigine, naming every ghost gum tree, cockatoo, and dingo in the outback. He was totemic. Now he writes a column people make fun of and consorts at a seventieth-birthday party / bar mitzvah with the likes of Saul and Gayfryd Steinberg, Robert and Georgette Mosbacher, Dr. and Henry Kissinger.

So there's a lot of Jerzy Kosinski and Betty Friedan in *Behind the Times*. (Abe, like Norman Mailer, is as loyal to his friends as a Mafia capo.) And a lot about AIDS coverage. (Diamond's at his meticulous best in arguing that this story, while the coverage for a variety of reasons was late in developing, finally got the attention it deserved. He is less persuasive on homophobia at the paper.) And inside stuff on everything from Abe's notorious "shit list" to the epic battle between editorial and advertising as if between warrior tribes of Pandavas and Kauravas four thousand years ago, throwing dice and juiced on soma, to determine whether Science or Fashion won the heart of a new Tuesday *Times*. We also learn that, since the Schanberg unpleasantness, an Op-Ed column no longer comes with lifetime tenure. Even Anna Quindlen had a three-year contract.

But something loftier troubles Diamond. The gray lady ain't what she used to be. Whether as a by-product of market research and unholy compromise between Ed and Ad, or because the new publisher is New Age and would like to be Downtown Hip, it's squishy. No longer the Paper of Record, it might as well be the *New York* magazine from which, in the seventies, it purloined service features and editorial talent. Everywhere you look: *trends*. And, in all those sections, even Sports, more *opinion*, a metastasis of columnists, a gush of yard goods. While only 8 percent of *Times* readers have household incomes of more than $100,000 a year, "Fashions of The Times" nonetheless devotes its glitzy self to upper-end designers like Yves St. Laurent, Karl Lagerfeld, and Calvin Klein. While Bryan Miller's salary and expense account added up to what it costs to maintain a bureau in Africa, his editor reassured him: "We get a helluva lot more bang for the buck out of the food column." Moreover, Diamond says, "the celebration of consumption in the new upscale sections inevitably weakened coverage of the unbeautiful city."

Is this true? I wonder. *Times* coverage of the Unbeautiful City has always been weak. My impression is that lately it's improved. A six-part daily means more features and more ads, but also more pages, in a fatter paper, with a bigger news hole. Sure, there's more sports "commentary," but there are also more stats. Nor, even if reader surveys favor them, is there anything wrong with the *idea* of so many Critic's Notebooks, though it would be nice if the critics actually had ideas. I don't mind Bernie Weinraub's actually reporting from Hollywood, so long as the paper maintains and publishes so many full-time critics, twice as many as the *Los Angeles Times* and the *Washington Post*. (But what caused the Saturday book review to disappear, like Poof the Magic Realist?) A new section on "Circuits" is at least as compelling as the old column on antiques. Do either steal space from hard news about Chicago, Detroit, Sarajevo, or Gdansk? Is there *less* metro coverage, or news from abroad, or guff from Washington? Certainly not that you'd notice in the plague of reporters after Rajiv Gandhi was assassinated, or Yugoslavia fell apart, or a deep-pore earthquake cleansing hit Joan Didion's Southern California.

Somebody else will have to do the figuring in column inches, because Diamond doesn't. He is, of course, a professor of journalism at NYU. What he really misses, among so many soft features, vagrant trends, meaningless polls, unintelligible charts, and lollipop thumbsuckers, is the appearance of impartial reporting. Just the facts ma'am. "Objectivity" in newspapers is something real to him, and this pre-Heisenberg faith is touching. I am weary, too, of a complacent postmodernism that insists there's no such thing as objective truth, linear progress, rational planning, standardized knowledge, coherent representation, or intelligent action; only spectacle, lifestyles, and language games, allegory and esthetics. But at all newspapers *someone* decides which story to cover, with what lead, for how long, after talking to and ignoring whom, and where to play it. These decisions are now and always have been subjective. Most subjective of all is: Whom do you trust? As Russell Baker tells us in *The Good Times* (1989): "No matter how dull, stupid, unfair, vicious or mendacious they might be, the utterances of the great were to be reported deadpan, with nary a hint that the speaker might be a dunce, a brute or a habitual liar. For a reporter to question the value of 'objective journalism' was worse than unthinkable. It was subversive. It was revolutionary."

Take a look at Baker's memoir. It's as friendly, diffident, and aw-shucks as his column. He tells us about his boyhood paper route, his college weekly at Johns Hopkins, his durance vile and giddy rise from police reporter to London bureau chief to White House correspondent for Baltimore's *Sun*; his abduction by Reston of the *Times* to cover the State Department and the Senate; and his annunciation as "Observer," so impossibly young and so impossibly charming. He tells us all this as if talent had nothing to do with any of it—just luck and a mother who nagged and a winning way with the surrogate daddies who urged him ever upward, an inky angel.

Of course, the story is more complicated. Longtime readers know that a Baker column, like a story by Cheever or Gogol, can turn on them and bite. He has his doubts, and between anecdotes about John Foster Dulles, Estes Kefauver, LBJ, and Evelyn Waugh, he hints at them: "Only a fool expects the authorities to tell him what the news is." And: "Bad taste is almost always the excuse editors fell back on when they lacked a persuasive reason to suppress news they didn't want to print." Looking in his mirror, he sometimes sees "a man content to wear out his hams sitting in the marble corridors of power waiting for important people to lie to him, a comicbook intellectual, a human pomposity dilating on his constitutional duty, a drum-thumper on a demagogue's bandwagon, a member of the claque for this week's fashion." He knows too many reporters who, for reasons of ego and social advancement, are also "players," much too buddy-buddy with the pols they are supposed to cover, and too many editors and publishers who look the other way in exchange for scoops and dinner-party invitations. They are in danger, he says, "of demeaning themselves and their papers, and betraying their readers by becoming propagandists. It's hard to become a player and stay in the business without ending up contemptible. Or a columnist."

You won't believe how many of us were promised Russell Baker's column, if we only waited patiently till he retired. Next year in Jerusalem . . .

*   *   *

The *Times* is the best newspaper in the United States today the way Victor Hugo was the best poet in nineteenth-century France. That is, when he was asked who the best French poet in the nineteenth century was, André Gide replied with a sigh, "Victor Hugo, *helas!*" But it *is* a newspaper. It's not some secret society of the Bavarian Illuminati, a Macedonian phalanx of Alexander Ragtime Gladboys, or the *Sefer ha-bahir* of the esoteric Kabbalists. Nor are its West Forty-third Street headquarters, in the middle of the Times Square redevelopment project it has so vigorously championed on its editorial page, some kind of Lubyanka, Berchtesgaden, Bayreuth, or Bomarzo, whatever we might have imagined if we only subscribed to Accuracy in Media on the right or *Lies of Our Times* on the left. "The *Times* is a centrist institution," Arthur Gelb told me when I quit on him, "and *you* are not a centrist." True enough. But the center had moved since 1967, when I'd been hired right out of the antiwar movement. And with Reagan's election in 1980, it seemed to me that this center had set up shop in a Knut Hamsun novel. And where did that leave those of us who were still reading early Dos Passos or the latest Günter Grass?

On the shit list, that's where. Those of us who go over the wall—who leave the Catholic Church, the Communist Party, or the *New York Times*—usually decide at last to jump because of something small. You may have swallowed a whole history of whoppers, but there's a fatigue to your faith. Without any warning the elastic snaps and you are hurled out of the closed system into empty space, and your renunciation, arrived at by increments, looks capricious. In my case I thought the brand-new *Vanity Fair* would be a serious magazine, as did many of my friends, and so we entered the halls of Condé Nast like the children who followed Stephen of Vendôme south to Marseille in 1212, expecting the Mediterranean to part like the Red Sea, allowing us to pass over to the Promised Land. We were sold instead into slavery in Egypt. Well, it wasn't *that* bad. But when we leap over the wall, we always imagine that *they,* whoever *they* are, will love us more in the outside world. They'll love us just as much, or as little, as we serve their interest.

It's crucial to remember this in thinking about the *Times*. From Talese, Salisbury, Baker, Robertson, Diamond, and even Goulden, we get fitful portraits of a corporate culture whose wage slaves are expected to internalize certain norms. And they do. But these are the norms of any other mainstream news organization, not to mention quite a few law firms, colleges, and foundations. They put on self-important airs. Max Frankel's management style by every account was kindlier than Abe Rosenthal's — creative violence! — but both were paid to superintend a bureaucracy that sees itself as a fourth branch of government, with its own pomp, protocols, PR flacks, foreign policy, and official secrets, lacking only its own anthem and a helicopter beanie. It may occur to you and me that, since we know in advance the authorities will lie to even as they leak on us, we ought to conceive of ourselves as their adversaries, not as their chums and peers.

But such a feisty notion belongs to an older idea of newspapering as a craft or trade instead of a club of professional perkies worried about summer homes, Cycladic vacations, Sullivanian analysis, engraved invitations to Truman Capote parties, and private schools for their sensitive children — back when our fingernails were dirty and we knew the romance of ink and lived in the high-school print shop and could read the type upside down, and the belching machine seemed somehow to connect brain and word, muscle and idea, hot lead and cool thought; before we got into the information-commodities racket, where we have more in common by way of class angles with Henry Kravis and Henry Kissinger than we do with papermakers and deliverymen; after which our real story is ourselves, at the Century Club or Elaine's or a masked ball charity scam — Alex Solzhenitsyn, Oscar de la Renta, and Leona Helmsley invite you to Feel Bad about the Boat People at the Museum of Modern Art — with plenty of downtime left over to make it to Yankee Stadium, where Boss Steinbrenner will lift us up by our epaulets to his skybox to consort with such presbyters of the Big Fix as Roy Cohn and Donald Trump, and you can't tell the pearls from the swine.

From Bill Greider in *Who Will Tell the People?* (1992), we learn that Thomas Friedman, the *Times* correspondent then covering the State Department, played tennis with the Secretary of State; that Brit Hume, covering the White House for ABC, played tennis with George Bush; that Rita Beamish of the Associated Press jogged with George; that George and Barbara stopped by and were videotaped at a media dinner party in the home of Albert Hunt, the *Wall Street Journal* bureau chief, and his wife, Judy Woodruff, then of the *MacNeil/Lehrer Newshour*, now on CNN; that one reason Andrea Mitchell, who covered Congress for NBC, showed up so often in the presidential box at the Kennedy Center was that she just happened to live with Alan Greenspan, the chairman of the Federal Reserve Board. From Eric Alterman in *Sound and Fury: The Washington Punditry and the Collapse of American Politics*, we hear about a George Will still ghostwriting speeches for Jesse Helms during his trial period as a *Washington Post* columnist, and prepping Ronald Reagan for one of his debates with Jimmy Carter, and then reviewing Reagan's performance the day after in his column, and later on writing a speech Reagan delivered to the House of Commons. About Morton Kondracke and Robert Novak collecting thousands of dollars from the Republican Party for advice to a gathering of governors. About John McLaughlin settling one sexual harassment suit out of court, facing the possibility of at least two more, and nevertheless permitting himself to savage Anita Hill on his own *McLaughlin Report*. About Henry Kissinger, on ABC television and in *his* syndicated column, defending Deng Xiaoping's behavior during the Tiananmen Square massacre without telling us that Henry and his consultancy firm had a substantial financial stake in a Chinese status quo. Objectivity, my tricorn . . .

We got a chuckle out of Bobby Ray Inman's Checkers speech, but what *was* Bill Safire up to, on his back channel to the late Bill Casey, lobbying for Ariel Sharon, if not conducting his own foreign policy? And what on earth are we to make of Inman's assertion that, during his tenure as NSA director in the Carter Administration, *Times* editors called him at night at press time to clear stories that might have national security implications: "There were lots of stories that I let go through," says Inman, "even though people didn't like it. There were others where the editors made the decisions to alter the terms of the story to protect intelligence sources and method." And, he says, they went on calling him after he left Washington for Austin, Texas, in 1982, "because they couldn't get an answer from the Government."

What this "center" does is situate itself in the middle of wherever the heavy-hitting action is. At such a location, a Molly Ivins will last about a minute, failing to internalize the decorous norms. A Dick Eder is hounded out of town, on his way to a Pulitzer Prize with another newspaper. Even a Hilton Kramer eventually quits, though he just can't help himself, slinking back each week in the *New York Post* to look under the bed, like Pat Buchanan, for a Marlon Riggs who might mess with his new criterion. And whatever these writers actually write will itself be Osterized by editors who know at Bomarzo just what's really happening in El Salvador, the way the deskbound decisionmakers playing kneesies at the State Department know better than the area experts and career diplomats who have somehow gone native and fallen in love with their client states. Hell, a reporter isn't even permitted to be a citizen of any other nation but the *Times,* to go to abortion rallies or endorse political candidates or show up more than once a season on a television program, any more than a *Times* critic is allowed these days to belong to an awards-giving professional society like the New York Film Critics Circle or the National Book Critics Circle. Not belonging to a union is obviously next.

Diamond devotes an interesting chapter to the *New York Times Book Review,* discovering no Watergates, not even a Whitewater, but missing the important point. The problem is not the occasional scandal—worse things happened on my watch than he reports here—but the *TBR*'s very commitment to judiciousness. If ever a lonely book needed a friend, it's at the *Times* on publication day. Whenever I'm asked if I miss the paper, I reply that I miss it every time I love a book, because *Times* readers will go out and buy one if you talk them into it. But talking them into it no longer seems part of the paper's mission. There's no drive to discover, nor passion to persuade. They have appointed themselves the hall monitors of an unruly schoolboy culture: This one gets a pass to go to the lavatory; that one must sit in a corner wearing a dunce cap. They hear only the bells in their own heads. Whether the fish in the barrel they shoot are rainbow trout, they're too lofty to care. It's all product. Nobody has explained to these solid citizens of the *center* that there is more honor out there on the margins, even in writing a bad book, than in any review ever written, or a collection of all of them, which would amount to little more than a food-chain chart on parasitology. Diamond likewise inside-infos us about theater critic turned Op-Ed columnist Frank Rich, his wife Alex Witchel, and what Robert Brustein did to their happy marriage in the pages of *The New Republic*. Well, I liked *Two Shakespearean Actors*, too. I even liked *Metro*, and when I went backstage at the Polish rock musical during intermission, the producer wanted to know what Frank Rich sees when he looks in a mirror. What he sees, of course, is the *Times*. That's what they all see. And the Broadway culture itself conspires at what it Richly Deserves. The producers, the theater owners, and the play-going public permit themselves to be spellbound and hypnotized by a single pair of eyes and ears, in a single seat or at a single winking VDT, just because his opinion is published in the newspaper that actually endorsed Al D'Amato, that picklehead, for the United States Senate. I mean, we are accustomed to seeking at least a second opinion before we eat at a Thai restaurant or buy a condom.

The *Times* and the reading public have a codependency problem. So do the *Times* and its refugees, those Boat People who left West Forty-third Street and can't stop screaming in their dreams about it. And so do the *Times* and its critics, left and right, who expect it somehow to be something it isn't, to represent their own politics, to do their own heavy-lifting historical work, the way so many of us waited around for the Supreme Court to ordain from on high our notions of social justice instead of hitting the streets and rubbing up a movement, some continental drift out of the abrading of tectonic plates. "Newspapers like the *Times,*" Ed explains, "have captured a demographic segment of the population highly desired by the advertisers. . . . Corporate America then pays the *Times*— and CBS, *Newsweek,* et al.—for the privilege of talking to that audience." That's what they're in business for, giving the advertisers what they want, like the "magnetized water" dispensed by Anton Mesmer in the dark days before the French Revolution to cure the credulous of their "disequilibrium" while ethereal music lisped on a glass harmonica.

One last thought about the Boat People. According to Goulden in *Fit to Print,* Abe Rosenthal was so mad at me for publishing in the *Times Book Review* in 1971 Neil Sheehan's long essay on war crimes in Vietnam that I "was bounced to the lesser job of daily critic." Well, maybe he was mad, but he never said a word to me. Far from being "bounced," I stuck around as *TBR* editor for another five years, and when I tried to quit, it took a year for them to agree on a replacement. I hated being a boss, I hated not writing, and my marriage was falling apart. And it was Abe, amazingly, who found room in his news budget for me, gave me a fancy title, and let me write about books, movies, sports, and anything else except politics. We had our noisy differences, but when in my life there were enormous changes at the last minute, he went out of his way to help.

Similarly, I'm said by Goulden—who never called me—to "dislike" Artie Gelb. In fact, it's hard *not* to like Artie Gelb; he's your goofy brother. He gave me a column, and I thanked him for it in a collection of them. Then he took it away. Then he dreamed up another one. Sure, like Abe, he had a memory hole

down which a lot of what I thought I knew disappeared overnight, and he seemed sometimes to invent a brand-new substitute truth the very next morning for breakfast. But I never
doubted *he* believed it, and, hey, this is the big leagues. Love it
or leave it. So I left it. It occurs to me that, if we are to be genuinely fair, all the Boat People will have to write novels that somehow deal with Abe's ferocious complexity and Artie's goofy
swoops, as though they were—and maybe they even wanted to
be, and maybe *we* even wanted them to be—our fathers. Oedipus! Peter Pan! Beyond this pop psych, there's something else.
"We made you!" they screamed at me, as if they'd published
what I wrote out of the kindness of their hearts, as if we hadn't
been *even* every day. I now wonder whether there wasn't about
our servitude elements of an abusive marriage—tantrums, fists,
and fear; excuses, apologies, and denials; dependency and self-
loathing; battered wives and battered writers. From such wed-
lock, the only thing to do is walk. Like Patsy Cline after the
Grand Ole Opry, we can always go back to the honky-tonks and
sing our old sad songs.

Editors Anonymous

I've always run poker games and whores and crime. You make the reality in court and press. I just ride and play the cards that were pushed on me to play. Mass killer, it's a job, what can I say.

(Charles Manson to Paul Krassner)

Like Willie Morris, Paul Krassner also lost a job. In fact, he lost several, including his post as movie critic for *Cavalier* magazine when he reviewed *M*A*S*H* as if it had been a Busby Berkeley musical called *Gook Killers of 1970*; and a radio show in San Francisco where, calling himself Rumpleforeskin, he didn't fit in with "formatted progressive rock." But the job I'm talking about is editor of *Hustler,* after six months in 1978, on the occasion of his "Last All-Meat Issue," "a six-page menu of nude women, spread with appropriate condiments, mustard or tomato sauce—as if they were *actual* pieces of meat, superimposed on various dishes, a frankfurter or a plate of spaghetti and meat balls." This sounds to me surprisingly like the last issue of *Harper's* under Willie Morris, which featured Norman Mailer's *Prisoner of Sex.* But then we are talking about little boys who never grew up, and their Boys' Own Books.

Like John Cowles Jr. who got rid of Willie, Larry and Althea Flynt who got rid of Paul came to problematic ends. Cowles, Willie tells us, descended into est, nude dancing, and Primal Scream. After Althea, a narcotics addict, drowned in her bathtub, Larry got himself a penile implant and a mail-order bride. Willie went back to Yazoo City, Mississippi. Paul was on the next plane to Egypt with Ken Kesey for a concert in front of the pyramids by the exceedingly Grateful Dead.

Willie's memoir, *New York Days,* got lots more ink than Paul will get for *his* memoir, *Confessions of a Raving Unconfined Nut: Misadventures in the Counter-Culture.* This is because Willie takes his Big City disappointments very seriously indeed, and so did the Manhattan reviewer types who dilated so much on their grudges in the mirrors of their slicks. Whereas Paul is a nomad instead of an opportunist, on acid instead of the tricycle of his career, a citizen of the limbic wastes. Too bad, though. Willie's best line in *New York Days* refers to his busted buddy-bond with Norman Podhoretz, after The Pod went right-wing neocon. (He quotes Oscar Levant on Doris Day: "I knew her before she was a virgin.") Whereas Paul . . . well, *Nut* is chockablock with nuggets, from the zinger to the set piece. It's all performance art, like the sixties. On the one sly hand, he will tell us: "Harmonic Convergence was just a bunch of virgins getting together to play their harmonicas." On the other hand, he turns Groucho Marx on to LSD. They trip out to Bach's Cantata No. 7. Groucho says, "I'm supposed to be Jewish, but I was seeing the most beautiful visions of Gothic cathedrals. Do you think Bach *knew* he was doing that?" To which Paul replies: "I don't know. I was seeing beehives and honeycombs myself."

But, who can trust him? He says Bobby Kennedy, the night he was murdered, had dinner with Roman Polanski and Sharon Tate. That Chandler Brossard not only ghostwrote Norman Vincent Peale's advice column in *Look* magazine but also made up the questions. That Carlos Castaneda was "one of the actors who got a blow job in *Deep Throat.*" All three or none of these things could be true, but the guy who says so also published in *The Realist* what he called "The Parts Left Out of [William Manchester's] Kennedy Book," reporting an act of necrophilia on Air Force One by new President Lyndon Baines Johnson on the exit wound in John Kennedy's corpse, as witnessed by Jackie—the same guy who, in *Chic* magazine, faked an interview with Nancy Reagan in which she confessed to having an affair with LA Chief of Police Daryl Gates.

Paul is the City College psych major who told a conference on "Media and the Environment" how to tell the difference between "news" and "dreaming": When you see something you don't know whether to believe, you should flap your arms like wings. If you seem then to be flying, it's a dream. This has been Paul's advice to himself since he was seven years old and gave up a career as a concert violinist, playing Vivaldi in black velvet shorts at Carnegie Hall in 1939, to become a standup comic, invent "Yippie," and correspond with Charlie Manson about Scientology.

Most of the reviews of Willie's book, like most of the book itself, were devoted to his days at *Harper's*. So be it. The only revenge a writer's got on the bean counters and back stabbers who buy and sell him like a yo-yo or a pork-belly future is to give us a book that pins them through their buggy little eyes down to a page of style, impales them on a consummate disdain. Even if Willie and his boys drank too much at Empire Chinese and ate too often at Elaine's, any magazine that in five years managed to publish Mailer on the armies of the night, Halberstam on the best and the brightest, Irving Howe on the New York intellectuals, and Seymour Hersh on the My Lai massacre was doing wonderfully well, thank you, no matter what they thought in Minneapolis. But Willie, whose sweet tooth for the elegiac is notorious, also has some nice passages on his Oxford days as a Rhodes Scholar, where his best friend was Dennis Potter, The Singing Detective. And on Manhattan as a ghostly moonscape where the anonymous dead stare up at you, their own ambitions dashed, "only fossils for the forensic anthropologists." And on poor Ralph Ellison being called in the late sixties an Uncle Tom, at Grinnell College in bloodthirsty *Iowa*. And on the last sad days of an angry Max Ascoli, selling *The Reporter* subscription list to Cowles, "the only man in my whole life," says Willie, "who ever refused to shake my hand." And, most movingly, on marriage, the first casualty of vaulting ambition, after which the liver and then the ego. As if possessed by Dostoyevsky, he stands outside an Upper East Side building waiting to stalk his wife's psychiatrist as once upon a time he'd followed Greta Garbo.

Willie and Paul both drop names. So should they. Why else leave the provinces, if not to meet Bacall and Groucho? Why else read memoirs? But except for Joe Heller, Norman Mailer, and Abbie Hoffman, the names they drop are very different. I won't tell you Willie's names—the Elaine's, Hamptons, *Commentary*, and Plimpton crowds—because they already know who they are and they shouldn't be encouraged. Paul's names include another sort of sixties, from Lyle Stuart who gave him his start in journalism to William Gaines at *Mad*, Hugh Hefner at *Playboy*, and Lenny Bruce in chains; Emmett Grogan of the Diggers and Timothy Leary in Algeria; Bob Dylan, Joan Baez, John Lennon, and Jerry Garcia; Ed Sanders, Cass Elliot, Dennis Banks, and Dick Gregory. Paul got around more. Not long before Squeaky Fromme took her potshot at Jerry Ford, Paul was chatting her up in a bathroom while she soaked. Minutes before Valerie Solanas tried to waste Warhol, Paul refused to have lunch with her. If, in *New York Days*, the sixties seem a bit abstract and canned, it may be because Willie lacked this . . . Left Coast brain. A Left Coast California-dreaming sort of brain is downwardly mobile and more inclusive, into the rabbit-hole with Patty Hearst and Harvey Milk. Just ask Alice. You can be sure that if Paul had met Alice Walker in Mississippi in the late sixties, on the eve of the publication of her first novel, he'd have importuned an article immediately. Willie didn't ask Alice. Willie seems not to have hobbed the knob with too many women writers.

I'm not saying *The Realist* in either of its incarnations—from 1958 till 1974, and from 1985 through at least last month—was *I. F. Stone's Weekly*. I am saying I'm glad that we cleared up a misunderstanding at Abbie Hoffman's memorial service, restoring me to Krassner's readership in time to make up for the low blow of Tina Brown's lopping me off *The New Yorker* comp list after twenty-three years. The former *Ramparts* "society columnist" has always been generous. Half his first *Cavalier* paycheck went to a Lenny Bruce in dire straits. His salary at *Playboy* helped support Bill Baird's free birth-control clinic. Proceeds from sales of his infamous FUCK COMMUNISM! poster paid for Robert Scheer's round-trip ticket to Vietnam. Besides running a one-man underground abortion referral service, he also subsidized remedial reading programs and a Lower East Side judo center. Before and after the sixties, he was a participatory democrat.

Well, yes, performance art. When, on election night in 1988, Hunter S. Thompson showed up two hours late at the Ritz, waving a rifle and wearing a rubber Richard Nixon mask, we were entitled to wonder whether the act had worn a little thin, if wild Borks weren't waiting for us in the mean American Bush. And when Ken Kesey, not long ago in *Further Inquiry,* had a chance and failed to rethink the reefer madness of his "wine and bongo time," during which one Merry Prankster flipped out and ran naked "into the goatherds, raving in thorny despair," after which the rest of them dumped her in a Houston loony bin and rolled on giggling into their Day-Glo night, well, we were entitled to wonder if, deep down in their Primal Tripping, they had any communal politics or elemental decency at all, any more common sense than God gave a tractor. Who's Tom Wolfe, if not a right-wing Warhol? Look where the vapors took Mailer.

As for the East Coast (Elaine's) brain: In these same sixties, *The New Yorker* was a better magazine than *Harper's,* and *Esquire* at least an equal, and the *New York Review* more audacious. *National Review* discovered more new writers at the beginning of the decade, as would *Rolling Stone* at the end. A wily and parsimonious Victor Navasky was about to take over *The Nation,* and some of us kicked up some trouble, too, at the *Times Book Review.* Fellows (and females) as fine as Willie will always eventually be dumped on by people like Cowles, as was Willie's buddy Bill Moyers at *Newsday;* his competitor Robert Manning, by Mort Zuckerman, at *The Atlantic;* Terry McDonnell, by Hearst, at *Esquire;* almost everyone who has ever worked for Si Newhouse, from William Shawn to Grace Mirabella; even Ed Murrow at CBS. In every one of our paternal institutions, brilliant young men find surrogate fathers and imagine, in this relationship of privilege and patronage and protection, that they can go on being brilliant on their own terms forever. But in a corporate culture, we *aren't* fathers and sons. We are landlords and tenants, owners and pets. It shouldn't surprise the brilliant young men, and yet it always surprises the brilliant young men, when the party's over and the pets are put to sleep.

Flap your arms if you think you're dreaming.

American Cassandra

In her prime, in the late 1930s, the syndicated columnist Dorothy Thompson was called a "breast-beating Boadicea," a "wet nurse of destiny," "the Clara Barton of the plutocrat in pain," "the Florence Nightingale of the wounded Tory intellect," and "our self-appointed anti-fascist Joan of Arc." According to H. L. Mencken, "She frightens me. . . . She looks like Hindenburg as a young man." To John Hersey, she seemed "an over-powering figure in a Wagnerian opera, a Valkyrie, deciding with careless pointing of her spear who should die on the battlefield." Alice Roosevelt Longworth said she was "the only woman in history who had her menopause in public and made it pay." And one of her own husbands, the Nobel-winning novelist Sinclair Lewis, told her: "You . . . you are . . . a . . . pudding . . . a bread pudding . . . made of the divine host."

Gee, they never said any of those things about Walter Lippman, with whom she alternated every other day on the front page of the second section of the New York *Herald Tribune*. And she was just as serious as Lippman about international affairs. And she'd actually done more homework, on foot in Central Europe. And on the most important story of her time, the Nazi madness, she was prescient and fierce—predicting not only that Czechoslovakia would fall after Austria, and Poland would follow Czechoslovakia, but also that surprise twist in Soviet foreign policy, the Hitler-Stalin pact. She was, moreover, the only American newspaper columnist of any consequence to fear for the fate of Europe's Jews. (Not once, in his thousands of columns, could Lippman ever bring himself to mention the death camps.)

But Thompson, however extraordinary, was a woman; and the way our culture chose to deal with her success was to make fun of her. Sinclair Lewis made fun of her in his suffragette novel, *Ann Vickers*; and again, as Winifred Homeward, the

Talking Woman, in *Gideon Planish*. Garson Kanin made fun of her in *Woman of the Year,* in which a highfalutin Katharine Hepburn was cut down to size by Spencer Tracy's sportswriter. Elmer Rice made so much fun of her *and* Sinclair Lewis in the original version of *Cue for Passion* that lawyers insisted on a rewrite. Even Lippman wrote his wife: "Did you ever realize how much Dorothy is like the Statue of Liberty? Made of brass. Visible at all times to all the world. Holding the light aloft, but always the same light. . . . Capable of being admired, but difficult to love."

After all this fun was made—after the *Herald Tribune* fired her because she supported FDR instead of Wilkie in 1940; after the New York *Post* dropped her because she was deemed too soft on postwar Germany and insufficiently supportive of Zionism in the Middle East; after three marriages, all those books, an ill-fated Broadway play that cost her $30,000, a script on Alexander Hamilton that Hollywood never produced, and, at the end of her career, the embarrassing earth-mother essays for *Ladies' Home Journal*—our culture chose to forget her. If she's shown up at all in recent decades, it's been in walk-on or supporting roles, in Mark Schorer's biography of Lewis, Ronald Steel's biography of Lippman, and Richard Kluger's history of the *Herald Tribune.*

From this mockery and amnesia Peter Kurth determines to rescue her. He's a prickly advocate, supportive and exasperated. His book goes on forever without arriving at any thesis but the "self-creation" of a heroine "sprung from nowhere." But *American Cassandra* nevertheless enthralls. In his passion to pin down gossamer wings of fact and to abolish internal contradictions, Kurth is assisted by Thompson herself from beyond the grave. She wouldn't stop scribbling. There are millions of published words to construe; thousands of remarkable letters, many never mailed; and a diary astonishing in its candor. The result is a Portrait of a Lady telling us everything about sex, money, and that brute face of the world Henry James wished not to know. It should make a terrific television miniseries.

Late in life she confessed, "I've always wanted to be blond—blond and kittenish." Imagine her, instead, in an upstate New York turn-of-the-century childhood, brown-braided, sturdy, freckled; a reader of Job, Dickens, Shakespeare, and *Leaves of Grass*; a Welsh immigrant clergyman's daughter. The daughter remembered the clergyman as "sublimely innocent," "a born poet" who "could pray a bird off a tree." She also recalled "a childhood untouched by neurosis," and so it may have been, at least till her mother died of a botched abortion performed by Dorothy's own grandmother *without* her mother's knowledge. The "born poet" remarried. The new stepmother wasn't so much wicked as hypochondriacal—"with an allergy to children." One Christmas she gave Dorothy a package containing a baby's bottle and a card: "Merry Christmas to a cry-baby." Dorothy rebelled and, at age fourteen, was kicked into exile. She spent five years in Chicago, where a couple of aunts taught her to do her hair, an English professor at a junior college for "the poor but proud" encouraged her literary ambitions, and she was the only female in the debating society. Syracuse offered a scholarship.

"It was a legend at Syracuse for many years that a date with Dorothy Thompson had meant a walk in the moonlight and a talk about Hegel." From stuffing envelopes at the Buffalo headquarters of the New York State Suffrage Party, she graduated to "organizer" and hit the road to live on fried steak, speak standing on farm wagons and meet, besides "large groups of working and immigrant women," factory workers, socialists, anarchists, "and a host of Jewish intellectuals." When suffrage won in New York in 1917 by 94,000 votes, she was off—first, to Greenwich Village, where she worked for an ad agency; and then to Cincinnati, starting up family-hygiene and nutrition programs for the poor. The mayor of Cincinnati thought that she was one of those "Bolsheviks," pushing "violence, pacifism, free-love and other obnoxious ideas."

At twenty-five, she was still a virgin, though an older woman had called her "a daughter of the Gods" and written her a hymn of praise. At twenty-seven, having published articles in the *Times,* the *Sun,* and the *Tribune,* she set sail for London, wanting to see the Russian Revolution for herself. Her father, wonderfully, advised her: "Because you are obliged to earn your own living, it will not always be possible for you to remain a lady. But I pray you, Dorothy—please promise me, that you will always remain a gentleman."

Kurth deals simultaneously with the woman and the career. I don't have to. Forget, for a minute, the woman. The journalist found herself, on that boat, with Zionists on their way to a conference on Palestine. Immediately she wrote about it. Her first scoop was an interview with leaders of the Sinn Fein rebellion in Ireland—including MacSwinney just before he starved himself to death. In Paris she wrote publicity for the Red Cross at a penny a line, while covering in Rome a metalworker's strike. In Vienna, a "dark and rotting place," "a city of dread," she interviewed everybody from Trotsky and Freud to Atatürk and, in 1922, wore a fur coat to her first revolution. Her circle included Brecht, Schönberg, Adolf Loos, and Oskar Kokoschka. In Prague she talked to Beneš and Masaryk and scooped the world on the Emperor Karl's risible attempt to seize the Hungarian throne. In Berlin in 1926—*Caligari,* Piscator, Expressionism, Orientalism, Nazism, jazz, and drugs—she socialized with Kurt Weill, Lotte Lenya, Alma Mahler, Klaus and Erika Mann, Maxim Gorky, and Albert Einstein.

In one breathless year, Thompson jumped from freelancing for the New York *Post* and the *Christian Science Monitor* to stringing for the International News Service to covering Austria, Hungary, Yugoslavia, Czechoslovakia, Rumania, Greece, and Turkey for the Philadelphia *Public Ledger.* The joke among her lazier peers in the press corps went like so: "Have you heard? Dorothy Thompson got into town at noon." "Good God, what happened at one o'clock?" The same correspondents, after a long Vienna night of schnapps, voted her first in a contest to determine "whose brains, among all those assembled there, would, if removed and pickled, make the best paperweight."

Picture this, in 1926: Revolution breaks out in Poland, Thompson's at the opera, and the banks are closed. So she knocks at night on Freud's door, borrows some money, and hops the next train to Warsaw. In 1927 she went to Russia with Theodore Dreiser. In 1928 she was back in New York, at the Algonquin.

I'm leaving out a marriage or two, a house in Italy, and a child. The career took her back to Europe in 1930–31 from Stockholm to Berlin, where she interviewed and despised Adolf Hitler ("the perverter of Nietzsche," "the champion of the blond beast"), and warned her readers that "unless things change radically, there will be war in Europe within the decade, before the 1930s are out. And I've been where it will start." After lecturing all over the U.S. on fascism, she returned to Germany in 1934 to look at the pretty flags: "They hung from all the houses . . . bright red with a black swastika in a white circle in the middle, and sometimes they hung from the second storey to the ground. They gave the streets an odd Chinese look." At a summer camp for Hitler Youth, she saw a banner: "YOU WERE BORN TO DIE FOR GERMANY!" Hitler himself expelled her from the Third Reich, "for the crime of blasphemy."

I'm leaving out affairs with H. R. Knickerbocker, Edgar Mowrer, John Gunther (maybe), and an actor who wore a hair net playing tennis. What next happened to the career, in 1936, was that Helen Rogers Reid, who ran the *Herald Tribune* while her husband drank, decided to hire Thompson as a thrice-weekly "On the Record" columnist. By 1940, she had seven million readers. She wrote in bed, in longhand, chain-smoking Camels, having spent the night before on Central Park West consulting a brain trust of Morris Ernst, Frances Perkins, Harry Hopkins, David Sarnoff, Christian Gauss from Princeton, and Max Ascoli of *The Reporter.* She was against Social Security, the WPA, organized labor, Roosevelt's court-packing plan, and the isolationist Charles Lindbergh (a "somber cretin"). Of the quarter-million words she wrote between 1938 and 1940, not counting her NBC radio program and her lecture series, three fifths were devoted to attacking Hitler and the cowards who sustained him.

In 1939, in England to address the House of Commons, she had lunch with Nancy Astor and dinner with H. G. Wells; went to the movies with Anthony Eden and spent the weekend with Winston Churchill. In New York, on her way to speak to Phi Beta Kappa, she stopped in at Madison Square Garden to heckle a rally of the Bund; storm troopers muscled her out the door. When a friend, the German refugee writer Ernst Toller, hanged himself in May 1939 at the Mayflower Hotel, Thompson told a PEN Congress:

> They will say that Hitler killed him. That is true enough. But commend him not to hate who had in him no steely power to hate. His fate was to love the world and mankind, and most unhappily. . . . Being a poet, he was afflicted—with nerves and imagination. . . . He looked upon the world with torn-open, incredulous eyes. They remained to the end incredulous eyes. They looked eagerly for beauty, serenity, dignity, justice, truth. What they saw appalled them. Toller was appalled to death.

I'm leaving out some lesbianism. She also predicted Pearl Harbor. From the war, when at last she got it, she hoped for a "rational reasonable peace," not the "insanity" of "unconditional surrender." This made her suddenly "pro-Germany" to *Post* readers, as her sympathy for displaced Arabs and her membership in the CIA-funded American Friends of the Middle East made her suddenly "anti-Semitic." She was for the United Nations, against atom bombs, and otherwise in the postwar period a conventional Cold Warrior, unless you count a vote in 1948 for the socialist Norman Thomas. She called McCarthyism "childish," but endorsed Congressional investigations into "subversive" activities, and had her muddle-minded doubts about free speech in "dangerous times." She managed to admire, simultaneously, Douglas MacArthur and J. Robert Oppenheimer. She found nothing new at all in Simone de Beauvoir's *The Second Sex*.

I'm leaving out the Dexedrine, the Bennies, the drinking, the flying saucers, and the commune in Vermont. On the long curve of her decline, she returned to the faith of her father, and something more mystical, a final Tree Goddess stage of advising readers of the *Ladies' Home Journal*: "A claim on the moon should be staked out, it seems to me, by the women of the whole world—including, of course, Russian women—to protect the chaste huntress, wielding love's bow, from the rape of the warriors." Asked by the Boston *Globe*. "What is the best thing you can say about yourself?," she replied: "I never wrote to be popular. It cost me a lot."

You're wondering about the woman: the miniseries. Her first choice was the Budapest-born, Sorbonne-educated Joseph Bard, "who looked like an Egyptian prince, his hair lay on his head like burnished wings." She married him, kept him, and he was too busy bedding her best friends ever to finish his magnum opus, *The Mind of Europe*. "Like all intellectual women," complained Joseph, "she thinks you can starch your prick at the nearest men's laundry."

In July 1927, the month of her divorce from gallant Joseph, she met her second husband, an Ugly American and a drunk: Sinclair Lewis. About him she'd later confide: "I say to myself, 'You are totally unimportant and you are married to a man of genius—if you give your life to making him happy it is worth it.' But it isn't! I can really do nothing for him. He is like a vampire—he absorbs all my vitality, all my energy, all my beauty—I get incredibly dull." About her, whom he'd beat up in alcoholic rages, he was quoted: "If I ever divorce Dorothy, I'll name Adolf Hitler as co-respondent." (She likes Europe more than she likes me!) They lasted long enough together to ruin a child.

Later, she'd write him: "I am glad that you are happy. I happen not to be. I am not happy, because I have no home, because I have an ill and difficult child without a father. Because I have loved a man who didn't exist. Because I am widowed of an illusion. Because I am tremblingly aware of the tragedy of the world we live in." A letter never mailed is more remarkable:

There are things in my heart that you do not dream of, things that are compounded of passion and fury and love and hate and pride and disgust and tenderness and contrition, things that are wild and fierce . . . and you ask me to write you conventional letters because you are in 'exile.' From what? From whom?

Give me Vermont. I want to watch the lilac hedge grow tall & the elm trees form, and the roses on the grey wall thicken, and the yellow apples hang on the young trees, and the sumac redden on the hills, and friends come and your two children feel at home. Who knows? Maybe some time you might come home yourself. You might go a long way and do worse. As a matter of fact and prophecy—you will.

In her unhappiness, she fell in love with the sculptor Christa Winsloe, author of the book *The Child Manuela,* from which the lesbian movie *Mädchen in Uniform* had been made. It wasn't Thompson's first lesbian experience, but her first (and last) lesbian love affair. Although she wrote an interesting poem about it, it seems not to have been a big improvement on her marriages to either the cad or the drunk: "I think, you see, that you are very much better than I am. I think, perhaps, that I have something which this very-much-better-than-I-am-person can use." Christa dumped her, in Salzburg, for the Italian basso Ezio Pinza!

The last important man in her life, with whom she fell in love at age forty-nine, was the refugee artist Maxim Kopf, a Vienna-born Czech Secessionist with a concentration camp in his resumé, described by the *Times* as "a coherent and disciplined Kokoschka." This seems, in Vermont, to have worked out nicely, at least after Thompson bought off Kopf's previous wife for $30,000. She liked his painting, detecting in it "a weird sense of unreality"—especially his *Resurrection*, with the body of Christ, or maybe of Apollo, "suspended, and somehow rising, against a backdrop of rose-red, the color of sunrise." I imagine that she might have seen her father, too, who had once explained to her that "Dorothea" means "the Gift of God."

While she was still on Central Park West, wanting it all, working twice as hard to get it; talking too much, explaining Europe to everybody who didn't want to hear; the object of so much satire and yet, like the first Cassandra, so often right where the wits were wrong; not, perhaps, an original thinker, but equipped with a built-in compass that pointed true north to a magnetic pole of decencies; run through by the century as if by a sword; a role model and a cautionary tale and, of course, a heroine, she declared: "I'd throw the state of the nation into the ashcan for anyone I loved." It's a measure of Kurth's biography that I don't believe her.

Whose Television,
for Which Public?

Eighty pages into his coroner's exam of public broadcasting, *Made Possible By* . . . , James Ledbetter complains
about the system's "Byzantine complexity and ineffi-
ciency." This is unfair to Constantinople. Public television is a
whole lot more Egyptian. Like Ptolemaic astronomy, it's tricked
up with epicycles to explain eccentric motions. Like Tutankha-
men's diadem, it's half vulture and half cobra. Like the Temple
of Luxor, it's a hodgepodge of art and politics, a dreamworld of
obelisks, scarabs, and bulls, and a monumental mystification.
Therein we find, as John Anthony West explained in *Serpent in
the Sky,* his meditation on the Sacred Science of the Pharaohs,
"priest-bound necrophiles worshipping a grotesque pantheon
of animal-headed gods."

None of this much resembles what the Carnegie Commission
on Educational Television had hoped for in its 1967 report,
Public Television: A Program for Action—a system inclusive of
"all that is of human interest and importance which is not at the
moment appropriate or available for advertising" and "a voice
for groups in the community that may otherwise be unheard,"
paid for by an excise tax on television sets. What Carnegie proposed, Congress would dispose of in the Public Broadcasting
Act of 1967, a product of both Great Society feistiness and what
public-TV historian Ralph Engelman calls a "utopian tradition," as old as Walt Whitman's fervor for the telegraph, in
which "a vital public sphere of communication can foster free
and diverse speech, a sense of community, and purposeful action." But because of Vietnam, the Great Society was already
running on fumes. What Congress omitted from this disabling
act was any means of funding such a sphere other than a begging
bowl. And so, from the start, the experiment was corrupted by
politics and money: the forked tongue and double penis of the
Egyptian serpent.

Ledbetter, media critic for *The Village Voice,* looks back with a savage eye on the last thirty years of public broadcasting and sees a betrayal of its utopian promise, an unseemly mimicry of commercial networks, and a culture of increasing accommodation to partisan politics, sectarian pressure groups, and that "military-industrial-entertainment complex" so beloved of *X-Files* Agent Mulder. In *Public Television: Politics and the Battle over Documentary Film,* B. J. Bullert, who had to take a day job as an assistant professor of communications at American University to support her habit of documentary filmmaking, examines the case histories of a half dozen controversial programs from 1985 to 1993, interviews the appropriate apparatchiks, and limns a sort of ethnography of the labyrinth. As in the old English proverb, "They agree like bells; they want nothing but hanging."

Inside today's Temple, priest-bound necrophiles include nine presidentially appointed members of the Corporation for Public Broadcasting board, "a dumping ground," says Ledbetter, "for the worst sort of political hacks"; the forty on-staff "gatekeepers" who decide on national programming for the Public Broadcasting Service; such alternative suppliers and distributors as the American Program Service, the Eastern and Central Educational Networks, the Public Mountain Network, and the Southern Educational Communications Association; 354 cantankerous affiliate fiefdoms that partake of these services for a fee and occasionally produce or "present" programs of their own; the aggrieved community of independent producers who can't get their work on the air; foundation folks who fund tapeheads; relevant panelists at the two Endowments; the 2 percent of the population that can be counted on to watch the stuff, and five million dues-paying public-TV "members," pledge-break groupies, tote-bag schleppers, Barney-doll fetishists, Muppet symps, and anybody who was ever kinky about adhesive-padded geckos.

The animal-gods, of course, include:

(1) The White House, any White House. All are equipped with telecommunications policy wonks whose sole purpose is to make their president, whoever, and his behavior, however, look spiffy. Clay Whitehead, who spiffed for Nixon, went so far as to seek to ban from PBS any public affairs programs whatsoever: no documentaries, no interviews, no panel discussions. (He was assisted by young Brian Lamb, before he became the Clairvoyant Master of C-SPAN.) The very first Reagan budget tried to cut appropriations for public broadcasting by half. Failing that, they brought in a declared enemy of the whole system, Pat Buchanan, to help vet appointees to the CPB board, and never mind that Pat got famous in the first place on *The McLaughlin Report*—that without public television, this pip might never have been heard to squeak.

(2) Congresspeople, whose reelection campaigns depend on big money, whose constituents are likely to consist of pale-faced churchgoing middle-class nuclear families, and who are thus disinclined to spend tax dollars on bad-news programs about corporate accountability, domestic violence, declining cities, race war, indeterminate sexuality, Southeast Asia, Latin America, and the Middle East. Till the 1994 elections, you'd have thought everyone in Washington agreed that Hollywood and network television were to blame for pandemic Sex-and-Violence. But after the triumph of a Guns-and-God Republican Congress, the emphasis shifted to a Culture War in which Keystone Khmer Newts sought to cleanse Phnom Penh of every pointy-headed intellectual with a tutu in his closet, every parasitic painter who ever suckered a dime from the Endowment, every Third World wetback here to steal a job, and every illegitimate child dieting unto attention deficit on food stamps, not to mention their welfare mothers and crackhead fathers and shyster lawyers and other codependents who should instead be growing rice and eating fish paste in the boondocks. And so the focus of media-bashing shifted to "left-dominated, elitist, minority-radical" public television, widely perceived as pro-

moting an ulterior agenda of multculti / femi-nazi / gay pride / socialized medicine / performance art.

(3) Big biz. While federal funding shrank from 86 percent of public broadcasting's total revenue in 1980 to 16 percent in 1995, corporate funding increased by 50 percent, to 27 percent of national program costs. (By comparison, Ledbetter notes that in 1995, six years after winning the Cold War, Congress authorized $500 million for Voice of America and Radio Free Europe broadcasts to un-Americans. He also notes that Japan, Canada, and Great Britain spend $32, $31, and $38 per citizen per year on public television, while we spend $1.09.) The corporations are so generous not because they desire to foster diverse speech, much less purposeful action, but because their advertising and PR agencies have persuaded them that tax-deductible "enhanced credits" constitute what Ledbetter calls "reputation laundering," sociologist M. David Ermann calls "milieu control," and Peter Spina, Mobil Corporation's general manager of corporate relations, calls "the halo effect." Herb Schmertz, the Mobil veep without whom *Masterpiece Theatre* would still be called *Masterpiece Theatre,* once explained that "cultural excellence generally suggests corporate excellence," by which he probably meant he'd sell more gas and stock shares to the upscale demographic that adores aristocrats because their houses are big and their servants are cute and, when they aren't eating immense amounts of overcooked food, they stand around on their broad rolled lawns like croquet hoops, waiting for history to pop through holes in their heads.

I I

Public TV has been in bed with the petroleum industry forever. Most of its startup money came from the Ford Foundation's Fund for Adult Education, whose first chief, in 1961, was Alexander Fraser, president of Shell Oil. For just as long, Ledbetter informs us, public TV has also been in the closet with the Department of Defense and its subcontractors. The first board of National Educational Television, predecessor of CPB, included the chairman of the Atomic Energy Commission and officers of IBM and General Electric; the first president of CPB was Frank Pace Jr., former chief executive of General Dynamics, Secretary of the Army during the Korean War, and a member of the boards of Continental Oil and Time Inc. Moreover, too poor to pay for long-distance phone lines to distribute programs to all of its affiliates simultaneously, PBS hoped to solve its "bicycling" problem with the new satellite technology, access to which in turn depended on what the military told the Congress about its "national security" needs and how sensitive Congress was to the feelings and the earnings of "domestic carrier services" like Western Union and AT&T, not to mention Sperry Rand, Martin Marietta, and Grumman Aircraft. And just as the usual players jockeyed for a piece of the eye in the sky, a Ford-funded Public Broadcast Laboratory series in the fall of 1967 had the *lèse-majesté* to insinuate that the Pentagon's version of what went down in Gulf of Tonkin had been fictitious.

Nor is it as if Humble Oil, U.S. Steel, Hills Brothers, Westinghouse, and Xerox hadn't been thanked for their donations in the sixties. But those expressions of gratitude were discreetly fleeting. Not even for McDonald's, on the children's program *Zoom!*, did we ever see a corporate logo—nothing like 1984, when Frito-Lay and Pizza Hut jumped out of a grocery sack to remind us that *MacNeil/Lehrer* would not have been possible without Pepsico; much less today, when *NewsHour* depends on $6.8 million a year from Archer Daniels Midland, the agribiz octopus whose fixing of prices and politicians got so much attention in 1995, everywhere except on *NewsHour*. I'm with Ledbetter (and Greenpeace) in suspecting that DuPont sponsors *Discover Underwater,* Waste Management International sponsors *Only One Earth,* and Gulf Oil spends more money advertising than producing *National Geographic,* to help us forget just who polluted the environment in the first place. I'm not surprised Kellogg and Nestlé paid for the *Eat Right* program on the

American diet; that *Childhood* was underwritten by Oreos and Fig Newtons; that investment houses like Franklin/Templeton bankroll a *Nightly Business Report,* Prudential Bache a *Wall Street Week,* Met Life an *Adam Smith's Money World,* American Express an *American Experience,* and Sears *The Puzzle Palace* kiddie show.

What else should we expect in a brand-named, theme-parked country where the whole visual culture is a stick in the eye—one big sell of booze, gizmos, insouciance, safari styles, and combustible emotions? Where the big-screen rerelease of George Lucas's *Star Wars* trilogy is brought to us by Doritos and the associated sale of stuffed Yodas, Muppet minotaurs, trading cards, video games, and a six-foot-tall Fiberglas Storm Trooper for only $5,000? Where the newest James Bond is less a movie than a music-video marketing campaign for luxury cars, imported beers, mobile phones, and gold credit cards? Where Coke and Pepsi duke it out in grammar schools and Burger King shows up on the sides of the yellow buses that cart our kids to those schools, in whose classrooms they'll be handed curriculum kits sprinkled with the names of sneaker companies and breakfast cereals? Where there is a logo, a patent, or a copyright on everything from our pro athletes to our childhood fairy tales, and Oprah is sued for $12 million by a Texas beef lobby for "disparaging" blood on a bun during a talk show segment on spongiform encephalopathy and Creutzfeldt-Jakob disease?

So the logo is our *logos.* So what? Ramses II, that pylon-happy Syrian-basher, so loved his own reign that he just couldn't stop putting up images of himself to which every sacred bark, papyrus-cluster column, and blue lotus with a yellow heart paid smarmy obeisance.

Ledbetter and Bullert agree that the "so what" resides less in what gets on public TV than what doesn't. Unisys, a computer manufacturer, is allowed to bankroll a 1992 PBS series like *The Machine That Changed the World* and General Electric does the same for PBS convention coverage. But an Oscar-winning 1991 documentary like *Deadly Deception,* critical of GE and the nuclear-power industry, can't get on the air because it was funded by a group boycotting GE products. And *Defending Our Lives,* also an Oscar winner in 1993, can't get on the air because it was produced in collaboration with a victims-rights advocacy group. And the splendid summer series of independent films, *P.O.V.,* isn't permitted to air a documentary about gays and lesbians in the workplace because labor unions helped fund it. That petroleum companies should be such fans of John Galsworthy and George Eliot is almost charming, unless we also know that a board member of the Metropolitan Opera – supportive Texaco tried to buy off PBS in 1980 if it agreed to drop *Death of a Princess,* a BBC account of the execution of a royal adulteress so offensive to Saudi Arabia that it threatened an oil embargo. And we remember that Gulf + Western canceled support of WNET in New York after the telecast of *Hungry for Profit,* a 1985 documentary on the rape of the rain forest. And we've noticed public TV's shamelessly shallow coverage of the Exxon *Valdez* oil spill and its shameful neglect of the role of Shell Oil in the murder of Ken Saro-Wiwa and the ravening of Nigeria. We may not even mind that Ken Burns is a wholly owned subsidiary of General Motors, lock, stock, and banjo — baseball and the Civil War can be counted on not to step on any corporate toes — except that *Rights & Wrongs,* Charlayne Hunter-Gault's program on human-rights abuses, can't get PBS funding because, according to program vice-president Jennifer Lawson, "human rights is not a sufficient organizing principle" for a TV series.

Ledbetter asks: "When General Motors and Mobil insist that fictional television should be about nineteenth-century England, and nonfiction television should be about business news, the U.S. civil war and villain-free celebrations of the animal kingdom, who is PBS to object?" By way of a Delphic answer, Bullert quotes a former PBS gatekeeper on what determines which shows get on the national schedule: "who's powerful, who's weak, and who cares."

III

The passage of Bullert through the labyrinth feels like all great mystic journeys toward Enlightenment, from Saint John of the Cross to a Sufi lapwing. There are voices and visions, ravens and hounds, dark nights and rivers of light. But since I'm pushing Egyptian dread, think of the independent film as a *ka* or a *ba* in the Book of the Dead—arriving by boat to plead its case at the Seven Gates of the House of Osiris; looked down upon by Watchers and Heralds; trussed up by the jackal-headed psychopomp Anubis; badmouthed by the ibis-headed prosecutor Thoth; scaling its heart against a feather from the headdress of Maat, the Goddess of Truth; found wanting and then gobbled by a beastly Ammit.

Even gatekeeper nomenclature needs a Rosetta Stone. As if hieroglyphed, "fairness" and "balance" translate into what William Hoynes in *Public Television for Sale* calls "goal ambivalence" and "a logic of safety," and Bullert calls "anticipatory avoidance" and "a culture of timidity." Thus *Dark Circle*, a documentary on the Rocky Flats nuclear weapons facility in Colorado and the Diablo Canyon nuclear power plant in California, got rave reviews at the New York Film Festival in 1982, the Grand Prize at Sundance in 1983, a proposal by KQED in San Francisco to present it nationally in 1984, a PBS rejection of that proposal *two years later,* and screenings on Ted Turner's superstation and premium-cable Bravo before finally achieving *P.O.V.* in 1989, after which it won an Emmy. While there was every reason for a pro-nuke Reagan and Rockwell International (plutonium triggers), Bendix (bomb packaging), DuPont (radioactive hydrogen), GE (neutron generators), Union Carbide (enriched uranium), and Monsanto (explosive detonators) to object to such a program, there's no evidence that any of them did. Instead, the system itself was suspicious of a *Dark Circle* support group that included Physicians for Social Responsibility and Mothers for Peace.

Likewise, a 1989 documentary, *Days of Rage: The Young Pal-*

estinians, was at first scheduled and then held up for seven months until it could be packaged between two short videos presenting an Israeli perspective on the *intifada,* followed by a panel discussion with a Likud tilt, after which the Israeli Consul General helped four New York businessmen to raise $382,000 to produce and air *A Search for Solid Ground: The Intifada through Israeli Eyes,* with absolutely no attempt to "balance" it with a Palestinian point of view. None of this was George Bush's fault, or corporate America's. Neither was the sudden dumping from the 1991 PBS schedule of *Stop the Church,* a filmed account of the ACT-UP action against St. Patrick's Cathedral. Originally meant for *P.O.V., Stop the Church* was dropped—in favor of *Binge,* a confessional video about a woman's weight problems—after all the bad publicity and affiliate defections attending another installment of *P.O.V.* that same summer, *Tongues Untied.*

Of the disputed programs that Bullert worries in detail, only *Roger and Me* had to fend off a major corporation. While *P.O.V.* turned down a rough edit in 1988, Michael Moore's whimsy did show up there four years later, after a wild theatrical run, and three million people saw it. In the meantime, so unkind was Moore's rendition of what General Motors did to Flint, Michigan, that GM yanked its commercials from any program inviting him to chat. Bullert thinks that *Roger and Me* would have won an Oscar if critics like Pauline Kael hadn't been so fetishistic about factual inaccuracies. Bullert has a poststructuralist sort of feeling that such nitpicks are in thralldom to the dominant discursive myth of "objective" journalism. She seems even to resent *Frontline,* the fearless PBS investigative series—whose own critique of GM, *The Heartbeat of America,* she says got less flak than Moore because of its traditional "news documentary style," old-fashioned on-camera reporter, pro forma interviews of "experts and key figures," and the related paraphernalia of humdrum "fairness." Independent filmmakers, full of passionate conviction, are presumed to lapwing on a higher plane. This is silly, as if scruples about accurate description were somehow superstitious or maybe even hegemonic. When NBC's *Dateline* rigged crash tests on GM pickup trucks to support a passionate conviction that side-mounted gas tanks are dangerous, it was bad for journalism and good for GM. When I review a book, no matter how I feel about it, I must have read it first and then quoted it accurately. I've also been an editor at *The Nation*, a magazine that's subjective (as well as subjunctive) about almost everything. Yet we require and prize our rigorous fact-checkers, who save us from being stupid in public.

Disputed facts had nothing to do with the 1991 *Tongues Untied* controversy. Marlon Riggs, a Berkeley journalism professor, never imagined himself on public TV. He had something to say to the African-American community and was in a hurry to say it before he died. *Tongues Untied* is the story of a gay black man with AIDS trying to explain, in a collage of skits, poems, dance, autobiography, newsreel footage, rap, camp, and music video, how it felt to be gay, black, and doubly disdained in straight white America. Some of this was funny: a doo-wop barbershop quartet singing "Baby Come Out Tonight." Some of it was angry: at straight black activists with no time for gay men; at a white gay subculture with no time for black men; at homophobic entertainers like Eddie Murphy. Some of it was dreadful: especially those poems. And some of it broke the heart: like listening to Billie Holiday. But ten or so minutes were shocking: even on *cable* TV we seldom see full frontal male nudity or black men kissing each other.

Never mind that it was scheduled well in advance, and safely tucked away, like all *P.O.V.* programs, at ten o'clock on a slow summer night so as not to perturb pledging. Never mind that affiliates got an advance peak in March and April "preview feeds." Even so, more than a hundred public-TV stations refused to show it, including seventeen in the top fifty markets, and others delayed the broadcast—to 1 A.M. in Miami, to 3 A.M. in Seattle. Newspaper articles about it alerted the Rev. Donald Wildmon, the gnome of Tupelo, whose American Family Association immediately issued a press release attacking a program they hadn't seen, and attacking as well the National Endowment for the Arts, for helping to fund *P.O.V.* Which in turn alerted Congress, where both the NEA and the CPB faced reauthorization hearings. Oddly, neither Bullert nor Ledbetter mentions that Pat Buchanan made a noisy issue of *Tongues Untied* in his mossback campaign for president in 1992. Every time he looked under the bed, Pat imagined Marlon and was filled with fear and trembling.

IV

As German liberals in the nineteenth century hoped that the first big-city newspapers would be "grand institutions of public enlightenment" but got *Berliner Morgenpost* instead, so liberal-minded twentieth-century Americans like Ledbetter, Bullert, and the Carnegie Commission long for government-subsidized noncommercial TV to amount to something equally exalted but get Ben Wattenberg every week going scuba-scuba glub-glub in his *Think Tank.* It's sad enough to remind you of a priestly inscription on a tomb at Heramopolis, lamenting the death of a child: "Though I had many friends, none was in a position to protect me. Everyone in town, men and women alike, is in mourning after what happened to me because everyone was attached to me. All my friends moaned, my father and my mother raised questions about death, my brothers prostrated themselves when I was taken away toward this province of misfortune, where one must present one's reckoning before the Master of gods."

But public television is not so sorry. Or: it has always been almost as sorry as it is now, and yet more, and other, than merely a muddle, a wound, and a whistling in the ether. Those of us old enough to have watched it back when it was still "educational" remember low-watt UHF hours on adult literacy, family hygiene, farming, and forestry. So we are not exactly shocked by reruns of Lawrence Welk, the listener-supported flavor of the happy-camper nineties. Those of us who reviewed its first few baby steps in "public" — *Banks and the Poor,* for example, which drove Nixon bananas — couldn't then have imagined anything as ambitious as a single installment of *Frontline* or *P.O.V.,* much less a season of them, and then a whole decade; or the Bill Moyers miniseries on the scandal of our intelligence agencies, *High Crimes and Misdemeanors*; or those home movies on the second American revolution, *Eyes on the Prize*; or even dreamt of Ofra Bikel's scorched-earth documentaries on the satanic-ritual-abuse hysteria.

Of *course*, public-television programs should include a *Tongues Untied.* After so many hours of the gentle Tasaday and the awful Ik, why not gay black Americans — fellow citizens who speak a different anguish? And of *course,* these programs should be funded out of a trust whose coffers are full from an excise tax on TV sets, or a tariff on the commercial networks, or a percentage of the $30-billion-plus spent each year on TV advertising, or a share of profits from the forthcoming sale of the digital broadcast spectrum, or even a check-off on our income tax forms. But we are radically naïve to think that a government-by-subtraction, in fearful flight from its responsibilities to the young, the old, the odd, the powerless and afflicted, for which prisons are a growth industry and schools are not, is about to *institutionalize* dissent, to pay, as it were, for an auto-critique. In a buck-grubbing, status-scrabbling, tantrum-yoga culture that measures everyone by his or her ability to produce wealth and morally condemns anyone who fails to prosper, the government now is just another market. And the market, as usual, sells us short.

On this depressing score, I learned as much from what's missing in Ledbetter and Bullert as I did from their painstaking exhumations. What's missing, for want of a better shorthand, is Helen Mirren. If almost half of PBS programming is public affairs, at least half is not. Between bouts of remedial seriousness, we have also enjoyed all six hours of Ingmar Bergman's *Scenes from a Marriage* and thirteen weeks of Paul Scott's *The*

Jewel in the Crown, Miss Marple and Julia Child, Eugene O'Neill and *Sesame Street,* the spoonbilled bee-eater and the midwife toad. Science makes wonderful TV. And children need *more* TV that respects them, not less—as so perversely recommended by a Ledbetter who'd prefer to see documentaries on the dire straits of inner-city classrooms. But both Ledbetter and Bullert are so monocular, so burningly focused on a politics exclusive of culture, they forget we seek options that please as well as edify; that *Mystery!* with Diana Rigg is a welcome alternative on Thursday nights to the penis jokes and prophylactic sneer of *Seinfeld*; that even a *Masterpiece Theatre* coasting on potboilers is sometimes preferable to an *X-Files* rerun about man-eating pigs. While I miss *The Great American Dream Machine* just as much as Ledbetter does, I mourn even more the passing of *American Playhouse,* the risk-taking series that invested in original films and plays, and adaptations of novels and short stories, from *Ethan Frome* with Liam Neeson to *A Raisin in the Sun* with Danny Glover; from *Sensibility and Sense,* Richard Nelson's playful reconsideration of the adjournment of minds among Lillian Hellman, Mary McCarthy, and Diana Trilling, to *Daughters of the Dust,* Julie Dash's painterly contemplation of turn-of-the-century Gullah culture, to *Paris Is Burning,* Jennie Livingston's hilarious and heartbreaking account of life in drag in lower Manhattan.

American Playhouse, mentioned a stingy once each in Ledbetter and in Bullert, is gone because its principal sponsor, the National Endowment for the Arts, fared worse than public television in the Culture Wars. It was easy enough, as Ledbetter observes, for the gatekeepers—as timorous, evasive, disingenuous, self-righteous, self-pitying, hassled, or burnt-out as they may appear in Bullert's pages—to buy off their right-wing critics in the early nineties. All they had to do was give Peggy Noonan her own series, *Values*; and Fred Barnes and Morton Kondracke their own series, *Reverse Angle*; and Tony Snow space for a *New Militant Center,* plus two hours to reform welfare by abolishing it; and Bill Bennett, the PBS cartoon that his *Book of Virtues* so richly deserved. But the NEA, lacking any blood ties to the local business / political power structures that coalesce around PBS affiliates, was helpless before its many enemies. And its disemboweling by yahoos is neglected in both these books. If *American Masters* seems more and more these days to settle for the sort of celebrity just as likely to show up on a low-budget A & E *Biography,* and if *Great Performances* panders for ratings with superstar overproductions like *The Three Tenors,* it is as much because the "peer panelists" who recommend grants at the traumatized NEA are looking over their shoulder at Congress as it is because PBS executive producers are licking the corporate boot on their throats.

I have served on two of these NEA panels, Literature and Media Arts, reporting to the National Council. They were happy part-time years. We met mostly in Washington or New York, but I remember Berkeley, where paranoia against Easterners like me ran amok even though I'd gone to college there. And Savannah, where we admired the house in which Conrad Aiken's father murdered Conrad Aiken's mother. And San Antonio, where Rosalind Russell rode a bouncy barge downriver, and six mariachi bands trailed us room to room in a hacienda full of shower stalls big enough to stable the horses of the Apocalypse, and Edward Villella and Clint Eastwood took us to a Dixieland jazz joint Eudora Welty had recommended. But mostly I recall long, smoky hours in hot little rooms, devising programs that would put poets into schools, novelists on radio, paperbacks into bookmobiles, dance on television. We were trying to keep difficult people from starving, because we believed that these difficult people, at their difficult task, would ultimately transfigure us. Think of it as a seeding for a Gross National Product of mystery and magic. Once we gave a grant to a poet who used it to write, instead, a best-selling novel. The poet's name was Erica Jong; the novel was *Fear of Flying.* Congress was livid, our budget was in trouble, and yet somehow the republic survived this zipless foofaraw, as it would subsequently survive *Tongues Un-*

tied. Whereas the NEA doesn't look as if it will make it to the millennium.

I should have imagined that any civilization worth the savor of its salt invests as much in surprising art as in libraries and museums, in land-grant colleges and national parks and public spaces to celebrate ourselves as citizens. That peer panelists— like the volunteers who person the phones during public-TV pledge breaks and the signers who simultaneously interpret Peter, Paul, and Mary for the deaf—are on the angelic side of the Johnny Appleseeds with jumping beans who deliver us from platitude, punditry, baby talk, psychobabble, laugh track, skin pop, and thumb in the eye; from cop shows against the Bill of Rights and abductions by sperm-sucking polliwogs. That we ought to be grateful for those ghosts in our machines who speak for our irregular sizes and shapes, our differing contours and textures and grain. That, as a nation, we are a lot more complicated than what we see on the hole in our wall.

But I would have been wrong. This is what Thebes looks like—self-serving monuments standing stunned under the sun god Ra, with most of the color in the tomb caves underground, waiting for Greeks to teach us that the human body has a belly button.

Part Four

AMERICAN IDENTITIES

Mary Gordon's Father
Runs Away from Home

"**I** love you more than God," David Gordon told his daughter Mary before dying from a heart attack when she was seven. His only child, than whom there's no brainier writer or reader, no more resourceful archaeologist of hidden meanings, has worried this bone like a hound of heaven ever since: "I didn't know, and still don't," she says in her aurora of a memoir, "if he meant he loved me more than he loved God or more than God loved me. It almost doesn't matter. It was a serious thing to say and it scared me."

It also sounds like a curse. No one, not even a parent, should have such power over our imagining of ourselves. Nor ought any child need to love him back so much, at whatever cost. But David taught Mary to read when she was three; to memorize the Latin Mass when she was five; to dwell in libraries and ideas. "He ripped a picture of Beethoven out of the encyclopedia and hung it near my toy box." The only other picture allowed in the house was a print of Holbein's *Thomas More*; no landscapes, no still lifes, certainly not any modern art, which he considered "dangerous, and ugly, too." Not even any television. Instead, the Easter show at Radio City, where the Rockettes dressed up as angels and nuns. And the *Six O'Clock Saints,* where Mary learned the story of Saint Nicholas, who reassembled little boys who had been dismembered and pickled. And in a magazine her father edited, *The Children's Hour,* tales of the superdutiful daughters of Prospero, Rip Van Winkle, and the Chinese mandarin Kuan-Yo.

In Lafcadio Hearn's "The Soul of the Bell," Kuan-Yo, an adviser to the emperor, supervises the construction of the world's most perfect bell. But the heated metals of gold, silver, and brass won't blend and the bell can't be cast. To save his life, Kuan-Yo consults the usual wise old man on the usual mountain, who explains that only the body of the usual spotless virgin can cause the metals to blend. Naturally, Kuan-Yo has just such a daughter, who promptly flings herself into the vat, crying "For thy sake, O father." Presto: ding-dong. "The perfect life," says a sarcastic Mary, "the perfect death, the graceful fall into the boiling metal. . . . Endlessly entombed, endlessly beloved, endlessly revered, the body turns to music, the perfection of the bell's tone repeats itself in the receptive and ecstatic air." And yet, not believing a word of Hearn, what she does in *The Shadow Man* is turn herself into a bell. "Ecclesiastical language is full of names for vessels," she tells us: "chalice, ciborium, monstrance, pyx; there must be containers to enclose, keep safe, keep intact, keep protected from the world's contamination the sacred matter . . ." The world contaminated her only father. Too late to protect him, Mary's bell will ring his vespers.

Because the David Gordon who wrote poems to his daughter—from whom she learned "the sovereignty of the mind and the imagination," for whom she named her son—was also the David Gordon who, in the twenties, edited a semiporn girlie magazine called *Hot Dog*; and, in the late thirties and early forties, wrote anti-Semitic articles for *Catholic International* and the Jesuit weekly *America*; and, in the early fifties, wrote speeches for Joe McCarthy. Even his biography of the poet Paul Claudel, written a decade after the terrible news of the death camps, was actually a diatribe against André Gide, modernism, and "the infection of the Jews": "The Jew Proust. The Jew Bergson. The Jew Masoch . . ." More astonishing, David Gordon had himself been born a Jew, only converting to Roman Catholicism in 1937, just in time to side with Franco in the Spanish Civil War and to complain in *America* about the international brigades of "Jewish soldiers" gone to Spain "to help murder nuns in Lincoln's name."

So he died on her, this changeling, and his secrets with him: "I am in a dark room, waiting to be allowed to see him, to wave to him. I have always been. I have always been waiting. I have always known that if they let me see him, he will never die. I know what the sight of me means to him. Everything." And what the death of him meant to her was a fall into her mother's Irish-Sicilian world of grudge and grievance; of polio, alcoholism, and Alzheimer's; of *My Little Margie* on Friday night television and something more mysterious on the bedroom wall: "A picture made of slats. You turned your head one way: it was the Scourging at the Pillar. Another turn of the head produced Jesus Crowned with Thorns. If you looked absolutely straight ahead, you saw the Agony in the Garden"—the world, in other words, of Mary Gordon's novels, of *Final Payments, The Company of Women, Men and Angels,* and *The Other Side.*

Though she wouldn't discover *Hot Dog,* pressed between pages of the *Catholic Encyclopedia,* until she was twelve, finding bared breasts, provocative bums, and Little Girlie Ginger sex jokes she flushed immediately down a toilet, it was not as if half-orphaned Mary, afraid of mayonnaise and gristle, hadn't known she was partly Jewish. Her father told her his ancestors had been wealthy and cultivated French Jews; that his grandfather had been a rabbi; that his father owned a saloon. (He also told her, or so she thinks she remembers, that he was an only child; that he had gone to Harvard with Walter Lippmann, seen Oxford's dreamy spires in the era of *Brideshead Revisited,* consorted in Left Bank cafes with poets like Claudel, and been blacklisted by the Anti-Defamation League of B'nai B'rith, which was why he couldn't hold a job driving a taxi or tending a bar.) In his absence, moreover, her mother's family had always been there to remind her, whenever she was reading, dreaming, or otherwise difficult: "That's the *Jew* in you."

The Jew in her? "For most of my life, I felt I had no right to claim Jewishness for myself because I hadn't suffered for it. . . . No one needed me to be a Jew. But what did *I* need?" A father, of course, who must have abandoned her because she hadn't been alert enough to love him more: "Maybe he was not really dead but was missing or banished, a political exile, and I, by the right word or signal, would be able to recall him." A *writing* father, from whom she inherited, like a recessive gene, a predisposition to semicolons and parallelisms, argumentative paragraphs that end in punchy accusations, and "some dream of purity. Some way of naming and distinguishing. Some taste for exclusion and embellishment. And a desire for a point of silence, emptiness, and rest." A film noir father who "lived as a man drowning," with his missing teeth, torn trousers, broken shoes: "The figure behind every story. The stranger on the road. The double, feared and prized, approaching from the distance." Had he lived, this Shadow Man would have seen to it that his daughter went to college in Quebec, or Belgium, or Ireland, certainly not to godless Barnard, where she became the leftist feminist and trained investigator who pursues him through these pages: the scholar, historian, literary critic, Magical Realist, and private eye who looks for him in library catalogues, census reports, deed bins, immigration archives, and other "caves of memory" in New York, New Haven, Providence, and Cleveland, in photo albums, microfiche plates, and dossiers marked "Loss," "Fascism," and "Kafka." The child Mary feared bicycles and seesaws and merry-go-rounds. The adult, a hedgehog and a fox, will go anywhere by any means to track her father down. "It's a less hopeless prospect for me to imagine that I can find him than to imagine that he can find me. I am, after all, the one who lost him. 'She lost her father,' I've often heard people say. 'She lost her father when she was very young.'"

Bad enough that David "did other things in his life than love me." It turns out he also lied a lot: "Facts nose their way into what I thought was the past like a dog sticking his nose under a lady's skirt. How I resent the insidious, relentless, somehow filthy nudging of these facts." He had been born not in Lorrain, Ohio, but in Vilna, Lithuania. His first name had been Israel, not David; his first language Yiddish, not English. Nor was he an only child; sisters stashed in mental hospitals and nursing homes, relatives of whom she had no inkling, possessed snapshots of a little Mary lovingly inscribed. Rather than owning a saloon, his father had worked in a dry-goods store. Instead of going to Harvard with Walter Lippmann, David was a railroad clerk. Far from rolling Oxford lawns with Evelyn Waugh, or Left

Banking with right-wingers, he never graduated from high school, never applied for a passport. He'd even been previously married to a flapper, and a stepfather to *her* son. Mary being Mary, she is more jealous of Yiddish than she is of any stepson. Yiddish was an elsewhere her father could go to, leaving her behind without her ever knowing it, as if "the legitimate daughter" was "too good" ever to meet "the love child" — this Other's discourse of shtetl and Ellis Island, of goose grease and cabbage leaves and steerage, of Chagall's dancing cows and dark men in fur hats "praying to a God who has no son or mother."

And so an angry daughter in mourning, the cracked bell, must imagine her father's passage from turn-of-the-century Midwest outcast ("the tumult, the vilification and self-hatred, the immigrant's terror, the weak son's dread, the Eastern Jew's American abashment") to the dandy and the pedant and the convert who tried to pass by reading Matthew Arnold and Walter Pater, by dropping names like Ovid or Dante, by pretending his "natural habitations" were the open spaces of Rome, the dappled woods of the Middle Ages, the majestic palaces of the Renaissance, hoping in the cramped rooms above the store "one day to awake without reproach." Bristling like a porcupine with empathetic intelligence, every needle an optic nerve, she'll watch him run into her future. She'll dream him up all over again, in an ecstatic trance, by meditation and incantation on such objects as his pink shirt, black comb, silver ring, and a prayerbook with a lamb's paw; on such fragmentary texts as Father Coughlin and Father Feeney, Chesterton and Belloc; on her "police artist" sketch of the face of his "stalker," with H. L. Mencken's mouth, Ezra Pound's hair, Henry Roth's eyes, and Bernard Berenson's skull. Because we know and she knows that the shadow will follow and fall on the fugitive, this luminous exertion breaks the heart:

> My father walks out of the meadow to the marble building. He is light with feverish joy but his forehead is cool. Words jump and dance but remain separate, do not swarm. Assisi. Provence. Languedoc.

Toscana. Chartres. Words rise up, white and shining, images of irides-
cent ease, words that do not accuse but absorb accusation. No need to
fear, no need to cringe or wait for the reproach. In the white silence
rimmed with green or gold, the dream of Europe, swallowing loath-
someness and hatred, insult, terror, dread.

Until it starts again. The buzz and hiss. The torment. "Everything
you do is wrong."

This shadow fell, as well, on her in the fifties, while her father
was writing speeches for Joe McCarthy and loving Mary more
than God, and his daughter was reading *The Children's Hour*:

I hear as if in a dream through thick fog . . . the news of the execution of the Rosenbergs. Mrs. Rosenberg in her boxy coat, her hat, her
pocketbook, like anybody's mother. I am told she, too, is trying to kill
me. She is a mother, but the deaths of children mean nothing to her.
Even the death of her own children would mean nothing to her. She is
a Communist. This is what Joe McCarthy and Roy Cohn are protect-
ing me from. But every time I see electric wires, a chain-link fence with
barbed wire on top, or an electric power plant, sometimes even a water
tower, anything sending something from one part of the official world
into our private lives, I am afraid for Mrs. Rosenberg. For the electricity in her body. To save me? You don't need to do that to her, I want to
tell everybody. It is impossible that people like me will be saved. We
will eventually be found out, and we know very well that you will be the
ones to do it. We don't know what we've done, but you know. Then we
will join Mrs. Rosenberg. Then our bodies will be shot through with
electricity. We will be shocked. (I have felt it when I touched the plug
of the electric toaster.) We will be shocked to death.

We are reminded of other memoirs, variously apposite. Some
Sartre, surely, for the precocious Baby Writer: a bratty Jean-
Paul inventing in *Words* a childhood self appropriate to his
speed-freak metaphysics, in the absence of *his* dead father glee-
fully certain he's free of superego. Some *Speak, Memory*
Nabokov, for sheer lyrical anti-Freudian stubbornness: the lepidopterist who claimed, as a child in prelapsarian Russia, to have
seen through the dining room window *his* father *levitate,* a glorious midair sprawl in a wind-rippled white summer suit against
the cobalt-blue noon sky, hoisted by happy peasants, prefigur-

ing an angel on a vaulted church ceiling, wax tapers, swimming lights, funeral lilies, and the open coffin. Maybe even Philip Roth, about whom Gordon has written so brilliantly, who came to understand *Patrimony* during his custodianship of his dying father: a shaving mug handed down by generations of Jewish immigrants; the excrement Philip had to clean up, as once he'd been cleaned up after as a baby; their mutual obsession with memory, never forgetting *any thing*; a distinctive voice: "He taught me the vernacular. He *was* the vernacular, poetic and expressive and point-blank, with all the vernacular's glaring limitations and all its durable force."

Or, for a female point of view on excess, secrecy, and dysfunction: Germaine Greer, who tells us in *Daddy, We Hardly Knew You* that *her* father Reg had lied his whole life to his wife and children about almost everything, from his ersatz South African origins to his phony war as a cipher clerk at an underground decoding machine in Malta, meaning there had been no excuse at all for his daughter's growing up in a house without music, books, flowers, cheese, or love. To which, add Carolyn See, who speaks in *Dreaming* of a grandfather dying drunk in a snowdrift and a grandmother blowing her head off with a shotgun and a father who churns out hardcore porn under a lifesized snap of a naked Marilyn Monroe and a mother playing tag at night inside high-voltage power stations with a pint of vodka in a Bible; of knowing that it's Thanksgiving because Uncle Bob sets himself on fire and that it's Easter because you're in Las Vegas, where the Risen Christ is a topless dancer on a skating rink performing "Spice on Ice."

But Gordon is *sui generis,* and so is her book: wounding, refulgent, and redemptive. "The detective in love with her client," she warns, "usually ends up murdering or being murdered." Besides, "we want the log of a voyage with a happy ending. The story we don't want to hear is the story of disintegration, diminishment, humiliation, loss. This is the America we can't imagine." Nevertheless: "There is some residue. . . . You didn't get it from your accusers; it was neither pitiable nor the stuff of shame. Perhaps it was the voice of God. The God of singleness and silence. The font of pure, accepting love." Insisting: "His name is not David, or Israel. It is My Father." Finally: "This man owes me his life, and he will live forever."

In the last astonishing pages of *The Shadow Man,* having exhumed her father, she reburies him, in an elsewhere of her own choosing, in a ceremony of her own devising, in a coffin strewn with the severed heads of roses. Her friends think she is crazy. Well, so was Joan of Arc. And Simone Weil. And Antigone. And Hildegard von Bingen, the twelfth-century "Sybil of the Rhine," who wrote poems, plays, histories, and sacred songs and refused to yield to local authorities the body of a radical buried in her convent graveyard.

Maybe she just loved him more than God.

Underground Gass

Your wife is fat. Your penis is tiny. Your children are sallow-faced louts. Your mistress dumped you because you have "a loathsome mind." Your colleagues in the history department at a Midwestern university are charlatans and poltroons. Your "post-Bomb pre-Boom" students on the banks of the Wabash are either boring pests or sexual prey. The preface you are writing to your magnum opus, *Guilt and Innocence in Hitler's Germany*—"This is to introduce a work on death by one who's spent his life in a chair"—has turned into a nightshriek. And you are also digging a tunnel in your cellar. To escape from what? From marriage, mind, and matter as if they were concentration camps: "There is no final safety from oneself. It is something we often say, but only the mad believe it, the consequences are so awesome, and so infinite. In that sense Hitler's been the only God. But must I always live in Germany?"

In the noisome 1960s, contemplating "first love, first nights, last stands," at age fifty and at the end of his rope, William Frederick Kohler—the malodorous mind that imagines *The Tunnel*—bares his teeth at everything that tethers him: childhood, ego, landscape, language, narratology, Western Civ. It goes without saying that he is also trapped in this Panopticon of a postmodern novel that William Gass has been torturing for three decades, as Giacometti tortured metals. Alice down a rabbit hole, Dostoyevsky underground, Orpheus descending: "I am distance itself," says K. "I stand alone on an empty page like a period put down in a snowfall." As his introduction turns into a howl (Henry Adams does *Mein Kampf*), a dozen fonts change points and riot in bolds and italics, outlines and shadows, sub- and superscripts. Type shifts shape to form cellar steps, male genitalia, a Star of David. The book tunnels itself—"as long as a chimney," carting up dirt, wading through bile, digging out from under cave-ins, excavating emptiness: *Holes. Wombs. Archaeologies.* There are also a surprising number of limericks for such a transgressive text, many about nuns, most obscene. Not that we can trust a word of it, but this is what we're told . . .

About K's childhood: Silence, exile, punning. He was born in Iowa and raised in Ohio. His arthritic father, a failed architect (Albert Speer? Ayn Rand?), hated him. His alcoholic mother, who forgot to invite any of his friends to his birthday party, went mad in a cyclone and died in an asylum, smelling of juniper like a shrub, combing glass out of her hair. Besides cyclones and a plague of locusts, there was also "The Sunday Drive" into the Heart of the Heart of the Country, achingly evoked in a brilliant chapter as long as a novella, only then to be despoiled, as if, with "a little Führer" at the steering wheel, internal combustion can only produce more poison Gass. "My father taught me how to be a failure. He taught me bigotry and bitterness. I never acquired his courage, because I caught a case of cowardice from my mother — soft as cotton — and I was born with her desperate orality, her slow insistent cruelty — like quicksand — her engulfing love." No wonder he will beat up on his own infant son.

About K's marriage: It's hateful. "Once upon a time, Martha and I slept naked, and we were all the flannel one another needed. Now she goes about layered in ghost garb like a contemporary text." She also collects heavy antique furniture with a view to opening a shop. Into these bureau drawers K will empty his dug-out dirt. "I think what bothers me most about you," she tells him, "is that you're not ashamed of what you are." Worse than her calumnies on his character are her criticisms of his prose: "Martha hates it when I shape my sentences. She says it doesn't sound sincere. . . . She says it falsifies feeling." What sincerity? What feeling? "What does my work do but simply remove some of the armor, the glamour, of Evil. It small-*e*'s it. It shakes a little sugar on the shit. It dares to see a bit of the okay in our great bugaboche. Inexcusable. Slander our saints if you will, but please leave our Satan undefiled by any virtue, his successes inexplicable by any standard." No wonder he will pounce on corn-fed coeds.

About K's education: He grew up mapping emotional climates, and longed to be a poet. Rilke is all over these pages; Homer and Virgil; Dante, Shakespeare, Goethe, and Blake; Baudelaire and Hölderlin; adumbrations of Yeats ("old clothes hangered in a closet"), T. S. Eliot (a party of Prufrocks), and Ezra Pound (whom he most resembles). But he abandons poetry to get at the uglier truths. As a graduate student in prewar Germany, where on Kristallnacht he may have hurled a stone himself, he trifles with the gypsy Susu, who pays with her head for violating Nazi dietary laws by eating the roasted thumbs of Jews, and finds his mentor in Magnus Tabor, "Mad Meg," author of *The Eternal Significance of the Caesar, The Death of Destiny,* and *The Failure of the Future,* an amalgam of all that's monstrous in Nietzsche, Spengler, and Heidegger. Tabor deplores the Greeks because "the German mind has been so sodomized by these splendid pederasts, we don't know which of our holes is for what"; he preaches that history is half provocation and half revenge, and either American or Mongol, liking "both size and winning"; he believes that "anything of which you could form a passionate conception automatically *was* because the pure purpose of things lay in their most powerful description." K laps it up, including the swastika: "Has ever a company contrived a better logo? Perhaps Mercedes-Benz." No wonder that Indiana will seem so disappointing upon his return to the States: "I suspect that the first dictator of this country will be called Coach."

About K's career: He got tenure early on, when it was easy, on the basis of his first book, *Nuremberg Notes,* which ridiculed war-crimes trials. Said a reviewer: "Professor Kohler has given to the German mind a public place in nature." Yes, he thinks: "Men may walk about it now like someone waiting for a bus, and feed the birds." What he does now is "inhale hate like hemp." It's okay to be anti-Semitic if you despise everybody else *too.* He encourages his own doctoral candidates to cobble up theses on fascist symps like D'Annunzio. On a pane of window, a white of page, a black of board, he spies "the utter absence of significance; it is the world as unread and unreadable." Under the sunporch he has stored his trunk of Nazi memorabilia: armband, swagger stick, schnapps flask, silver braid, black boots. He dreams of and designs similar insignia for an imaginary Party of the Disappointed People (PDP), every resentful manjackboot of them a Prufrock: "My god, to be a man as I am—smothered with women and children like a duck with onions . . ." But: "History startled me. Melting one small Jew to keep the ovens cool. And then another . . . Schopenhauer, you old fool, this world was never my idea." K will never be a Coach.

There is no light at the end of this *Tunnel,* not even a whimper, merely a pun, like a shaggy God story, except that God is dead and so are Author Gods. As if he were Isaiah Berlin's evil twin, Gass kills off everybody who was anybody in the Western intellectual tradition—from Plato to Wittgenstein, Pythagoras to Spinoza, Democritus to Durkheim, Aquinas to Unamuno, Tacitus to Gibbon, Parmenides to David Hume. Off with their chockablock heads: "Hegel, Bergson, Toynbee, Marx, Buber, Sartre, Niebuhr, and other dead-again Christians." Poets like Pindar and Milton and Wordsworth and Cavafy. And novelists too: Cervantes, de Sade, Pavese, Céline (of course!), and Nabokov. In the service of what? In the service of Kohler's disillusionment. In this most savage of academic novels (by comparison, Mary McCarthy is Mary Poppins), K's a Nabokovian himself, more like a Kinbote than a Pnin, but witless from his blind misreading of the black and white spaces. He has come to the conclusion that all history—of kings, princes, classes, clans, forces, causes, genius, fortune, gods, heroes, prima donnas, coincidences, conspiracies, cabals; of Chinese stages and Russian periods and Soviet steps and forward leaps and new world orders; of the study of language, the science of men in time, or the process by which consciousness seeks to contain its sievelike self—is a cover-up for what any one man, tribe, culture, or nation-state will do to another if they ever get the power and the chance. "Who of us has not destroyed our enemies in our heads? Suppose but a whisper of our wishes leaked out and half a continent was ready to rise and do our bidding?" We've been at it since Carthage: "Nature punishes gluttony, not avarice or hate. To Nature it's important that you get a good night's sleep." Who, knowing that we are born stupid and die dumb and leave behind our little lumps of language like a turd, wouldn't become a "friend of Fascist thought"?

No wonder Primo Levi threw himself down a Turin stairwell.

To empty this Kohler out on us, gravedigger Gass has composed a kind of anti-canticle, an aria of obloquy. Each paragraph, each sentence, every clause, every phrase, has been burnished breathless, willfully wrought, stippled stark. Not a lyric but it's laced with acid. Not a whale tooth but it's scrimshawed. The eye can't rest, nor the mind mist. But isn't this the whole idea? "Syllables catch fire, General. Towns do. Concepts are pulled apart like the joints of a chicken. Substance. Listen to the mind munch. Consonants, General, explode like grenades. Vowels rot in some soft southern mouth, and meaning escapes from the oooos like an ass." So much for high culture. Consciousness is noise: Bach and Buchenwald. One thinks of Ezra Pound, that "broken bundle of mirrors" by the waters of Rapallo, wandering Lear-like into his Waste Land madness, a flotsam of Homer and Confucius, of Li Po and T. S. Eliot, troubadours and Rosicrucians, Mussolini and Social Credit; that godfather of modernism who was ignorant of Marx and uncomprehending of Freud; that critic of literature who'd never read the Russians; that critic of art who'd missed Picasso's point; a tone-deaf composer of tuneless operas with his Brain Sperm and Funny Money theories and a hatred of "the democratic virus." "Pull down thy vanity!" the old goat cried, and his vanity pulled him so far down that he was vile. Now meet K, for whom history is "horse drop, cow plop, nose snot, rope knot, flesh rot, ink blot, blood clot, street shout," whacking away on his little weenie, a one-man marching band of the banality of evil. Gass has written a splendid, daunting, loathsome novel.

Amazing Grace

Never mind how wonderful it is that Grace Paley should have imagined an alter ego named Faith Darwin. One of them is about to undergo an enormous change at the last minute. "Just when I most needed important conversation, a sniff of the man-wide world, that is, at least one brainy companion who could translate my friendly language into his tongue of undying carnal love, I was forced to lounge in our neighborhood park, surrounded by children." Like a Transcendental angel out of Emerson, she's twelve feet up in a sycamore tree, from which she can see almost everything except the horizon of that "sensible, socialist, Zionist world" her mother had dreamt of—a future full of faith and grace.

"What a place in democratic time!" she thinks. Aloft, this "Faith in a Tree" will also consider motherhood: "I own two small boys whose dependence on me takes up my lumpen time and my bourgeois feelings." And the older fathers in the park: "every one of them wearing a fine grey head and eager eye, his breath caught, his hand held by the baby daughter of a third intelligent marriage." And the blue-eyed, boy-faced policemen: "They can see that lots of our vitamin-enlarged high-school kids are planning to lug their guitar cases around all day long. They're scared that one of them may strum and sing a mountain melody or that several, a gang, will gather to raise their voices in medieval counterpoint." And herself: "I often see through the appearance of things right to the apparition itself." Plus her son Richard, her friends Kitty and Anna, the PTA, the Board of Ed, the People's Republic of Ubmonsk, "the rise of industrialism and group therapy," and the God of the Jews:

If it's truth and honor you want to refine, I think the Jews have some insight. Make no images, imitate no God. After all, in His field, He is pre-eminent. Then let that One who made the tan deserts and the blue Van Allen belt and the green mountains of New England be in charge of Beauty, which He obviously understands, and let man, who was full of forgiveness at Jerusalem, and full of survival at Troy, let man be in charge of Good.

We have been here before Faith, inside this American English with a Yiddish accent, vitamin-enlarged, as it were, by a medieval counterpoint that modernized our postwar literature, that jumped our beans. We hear it in the brilliant twitchy speakfreak patter of a Bellow—mandarin and colloquial, sentimental and neo-Baroque, Talmudic mutter and gangster slang; the long irony, the low laugh, the short fuse. ("Orpheus, the son of Greenhorn. He brought Coney Island into the Aegean and united Buffalo Bill with Rasputin.") And whenever Malamud is feeling bad, before he goes up in a magic barrel to consort like Chagall with cows, candles, and violins. ("Have a little mercy on me Lesser, move so I can break up this rotten house that weighs like a hunch on my back.") And even in the fractured liturgies of S. J. Perelman. ("To Err is Human, to Forgive, Supine.") And maybe in the idol-smashing of an Ozick. ("His intelligence was a version of cynicism. He rolled irony like an extra liquid in his mouth.") But in Paley's wonderful stories—about what mothers should have told their daughters, and men don't know about women, about friendship, death, and making do, about reading Dostoyevsky and running for your life—the political accent is always *grave,* levitating leftward: socialist/anarchist/pacifist/ feminist. To a table where the bread is kneaded with the baker's tears and there's blood in the chicken soup, she always brings a surpassing generosity, a radical optimism, and our marching orders.

What happens to Faith in her tree in the park is the politics of witness:

> a banging of pots and pans came out of the playground and a short parade appeared—four or five grownups, a few years behind me in the mommy-and-daddy business, pushing little go-carts with babies in them, a couple of three-year-olds hanging on. They were the main bangers and clangers. The grown-ups carried three posters. The first showed a prime-living, prime-earning, well-dressed man about thirty-five years old next to a small girl. A question was asked: would you

burn a child? In the next poster he placed a burning cigarette on the child's arm. The cool answer was given: WHEN NECESSARY. The third poster carried no words, only a napalmed Vietnamese baby, seared, scarred, with twisted hands.

The cops roust these troublemakers, but Faith has received their transmission:

> And I think that is exactly when events turned me around, changing my hairdo, my job downtown, my style of living and telling. Then I met women and men in different lines of work, whose minds were made up and directed out of that sexy playground by my children's heartfelt brains, I thought more and more and every day about the world.

When a young Malamud had been too long-winded telling a tale, his father used to asked him: *"Vus noks du mir a chinik?"* What tune are you banging on your pot?

Then, as often happens in stories, it was several years later.

("Listening")

This was late in the eighties, on Second Avenue in Manhattan across the street from the Israeli Consulate, next door to National Public Radio. From the window of a bus, I saw they were demonstrating—something about the *intifada*. So I got out, walked around, and met the New Jewish Agenda—and there, of course, was Paley, appalled by rubber bullets and broken hands. I wanted to tell her to go home and write another story. I would agitate in her stead. For decades, no matter where, every time I went to demonstration, she was already there. I also knew that when I failed to show, she'd be there anyway. Why not a bargain? Couldn't she call when she felt a demonstration coming on? I'd go *for* her. She'd stay home and "invent for my friends and our children a report on those private deaths and the condition of our lifelong attachments." I would gladly serve as a decoy, a beard, or an umbrella, while she was secretly committing magic.

This is to miss the point of a woman who'd already looked into "the square bright window of daylight to ask myself the sapping question: What is man that woman lies down to adore him?" Yeats said famously: "The intellect of man is forced to choose / Perfection of the life or of the work." He wasn't happy about it, adding: "That old perplexity an empty purse / Or the day's vanity, the night's remorse." But it was a male piggy thing to say. The Paley who wrote the stories for *The Little Disturbances of Man* (1959), *Enormous Changes at the Last Minute* (1974) and *Later the Same Day* (1985), and who now publishes *Just as I Thought*—that Paley had never been up a sycamore tree. For her, writing stories and going to demonstrations were both, and equally, the normal respiration of intelligence. It's clear from this collection of essays, speeches, and reminiscences, this rich compost heap of travel notes, position papers, prefaces, and afterthoughts, that she was born with a pot and plenty of tunes to bang on it:

> I had this idea that Jews were supposed to be better. I'm not saying they were, but they were supposed to be, and it seemed to me on my block that they often were. I don't see any reason in being in this world actually if you can't in some way be better, repair it somehow. . . . So to be like all the other nations seems to me a waste of nationhood, a waste of statehood, a waste of energy, and a waste of life.

From the very beginning seventy-seven years ago in the East Bronx, she has been agitating. Her doctor father was a socialist, her uncle Grisha an anarchist, one aunt a Zionist and another a communist. She learned early on never to carry the flag at a protest march; a cousin had been gunned down in Russia in 1905 because the red banner was such a nifty target. She wore, at age nine, the blue shirt and red kerchief of a young socialist Falcon and fought in gang wars between the Third and Fourth Internationals. She was suspended at age twelve from junior high for signing the antiwar Oxford Pledge, and staged agitprop plays with titles like *Eviction!* She was married at nineteen, and the abortion she'd later write a story about, as she helped organize one of the first abortion speak-outs in the country in the late sixties, also caused the doctor who performed it to be arrested and imprisoned. Her first jobs included opening doors and answering telephones for doctors like her father; typing bills at an elevator company; secretary to the fire chief on a North Carolina army post; superintending linens in a rooming house; fetching for professors of zirconium and titanium at Columbia; the Southern Conference of Human Welfare and the New York Tenants Association; housewife, mother, teacher, writer, angel.

And see where she went: Into geographies of disobedient mind and language, out among fractious worlds. To Cooper Union, the ILGWU, and May Day parades. To Margaret Sanger's Sixteenth Street birth-control clinic, the Whitehall Induction Center, Wall Street, and the Pentagon; to a World Peace Congress in Moscow, where she consulted with Sakharov, and a conference in Puerto Rico on bilingual children and public education; to Hanoi, from which she brought back prisoners of war ("You are assumed by your hosts to be an important person in your country, whereas you are really a kind of medium-level worker in one tendency in the nonviolent direct-action left wing of the antiwar movement"), and to Nicaragua and El Salvador, where she met the Mothers of the Disappeared. Have I mentioned the Greenwich Village Women's House of Detention, to which she was sentenced for sitting down to impede a military parade, where she spent six days reading William Carlos Williams while bonding with prostitutes? "If there are prisons, they ought to be in the neighborhood, near a subway—not way out in distant suburbs, where families have to take cars, buses, ferries, trains, and the population that considers itself innocent forgets, denies, chooses to never know that there is a whole huge country of the bad and the unlucky and the self-hurters, a country with a population greater than that of many nations in our world." Nor ought I to neglect the actions against missile sites and nuclear power plants like Seabrook and Shoreham, in upstate New York towns like Waterloo, where she was greeted with signs that said: NUKE THE BITCHES TILL THEY GLOW, THEN SHOOT THEM IN THE DARK.

"The slightest story," she tells us, "ought to contain the facts of money and blood to be interesting to adults." All the while that she wrote hers, opposing people made of blood and bone to connections made of oil and gold, all the while she was teaching her students to read the biographies of Emma Goldman, Prince Kropotkin, and Malcolm X and the fiction of Isaac Babel and Christa Wolf ("Send these words out, out into the airy rubbly meaty mortal fact of the world, endless love, the dangerous transforming spirit"), she seems seldom to have missed a meeting of the Clamshell Alliance, the War Resisters' League, Women's Strike for Peace, the Fellowship for Reconciliation, the American Friends Service Committee, Jews for Racial and Economic Justice, Ploughshares, Sane/Freeze, even PEN. And she seems always to have found a community where someone says: "This is where *my* trouble is; this is where it hurts. And then someone else answers, Me too. And listen. This is what I did about it." Except for Studs Terkel, Gloria Steinem, Pete Seeger, Joan Baez, Ed Doctorow, and a few other faithful, I don't know where the rest of us went instead. Maybe, in a Duke sweatshirt or a Sorbonne zoot suit, we were on the barricades at a Paris Commune faculty meeting, writing a campus speech code.

First they make something, then they murder it. Then they write a book about how interesting it is. ("The Long-Distance Runner")

"If you're a feminist," she says, "it means that you've noticed that male ownership of the direction of female lives has been the order of the day for a few thousand years, and it isn't natural." To which she adds: "It seems to me that privilege is obligation, that if it's easier to go to jail, so to speak, or more possible, then direct actions that may lead to arrest are exactly what we ought to undertake when that is what's called for. . . . Some of this will probably seem naïve to some people. It's a naïveté it's taken me a lot of time and thinking to get to." And then, a kind of coda: "There are things about men and women and their relations to each other, also the way they relate to the almost immediate destruction of the world, that I can't figure out. And nothing in critical or historical literature will abate my ignorance a tittle or a jot. I will have to do it all by myself, marshal the evidence. In the end, probably all I'll have to show is more mystery—a certain juggled translation from life, that foreign tongue, into fiction, the jargon of man."

That honorableness should be so straightforward comes as a cattle-prod shock to those of us who hopped away from the sixties on the pogosticks of our careers. In Paley, life, literature, and politics converge—nonviolently, of course—in a cunning patchwork quilt of radiance and scruple, of witness and example, of nurture and nag, of subversive humor and astonishing art—a Magical Socialism and a Groucho Marxism. Just listen to bits and pieces of what her stories teach us, better than Buddha:

> My husband gave me a broom one Christmas. This wasn't right. No one can tell me it was meant kindly.

> I cradled him. I closed my eyes and leaned on his dark head. But the sun in its course emerged from among the water towers of downtown office buildings and suddenly shone white and bright on me. Then through the short fat fingers of my son, interred forever, like a black-and-white-barred king in Alcatraz, my heart lit up in stripes.

> Don't put yourself on a platter. What are you—a roast duck, everything removable with a lousy piece of flatware? Be secret. Turn over on your other side. Let them guess if you're stuffed. That's how I got where I am.

> Wherever you turn someone is shouting give me liberty or I give you death.

> Then for a little while she talked gently as one does to a person who is innocent and insane and incorruptible because of stupidity.

> It's a terrible thing to die young. Still, it saves a lot of time.

> Though the world cannot be changed by talking to one child at a time, it may at least be known.

> Hindsight, usually looked down upon, is probably as valuable as foresight, since it does include a few facts.

> I am trying to curb my cultivated individualism, which seemed for years so sweet. It was my own song in my own world and, of course, it may not be useful in the hard time to come.

It's very important to emphasize what is good or beautiful so as not to have a gloomy face when you meet some youngster who has just begun to guess.

As if to punish us for our mayor, Citizen Paley has left the city she made so vital on the page that provincials like me could imagine no other capital or homeland—a Galapagos of jazzy thought, passionate conviction, smart mouths, odd birds, and republican virtue. I know she's up there bothering Vermont about dairy farmers and river polluters, disrupting meetings of school boards and zoning councils, causing trouble for the czar. But we need her more here now in Mussolini meantime—as beautiful as blue Van Allen belts, more forgiving than Jerusalem—than we ever did back when she was Falconing. "Let us go forth," she writes, "with fear and courage and rage to save the world." Ashamed of myself in her moral corona, I look for Faith in every tree.

Morrison's Paradise Lost

So abundant, even prodigal, is Toni Morrison's first new novel since her Nobel Prize, so symphonic, light-struck, and sheer, as if each page had been rubbed transparent, and so much the splendid sister of *Beloved*—she's even gone back to Brazil, not this time to see the three-spoke slave collar and the iron mouth-bit, but to check out *candomblé*—that I realize I've been holding my breath since December 1993. After such levitation, weren't all of us in for a fall? Who knew she'd use the Prize as a kite instead of a wheelbarrow?

And I realize I've been holding my breath even on those occasions—under a tent at Caramoor, once in a cathedral—to which I've been invited as a designated partisan, after which I'm guaranteed a standing ovation because, of course, I'm followed by the Laureate, who reads from her novel-in-progress, which begins: "They shoot the white girl first." All week long in Stockholm, after the embassy lunch and the postage stamp with her face on it, before the concert and the banquet, between madrigals and snowflakes and candle flames and the joyride in the Volvo limo behind a police escort to the great halls and the grand ballrooms and the singing waiters and the reindeer steak, I had thought of Pecola, pregnant with her father's baby, believing that if only she had blue eyes she'd be loved as much as Bojangles had loved Shirley Temple. And of Sula, who when she loved a man rubbed the black off his bones down to gold leaf, then scraped away the gold to discover alabaster, then tapped with a hammer at the alabaster till it cracked like ice, and what you felt was fertile loam. Of Milkman in *Song of Solomon*, who went south from Detroit to a ruined plantation and a cave of the dead, who learned from blue silk wings, red velvet rose petals, a children's riddle song, and a bag of human bones not only his own true name but also how to fly all the way back to Africa. Of the horseback ghosts of the blind slaves in *Tar Baby*, where Caliban got another chance against Prospero. Of Sethe in *Be-*

loved like a black Medea with a handsaw and Denver who swallowed her sister's blood and Beloved swimming up from blue water to eat all the sugar in the world: *Beloved,* that ghost story, mother epic, folk fable, fairy tale, and incantation of lost children, men like centaurs, lunatic history and babies offered up like hummingbirds to shameful gods. Where had it been hiding, this book we always needed? Who now can picture our literature in its absence, between Whitman and Twain, the Other in Faulkner and Flannery O'Connor? Before *Beloved,* our canon was wounded, incomplete. Until *Beloved,* our imagination of America had a heart-sized hole in it big enough to die from, as if we'd never seen black boys "hanging from the most beautiful sycamore trees in the world." And finally *Jazz*: as if Sidney Bechet had met the Archduke Trio or Ellington gone Baroque; a novel that wrote itself by talking to us, a story that confided: "I love the way you hold me, how close you let me be to you. I like your fingers on and on, lifting, turning. I have watched your face for a long time now, and missed your eyes when you went away from me. . . . Look, look. Look where your hands are. Now."

After her dispossessions and her hauntings, her butter cakes and baby ghosts, her blade of blackbirds and her graveyard loves, Not Doctor Street and No Mercy Hospital and all those maple-syrup men "with the long-distance eyes": *Just look where she was now.* We stood at our banquet tables in Stockholm's City Hall, in white tie and ball gowns and trepidation. A trumpet fanfare sounded. Above us, past a gilded balustrade, the processional began. The winner of the prize came down the marble steps at last, on the arm of the King of Sweden. Never mind that I am pale and I am male. She'd taught me to imagine the lost history of her people, to read the signs of love and work and nightmare passage and redemptive music, to hear the deepest chords of exile. I was proud to be a citizen of whatever country Toni Morrison came from. And that night she gave lessons to the noble rot of Europe on what majesty really looks like.

All of this — up in the air, dancing on the vaulted ceiling.

"They shoot the white girl first." In her lecture to the Swedish Academy, she had spoken against the punishing speech of the organs of obedience, used to "sanction ignorance and preserve privilege"; against the "obscuring" and "oppressive" language of state, the "calcified language of the academy," the "faux-language of the mindless media," the "policing languages" of "racist mastery," and the "seductive, mutant language designed to throttle women, to pack their throats like paté-producing geese with their own unsayable, transgressive words." Rather than these obscenities, she proposed a tongue that "arcs toward the place where meaning may lie." Word-work is sublime, she said, "because it is generative; it makes the meaning that secures our difference, our human difference." Death may be the meaning of life, but language is its measure. Language alone "protects us from the scariness of things with no names. Language alone is meditation." Meditating, she had found brave words like "poise," "light," "wisdom," "deference," "generosity," "felicity," and "trust."

To these, we must now add "solace." Like Schopenhauer and the sorrow songs, *Paradise* seeks consolation. Part history and part Dreamtime, part opera and part Matisse, it would be surpassing and transcendent if only for the notion of a "Disallowing." But its rainbow parabola also includes Reconstruction and the Trail of Tears, Vietnam and civil rights, patriarchy and ancestor worship, abduction and sanctuary, migration and abandonment, sex and ghosts. Considering degrees of blackness, reversals of color-blind perspectives, and above all longings for home, it will raise a ruckus and rewrite God.

> *Bodacious black Eves unredeemed by Mary, they are like panicked does leaping toward a sun that has finished burning off the mist and now pours its holy oil over the hides of game.*
> *God at their side, the men take aim. For Ruby.* (Paradise)

In a house shaped like a cartridge, in a state shaped like a gun, the fathers and sons of the nearby all-black town of Ruby shoot down running women as if they were deer. *They shoot the white girl first.* Not the least of many mysteries in *Paradise* is how hard it is to figure out which of the five women attacked by a fearful lynching party in a former convent in a godforsaken Oklahoma in the 1970s is, in fact, white. Slyly, Morrison is reminding us that skin color, about which we tend to get hysterical, is only a single datum, and maybe not the decisive one, in a universe of information. We do know the lynchers are "blue-black people," called "8-rock" after coal at the deepest level of the mines. To understand how it happened—this act of violence at the heart of every Morrison novel, the wound that will not heal—we must first learn the stories of the convent and the town, then the dreams of the players and finally the template's design. We are vouchsafed all three simultaneously, in flashes of lyric lightning; in "the cold serenity of God's wrath"; and in raptures, seizures, or eruptions of volcanic consciousness ("You thought we were hot lava and when they broke us down into sand, you ran").

The "big stone house in the middle of nowhere" began as an embezzler's mansion, with lurid appointments of nude Venus statuary, nipple-tipped doorknobs, and vagina-shaped alabaster ashtrays. After this Gatsby's imprisonment, it was taken over by nuns and turned into Christ the King School for Native Girls, most of whom would run away from the God who despised them. But these nuns brought with them their own luridities, including an etching of Saint Catherine of Siena on her knees offering up a plate of breasts. And when the last nun died— leaving behind only Consolata, the child they'd stolen decades ago from Rio's slums—the convent became, without even thinking about it, a sanctuary for young women orphaned or broken on history's wheel, a safe house for the throwaway, castaway female children of the sixties and seventies, on the road and looking to hide from angry fathers, abusive husbands, dead babies, boyfriends in Attica, rapists, Vietnam, Watergate, black water, and little boys on protest marches "spitting blood into their hands so as not to ruin their shoes."

Something will happen in 1976 to this haphazard ad hoc community of "women who chose their own company," these wild-thing Sulas—to Consolata in the cellar with her wine bottle and her bat vision; to Seneca in the bathtub, the "queen of scars," making thin red slits in her skin with a safety pin; to Mavis, who hears her asphyxiated twins laughing in the dark; to Gigi/Grace, who seeks buried treasure; and to Pallas/Divine, who could be carrying a lamb, a baby, or a jaguar. They are suddenly full of "loud dreaming." They chalk their bodies on the basement floor. They shave their heads and dance like holy women in the hot rain: *If you have a place that you should be in, and somebody who loves you waiting there, then go. If not stay here and follow me. Someone could want to meet you.*

And the nearby town: ah, Ruby. Although Morrison doesn't say so, the ancients believed that rubies were an antidote to poison, warded off plague, banished grief, and diverted the mind from evil thoughts. A "perfect ruby" was the Philosopher's Stone of the alchemists. We may also remember Dorothy's slippers in *The Wizard of Oz*. Ruby, Oklahoma, is likewise a refuge as well as a fortress, a Beulah, Erewhon, or New Shangri-la, not to mention the promised land of Canaan, and the last stop of a long line that began with the passage from Africa, that included landfall, slavery, and civil war, Emancipation and Reconstruction—a proud community of freedmen, of gunsmiths, seamstresses, lacemakers, cobblers, ironmongers, and masons:

> They are extraordinary. They had served, picked, plowed and traded in Louisiana since 1755, when it included Mississippi; and when it was divided into states they had helped govern both from 1868 to 1875, after which they had been reduced to field labor. They had kept the issue of their loins fruitful for more than two hundred years. They had denied each other nothing, bowed to no one, knelt only to their Maker.

In 1890, armed with advertisements of cheap land for homesteading—at the expense, of course, of the Choctaw, Creek, and Arapaho who happened to live there—they "took that history, those years, each other and their uncorruptible worthiness" and walked to Oklahoma, fifteen families looking for a place to build their communal kitchen, to inscribe on this

brick altar of an Oven a ferocious prophecy ("Beware the Fur-
row of His Brow"), to seed their fields and their women and
make a home they called Haven—one of many all-black towns in
the territory of the time, like Taft, Nicodemus, Langston City,
and Mound Bayou. Following a spectre into the wilderness,
they'd endured black-skinned bandits, "time-sharing shoes,"
rejection by poor whites and rich Choctaw, yard-dog attacks,
and the jeers of prostitutes. What they hadn't prepared for—a
humiliation that more than rankled, that "threatened to crack
their bones"—was the "contemptuous dismissal" they received
from Negro towns already built. This was the infamous "disallowing." And the reason for it is the secret of Ruby, which is
where nine of the families went next, in 1949, after the men came
home from war to Haven, to find America unchanged: "Out
There where your children were sport, your women quarry, and
where your very person could be annulled." Disallowed like the
ex-slaves before them, the ex-soldiers dismantled their Oven
and pulled up their stakes and struck out again. For Ruby.

Prosperous Ruby: wide streets, pastel houses, enormous
lawns, many churches (if only one bank), and flower gardens
"snowed with butterflies"; household appliances that
"pumped, hummed, sucked, purred, whispered and flowed";
Kelvinators and John Deere, Philco and Body by Fisher. No
diner, no gas station, no movie house or public telephone, no
hospital or police, no criminals and no jail, no "slack or sloven
women," nor, of course, any whites. "Here freedom was a test
administered by the natural world that a man had to take for
himself every day. And if he passed enough tests long enough,
he was king." It was as if Booker T. Washington had gone to
bourgeois heaven without having to die first dirt-poor. Because
nobody ever dies in Ruby, either. That's the deal they made with
God, the guy with the Furrowed Brow. It's payback for the Disallowing.

I'll explain the Disallowing in a minute. But you should know
that something is also happening in Ruby in the seventies. A
new reverend, a veteran of the civil rights movement, messes

with the minds of the children. (He actually thinks that "a community with no politics is doomed to pop like Georgia fatwood.") Somebody paints, on their sacred Oven, a jet-black fist with red fingernails. Not only do daughters refuse to get out of bed and brides disappear on their honeymoons, but the women of Ruby begin to question the Fathers, who get angrier and noisier:

> They dug the clay—not you. They carried the hod—not you. They mixed the mortar—not one of you. They made good strong brick for that oven when their own shelter was sticks and sod. You understand what I'm telling you? . . . Act short with me all you want, you in long trouble if you think you can disrespect a row you never hoed.

Naturally, the convent women are blamed. Hadn't they shown up at a wedding reception to which they should never have been invited in the first place, "looking like go-go girls: pink shorts, see-through skirts; painted eyes, no lipstick; obviously no underwear; no stockings"? Haven't our own women, who can't drive cars, been seen on foot on the road going to or coming from secret visits there—for vegetables, for pies, and maybe even for abortions? "The stallions were fighting about who controlled the mares and their foals," thinks Billie Delia, who as a child rode bare-bottomed on a horse until they reviled her for it. Graven idols, black arts, narcotic herbs, lesbian sex!

Besides—"out here under skies so star-packed it was disgraceful; out here where the wind handled you like a man"—the women of the convent are not 8-rock.

> *For ten generations they had believed the division they fought to close was free against slave, rich against poor. Usually, but not always, white against black. Now they saw a new separation: light-skinned against black. . . . The sign of racial purity they had taken for granted had become a stain. The scattering that alarmed Zechariah because he believed it would deplete them was now an even more dangerous level of evil, for if they broke apart and were disvalued by the impure, then, certain as death, those ten generations would disturb their children's peace throughout eternity.*

The fifteen families on their way to the promised land were Disallowed by "fair-skinned colored men," "shooed away" by "blue-eyed, gray-eyed yellowmen in good suits," *because they were too black*: so black they must be trashy. And so they became "a tight band of wayfarers bound by the enormity of what happened to them. Their horror of whites was convulsive but abstract. They saved the clarity of their hatred for the men who had insulted them in ways too confounding for language." What this meant for Haven and for Ruby was that anyone marrying outside the coal-black 8-rock bloodlines, "tampering" with the gene pool, was an outcast, no longer welcome in a community "as tight as wax," no longer even represented in a Christmas schoolroom reenactment of the Nativity that hybridized the birth of Christ with the trek story and the creation myth of the 8-rock forefathers. So what if all those generations kept going "just to end up narrow as bale wire"? In Ruby, nobody dies.

Until they do. And even then, at least in *Paradise,* they don't. Because the midwife Lone is there to teach Consolata how to raise the dead. And Soane's boys who died in Vietnam are as likely to show up leaning on her Kelvinator as Mavis's twins, who died in the mint-green Cadillac, will be heard laughing in the convent dark. And Dovey has a "Friend," who may be the apparition that led the fifteen families to their Haven, who visits her in the garden on his way to someplace else. And the fire-ruined house in the wilderness where Deacon meets his secret love is full of ash people, fishermen, nether shapes, and a girl with butterfly wings three feet long. And in the meadow where the convent women run from the guns of Ruby, there is a door. And on the other side of the door is solace and Piedade, who'll bathe them in emerald water and bring shepherds with colored birds on their shoulders "down from the mountains to remember their lives in her songs."

Something astonishing happens here. While, as usual, Morrison is complicating our understanding of black communities, with their very own scapegoats and pariahs as well as their raven-wing circles of sorrow, she also prestidigitates another kind of Reconstruction. Having reminded us in her Harvard lectures, *Playing in the Dark,* of the invisibility of black Americans in our classic literature—and yet their gravity and torque, and yet their ghostly resonance—she not only rewrites that literature (Hawthorne and Melville) but our history as well (from the Middle Passage of a *Mayflower* to colonial New England's City on the Hill to the destiny-manifesting westward Voortrek), and even our sacred texts (the Declaration of Independence, Lincoln's Second Inaugural). And in this rewriting, with its Xenophon and Moses and Balboa, odysseys and iliads, expulsions and displacements, lost tribes and diasporas, she dreams a second Republic "of longing, of terror, of perplexity, of shame, of magnanimity," in which white people are entirely spectral, a cloud on the water, a shadow mind.

Piedade; Pietà. Consolata; consolation. Hunted; haunted. Convent, covenant, coven. Morrison names: Seneca, Divine, Elder, Drum, Juvenal, Easter, Royal, Pious, Rector, Little Mirth, Flood, Fairy, Praise, Pryor, Apollo, Faustine, Chaste, Hope, and Lovely. She evokes: late melon and roast lamb, wild poppies and river vine, burnt lavender and broken babies; cherubim and body bags. And she redeems: There is a ghost for every family secret and every horror in history, and the language to forgive them. If we knew how she did it, we'd have literary theory instead of world radiance. I was holding my breath, and she took it away.

Part Five

THIRD WORLDS

Said's Culture and Imperialism

As Marlow helpfully pointed out in Conrad's *Heart of Darkness*: "The conquest of the earth, which means the taking it away from those who have a different complexion and slightly flatter noses than ourselves, is not a pretty thing when you look at it too much."

After too much looking, Edward Said in 1978 issued his magisterial report, *Orientalism*. Orientalism, he explained, is a "text" compiled by scholars, social scientists, and colonial administrators; a "trope" embellished by novelists, dramatists, even painters; and a *"distribution* of geopolitical awareness" in our libraries, our museums, our theaters, and our heads, to bolster the self-esteem of the West. We need and therefore hallucinate an "Orient" that's changeless, passive, and dependent; a sexy Other to which we can feel superior and thus excuse ourselves for a little imperialism here, a lot more racism there, and a fantasy life that's distinctly kinky.

Consider, as Said did, the culture-bound presumptions of Renan, Massignon, and Fourier, of Balfour and Disraeli. Or the metaphorical excesses of Goethe, Hugo, Lamartine, Lord Byron, and Richard Francis Burton. Or the ethnocentric arrogance of fledging philologists who suddenly decided that the Indo-European language group was "organic" while the Semitic group wasn't. Or our continuing ignorance and adamant disdain of Islam, as if Constantinople's sacking were a scary bedtime story still, like the Mongol hordes. Or the baggage we take along with us as tourists, "tyrannical observers," and the booty we bring back, like Elgin and his pilfered marbles — fancies and confabulations like an "Arab mind," a "passive, feminine, silent and supine East," and all that "unimaginable antiquity, inhuman beauty, boundless distance," wasted on natives who are dark, little, and lazy; our image-clusters of Eden and Troy and Sphinx; of Isis, Astarte, and Sheba; of hanging gardens and cruel Turks and bad hygiene and dangerous sex, especially with little boys.

Although Said, as much a child of the academy as of Egypt and Palestine, borrowed concepts of "hegemony" from Gramsci, and of "archaeology" and "discourse" from Foucault, what he really told us is that "Orientalism" is a masturbatory fantasy. From this rich and difficult book, like a giant banyan, fruit and colors fell, even popularizations. Ariel Dorfman's decodings of pop-cultural subtexts in *The Empire's Old Clothes* are as much Saidic as they are Marxist. (Think of the *Babar* children's books. By what divine right, Dorfman asks us, is this French schoolmarm teacher's pet the King of the Elephants, and why should he wear panties like a lamb chop? Only France, condescending to its African colonies.) Just as Saidic was Lucy Hughes-Hallet's demystification of *Cleopatra: Histories, Dreams and Distortions*. (Ever since Actium, from Shakespeare to Pushkin to Heine, from Tiepolo to Berlioz to Cecil B. DeMille, men fantasize whatever Cleo they think they need to mask how they really feel about female sexuality and the duplicitous, lassitudinous, nymphomaniacal "Orient": lover, killer, bimbo; dominatrix, sex kitten, camp; "pornography, window-shopping, and tourism.")

You'd have thought, after such a brilliant explosion of the trope, nobody would dare float it ever again. But then the Gulf War happened, and what we heard from technoblab spokestrolls in the Pentagon glitterdome was very much the same as what we heard from "Arab Experts" on the nightly crisis news, and what we read in such respectable quarterlies as *Foreign Affairs*, which told us that winter that Saddam's Iraq was "a brittle land, a frontier country between Persia and Arabia, with little claim to culture and books and grand ideas." *This*, about a Mesopotamia where we learned to write articles in the first place, even for *Foreign Affairs*; about a Basra that may have been our Garden of Eden; about a Baghdad that was, from centuries nine through twelve, the seat of Abbasid civilization; about Abraham's birthplace, Jonah's tomb, Nebuchadnezzar's fiery furnace. So much for Sumer, Nineveh, and Babylon; for Samara and Ur; for the first cities, and the original wheel, and a dolt like Hammurabi.

During the Gulf War a sign in a Manhattan bookshop said: PLEASE DON'T THROW BOOKS BY EDWARD SAID ON THE FLOOR. It was as if he had never written *Orientalism*. And so it's back to the drawing board, the shooting script, the rack and the zoo.

See Jane sit, in the poise and order of *Mansfield Park*, not much bothering her pretty head about the fact that this harmonious "social space," Sir Thomas Bertram's country estate, is sustained by slave labor on his sugar plantations in Antigua. Even Jane Austen, as early as 1814, bought into empire's easy assumptions and long perspectives—of a Greater civilizing Britain, entitled to garden where it wished, in violence and in shadows.

Watch Al run away, in *L'Etranger*, from nameless, faceless Arabs, as if existential anguish were appropriate to the Nazi occupation of France but somehow beside the point when it came to French colonial rule in Algeria. Even Albert Camus, as late as 1942, was not immune to Napoleonic notions of belonging wherever you happened to be, of an "ontological" prior claim to somebody else's geography, by force of arms, squatters' rights, and ethnographic pseudoscience.

How compelling, *still*, says Edward Said, are "the images of Western imperial authority":

Gordon at Khartoum, fiercely staring down the Sudanese dervishes in G. W. Joy's famous painting, armed only with a revolver and sheathed sword; Conrad's Kurtz in the center of Africa, brilliant, crazed, doomed, brave, rapacious, eloquent; Lawrence of Arabia at the head of his Arab warriors, living the romance of the desert, inventing guerrilla warfare, hobnobbing with princes and statesmen, translating Homer, and trying to hold on to Britain's "Brown Dominion"; Cecil Rhodes, establishing countries, estates, funds as easily as other men might have children . . . the concubines, dancing girls, odalisques of Gérôme, Delacroix's Sardanapalus, Matisse's North Africa, Saint-Saën's *Samson and Delilah*.

And this before analyzing Conrad, who knew the worst about

the West in Africa and South America, but couldn't imagine alternatives; or *Kim,* in which a carefully observed, various, and vital India was nevertheless, for Kipling, an English schoolboy's very own playing field, a blue balloon, a Great Game. Nor has he begun cataloguing such paraphernalia of empire as Ireland, Hegel, Picasso, belly dancing, Caliban, French postcards, Baden-Powell's Boy Scouts, or Verdi's famous "Egyptian opera," the occasion of the single joke in all of *Culture and Imperialism.* Like Verdi's earlier operas, winks Said, *Aïda* "is about a tenor and a soprano who want to make love, but are prevented by a baritone and a mezzo."

In *The World, the Text and the Critic* (1983), Said suggested that Conrad might have been thinking about himself when he described the "autistic art" of deranged and innocent Stevie, the ultimate victim of paranoid geopolitics in *The Secret Agent*:

> seated very good and quiet at a deal table, drawing circles, circles; innumerable circles, concentric, eccentric, coruscating whirl of circles that by their tangled multitude of repeated curves, uniformity of form, and confusion of intersecting lines suggested a rendering of cosmic chaos, the symbolism of a mad art attempting the inconceivable. The artist never turned his head; and in all his soul's application to the task his back quivered, his thin neck, sunk into a deep hollow at the base of the skull, seemed ready to snap.

Page-bound circles, blank white space, silence and mystery: at the receding center of the multitude of Conrad's words, his dark heart and his Inner Station, was something indescribable, "the folly" or "the horror." Says Said, "I think it entirely likely that Conrad imagined Stevie as a kind of writer viewed *in extremis* who, in being taken for a sort of pointless idiot, is limited terribly to two poles: inscribing a page endlessly or blown to bits and without human identity."

Culture and Imperialism (1993) is likewise a coruscating whirl. Out of these circles of criticism, of tropes and icons, of theories of reading and ideologies of empire and "magic totalities," Said, American and Arab, professor and polemicist, seeks a space of his own. By "a kind of geographical inquiry into historical experience," in "narratives of emancipation and enlightenment," he will deliver himself from "exilic marginality." A grabby imperializing West has gobbled up not only Conrad's blank spaces on the map—tin, gold, and silver; rubber, cotton, and opium; spices, sugar, and slaves—but also the blank spaces in our heads; our structures of "attitude and reference"; entire sciences like anthropology and linguistics; the very geography of thought.

But oh those "intersecting lines." If *Orientalism* was Said's *Midnight's Children,* a kind of origin myth, then *Culture and Imperialism* is his *Satanic Verses,* an epic of migration and metamorphosis, a Boat People *Iliad.* He insists that we decipher ourselves, full of bad faith and self-aggrandizing "social space." He demands that we consult the Southern and Eastern Other, a rich literature of opposition and resistance. He is writing as well for the Third World; xenophobic nativism and nationalism, sectarian and communal violence are not what "liberation" ought to have been about. Meanwhile he's furious at his own academy, where a claustrophobic "identity politics" bares its fangs at "investigators of the aporias and impossibilities of reading." He has strong opinions on the Gulf War and a superpower New World Order, and perhaps they belong elsewhere. He argues that imperialism invented the novel, that modernism substituted art for empire, that postmodernism is a reactionary denial that any of this ever happened, or matters—arguments that need at least another book. He is easily distracted, answering too many fire alarms, sometimes to pour on more petrol. And he must begin by distinguishing among imperialisms rather breezily, as if in an irritated rush to get to his preferred punching bags:

> What I am saying about the British, French, and American imperial experience is that it has a unique coherence and a special cultural centrality. . . . [Besides:] Before the Anglo-French competition, the major distinguishing characteristic of Western empires (Roman, Spanish, and Portuguese) was that the earlier empires were bent on loot, as Conrad puts it, on the transport of treasure from the colonies to

Europe, with very little attention to development, organization, system within the colonies themselves.

Is this true? In Latin America, we'd have to ask a Bolívar, an Octavio Paz, and the Mayas, Incas, and Aztecs. Whatever happened to nonwesterners like the Manchus in China, the Mughals in India, Abassids and Ottomans? Do languages count, or religions, like Christianity and Islam, devouring in their messianisms most of the available imaginative space? Russians have much to answer for; so do Austro-Hungarians. The Hellenes also threw their weight around. After Alexander and his Noble Companions danced naked with garlands around the Aristotle sepulchre in Troy, they'd go on to mess with the centrality of many cultures, from Tyre to Gaza to Persepolis, from Babylon to the Hindu Kush, from dynastic Egypt to the Peacock Throne. And Genghis Khan gobbled up twice as many square miles as Alexander with an arrow in his armpit. The bad news is that all the ancient civilizations were based on gold and slaves. Even the Moors owned Slavs and Celts. For the Japanese, Koreans. When Akbar betook himself four hundred years ago to the ghost city of Fatehpur Sikri, intending there to synthesize the great religions, he played chess and Parcheesi with slave girls as pieces.

But when it comes to sheer size, Genghis and Alexander were pikers compared to Europe's nineteenth-century imperial enterprise. In 1800, western powers controlled about a third of the globe. By 1914, says Said, "Europe held a grand total of roughly 85 percent of the earth as colonies, protectorates, dependencies, dominions, and commonwealths." And to justify all this geography, they had the best and the brightest of clerks scribbling their limpid excuses.

There was what Said calls "a cultural discourse regulating and confining the non-European to a secondary racial, cultural, ontological status," which permitted the conqueror to rationalize his conquest as "civilizing." Presumed in this discourse was an "ideological vision . . . sustained not only by direct domination and physical force but much more effectively over a long time by *persuasive means,* the quotidian processes of hegemony." These processes included the building of colonial cities (Delhi, Algiers, Saigon); the manufacture of agitprop (sheet music, almanacs, toy soldiers, brass band concerts, music-hall entertainments, board games); the inventing of new media (journalism, travel photography), new artistic styles (exotic painting, monumental sculpture), and new sciences (sociology, anthropology, psychology) all flacking for empire. The result, in the West, of this monopoly of "representation" was a sense of "entitlement," as if the idea of empire functioned "very much like the servants in grand households and in novels, whose work is taken for granted but scarcely ever more than named." The result in the East and South was servitude, resentment, and ultimately revolution . . . another, bloodier sort of narrative.

As the manticore explained to Gibreel in Rushdie's *Satanic Verses*: "They have the power of description, and we succumb to the pictures they construct."

Oh, look, French and German grammarians have discovered Sanskrit! English, French, and German poets and artists have discovered the great Indian national epics, and Persian imagery, and Sufi philosophy! English, French, and German grammarians, poets, artists, ethnographers, archaeologists, historiographers, and tourists have discovered ancient Greece, which civilization, by wishing away its inconvenient Semitic and Egyptian roots, is "Aryanized" and squeaky-clean!

On Conrad and Kipling, Said, predictably, dazzles. About E. M. Forster and Graham Greene, we could use more pages. Anthony Burgess and Paul Scott are omitted entirely. But what an artful dodge it is through the scrum of the rest of the English novel from Defoe and Dickens to Joyce Cary and Jean Rhys. We are led by Thackeray, in *Vanity Fair,* to believe there is something *off* about Joseph Sedley's money because it's Indian. Bertha Mason, Rochester's deranged wife in *Jane Eyre,* is of course West Indian. Why, Said wonders, should we duck our heads and pass on by, rather than stop and think, not only about the Bertram sugar plantation in *Mansfield Park,* but later on, Charles Gould's San Tomé mine in *Nostromo* and the Wilcox Anglo-Imperial Rubber Company in *Howards End*? The empire is the ghost at banquets of George Eliot (*Daniel Deronda*), Disraeli (*Tancred*), and even Henry James, who sent Ralph Touchett off to Egypt and Algeria in *Portrait of a Lady.* In at least this one presumptive respect, high art is not to be distinguished from the manufacture of Conan Doyle, Rider Haggard, and Robert Louis Stevenson.

Edmund Spenser was not much worse on the Irish question in the sixteenth century than David Hume was in the eighteenth or Matthew Arnold in the nineteenth. For Thomas Carlyle, *The Nigger Question* — "ugliness, idleness, rebellion" — was answered readily enough "with beneficent whip, since other methods avail not." Just listen to Ruskin go on about the English, "still undegenerate . . . a race mingled of the best northern blood," worthy of "seizing every piece of fruitful waste ground she can set her foot on," to "guide the human arts, and gather the divine knowledge, of distant nations, transformed from savageness to manhood." But such arrogance was pandemic, from historians like J. R. Seeley to legal scholars like Sir Henry Maine, to geologists like Roderick Murchison, to literary critics like Arnold, to revolutionaries like Marx and Engels. Marx swallowed whole Hegel's view of the Orient as static, despotic, and irrelevant to world history. Engels judged Algerian Moors a "timid race" because repressed, but "reserving nevertheless their cruelty and vindictiveness while in moral character they stand very low." Arnold supported martial law and a massacre of Jamaican blacks in 1865. Although they should have known better, the working-class and women's movements were just as besotted by empire as the male intellectuals with their rubber ducks and wooden swords.

Spinning from England to France like a Sufi dervish or a modern molecular physicist, Said is at his most ingenious. When Napoleon invaded Egypt, he took French science with him, and all those archaeologists, historiographers, and linguists came back to mount, with solemn academic seriousness, Universal Expositions of the "Orient" — Asia and Africa "staged" for the European theater. It's not just that Verdi, to get some idea of what Egypt looked like back when it was still important, consulted Egyptologist Auguste Mariette before turning priests into harem girls. It's that Mariette himself relied on the archaeological volumes of Napoleon's *Description de l'Egypte,* and on Jean-François Champollion's dreamy reconstructions of temples and palaces from his own reading of the hieroglyphics. Archaeology as Grand Opera: suddenly, a culture of death!

So, too, do the ethnographic hierarchies of Gobineau, Renan, and Humboldt show up in nineteenth-century French fiction. See Balzac's academic knowingness, in *La Peau de chagrin* or *La Cousine Bette.* Or Loti, Daudet, and Maupassant. If Stendhal is impossible to read without meeting an iconic Napoleon, imagine the goggles Flaubert wore to write his Carthage novel, *Salammbô*: as in the twentieth century Gide would wear goggles to North Africa and Malraux to Indochina. About Camus ("an extraordinarily belated, in some ways incapacitated colonial sensibility," says Said): You can take the boy out of the *pied noir,* but not the *pied noir* out of the boy.

I should say that Said is unkind to Conor Cruise O'Brien, who first suggested this reading of Camus in a 1970 essay. But O'Brien, after his original enthusiasm, has turned on Third World nationalism, like V. S. Naipaul, and Said holds a grudge. At least Camus is snatched back from the Freudians. I can still recall a dumbfounding college lecture on *L'Etranger,* back in 1957, which concluded: "Of course, the Arab is Meursault's mother." And I wonder now why Said's so silent on Sigmund, surely a greedy and culture-bound King Baby, whose name is dropped only in passing in *Culture and Imperialism* to help explain Fanon and mentioned not at all in *Orientalism.*

Tocqueville deplored the American treatment of blacks but not French treatment of Muslim Arabs: a nice shot. But surely

Malraux deserves more than a page and a half on *La Voie royale.* (How come all the "Chinese" revolutionaries in *La Condition humaine* just happened to be Europeans? And what was his notorious "Museum Without Walls" if not an expropriating Universal Exposition?) Jean Genet gets credit, like Albert Memmi, for having "crossed to the other side," but their work is undiscussed. Since I'm at it, doesn't Marguerite Duras deserve at least a footnote? And while Larteguy novels like *The Centurions* and *The Praetorians* may not be high art, they directly addressed French behavior in the late imperial stage in Indochina *and* Algeria.

But compared to *Culture and Imperialim*'s American section, the French chapters are exhaustive. Melville was more complicated than Said lets on. Consider Thoreau and the war with Mexico. Toni Morrison, Robert Stone, and Don DeLillo require more than a name-drop. Maxine Hong Kingston isn't even mentioned. Nor Norman Mailer's imaginary Egypt. Nor Hemingway, Bellow, and Updike, who wrote novels about Africa. Nor Mary McCarthy and Susan Sontag, who went to Vietnam. Nor Joan Didion on Latin America, Diane Johnson on Iran, Denis Johnson on Nicaragua, Mary Lee Settle on Turkey, and Allen Ginsberg in Calcutta. Silence!

Said's in a hurry. Rushdie's chimeras are gaining on him: *men and women in the guise of eagles, jackals, horses, gryphons, salamanders, warthogs, rocs . . . water-terrorists.* He wants to speak of "the importance of subjectivity to historical time" and "the far from accidental convergence between the patterns of narrative authority constitutive of the novel on the one hand, and, on the other, a complex ideological configuration underlying the tendency to imperialism." But modernism looms: "extremes of self-consciousness, discontinuity, self-referentiality," as if windblown from the blank spaces. The plague, in Mann's *Death in Venice,* is from Asia. For Europe to deal with its uneasy sense of vulnerability from the dark places, "a new encyclopedic form became necessary, one that had three distinctive features":

First was a circularity of structure, inclusive and open at the same time: *Ulysses, Heart of Darkness, A la recherche, The Waste Land, To the Lighthouse*. Second was a novelty based on the reformation of old, even outdated fragments drawn self-consciously from disparate locations, sources, cultures: the hallmark of modernist form is the strange juxtaposition of comic and tragic, high and low, commonplace and exotic, familiar and alien. . . . Third is the irony of a form that draws attention to itself as substituting art and its creations for the once-possible synthesis of the world empires.

These are texts a critic like Said not only construes but *loves*, as Chamcha in *The Satanic Verses* loved Pamela, the woman and the novel. But we're postmodern, Post Toasties, like Rushdie's Flatland and his extraterrestrial sitcom with the space rock calling itself Pygmalien. England didn't love Chamcha, and postmodernism doesn't love Said. All the energies poured into "novel and demystifying theoretical praxes . . . have avoided the major, I would say determining, political horizon of modern Western culture, namely imperialism." Even Frankfurt School critical theory, with its "seminal insights into the relationships between domination, modern society, and the opportunities for redemption through art as critique, is stunningly silent on racist theory, anti-imperialist resistance, oppositional practice in the empire." Silent, too, are neopragmatism, deconstruction, discourse analysis, the old Marxism, and the New Historicism, all those cults and "jargons of an almost unimaginable rebarbativeness," off in "the country of the blue," weightless, as if history had no gravity. "This massive avoidance has sustained canonical inclusion and exclusion: you include the Rousseaus, the Nietzsches, the Wordsworths, the Dickenses, Flauberts . . . and at the same time you exclude their relationships with the protracted, complex, and striated work of empire." Our discourse takes "no cognizance of the enormously exciting, varied postcolonial literature produced in resistance to the imperialist expansion of Europe and the United States in the past two centuries. To read Austen without reading Fanon and Cabral . . .

is to disaffiliate modern culture from its engagements and attachments."

And so, like the Wandering Jew in *Ulysses,* we come full circle.

In Madrid six years ago, in the funky subway, I saw a college student reading *One Hundred Years of Solitude.* In Spanish, of course. It was easy to imagine, on the London Tube, an Oxford decadent simultaneously absorbed in Naipaul or Rushdie. Or Chinua Achebe. Or Wole Soyinka. In English, of course. How must it feel to realize, in an ancient imperial city, that the genius of your language had removed itself to the former colonies, transmitting as if from exile?

"The holy centaurs of the hills are vanished," lamented Yeats; "I have nothing but the embittered sun."

It is Said's passionate conviction that—partly because of imperialism—"all cultures are involved in one another; none is single and pure, all are hybrid, heterogeneous, extraordinarily differentiated"; that crossing borders, dispossession, and exile are the modern norms; that all readers ought to be nomads and all reading "contrapuntal"; that we are in our "history-making" less the "symphonic whole" imagined by Vico, Herder, and the Schlegel brothers than "an atonal ensemble" of complementary and interdependent ecologies and rhetorics, "inflections, limits, constraints, intrusions, inclusions, prohibitions"; and that even the canon itself cannot be read without reading its opposition, a resistance to its presumptions in alternative historiographies, slave narratives, notes from the underground, the literature of prisons and women.

Read then; engage; attach. Upon these mindscapes we will meet the slice of the strange, the surprise of the Other, a witness not yet heard from, archaeologies forgotten, ignored, or despised; magic tricks, radiance, bloodthreads of a mother tongue, passionate conviction; juxtapositions, miscegenations, transplants, hybrids; atavisms and avatars, landlords and tenants, ghosts and gods; grace notes and cognitive dissonance; chaos theory, with lots of fractals. What could be more postmodern than a list?

Read, besides Fanon and Cabral and the usual Latin American suspects—Cortázar, Borges, Paz, Fuentes, Neruda, Asturias, Cabrera Infante, García Márquez—also César Vallejo, Nelida Piñon, and Alejo Carpentier; Manuel Puig, Ernesto Sábato, and Mario Vargas Llosa; Isabel Allende, Reinaldo Arenas, José Donoso, and Juan Carlos Onetti. Read, just to mention the Caribbeans, C. L. R. James, Walter Rodney, George Lamming, José Martí, Eric Williams, Edward Braithwaite. Read Aimé Césaire of Martinique, Faiz Ahmad Faiz of Pakistan, and the Saudi Arabian Abdelrahman Munif. Besides the Nigerians Achebe and Soyinka, the Kenyan Ngugi wa Thiong'o, the Sudanese Tayib Salih, the Algerian Kateb Yacine. Bessie Head, Alex La Guma, Anta Diop, Paulin Hountondjii, V. Y. Mudimbe, and Ali Mazrui. To whom I'd add some names not mentioned by Said, like Ousmane Sembéne of Senegal; T. Obinkaram Echewa, Buchi Emecheta, Amos Tutuola and D. O. Fagunwa of Nigeria; Ama Ata Aidoo of Ghana; and the Palestinian Christian Anton Shammas.

Boat people, all of them, the fathers and children of Said. Like Caryl Phillips, Nawal El Saadawi, Michael Ondaatje, Tahar Ben Jelloun, Pamoedya Anarta Toer. . . . After the Great Debate on Great Books at Stanford, they added one woman and one wog: "not a pretty thing when you look at it too much." Maybe as well as his *Satanic Verses, Culture and Imperialism* is also Said's *Haroun and the Sea of Stories,* a geography, ethnography, and psychology of Earth's second moon, Kahani, divided into Day and Night, where the Children of Light, called Guppees, are custodians of Stories, and their parliament is called a Chatterbox, and instead of an army they have a library, and instead of soldiers, Pages. Whereas the Creatures of Darkness, Chuppees, worship the idol of Bezaban ("tongueless"); are enslaved to Kattam-Shud ("finished"), Foe of Speech, Prince of Silence,

Arch-Enemy of All Stories; and sew up their lips with twine in a Cult of Dumbness. On Kahani, Haroun learns that by Naming we create Being, and that the world is full of things we haven't yet seen but nevertheless believe in, like Africa, submarines, kangaroos, pagodas, Mt. Fuji, and the North Pole, as well as the past ("did it happen?") and the future ("will it come?").

What is it that we miss, not reading Fanon, Cabral, Rushdie, or even Nadine Gordimer; not bothering our pretty heads about sugar and slaves in Antigua? Just maybe the Zulu Tolstoy in whose existence Saul Bellow refuses to believe. For instance, as if by prescription from Dr. Said, a new novel by Ahmadou Kourouma called *Monnew,* translated into English by Nidra Poller, which sneaks up on us from ambush like a masterpiece.

"Monnew" means outrage, defiance, contempt, insult, fury, and humiliation. It's a Malinke word from West Africa. It's used, in this extraordinary novel about a fictionalized Ivory Coast, to describe the seasons of shame in the Kingdom of Soba, in the Land of Mandingo. These seasons correspond not only to the period of French colonialism but, if I understand Ahmadou Kourouma correctly, to characterize as well as the corrupt black nationalism and one-party state that took over after the French fled. I am aware of no other novel that so richly evokes what colonialism felt like to its African victims, or how the historical and metaphysical baggage of the imperium was even translated into a culture half animist and half Islamic; and certainly none as loving or skeptical, as pyrotechnic and somehow jaunty.

"What truth is there in this version of events?" Kourouma asks. He asks it of the griots, the professional praise-makers in the court of Djigui, the last King of Soba; and of the Parisian journalists who are the griots of France; and of historians; and of himself. We're also told that, "when the grey lizard cuts out a pair of pants for himself, he makes sure to arrange a hole for his tail to stick out." What Kourouma does, in fact, is to reimagine most of the nineteenth and twentieth centuries, including Hitler, Stalin, Pétain, and de Gaulle, through a brilliant prism of tribal myth and metaphor, a Technicolored idiom. His own tail sticks out.

Imagine this King, of the Keita dynasty, whose totem is the hippopotamus. Surrounded by griots, marabouts, soothsayers, and fetishists, beating on tam-tams, tootling on balafons, in bad times he'll sacrifice so many cattle, chickens, goats, sheep, albinos, and dwarves that the birds themselves are drunk on blood. "Because of the sacrifices, his words became multidimensional, and, with the help of our ignorance, he seemed and believed himself to be incommensurable."

But none of this, not even the gifts of horses and virgins, can "rectify" the destiny of Soba, nor slow down the uncircumcised onion-stinking French, those Nazarene Toubabs with "their sorcery of technological savoir-faire." The little cock that sings in the middle of the night will lay a lizard egg; a goat gives birth to a pig; and, triumphant, the French bring in their scientists and administrators. They announce that they've abolished slavery, but they ordain instead a per capita tax, "cash crops," forced labor, and military conscription. In return, besides mirrors, umbrellas, needles, head rags, enamel plates, and red *chechia* with pompoms at the trading post, the Toubabs promise the King of Soba his very own railroad train. He sells out his people.

Only at the end of his 125-year reign—after one of his sons usurps his office; after he's been to Paris and Mecca; after drought and famine and meningitis and death on the battlefield in two world wars against the Germans; after the soul-eating owls and the double hedge of zombies and the great fire smothered by the feathers and flesh of vultures—only then does King Djigui realize that he has been deceived, by himself as well as the French. "The one wound that never closes," we are told, "is the one left by the crocodile come and born of your own urine." And so this King, suckled by a manatee, a panther, and a buffalo, having "attained the immunity of those serpents on desert rocks who die only by suicide, by biting their own tails," having partaken "of a concoction that makes us intrepid," at last says no. Nor does he intend to die like Adolf Hitler:

The planes, tanks and submarines of the triumphant armies pursued Hitler all the way to Berlin, where, caught by surprise, he took refuge in the anteater bowels of his palace, like the emperor Soumaro Kane in the mountains of Koulikoro in 1235, after the battle of Kirinia, and El-Hadji Omar Tall in the grotto of Djiguimbere near Baniagara in 1864 after the battle of Macina. But Hitler was a Toubab infidel. Unlike Soumaro he didn't know enough magical practice to turn himself into a vulture; he didn't have enough Koranic knowledge, like El-Hadji Omar, to become an echo. It was like a mouse that Hitler was smoked and grilled in the bowels of his palace along with his wife and dog.

Perhaps as it is prophesied, Djigui will turn into a butterfly "more beautiful than a blue of Sanaga," and "this butterfly will fly from Soba to the deepest waters of the Niger River and will spin around over the water until from the depths emerges, as he does every eighty years, the oldest hippopotamus in the world, the totemic ancestor of the Keita, and the butterfly will melt into the hippopotamus and the dynasty will return to the matter from which it emanated." Even so, Kourouma tells us, his people will be left "skeptical, skinned, half-dead, half-blind, voiceless, in short, more Nigger than ever before."

Discourse analysis, meet magic. Consulting *Monnew*, an African amazement, the autumnal patriarch in García Márquez occurs to me, and Simón Bolívar in his labyrinth. But also Vedic warriors, and samurai, and the bare ruined choirs of Great Zimbabwe, and Shakespeare's kings.

Doris Lessing Goes Back to Africa

She is eight years old in Africa. Her bitter, disappointed parents have shipped her off to convent school. Had you known that Doris Lessing spent four years in a convent school? That so admiring was she of holy water, rosary beads, sanctus bells, and a coffin as pink as a cake, in the shape of a violin, she actually converted, for a couple of minutes, to Roman Catholicism? That after her mother explained the Inquisition, she promptly quit religion, as she would quit piano? Anyway, she is eight years old, at night, in her convent dormitory bunk:

> The red light that burned always in front of the Sacred Heart and its bloody gouts lit the room with red. The nun in charge of us little ones came to stand in the doorway, the light behind her. In heavy German accents she said, "You little children believe you are safe in your beds, you think that do you? Well you think wrong, you think the holy God cannot see you when you lie under the sheet. But you must think again. God knows what you are thinking, God knows the evil in your hearts. You are wicked children, disobedient to God and to the good Sisters who look after you for the glory of God. If you die tonight you will go to hell, and there you will burn in the flames of hell, yes I tell you so, and you must believe me. And the worms will eat you and there will never be an end, it will never end."

I begin here because when I sat down to review *The Golden Notebook* in 1962, for Pacifica Radio in Berkeley (another sort of convent school), the Author Herself was this red-eyed God. She saw me under my sheet. She knew my wicked heart. She told me everything I didn't want to know about sex and history. Irving Howe said at the time that he felt he'd eavesdropped on "the way intellectual women really talk to one another when they feel free and unobserved." But it was scarier than that to me. In my vanity and petulant neediness *I'd been found out.* As promptly as the young Doris quit religion, I sought to modify my swinish swagger. Henceforth, at least in public, I would try to behave as if Anna Wulf were watching and reported me to Molly. This was ridiculous, as both my wives will tell you.

She had seen through more than me, of course. She'd seen through capitalism, colonialism, racism, and sexism, as well as Marx and Freud (Mother Sugar!). There was something pre-emptive about her burning eye, her scorching lens. Before many of us had a chance to entertain any of her illusions, to flunk any of her tests, Lessing disdained them. Like some Aztec Mother Serpent, she had shucked these skins in a slouch to sacrifice. Aspiring, like Anna, to "create a new way of seeing," embroidering her golden notebook from braids of red and yellow, black and blue, she had already moved on—toward desolation, maybe even deconstruction; as if, as much as all those *isms,* the realistic novel had also let her down. After the indignant politics, the unruly passions, and the ferocious intelligence of the African stories, *The Grass Is Singing,* and the first four volumes of the *Children of Violence* series, she arrived at a chilly omniscience and a lonely impasse. Knowing *everything,* Anna Wulf is still a mess. Although *Under My Skin* abounds with unpleasant smells from the past—horses, camphor, petrol, paraffin, chamber pots, dead fish, wet wool, the habits of nuns, her father's crotch— none is so redolent as the very *idea* of Anna's compulsive washing of herself in *The Golden Notebook* so that she won't smell of her own period.

Equally preemptive was the extraliterary gossip. A year before *The Golden Notebook,* I'd read and reviewed Clancy Sigal's *Going Away,* which seemed to me superior, as a vagabond novel, to Jack Kerouac's *On the Road* and John Updike's *Rabbit, Run*: A young American radical, having barely survived the labor movement's purge of its own left wing in the late forties, finds himself facing another blacklist, in Hollywood in 1956. He hits the highways in a DeSoto convertible. He listens on the radio as Soviet tanks crush Hungarians. And everywhere he stops to look up old friends, he discovers sellout, burnout, and despair. By the time he gets to New York and a ship, we know that he is heading not only for England but also for a nervous breakdown.

What happened to Sigal in England was there to be found in *The Golden Notebook,* whose last hundred pages were devoted to a young American radical fresh from Hollywood and despair, calling himself Saul Green, who moves in with Anna as Sigal had moved in with Lessing. Sigal then got *his* novelistic innings in *Zone of the Interior* (1979), all about a young American radical named Sid Bell who's written a novel called *Running* and lives in London with an African-born British writer named Coral, who sends him with his nervous breakdown to Dr. Willie Last, who so much resembles R. D. Laing that *Zone of the Interior* can't be published even today in litigious England. (At a literary cocktail party in London in the early seventies, A. Alvarez announced that "George Steiner and R. D. Laing are the two most dangerous men in England." This is the only genuinely thrilling thing anybody has ever said to me at a literary cocktail party.) As late as 1992 in *The Secret Defector,* Sigal was still at bat. A no-longer-young American radical, a sixty-year-old Gus Black, re-plays his love affair with an African-born British novelist named Rose, who had once written about him in a novel called *Loose Leaves from a Random Life* in which his name was Paul Blue. Gus refers to himself as "the Hopalong Cassidy of the picket line" and "the Rhett Butler of surplus-value." Rose is funnier: "My little Red Peter Pan," she says.

Callow is how I felt in 1962. First Mary McCarthy left Philip Rahv for Edmund Wilson, even though he beat on her and stashed her in a psychiatric hospital as if she were Clancy Sigal. Then Simone de Beauvoir writes a novel, *The Mandarins,* about sleeping in Chicago with Nelson Algren, while Jean-Paul, the chain-smoking pillhead, is back in Paris reading *Madame Bovary.* Now this. Our mentors were not only so far ahead of us on the barricades that we'd never catch up, but also in the bed-rooms. I felt like Doris, at age fourteen, at the garden party at Old Umtali Mission, drinking tea and eating cake with black people who for once aren't servants, chattering away to two old men who tolerate her gravely, until one at last says gently: "You see, I am very old and you are very young." This she describes as one of those special moments "when one is alive, and notic-ing, as if injected unexpectedly with some substance whose gift is that you should see clearly." Another such moment, in *Under My Skin,* is seeing her parents in a cloud of smoke as a pair of pathetic, gray, *old* people, *stuck together*: "I am never going to be like them. I shall never sit drawing disgusting smoke into my lungs holding cigarettes with fingers stained orange. Remember this moment. Remember it always. Don't let yourself forget it. *Don't be like them.*"

And so Martha started Questing, as Anna would later cry Wulf. And this Quest would end in the concluding volume of the *Children of Violence* series, in *The Four-Gated City* (1969), when Martha went through a wall like the Hound of Heaven, out of the modern world of technology and genocide, into some distinctly *other* realm beyond realism or coherence to seek in prehistoric recess, half-remembered myth, unconscious memory, and fractals of dream and madness some animating principle; to find an ancient metropolis betrayed in the childhood of the race, and a clairvoyant priesthood prophesying plague. Our only hope was drastic biological mutation.

Wow. So much for wrestling with the century, pinning it down, breaking its arm. One of the many things for which the century ought to be held accountable is that it discouraged Doris Lessing. From the disintegration of Anna's personality in *The Golden Notebook,* and Mark Coldridge's vision of emancipating mutants in *The Four-Gated City,* and Charles Watkins's tortured understanding of himself in *Briefing for a Descent into Hell* as a fragment of the consciousness of superior beings sent down from Venus, we were apparently to conclude that traditional narrative, conventional characters, details of domestic feeling, the hard-won integrity of an "I" that suffers and is culpable, maybe even feminism, were all as illusory as the class struggle and the Oedipus complex. As if on the altar of R. D. Laing she submitted madness as a proof of grace.

No wonder, then, that she went into Outer Space. I mean, she wrote her way out of Africa, and England, and the West, and This World, to disappear for the five volumes of the *Canopus in Argos* series. Sure the Queen of Zone Three was neat. So was the glacier on Planet 8. But who wants to be looked down on from three different galactic empires, in five different evolutionary time zones, whether by benign Canopeans, anxiety-ridden Sirians, or brutish Shammats? Stuck with reviewing each new novel in the sequence because nobody else at my newspaper was willing to go back and catch up with its woo-woo predecessors, I tried to make a case for Sufi mysticism and the flap of 'Attār's lapwing across the Seven Valleys, from enlightenment to Annihilation of the Self: Idries Shah meets Erich von Daniken. If Yeats was allowed to believe in faeries, Pound in funny money, and Bellow in Anthroposophy, why not Lessing in flying saucers? But it's no fun to be dismayed by a writer you are compelled to read because so much of what you know, you got from her in the first place. I was out of "alignment," like one of her Shiskastans, as if Canopeans had turned off the faucet of the "substance-of-the-we" feeling, meaning that famine, war, pestilence, and unkindness to small animals were in store for all of us. Here and now, we were hurting—in our history and our intimacy. It seemed to me that we were in no way healed by metaphors of dervishes, from Rumi's Persian poetry or from modern particle physics.

She came back from Outer Space, of course: from the blue air and the archetypes and the whistle of the ether. There was her odd prophetic book on Afghanistan, and the two novels under the Jane Somers nom de guerre, and *The Good Terrorist*—a kind of bookend to *The Summer Before the Dark*, the satanic flip side of Woman as Organizer and Mother as Minister of Caring. And then, in 1988, *The Fifth Child*, her short and terrifying "Neanderthal baby" novel. Against Ben, who strangles cats, his own siblings lock their bedroom doors at night. He will join the "hostile tribes" of bikers and rapists at the gates of a burning city, and I will eat, if not crow, then maybe one of those doomed beasts on Planet 8 whose "horns at their base were thicker than our thighs." Who, after such a book, could help but flinch from looking into the eyes of our own children?

Finally, as if warming up for this autobiography, between

writing a libretto for a Philip Glass opera and the story line for an "adult" comic book: *African Laughter,* her account of four different return trips to the territory of her girlhood, the domain of her brother, once white Rhodesia, now black Zimbabwe. These are not sentimental journeys. In 1956, almost by accident, she discovered she was a Prohibited Immigrant on account of her books. In 1982, just two years after Independence, she was back again, listening to the rancorous "monologue" of the remaining white settlers, meeting the corrupt new class of black civil servants, dodging hated North Korean soldiers imported to police a war-torn nation, and taking notes in bars, at clubs, on the veranda, and on the road. On this road she had a terrible auto accident. But she returned in 1988 to look into the schools, talk to missionaries and consultants, examine fish fossils and Bushman paintings, hear about AIDS, and hitch herself to young Book Team idealists who work with women in rural villages writing a collective history of grievance. The following year took her to suburbs, supermarkets, and commercial and communal farms; to the angry poetry, woeful hospitals, and sad new townships. What she found in the bush was silence: The animals and birds are going or gone. And drought: Southern Africa is drying up. And AIDS: In Zimbabwe alone by the year 2000, one million will perish out of a population of nine million. But at least they feed themselves, with a surplus to sell to South Africa or to donate to famine relief in the Horn. They are on the move, like the Book Team. They even write some novels we ought to be reading and Harold Bloom hasn't. And if they laugh enough, maybe the rains will come.

Doris Lessing was seventy-five years old just in time for the first volume of her autobiography—exactly my own mother's age. The burning eye is now a basilisk's. She reports a recurring dream: "I was in a dusty eroded landscape. I stood by a gulf or ravine, where the layers of Time's upheavals lay one under another. . . . Right at the bottom of the pit was a shape like a big lizard—no wait, it was a lizard, an ancient dragon, preserved there for millennia. But it wasn't dead, for its dust-glazed eye stared out at nothing, then slowly swiveled up, like a chameleon's, at me. Or, in other dreams, the eye stared out ahead, and after centuries, blinked." To which she adds helpfully: "Recently I saw a documentary made by Japanese and Chinese filmmakers of the part of the Chinese desert on the old Silk Road where the sands move about, covering ancient cities and exposing them as the winds blow, revealing the frail mummy of a young woman, still beautiful, with her shreds of wind-torn silk still clinging to her, and then burying her again. That is what the old lizard's eye sees while it blinks, once."

We see her too, in wind-torn silk: a baby in Persia, a girl in the Rhodesian bush, a young adult in Salisbury and Jo'burg and Cape Town. By way of antecedents, she's quite a double helix, from the "well-off working class" and the upwardly mobile civil service. Shake the family tree and down fall bootmakers, bank clerks, dissenting clerics; mariners and medics; a cousin to the painter Constable; a farmer who versified; a soldier on her father's side who fought in the Charge of the Light Brigade; a widow on her mother's who captained her own barge. D's father lost a leg in the Great War and never stopped talking about the trenches until the day he died of diabetes. Her mother met him in the hospital, where she had gone to become a nurse instead of the concert pianist her own father wished for. A young doctor, her great love, had perished at sea from torpedos, but D's mother "wanted children, to make up to them what she had suffered as a child."

Imagine such minor players on the great stage of the British imperium after two and a half years in Kermanshah, where Doris was born in a Persian garden near a Persian bank; after the nightmare passage, by oil tanker on the Caspian and a lice-ridden train across war-torn Russia, to "wet, dirty, dark and graceless England" in 1924; after porpoises and flying fish, sunsets and sea gulls, on the boat ride to Cape Town—striking for the African interior by prairie schooner behind a team of oxen, north to the flaming skies and termite heaps, where the maize crop failed and so did tobacco; were gold didn't pan out and neither did social ambition. But imagine too the novelist as Artemis or Diana. By age twelve, Doris who never went to college knew how to set a hen, raise rabbits, worm dogs, churn butter, cook and sew and go down mine shafts in a bucket, make cream cheese and ginger beer, drive cars, walk on stilts, and shoot pigeons and guinea fowl: "This is real happiness, a child's happiness: being enabled to do and to make, above all to know you are contributing to the family, you are valuable and valued."

Not that she wasn't at the same time reading, when the nuns let her: *Anne of Green Gables* and *The Girl of the Limberlost*; Kipling, Dickens, and Thackeray; G. B. Shaw, John Bunyan, Lewis Carroll, *All Quiet on the Western Front.* When she finally left that unhappy home where her mother loved her brother best, for the telephone exchange, the typists' pool, the dance hall, and the Left Book Club she would add Virginia Woolf to Olive Schreiner, and Lawrence, Proust, and Mann to Robert Louis Stevenson. Carlyle! Ruskin! She'd also abandon *The Observer* for *The New Statesman.* As a hard-drinking Young Married, trying to write her first novel, she discovered the Russians "like a thunderclap": Dostoyevsky, Turgenev, Chekhov, Bunin, Tolstoy. After which, as she had abandoned the "spineless social democrats" for the "kaffir-loving" local Reds, she would abandon dull Frank Wisdom and their two small children for Gotthold Lessing and the Revolution. (One thinks of the Russian Novel Party that Mary McCarthy threw at Bard, where everybody had to dress up as a favorite character, and Mary was Anna Karenina.)

Gotthold, she says, "looked like Conrad Veidt, all right in films but too much of a good thing in life." He was a Communist, a German, an enemy alien in World War II, and lousy in bed: "It was my revolutionary duty to marry him. I wish I could believe this was just one of our jokes, but probably not." To her children by Frank, she explained that she had to leave them to make a better world; "one day they would thank me for it. I was absolutely sincere. There isn't much to be said for sincerity, in itself." Gotthold, the father of her third child, the one we hear so much about in *The Golden Notebook* and in Clancy Sigal's *The Secret Defector,* is omitted from *A Ripple in the Storm,* the most strictly autobiographical of her *Children of Violence* novels, because he was still alive when she wrote it, "and I was bringing up his son." After this son, whom Gotthold deserted for East Germany, Doris, alarmed at her habit of having children by the men she loved and/or married, had her tubes tied.

Oddly, the least interesting bits of *Under My Skin* are the ones devoted to the Rhodesian and South African Communists. In *Ripple,* and in *The Golden Notebook,* they are made fun of but also forgiven. There is a forlorn dignity to them. Who else, after all, ever bothered seriously about the "Natives"? Here, however, they are vicious, as well as self-deluding:

> Yet we still believed that the future of the world depended on us. It never occurred to us to ask what qualifications we had for changing the whole world, and for ever. Or, for that matter, what qualifications Lenin had. If we had been told, and had been prepared to believe it— unlikely—that we were the embodiments of envy, vindictiveness, ignorance, our attitude would have been the same as when people say that such and such a priest is delinquent or even criminal: he represents God and his personal qualifications are irrelevant. We believed we personified the choices of History. The character of every one of us was as unlikeable as at any time in our lives: meanwhile we never stopped dreaming about utopias. Perhaps there is a connection.

But Lessing has given up on the Enlightenment and every variety of social engineering that came after it. If, after Africa, she had to disenthrall herself from Marx and Lenin and Freud and Laing, once upon an even *earlier* time it was her mother she had to escape—first "in a kind of inner emigration" and later to the big city, the garish politics, and the bad marriages. She spends a lot less time and space on the temptations to world-saving than she does in wondering where in such a girlhood of sunflowers, leopards, and pythons she got her sense of social injustice and her truculence about all authority. Over and over she asks, "Why do we expect so much?" The Great War, followed in 1918–19 by the flu epidemic killing an estimated 29 million Europeans, obviously had something to do with "a dark grey cloud, like poison gas, over my early childhood." How could it not "unless you believe that every little human being's mind is quite separate from every other, separate from the common human mind. An unlikely thing, surely." But her mother was special, and so was her father, with his wooden leg and rant. As if they were guinea fowl, she shoots these parents; then turns a musket on herself: "There is really nothing we can do about what we were born with." And: "Our lives are governed by voices, caresses, threats we cannot remember." And: "It was not my parents' strength that threatened me, it was their weakness."

It's taken me more than thirty years to realize that, as hard as she is on men, Lessing has always been harder on women, knowing as she does the worst about "a basic female ruthlessness, female unregenerate," coming from "a much older time than Christianity or any other softener of savage moralities," for whom *"It is my right."* When she sees "this creature emerge in myself, or in other women, I have felt awe." It is something like this same awe that she feels for her own young body, in and out of Erotic Longing; listening to jazz or to Caruso on the wind-up gramophone singing "The Volga Boatman"; setting fire to the thatch on the storage shed; about to fly up in our hearts. Nor has she patience for whining or victimhood. Again: "Why are we so bitterly surprised when we—our country—the world—lurches into yet another muddle or catastrophe? Who promised us better? When were we promised better? Why is it that so many people in our time have felt all the emotions of betrayed children?"

It can only come out of some belief, one so deep it is well out of sight, that a promise of some kind has been made and then betrayed. Perhaps it was the French Revolution? Or the American Revolution, which made the pursuit of happiness a right with the implication that happiness is to be had as easily as taking cakes off a supermarket counter? Millions of people in our time behave as if they have been made a promise—by whom? when?—that life must get freer, more honest, more comfortable, always better. Has advertising only set our minds more firmly in this expectant mode? Yet nothing in history suggests that we may expect anything but wars, tyrants, sickness, bad times, calamities, while good times are always temporary. Above all, history tells us nothing stays the same for long. We expect gold at the foot of always renewable rainbows. I feel I have been a part of some mass illusion or delusion. Certainly part of mass beliefs and convictions that now seem as lunatic as the fact that for centuries expeditions of God-lovers trekked across the Middle East to kill the infidel.

This seems to me insufficient. But I have all her other books to read, and they are full of whatever may be left out here, as she is about to leave for England and world literature. By now I should know that you don't tell a great writer what she should write about; you take what you can get from her. You're lucky she will talk to you at all. And if her weather report from the burning city, the bush, the barricades, or the void dismays, so be it. "Writers don't give prescriptions," said Chinua Achebe in *Anthills of the Savannah*: "They give headaches." When the biologist Lewis Thomas was asked what we should send up in a rocket to speak on our behalf to whatever alien civilizations might be watching in outer space, he said: "I would send the complete works of Johann Sebastian Bach. But that would be boasting." *I* would send the complete works of Doris Lessing, on CD-ROM. But then, Up There, they've probably already met her.

At Oliver Tambo's Funeral, 1993

By some sort of particle acceleration peculiar to the charismatic sciences, Nelson Mandela, even sitting down, is bigger than the rest of us. It's not so much his aura as his gravity and torque. Around the still center of the seamed face at the tiny table in the huge reception hall of the Carlton Centre in downtown Johannesburg, the colors of his revolution spin. Accustomed as we are to American presidents who come on stage like the elephants in *Aïda*, Mandela's repose seems sculptured, like music in a poem by Rilke: "when the innermost point in us stands / outside, as amazing space, as the other / side of air: / pure, immense, / not for us to live in now." Had there been a receiving line, we'd have rushed like groupies to pump his hand. But we were asked instead to hunker down and *chat,* at a kind of power prayer mat. Not even a groupie presumes such trespass. In another poem, Rilke met an angel, a very tough audience: "You can't impress *him* with a glorious emotion; in the universe where he feels more powerfully, you are a novice."

Of course, they're conserving his energy. He's seventy-five years old. Whatever happened to him in the mythic realm during twenty-seven years on Robben Island and at Pollsmoor, the body took a beating. The clock of the revolution is slower than the clocks of the revolutionaries. Cyril Ramaphosa, secretary-general of the ANC, is not getting any younger at the negotiating table with the de Klerk government. We are here tonight because Mandela's comrade, Oliver Tambo, died of a stroke last week at age seventy-five, and all morning and half the afternoon there'd been one of those operatic funerals, and Mandela wanted to say thank you to mourners from abroad. If you've ever wondered just how inclusive the ANC really is, it is inclusive enough to have included *us* in the cortege and in the Super Suite at the FNB soccer stadium in Soweto. But Tambo himself was struck down after eight hours in the blazing sun at another funeral in a Soweto soccer stadium for a much younger man, Chris

Hani, murdered in April at age fifty. There may also be a contract out on Joe Slovo, age sixty-seven, who said of Tambo this afternoon: "He died before he could vote."

No wonder Richard Stengel put his history of sneakers on hold to tape the world's most famous political prisoner on his jailbird years. A memoir already exists of the apprenticeship. Without the view from Robben Island, there can be no bestseller, never mind a new South Africa. On the Cape Town waterfront, I saw a sign: "Robben Cruises: Historical Island of Exile and Banishment! Penguins and Prisoners!" There were daily departures, at 10 A.M. and 1:30 P.M., of a yacht called, I kid you not, the *Alter Ego*.

It's easier to talk to Jesse Jackson, for whom at least we voted. His face is puffy, and one slinged wing is wounded from an auto accident. But he's swift to arrange photo ops for the eighteen-strong American delegation to the Tambo funeral . . . for Donna Shalala, who delivered Clinton's condolences in Soweto, being the only member of Bill's administration except for Ron Brown who had ever met Tambo, and who also seemed to endorse the ANC in the forthcoming (and yet ever-receding, like the green light of Gatsby's "orgiastic future") first nonracial election in South African history; for Maxine Waters, the Congresswoman and angel of righteousness from Watts; for Randall Robinson of the American Committee on Africa; and for Maya Angelou, who read another poem in Soweto and with whom we *did* hunker down, in the soccer stadium parking lot, behind the smoked windows of our respective limos, to compare notes on Toni Morrison.

Perhaps you are wondering why Carol Moseley-Braun, our only African-American senator, isn't here. I don't know for sure why she isn't here, any more than I know for sure why *I am*. But Moseley-Braun has been making pro-Inkatha Freedom Party noises, as if the warrior-thugs of Chief Mangosuthu Gatsha Buthelezi weren't, with helpful hints and tear gas from "Third Force" cells inside the security police, doing their murderous best, everywhere from Edendale to Boipatong to Alexandra township, to torpedo any negotiated transition government that might be disinclined to guarantee the $1 billion a year Pretoria forks over to Buthelezi's KwaZulu "homeland." And the word in Johannesburg is that Mosely-Braun is pro-Inkatha because her campaign manager / fiancé Kgosie Matthews is pro-Inkatha; and Kgosie's pro-Inkatha because his father, Joseph Matthews, is Buthelezi's chief of staff—nice work, and also a wonderful instance of upward failure if, like Joseph, you succeeded Nelson Mandela in the early 1950s as secretary of the ANC Youth League, and once belonged to the central committee of the South African Communist Party and used to be, in London exile, the managing editor of the ANC magazine *Sechaba,* before becoming in the mid-seventies the assistant attorney general of Botswana, from which you skipped bail in 1984 to avoid trial in Gaborone on a charge of having embezzled 130,000 rand from somebody's trust fund, before or after which surplus value you seem to have developed doubts about Marx.

Toni Morrison as a member of the American delegation to Tambo's funeral would have been a stroke of genius, but Clinton's not a genius. We *do* have Nadine Gordimer, who's already won *her* Nobel Prize for Literature. It's been a decade since I sat in silence in a living room on the East Side of Manhattan while Eliot Janeway explained South Africa to Nadine Gordimer. It's been merely a year since I sat in silence in front of my television set while Susan Sontag explained to Nadine Gordimer that the old categories of Left and Right no longer apply to our postmodern era. To which Gordimer wickedly replied: "Well Susan, I still agree with Jean-Paul Sartre. Socialism is the horizon of the world." I am very happy to see Nadine Gordimer.

Nevertheless, it isn't working out the way she predicted in *A Sport of Nature,* is it?

No, Gordimer agrees, it isn't. The triumphant revolution at the end of her *Sport* may have been, she suggests, just wishful thinking on her part. On the other hand, it may well be working out as she imagined in *July's People.* In *July's People,* after a civil war, their black gardener saves the lives of some white liberals by hiding them in his village. There is more rue than you may imagine in Gordimer's bifocal vision. She is fond of quoting Nosipho Majeke's disdain of "the role of the liberal" as the "conciliator between oppressor and oppressed." After the revolution in *A Sport of Nature,* there is a role for white people in the new South Africa. After the civil war in *July's People,* not only isn't there a role; there isn't even any *place.*

Yet tonight in Johannesburg, there is a gleam in Gordimer's eye. Look, over there by the food: Kenneth Kaunda! Five years ago, when South Africa's laws "were made of skin and hair," most of these people couldn't get into this country, not to mention this hotel. Gordimer is almost as old as Mandela, but also, to quote Barbara Kingsolver, "beautiful beyond the speed of light."

In *July's People,* Gordimer quoted Gramsci: "The old is dying, and the new cannot be born; in this interregnum there arises a great diversity of morbid symptoms." I've always wanted to quote Gramsci myself, and now at last I have.

All this was after the funeral, at which, subsequent to their somersaulting like athletes at pregame calisthenics, the Spear of the Nation drilled for the multitude to tunes like "We Shall Gather by the River," "Onward Christian Soldiers," and "The Battle Hymn of the Republic"; and the multitude itself sang "Nkosi sikelel' i-Afrika"; and Olaf Palme's widow spoke, and Maya Angelou read her poem, and Donna Shalala got her four minutes, just before the PLO, immediately after Cuba; and there was one mention of Walt Whitman's "O Captain!," and several of Moses not making it to the Promised Land, and a flower guard of Young Pioneers and a tumult for Mandela's gentle tempered steel. . . . It was like every movie about South Africa you've ever gone to where you felt bad without getting hurt, and every minute was broadcast live on South African television.

And Tambo's funeral was after a very European Cape Town, from which we drove to the tip of Africa to look for whales, eagles, Vasco da Gama, and Antarctica, with side trips into the wine country and the Cape Dutch Junker-Huis plantations, with their willow trees, pediments, duck ponds, and slave chapels, past "coloured" townships like Bombay slums and squatter-camp shanties new to the Cape since the abolition of the pass laws, where you're charged five hundred rand for permission to use a loo and have to steal a grocery cart in order to transport jars of water from the only well for a complex of two thousand families; to look for horned bok, hartebeest, clotted cream and scones not far from Chapman Road, with its breathtaking precipice to the sea, into which AIDS victims, who've come to a more liberal-minded Cape from all over the rest of morbid South Africa, hurl themselves to death. There are NAMES Quilt panels on the wall in Tutu's St. George Cathedral in Cape Town because there's an AIDS epidemic, as you'd expect in a country that invented hostels for single men on eighteen-month contracts to work in mines and factories and carouse with prostitutes in shebeens till they're laid off, return to their "homelands," and spread around the HIV.

How nice to see the imperial digs of Cecil Rhodes. How gratifying to be reminded that the stovepipe Boers with their Solzhenitsyn beards weren't the only heavies in South Africa. What Cecil wanted was a map of Africa entirely pink: "From Cape Town to Cairo," this most Lonesome Dovey of Victorian adventurists was fond of explaining through a cloud of cigarette smoke, under a broad-brimmed cowboy hat, behind a Mark Twain / Joseph Stalin mustache, with his Maxim machine guns, his DeBeers diamonds, and his bought missionaries. I say Lonesome Dovey because what happened here in the nineteenth century so closely resembles the history and cinematography of our own American West—from broken treaties with inconvenient indigenous populations to exuberant invasions, gleeful slaughters, and "native reserves"; from "pioneers" in prairie schooners to homesteaders cashing in on landgrab to private armies deployed by mining companies, railroads, and robber barons to secure mineral rights to the gold and diamonds from luckless Matabeles like Lobengula; from an Anglo-Saxon rhetoric of "civilizing" savages to a manifest destiny of Master Racism. And Lonesome Dovey, too, because this vicar's son who left England at age seventeen for a Kimberley hole in the ground to earn money for the very first Rhodes scholarship to Oxford, seems to have been bitterly alone most of his forty-nine years, unless we count the handsome young male secretaries, like big blond collies, to whom he was passionately devoted.

According to the new Antony Thomas biography, recommended by Nadine Gordimer, Cecil was indeed a repressed homosexual, although most of his associates in empire-building would eventually find women willing to marry them. (It might even be said that most of the English brought with them to Africa their own dark continence.) And, personally, I'm anyway inclined to blame class more than sex for the geography-gobbling and the skin game. Where else but in the colonies could the sons and daughters of a pinched middle class get to behave as willfully as aristocrats, with prime acreage, plantation houses, and hot-and-cold-running servants? They might get off the boat without much baggage, not even the notion of white superiority. But the sheer expanse of what awaited them—horizons on which to graze and gorge; frontier lawlessness; a Norman Rush of sunsets like peaches scrambled in blood—inflated the appetite. If young Cecil was nice at first to natives, his grown-up, aggrandized Rupert Murdoch self saw to it that Africans didn't get a decent education, taxed them into servitude, and wrote the first "pass" laws half a century before apartheid. Just in time for the Boer War, he also invented concentration camps.

To get to the funeral we took a Trans-Karoo express train from Cape Town to Johannesburg, City of Gold, that wound in the mineral earth from which moon colonies of glass tubers and steel spheres blossom, forty percent of it empty office space; to those suburbs with the ten-feet-high solar-powered security gates behind which whites themselves are trapped when their beep-me gizmos fail; to those streets of which even a warrior-poet like Nicaragua's Danny Ortega is so frightened that he decided not to show up at an ANC conference on cultural policy;

and, of course, to those black townships, out of sight if not of mind, where two million people try to get by in a treeless desolation, in which desolation, till recently, they weren't permitted to own property, not even a cold-water matchbox house, or start a business, not even a taxi van, only shebeens; and if the Zulus from the hostels don't get you, the *tsotsis* on the corner will.

And then *we* would go to Soweto with Babylon Xeketwane, who lives there with his wife and children, who works in the hostels as a sociologist, and who also took us to the busiest hospital in Africa, one big emergency ward like Soweto itself, except that Babylon with his Malcolm X cap, his graduate degrees, and his fifteen years in Alcoholics Anonymous won't move out because the kids need a non-*tsotsi* role model. You should see *his* matchbox, with its desperate rosebush. Or Walter Sisulu's equally modest digs on a street they named for him while he was away. And then look at the house belonging to Winnie Mandela, Nelson's wayward wife, which is a block unto itself, a palace and a fortress, paid for, she says, by royalties from her books, and patrolled by lolling bullyboys. We were warned that if Winnie didn't get off on the appeal of her murder charge, there would be martyrdom and trouble. Well, she's since got off. Now what?

As if to get as far away as possible from Soweto, we would also visit the Voortrekker shrine outside Pretoria, that pile of Aztec-Swastika Monumentalist Squat, that Calvinized radiator set in a "Laager Wall" of wagon wheels with its Hall of Heroes and Black Wildebeest, its sacred dome and cenotaph, its frieze and flame and God-blessed Ray of Sunlight that falls at noon each sixteenth of December on the Covenant. It ought to come as no surprise that this monument was dedicated in 1938, on the one-hundredth anniversary of the perfidy of Dingane, after many of the future architects of apartheid had just returned from German universities, where, from Fichte, Herder, Schleiermacher, and the brothers von Schlegel, they had picked up that Romanticism of *Volksgeist* and *urtümliche Bindungen* so indispensable to the National Socialist style. The dedication itself, as Allister Sparks reports in *The Mind of South Africa*, with its symbolic ox-wagon pilgrimage, and torch-bearing relay-runners, and hill-top bonfires, and girls in *kappies* burning their kerchiefs, was pure Nuremburg. Odd that they should speak a patois, Afrikaans, invented by their own slaves—an onomatopoetic pidgin Dutch crooned by black nannies into the helpless ears of white Christian fascist babies. But no odder than the fact that these odd people, having skipped the Enlightenment *and* decolonization, the eighteenth *and* twentieth centuries, created the most heavily nationalized economy outside the Soviet bloc, one big welfare state–capitalist trough, in which whites not only owned 87 percent of the land and 95 percent of the industry but more than half of all Afrikaners had government jobs! And still the best they could do was develop a bad-faith culture whose own elite—the Rian Malans, the Breyten Breytenbachs, the André Brinks, and the J. M. Coetzees—reviles it. Now that the pontoons and whistles have fallen off apartheid's Dutch Reform theocracy, they are, of course, privatizing like gangbusters.

Although I wouldn't get to read Norman Rush's wonderful novel *Mating* until we arrived by model airplane, four-wheel dawn patrol, and pogo stick at the termite mounds and game reserves of Botswana, in the Kalahari whereabouts of matriarchal Tsau, there are a couple of passing paragraphs on Afrikaners worth pasting in your memory book. For instance:

> The craziness of the Boers comes out of nationalism, [Denoon] said. The Boers have only had this feeling of being in charge in South Africa since 1948 or 1950, which is recent, when they finally overcame the British. They had just gotten their feet under the table, so to speak, when of all people the *kaffirs* start telling them it's all over, dinner will not be served. All they get is starters. The Boers reminded him of America, which only got to run a Pax Americana from the end of the Second World War until the sixties. Tantalized nationalisms are the worst. . . . Secondly, apartheid has to be looked at as an instance of a generically male form of madness having to do with sport. He said You're looking at a particular game of performative excellence, like the shepherds in Crete who base their hierarchies on successful sheep rustling. Oppressing blacks is a national blood sport. We should consider the handicap the Boers accept. A tiny minority is holding down

a gigantic black majority getting larger and more furious by the day. If the Boers can do it it's better than winning every medal in the Olympics, which the Boers can't play in anyway. The game is called Triumph of the Will.

And then, one page later, this cultural-anthro riff:

Possibly the dumbest thing the Boers ever did was allow kung fu movies into the townships. They thought they were letting in cultural trash to distract the masses. Mark my words, someday somebody will trace the influence of kung fu movies on the liberation struggle and it will be substantial. Because kung fu movies, which are in fact trash, nevertheless teach over and over again an important lesson: you've got to get revenge. Christianity says you don't, the reverse, and for years the educated black leadership went with that. But here comes something else, a set of brilliant how-to illustrations, that says to young men Join into groups, use your bare hands against the enemy—the corrupt kung fu groups that support the gangsters or the evil dynasty—accept discipline and adversity, team up, never give up, avenge your brothers. And by the way, here and there include women as fighters.

After the funeral, the Carlton, Soweto, and the shrine, a computer-systems expert explained that even though Apple slipped Mandela a PowerBook of his own, Apple is frozen out of the South African software market because Apple alone honored the sanctions and won't come back until Mandela asks them personally. (To do so before would jeopardize its contract with the City of Los Angeles, predicated on divestment.) And the human rights lawyers agreed over dinner, prior to heading off to Barney Simon's new play at the Market Theatre, that while class is really a more important issue than race, race is what drove everybody crazy. And the poli-sci feminist opined that "the oldest and most enduring nonracial institution in South Africa is patriarchy." And I discovered a treasure trove of *black* South African literature—Bessie Head, Alex La Guma, Todd Matshikiza, Mandla Langa, Miriam Tlali, and, especially, Es'kia Mphahlele—that I would read, with Rush, between elephants in Botswana and Zimbabwe, in the safari camps to which so many white South African refugees and ex-Rhodesians have already fled with their pet owls, their black guns, and their sullen resentments to re-create their own private wet-dream bush. And everybody in Johannesburg is already freaked by a visiting American scholar's research paper.

In "Voting for a New South Africa," Andrew Reynolds argues that the ANC might actually lose a free election to the Nationalists because (1) de Klerk, with his Saatchi & Saatchi ad campaign, has managed to dissociate himself from apartheid; (2) 42 percent of South Africa's blacks are illiterate, and a significant chunk of illiterates won't vote; (3) having to prove age or citizenship will disenfranchise 28 percent of black would-be voters; (4) high levels of intimidation could dissuade as many as 16 percent of black voters from trying to vote at all; and (5) an ANC plurality isn't good enough if other parties refuse to join them in forming a government. Add to this worst-case scenario the facts that half of South Africa's black population is under 18 years of age and won't be eligible to vote; that no South African black's ever voted before, and the rules for disallowing ballots are counterintuitive (no crossing off names, no pictures of candidates, an "X" for approval, not a check mark, whereas an "X" means "wrong" on the paper your child brings home from school when he or she isn't boycotting); that four million "coloured" South Africans are conservative Muslims (*The Satanic Verses* is still banned here) with no stake in the ANC; that a Zionist Christian Church membership, consisting of as many as five million apolitical teetotallers, has been heavily recruited by the Nationalists; that the Inkatha Freedom Party will draw 11 percent of the vote; and that less than 2 percent of the whites will back the ANC. This isn't even to mention a Pan-Africanist Congress busy trying to dissociate itself from its own dog-food terrorist army, Black Consciousness malcontents, twilight-zone Unity Party Trots, Conservative mossbacks, and a neo-Nazi Afrikaner Resistance Movement that probably murdered Chris Hani. I'm more optimistic mainly because Reynolds relies on the voting models of Samuel Huntington in *The Third Wave,* and Huntington is usually wrong. But it's not a cheerful prospect unless you're one of those deformed and deracinated soft-body die-hards, so much in thrall to what Rush calls "militant nostalgia" that you're actually rooting for a bloodbath.

Nelson Mandela won't let it happen. There is a religious ritual in southern Africa that requires two brothers who have fought to sit down together and eat ashes from the same urn. So will they be reconciled with their ancestors. To refuse this cleansing ceremony is to become an outcast. Forgiveness itself is a value, perhaps the only one that can possibly explain Mandela's behavior after twenty-seven years in prison. If there is reason to be optimistic at the Carlton Centre, it's because Mandela seems willing to eat ashes from anybody's urn. And so the stillness and gravity at the center, the spin of colors around it, the centrifugal force of so many years of exile, such a prison literature, all that music . . . seems to levitate. "The past," says Gordimer, "is not a haunting, but a preparation." Dancing on the ceiling of the Carlton, like a high-kick Hasid, like Chief Luthuli and Mahatma Gandhi, like dolphins and Etruscans and Rilke's angels and Chagall's violins, is the Revolution.

Discovering David Grossman

David Grossman, the thirty-seven-year-old Israeli troublemaker and magician, has shown up backward in this country. In order, in Hebrew: In 1983 he published this remarkable first novel, *The Smile of the Lamb,* about the occupation of the West Bank. ("It's as if some tormented Russian playwright cast us, of all people, in the role of conquerors and murderers . . . and the gun in Act One of our historic pageant about, say, the pioneering period a hundred years ago is now shooting at us, and we hear the curtain going down, but no applause.") In 1985 came his astonishing *matrushka* doll of a Holocaust novel, *See Under: Love,* from which Chagalls took wing—dead souls, black gloves, phantom brides, violins. ("We must never for a single moment forget to have mercy, because otherwise we're no better than 'they' are, may their names be blotted out.") And in 1987, in *The Yellow Wind,* he went as a reporter to the West Bank and Gaza to talk to Palestinians and Israeli settlers both. ("The impresarios of history are beyond my comprehension. They amuse themselves . . . with overly large toys, and the game may come down on all our heads. For instance the game called 'Blow Up the Dome of the Rock and Wait One Turn for the Arab World's Reaction.' . . . These are historical people, and historical people become—at certain moments—hollow and allow history to stuff them, and then they are dangerous and deadly.")

In this country, in English, we got *The Yellow Wind* first, in 1988, followed by *See Under: Love* in 1989, and then *The Smile of the Lamb.* I bother with this chronology so that we can see Grossman clearly. He was worried about what Israel looked like in its shaving mirror, before the invasion of Lebanon. He more or less predicted something like the *intifada* before it surprised everybody else, including Arafat; and he understands it in terms surprisingly reminiscent of Frantz Fanon. Almost alone among the Peace Now writers on what remains of the Israeli Left, he declined to jump on the Gulf War / Snuff Saddam bandwagon. Like a high-hurdler hounding after his own soul, in book after book he puts on moral muscle tone. By process of ever more passionate empathetic identifications with the Arab Other, he seethes with scruple. As late as March 1991—in spite of Palestinian cheers for Iraqi Scuds; in spite of "smart" bombs and Pac man briefings from the Pentagon columbarium; in spite of gee-whiz technoburble from the Hertz rent-a-generals in their network isolation booths —there he was, in an interview with Bill McLaughlin on *CBS Sunday Morning,* still insisting: "You do not make peace with a nice enemy. You do not even make peace with a reasonable enemy. You make peace with an enemy. Our mission is not to educate the Palestinians. Our mission is to create stability in the area for *our* sake. . . . I think this could be achieved only if we listen to the Palestinian suffering and misery."

Let's see where he began, to get so far alone.

Of the four voices who tell us alternating stories in *The Smile of the Lamb,* three belong to characters who would be comfortable in any serious European novel. Uri, the smiling lamb himself, is an idealistic young Sephardic Jew who hopes to bring hospitals and electricity to an Arab village on the West Bank in 1972. Katzman, a Polish survivor of the Holocaust, is the military commander of this zone of the Occupied Territories; he brought Uri into his service, ostensibly to help do "justice," but in fact to "contaminate" Uri with Katzman's own cynicism and hopelessness. Shosh, an unorthodox psychotherapist working with juvenile delinquents in Tel Aviv, may be married to Uri but she's sleeping secretly with Katzman. While the Israeli military demolish houses so that arrested Palestinians will have no place to come home to, cut down trees to eliminate snipers' nests, put on the thick skin and the uniforms of the bully, Katzman, Shosh, and Uri talk a lot, to each other and to themselves, about their motives and illusions. My, how they talk, with theories on everything, as though on loan from Turgenev or Malraux or Thomas Mann, tending to the oracular. Katzman thinks of consciousness "as a kind of sponge that can absorb the most voluminous fictions and lies, and then wring them out again as fresh truth." He thinks of justice not as a social or ethical convention but as "a hormone secreted at varying levels of intensity. Something a sensitive brain produces as a response to injustice, the way it does in response to sexual stimuli." He believes Uri to be "one of those holy fools . . . rash enough to let the world filter through to him"; can anyone so vulnerable survive in "this disaster area"?

Shosh spends a good portion of her time, when she isn't engaged with her delinquents in a "love" therapy that's part Trojan horse and part Stanislavsky method, theorizing into her tape recorder: "The human inclination to deceive will use anything, even love, as a lethal weapon." And: "The pretty names we give emotions are like the names that sailors give approaching typhoons in the vain hope of appeasing them, of making them easier to understand." To Uri, she lays down "the law of indemnity for dreams and fantasies," and accuses him of being a "do-gooder" only because "you don't have the guts to hurt anyone."

Uri—well, Uri suffers. All he ever wanted to do was good, among earthquake victims in Italy on his vacation, among Arabs on the West Bank. But he's subverted by superior theorizers. "I'm going through what you might call a reverse conversion right now," he says; "I'm learning not to believe." And: "It's only anguish, calling me louder than the other voices. Like a craving. Like a passion. For a woman, let's say. Yes." Finally, he hasn't much strength left, "not enough to take revenge, and not enough to forgive either. Only enough to sleep and not to be."

Now meet Khilmi, the novel's fourth storyteller and its afflatus. At last: an Arab. Perhaps conveniently, he is also mad, a one-eyed humpback in a silk robe and a black beret, who goes on too much, in his grape bower, his cave, his magic barrel, the cleft of his terebinth tree, about "his patron and protector" the hermit Darius and a hunter "who draws lions in the sand."

Khilmi belongs to another literature entirely, the Koran and *Arabian Nights*. In place of our "once upon a time," he substitutes an Arabic equivalent, *kan-ya-man-kan*: "there was or there was not." In "splashes of color and points of memory," he dreams an epic of panthers and dervishes; of lanterns from Bethlehem and candles from Nablus; of harvest songs, locust plagues, donkeys with samovars, the awful English and terrible Turks, Emir Abdullah and King Hussein, "whose soldiers slaughtered us without mercy." We hear about *rababa, darbekas,* and the singing of the prophets Noah and Mussa; about beloved Job, the twenty-eight stations of the moon, and Sha'aban with his bottles of powdered hyena testicles and jars of ravens' blood and jackal claws, off to kill a Syrian bear. What Khilmi, flying over his "invisible village," sees through the blue tunnel of his blind eye is Palestinian history. What he listens to on his transistor radio, from Fayruz in Beirut, from Um Kultum in Cairo, is a lamentation of "the weeping, fallen and forsaken people."

Against the logic of power, the instrumentalism and the bad faith of the Israelis, Khilmi is the embodiment—and the emancipation—of the repressed: memory, history, landscape.

See him grow up speechless and unwanted, tethered like a dog to a courtyard tree. See him take in Arab children as unwanted as he was. See one of these "moonchildren" join Al-Fatah, and die in a skirmish with Israelis. Khilmi believes in nonviolence: "Softer than a feather. More fragile than an egg . . . stubborn patience and infinite weakness. They will not be able to bear it." And: "We should have drawn into ourselves. Each person to his house and village in silence, to wait. . . . Then you would be struck with terror. Perhaps you would resort to violence. Think of it: a million people never touching you at all. Silence growing. In the beginning, you may shoot us, but we will kick a hole through our killers. And you are not made of very hard stuff." But his adopted son is dead. And so Khilmi takes a hostage: the ever-willing Uri.

Causing Katzman to think: "You have to be as crazy as Uri to step out of your life and view it from the outside, to rub your eyes and wonder how such a thing had happened. *How we had all been turned into hostages.*" Whereas Uri, as always, sees things differently: "We're all *kan-ya-man-kan* around here, and the only real thing about us is the pain we bring."

Besides *kan-ya-man-kan*, Khilmi speaks another language he's taught his moonchildren, an "infant tongue" with only a word or two of human speech ("longing," "caress"); stories "carved in water," "quarried in the wind"; "shadowplay" and bird gibber; parables of plants, of crushed leaves and twisted stalks, or, "to cure sadness," a broken thistle. Compare this speech to what a therapized Shosh talks into her tape recorder: "magnetic residue." Or the hateful scribblings of Al-Fatah: "words so hot [they] did not see whose blood had been spilled in ink." Or the infant tongue that Katzman, like Khilmi, spoke only to his father, in the pit where they hid from the Nazis, "a private language" based on Ariosto, about whom his scholar father was writing a book the son was forced to memorize. Shosh thought Katzman was "the person who could translate me into a foreign language" but he's only "the steam that reveals the invisible ink spilled on the page long ago." She's also furious to find that her own father, the liberal hypocrite Abner, is the very poet who, under the pseudonym Aviv Raz, "named the names, who kneaded me into words—no, not words—but shattered syllables, swollen letters that sank into me with a cold flame."

Lamb is an anthology, a Rosetta Stone, of secret languages, symbolic systems of communication. Kites talk, "long-tailed paper bats, colorful rhomboids with crosses of nickel and bamboo." And so do military orders, when you do harm: "How convenient military language was for such occasions. Sometimes Katzman felt it was his mother tongue, having lost his Polish and never mastered Hebrew." And so does a game of Scrabble, spelling out, like a Ouija board, words like "timely," "victim," and "yearning." There's even a sign language for lovers: Katzman and Shosh devise "a sly language of signals and insinuations" to use in Uri's presence. When she kisses Uri on the nose, it means she'll be waiting for Katzman the next day, when Uri has gone to the West Bank to do good. (If this sounds like the Judas kiss, well, "lamb" also has a Christian resonance. Maybe Jesus was the first Middle Eastern hostage.) And *against* all these languages, there's a surprising number of mutes. And suicides: a sign language that speaks of nothing left to say. If, sometimes, the fathers are assisted in their suicides by their sons, the children almost as often kill themselves, feeling betrayed by their parents and their surrogate parents.

Obviously Grossman intends his Occupation to stand as a metaphor for a whole range of distorted relationships: for power, deceit, and betrayal; for violations of privacy and intimacy in the bedroom, at the therapist's, wherever there's a West Bank; for the fictions we invent to excuse and suppress these violations and betrayals; *kan-ya-man-kan*. Just as obviously, Khilmi is an imaginary Arab—too much a fantastical construct of exotic bric-a-brac and secondhand *sumud* (long-suffering, endurance) to represent a Palestinian reality with its own fair share of innocent Uris, cynical Katzmans, deracinated Shoshs. Grossman will have to ride *The Yellow Wind* to Bethlehem, Nablus, and Wadi Alfuqin. But in an enormously ambitious first novel, he demanded of himself meaningful answers to the hard questions. And he was only warming up.

To summarize *See Under: Love*—so lavish, so heedless—is to risk ridicule. Briefly:

Momik is a nine-year-old *alter kopf* in Tel Aviv in the fifties. His survivor parents won't talk to him about the camps. He thinks of the Nazi as a Beast in his cellar to whom one feeds Jews. Then there's his great-uncle, Anschel Wasserman, who once wrote adventure stories for children, who likewise survived the camps, but whose witness is unintelligible, a sinister gibberish. Momik will grow up, after a bout of madness, to become a writer obsessed with the Holocaust. In Poland, at Gdansk, Momik talks to the sea, and the sea tells him a story about Bruno Schulz, the Polish-Jewish writer murdered by the Nazis. Momik and the sea then imagine, together, Schulz's lost masterpiece *The Messiah*: just like Cynthia Ozick. Then Momik, alone, imagines his great-uncle Anschel in the death camps.

Anschel in this imagining is a Scheherazade in reverse. He tells a serial story every night to the Nazi commandant, Herr Neigel, in return for which, every night, Neigel shoots him, though the bullets buzz right through his head, breaking mirrors and windows. The story Anschel tells derives from his adventure series *The Children of the Heart,* about superheroic kids who fly, by a "Leap in Time" machine, to the assistance of Beethoven and Galileo, Edison and Pasteur, slaves, gladiators, Armenians, and Robin Hood. But Anschel's heroes are now old, hiding out with Momik's childhood friends in the Warsaw Zoo, a "Resistance" of artists and dreamers. So absorbing is Anschel's story that the Nazi pretends in letters to his wife that he has written it himself, that it represents his secret thoughts, that there remains to him some decency. So consumed is Neigel with Anschel's characters that he wants to add to them one of his own—*and they let him.*

Finally, while we are wondering whether Anschel's story is really another crack at trying to imagine Schulz's *Messiah*, Grossman's novel turns into "The Complete Encyclopedia of Kazik's Life," at once the tale of a fabulous child of the dreamers in the Zoo and a glossary of the Holocaust, in which Anschel's characters are mixed with Grossman's characters, including Momik and Anschel, abolishing narrative, trying the patience, boggling the mind.

Now, then: The little-boy Momik section of *See Under: Love* is a brilliant novella in and of itself. This is how children, natural detectives, piece together the face of the unknowable, from animals tortured in the cellar and lunatics on the street and entries in the encyclopedia and the numbers tattooed on arms. This is how writers are doomed to their obsessions before they're old enough to defend themselves, having gone to bed to suffer history's nightmares, not their own. To God, Momik's mother says in Yiddish, "Maybe you could play with some other family?"

The Momik-in-Gdansk-with-Bruno-Schulz section is woozy. Of course, "a new grammar and a new calligraphy had first to be invented" for "the day the world would shed its scales like a fabulous lizard." And it's affecting to think of Schulz bending to kiss Munch's *Scream*, connecting Munch, Kafka, Mann, Hogarth, and Goya to a network of truth-tellers—"weak links" in a system of social and language control. But Schulz as a salmon is a bit much, especially after he acquires fins; and so is the talking sea (probably a nod to Günter Grass), "a woman's psyche in a body of water," sleeping "deep in one of a thousand lunar basins"; and the reimagining of the lost *Messiah*, in which all of the citizens of a Polish village turn by "magical forgetting" into artists, "firsthand souls," "mute essences" without language or a past, is a distinct disappointment after Ozick's dazzle in *The Messiah of Stockholm*.

Whereas the Anschel-tells-a-story-to-a-Nazi-Esau section is a Brothers Grimm for modern Europe with Hannah Arendt as the fairy godmother. What a problem Anschel represents for Herr Neigel: "A Jew who cannot die! What if other Jews were to catch on to undying now?" And what an opportunity for Anschel, this switch from commercial fiction to the real stuff of Sholem Aleichem, Mendeleh Mocher Sephorim, Tolstoy, and Gorky, not to mention the fantastical complications of Moharan, a little Zohar, a peek at Angel Raziel and the Book of Transmigrations. In the Warsaw Zoo: a minotaur. And Prometheus, a "time-stealing" circle of 360 mirrors "gleaming in the moonlight like icy tombstones." And The Scream, a mechanism of soldered drainpipes to contain "the purest octave of human anguish . . . the cry of the naked soul." And Kazik, born into this Scream and thus deaf to it, who will live his whole helpless life in a single day. And Otto, the guerrilla leader of the Children of the Heart, who weeps. This Zoo, of course, is an Ark.

To pass from Anschel in the death camp and the Zoo to an Encyclopedia (in Hebrew and English) including everybody we've already met (except Anschel) and some we haven't (picked up off the ghetto streets, seized from Yiddish literature) is to be confounded again, as with the talking sea. We're reminded too much of Primo Levi's *Periodic Table* or Danilo Kiš. And so many excessive characters—a Russian physicist with "golden hands and a closed heart," a lamed *vanik* who smells of herring, an American magician, a soul-stealing biographer and human glossary, a masturbating student of the Kabbala, an alchemist of human feelings, a beautiful woman who seduces God and then stabs Him—we stagger from the novel as if from an hallucination, blinded by pyrotechnics, having forgotten what it was we wanted and needed to know.

Something, however, has been rescued: a saving remnant; a quality of mercy. Momik, "a regular Holocaust homing pigeon," asks Ruthy (all right, I haven't told you who Ruthy is, but there are other women in Momik's life besides the talking sea, and they give him a hard time): "How can life go on after we've seen what a human being is capable of?" And Ruthy replies:

> Some people are able to love. Some people reach the opposite conclusion. There are two possible conclusions after the Holocaust, aren't there? And there are people who love and feel compassion and do good without any connection to the Holocaust, aren't there? Without thinking about it day and night. Because it was a mistake? Why not look at it like that, Shlomik?

He can't, of course. But maybe we can, some of the time, if only because in these pages we have also been into the White Room, where "you sit as if you were inside a kaleidoscope but this time the glass fragments are you," and whatever you happen to think about the Holocaust immediately materializes, "and if you don't answer the Sphinx correctly, you'll be eaten up." And we have seen, like Horatian (I'm not explaining Horatian either), those "fabled creatures" flickering on the darkened ghetto street: "colorful seahorses, tiny and winged; forest elves gleaming in precious light; Cinderellas, witches, unicorns, phoenixes and Peter Pans." These flickers prove to be the phosphorescent pins made and sold in the ghetto to keep Jews from bumping into each other in the blackness after curfew. After these pins, thirsty for meaning, Horatian goes to Otto and is allowed to drink Otto's salty tears. Otto "always found it easy to cry."

Somehow in these fables and pins, as if from the Ark after an impossible passage, what we see through Otto's salty tears is a corona of moral awareness—an embracing rainbow. To have found anything of the sort in a contemporary "metafiction," its saddlebags stuffed with every imaginable postmodern excess of unfeelingness, amazes.

Meeting David Grossman

Early on in *The Book of Intimate Grammar*—before he has fallen in love with Yaeli in her black leotard, before he is betrayed by his best friend Gideon, before his father, with a hammer, attacks the face of modern art, before his country goes off to the Six-Day War—in a schoolroom in West Jerusalem during English class, young Aron Kleinfeld discovers "the present continuous": "I em go-eeng, I em sleep-eeng. You don't have that *eeng* tense in Hebrew."

> "I em jum-peeng . . ." Jumping far, far out in space, halfway to infinity, and soon he was utterly absorbed and utterly alone; jum-peeng; it was like being in a glass bubble, and someone watching from the outside might think Aron ees only jum-peeng, but inside the bubble, there was so much happening, every second lasted an hour, and the secrets of time were revealed to him and the others who experienced time the way he did, under a magnifying glass.

The "present continuous" is Aron's stream of childhood consciousness. By a process he calls "Aroning," he will henceforth "dive in" as often as possible, to float, to swim, to drown in this "intimate grammar" of pumpkin seeds and elevator shoes and Mozart, where he's a magician like Houdini, a spy in Egyptian intelligence, or the first Israeli bullfighter; where every surface of the Holy City throbs with subcutaneous meanings, coded messages, invisible writing, Kabbalistic signs; where red shirts on a laundry line semaphore of friends in need, and scribbles on a sidewalk signal airplanes overhead; where food is a sacramental menu of values and emotions ("the sugars of friendship and the starches of perseverance and the carbohydrates of loyalty"); where time is so relative that minutes on a clock have not only different speeds, but animistic phases (between a slow horse and a vanishing atom, phases of fox, of mouse, mosquito, and germ); and where words, pronounced "with deep devotion," have lazy halos and can be plucked like strings:

there is a little light in everything, even the steel wool of scrubbing panels has a mysterious spark, even the dark grapes have a dusky gleam, or a thick drop of blood on the tip of your finger . . . and certain words, if you know how to pronounce them in a special way, not from the outside but as though you were calling their names, right away they turn to you, they show you their pink penetralia, they purr to you and they're yours, they'll do anything you want; take "bell," for instance, he rolls it over his tongue as though tasting it for the first time ever, "bellll," or "honeysuckle," or "lion" or "legend" or "coal" or "melody" or "gleam" or "velvet," melting on his tongue, sloughing off their earthly disguises, till suddenly there is red heat, a cinder of memory spreading its glow as it slowly disappears into his mouth, for Lo, this hath touched thy lips, and thine iniquity is taken away, and thy sin is expiated.

Like David in *Call It Sleep,* Aron has visions. Like Alex in *Portnoy's Complaint,* he spends too much time in the bathroom. Like Oskar in *The Tin Drum,* he refuses to grow up. At first he can't; later he *won't.* (Such a shrimp, his Uncle Loniu worries at the bar mitzvah: "Is this why we came to Israel with the sun and the vitamins and the oranges?") But who needs it? Pimples on the face, hair in the armpit, cracking of the voice, pornographic playing cards, patriotic sloganeering, Picasso's *Guernica?* Better to go "Aroning." With his imaginary dog, his broken guitar, his "jinxed shoes," and the blood covenant he strikes with Gideon in the cave where they bury the basalt stone, he will revel "in the possibilities that glittered between the wires, flitting in and out, to and fro; and in the process something would melt, and unfold to him in all its glory, yes, oh, yes, that's what he wanted, free passage through the fortified wall."

You think immediately of Momik in *See Under: Love.* Aron is his secret brother. As Momik was a child of survivors in Tel Aviv in the 1950s, so is Aron a child of survivors in Jerusalem in the 1960s. As Momik, in order to assuage a Nazi Beast he believed to be waiting in his cellar to devour Jews, would sneak down at night to feed yogurt, cucumbers, and chicken drumsticks to hedgehogs, lizards, turtles, and a raven, so Aron, in the Kleinfeld bomb shelter, seeks to raise a vegetarian cat, no meat and no bones. Nor is this cat Aron's only experiment. He tinkers as well with his tear ducts and laugh glands. He collects and smokes the butts of cigarettes to cause and assess a sneeze. He steals a giant magnet from the science lab at school and sleeps with it under his pillow. He establishes, in the bush, his own hospital for wounded words.

But Momik grew up to be a writer, looking for Bruno Schulz. Whereas Aron, who might have been, if not Babel's Di Grasso, at least a Gimpel out of I. B. Singer, won't grow up at all. He is exactly the same height and weight, after his bar mitzvah, as he had been at age ten and a half. Once upon a time he had a knack, but "the wunderkind has lost his wunder." Pouring the kiddush wine on Friday nights, his hand trembles; the wine spills. He is afraid of the electric eye at the supermarket that opens the glass door. He is "misclassified with a hasty glance" by movie ushers, substitute teachers, the new nurse, little old ladies, and "the crow that raids the trash bins who isn't quite sure whether Aron has reached the age where they stop throwing stones." It's as if he had been pickled and jarred, as his mother, with the banana hairdo, pickles and jars everything in the vegetable kingdom: peppers, olives, sauerkraut, carrots. While his father, a paper-pushing clerk who used to work in a bakery, moons over the neurasthenic Miss Edna Bloom next door "shivering like a delicate salamander." And his grandmother, crazy Lilly, who used to dance in a Polish nightclub, whose high heels Aron hides in the cellar, wants to give him a fire engine for his bar mitzvah. And his older sister, overweight Yochi, deserts him for the army. And his best friend, the green-eyed, "pure and noble" Gideon, will no longer play their games. And the love of his young life, the exquisite Yaeli, in whose likeness he has fashioned a sweet challah, prefers the company of Gideon, with his geopolitical expansiveness and Boy Scout warrior strut. (Poor Tonio Kroger, alone with his difficult art!) There is a buzzing, a "chirring," in his ears:

You don't stand a chance. . . . There's nothing in the world that isn't me. I'm the things of the world and the people who use them. I'm steel and rubber and wood and flesh. I'm cranks and valves and gears and pistons. I'm the blade that cuts. I'm the screws you have to remember which way to turn on the first try. I'm the knots in your shoelaces and the cord for the blinds. . . . I am the scourge of the broken plate and the light bulb exploding in your hand and the glass that shatters when you clink l'chaim.

Well, puberty. God help us. And there are certainly enough of them to go around, gods that is, in Jerusalem. And absolutes. And so many fortified walls between Aron and free passage: the Bet ha-Kerem housing project, the hospital where they send crazy Lilly, the school where time is relative, the cave of the childhood covenant, the abandoned refrigerator in the junkyard. And if not God, then Freud: Enraged by his mother, Aron strikes at her hands, which hold bottles full of milk. Massaged with too much enthusiasm by his sister Yochi, he is frantic, thrilled, almost abused. Grappling with Gideon, he is so much the lover scorned he might have been reading Leslie Fiedler. And when his father undertakes to knock down a wall in Edna Bloom's apartment, with its rug-checkered floors, its ivory figurines, its black leviathan of a piano, its volumes of Indian art, its reproductions of Degas, van Gogh, Picasso, and Magritte, those snow-filled globes of swans, clowns, dancers, and children trapped under glass—after first fiddling with her fig tree (come *on*, Grossman!)—and ends by reducing the whole flat to dust and rubble in an orgy of furious destruction, we have passed with Aron through and beyond a Viennese underground of eros and thanatos into the medieval realm of the *Sefiroth* and *Zohar*, of transcendental sexuality. No wonder that Aron, walking, eating, sleeping, Aroning, dreams of a "misty courier" crossing a white plain, a scaffolding of bones, a red-black sea of clotting blood, and a fissured egg of yellow coral covered with a frosty film: "Aron to Aron, where are you now, over . . ."

Not quite so suddenly, sex disgusts him, and food, too (custard, falafel and salami, Creambo and Yemenite *skhug*); the "code of mass" and "the canon of the flesh." How would you feel if what you really wanted for your bar mitzvah was a new Yamaha guitar, and what your father gave you instead was "very special": the army shaving kit with the razor, the foaming block, and the little tray he used during the Sinai campaign? To accompany, perhaps, the key ring in the shape of a Mirage jet given out in honor of Independence Day by the Delek gas company. Because war fever is heating up all over Israel, except in Aron's head. Even words have lost their savor: *longing, wandering, heron, diamond, autumn, lonely*— "all culled from the Hit Parade on the radio, an excellent source of words; in the middle there was news, Nasser Kasser Basser Yasser, and later that afternoon he would be releasing 'lamb' and 'twilight' and 'midnight' and 'kiss me by the sea.'" Comes the dark, however, and no place for Aron in Nighttown in Jerusalem:

> noisy shouts and patriotic songs blared over the loudspeakers, and the smell of burning in the air after the fireworks, how the night suddenly burst into color, with a pang of longing he thought of Yaeli, and people kept bumping into him, saying, Hey, kid, watch where you're going; he was out of step, out of sync, he always ruined everything, someone hit a sour note on the accordion: "Sing, oh water / Flow to the Negev." "Flow," that's nice, and there are public showers there but what about the flow of blood, and carefully he extricated the word "flow" from the general clamor, stripping it gently and whispering it backward thrice with great intensity; "Wolf wolf wolf," his mouth clamped shut so none of the outward pollution would infiltrate, the tumult and the smoke and the crowds, till the dusty, sweaty sheath of "flow" dropped away like a cast-off skin, with its shrill notes and dissonances and random undertones; he hid it inside him, in the intimate new center, quickly checking over the other words he had smuggled in over the past few days: "supple," "lonely," "gazelle," "profoundest secrets," "sacrifice," "tears," words that had welled out of an endless stream, and now "flow"; for seven days he would refrain from saying it aloud, till it was purified, till it was his, his alone.

But Aron hasn't seven days, not even Six. He must engineer his exodus, his shaman Houdini disappearing act and Great Escape, from a maze of meanings and a wheel of signs. He is acquiring too much density even as he cracks. With Roman coins and onion skins in his pockets, and nylon bags on his fingers, and magnets under his pillow, Aron—who wants only to tell stories, interpret dreams, fend off famines, lead children in song with his golden flute, and "trap the lustrous auras of this world in glassy marbles"; for whom language is contaminated and food constipating and flesh corrosive; who declines to grow up even as Israel in the Six-Day War is about to burst its borders, to break down Edna's walls; terrified of the sexuality and aggression of adulthood, the lust for power and appetite for territory of modern statecraft, the destructive dissonance of modern art, the raging hormones of gluttonous history itself—Aron falls inward, on a spiral track through voltages of feeling and magnetic fields of words, down to an abandoned refrigerator in a West Jerusalem junkyard, to await deliverance by magic, like an angel in a cyclotron.

So: Did Aron perish in that locked box in 1967, or somehow, with a broken guitar instead of a tin drum, prestidigitate himself?

This is the wrong question to ask David Grossman, on the outdoor terrace of the King David Hotel on a summer Sunday afternoon of ice cream and sparrows. He has dodged it too often in the three years since *The Book of Intimate Grammar* was originally published in Israel, where high-school students already read it before sitting down to final exams; where A. B. Yehoshua teaches a seminar on Aron at his impasse. Grossman still thinks about Aron; he may not be done with him any more than he is done with Momik. But Aron is an imaginary character. A residue, a caution, and a confabulation, he belongs now to the readers of his grammar, who'll have to make up their own minds. Anyway, if Aron *weren't* alive, his book could never have been written. And if he *has* survived, it is at a price. To be normal, after having been Aron, is to be coarsened. To fit in is to be diminished.

Besides, while Grossman was waiting for the poet and perfectionist Betsy Rosenberg to finish her loving translation of *Intimate Grammar* into English, he wrote and published two more books—*Sleeping on a Wire,* a series of interviews with troubled Israeli Arab citizens, and *The Zig-Zag Boy,* a novella for children on Israel's adult best-seller list. Red-haired, horn-rimmed, affable and evasive, he would have us believe that Aron's problems are existential, not political. I'm not buying it. I've been Aroning myself, in the *past* continuous. Grossman was thirteen years old himself during the Six-Day War, living like Aron in Bet ha-Kerem. "I was terrified," he says, "when they told us on the radio, on the Hebrew-speaking station in Cairo, that they would throw us into the sea. I was a child in Jerusalem. I didn't know how to swim very well. I took it in a concrete way, this threat. I am sure that I'm not going to live until the next Rosh Hashanah."

At age thirteen, he had already been a child actor on Israeli radio for four years, after winning a Sholem Aleichem contest, standing on a special "Grossman box" to reach the microphone and to speak in tongues. Following army service just in time for the Yom Kippur War, he returned to radio to become the anchor of a popular newsmagazine program, from which he was dismissed, to which he was restored, in a pattern of troublemaking that continues unto this summer Sunday. Imagine devoting your first novel to Israel's morally corrupting occupation of the West Bank. And daring in your second to write about the Holocaust when your parents weren't even survivors. Jewish Defense League hoodlets disrupted his American tour for *The Yellow Wind.* In the middle of the Gulf War, when the PLO made common cause with the Beast of Baghdad, as Scuds came down on Tel Aviv, still, on television, he insisted that peace was possible "only if we listen to the Palestinian suffering and misery . . . We were shaped by the same wound for almost a century."

But Grossman today would really rather talk about his son, who'll be waiting for him after soccer. And the Slavic planes of my wife's face, from the Pale of Settlement. And the red-headed

Syrian soldiers he met during the Lebanon mess, an odd camaraderie of carrottops.

It occurs to me that the last time I was in Israel, for the Jerusalem Book Fair in 1983, in the middle of that very same Lebanon mess, Grossman's novel *The Smile of the Lamb* hadn't yet been published, although it was about to be. Missing the story, as usual. Inquiring, instead, at the Sling-Shot Bar of this very same King David, where Edmund Wilson and Saul Bellow both got haircuts, where V. S. Naipaul had gloomed in the lobby, where Menachem Begin once planted a bomb, exactly how one went about meeting the famous mayor. Being told: Just stand still; he'll find you. And of course he did, minutes later, Teddy Kollek with a tree in one hand, a caduceus in the other, and a minivan outside to make sure we didn't miss an important goat. "Balzac would have taken to the mayor," wrote Bellow in 1976. "Kollek is to Jerusalem what old Goriot was to daughters, what Cousin Pons was to art objects." They've dis-elected Teddy now; installed in his stead a bloodthirsty clown, Ehud Olmert, who will defend against a visit by Arafat with a wall of West Bank settlers. I did see Citizen Kollek the other day at breakfast. And guess who walked right by his table without noticing? Alan Dershowitz himself, in town for a presidential forum on Israel-Diaspora relations, and probably billing O. J. Simpson.

My best moment in 1983 may have been seeing the Western Wall with Swifty Lazar at midnight. Or, barefoot at Haram esh-Sharif, my first two mosques. Or Masada, like the Alamo. My worst moment . . . maybe not at Fink's, a bar for journalists and Eurotrash, where I declined the offer of a hitch by jeep to the Lebanon front. Maybe at the party in Amos Elon's flat, full of Peace Now people, all of whom were bad-mouthing Jacobo Timerman. You recall Timerman. For being the sort of Jewish troublemaker who published in his Buenos Aires newspaper the names of the "disappeared," he was kidnapped by the sort of people who believe in a Zionist plot to gobble up Patagonia; and spent the next thirty months "talking to Susan," a machine that applies electrodes to one's genitals; and was then sent off by bloody parcel post to Israel, where he wrote *Prisoner Without a Name, Cell Without a Number,* in which he just happened to mention the acquiescence in his abuse by Argentina's silent Jewish community. Well, this ingrate had chosen in 1983, in the pages of *The New Yorker* and in a book called *The Longest War,* to criticize Israel's invasion of Lebanon—for which, by Peace Now people in Amos Elon's flat, he was now reviled. How *dare* he, having arrived so recently, having skipped not only the Holocaust but 1948, 1956, 1967, 1973 . . . "I see," I said. "He was tortured in the wrong language."

Jacobo Timerman went back to Argentina. "He should have stayed," says David Grossman, who hasn't even left Jerusalem, though A. B. Yehoshua has gone to Haifa for quiet time and peace of mind, and Amos Oz, after the reviews of *Fima,* is hiding out in the desert, and as we sit with our fingers crossed—Peace Now!—I'm semi-ashamed of myself. How is anyone here to know, and why should anybody care, that I was once upon a time a dilettante (or delicatessen) Zionist, a secular-humanist sabra-in-my-head, before Edward Said and Lebanon and the *intifada?*

Where have you gone, my blue-eyed goy? If you grew up lonely on the beach in Southern California in the 1950s, as alienated as an Aron from the sports-car culture and the pompons, the drive-in church and the grunion and surfer cults, you chose your emancipating fantasy from a rich debris of driftwood: James Dean, Jackie Robinson, Robert E. Lee, Mahatma Gandhi; bog-Irish semi-poet singing "Danny Boy"; Wobbly with cowboy boots; Bolshevik, but like Trotsky, scribbling as the alpenstock came down; *Mr. Keen, Tracer of Lost Persons.* It is really no more preposterous, after a boyhood reading of Arthur Koestler's *Arrow in the Blue* and *Thieves in the Night,* George Eliot's *Daniel Deronda* and Theodor Herzl's *The Jewish State,* to have dreamt yourself a kibbutznik, some sort of soldier-scholar, reading Marx and listening to Mozart after you've milked the cows . . . before communal sex. Instead of sand dunes and swamps, orange trees and potash; the white donkey and the red heifer and socialism with a suntan. Adolescence is all injury anyway; wounded feelings; blank incomprehension. So you appropriate the sufferings of a people to whom crimes beyond imagining have already occurred, and lay claim simultaneously to the great realms of modern thought, to the tragic determinisms of Marx and Freud, Einstein's relativity, Kafka's paranoia. And then you do something about it. Europe didn't work out. Let's start over again, from scratch. It's as if you turned the pages of *Partisan Review* with a sword.

Mordecai Richler has a genuine claim to such ambitious boyhood fevers. In his postwar Montreal neighborhood *aliyah* was a lively option. The disappointment of *This Year in Jerusalem* is that, while he remembers well enough, he doesn't make us feel it. Like Sartre in *The Words* inventing the homunculus he should have been in order to become the Sartre he thinks he is, Richler can't see his pimples for his cosmopolitanism. You'd never know he'd been an Aron. He seems merely to have read about him in a London library. And what he sees in Israel, from the Liv Ullmann Terrace of the Jerusalem Cinematheque, overlooking Moloch's Gehenna, hearing drums and the screams of children, fails to gladden such a practiced eye. *This* we feel. Toward the end of *Solomon Gursky Was Here,* Richler told us: "THE SYSTEM WAS INSPIRED, BUT IT IS MAN THAT IS VILE. IT WON'T WORK. THE SERMON ON THE MOUNT. THE MANIFESTO. THE WORLD CONTINUES TO PAY A PUNISHING TOLL FOR OUR JEWISH DREAMERS." The ravens got Solomon before he saw the Cinematheque or the Ben-Yehuda pedestrian mall or the concrete, aluminum, glass, and plastic prefab construction of a Gush Emunim settlement. But what Richler seems to be saying in his Ecce Homo *Canadiensis* memoir is that Israel won't work, either.

I was going to compare Richler's once-over-lightlies with those of Philip Roth in *Operation Shylock.* And then look at the lacerations of an Amos Oz. And mention, in passing, Shulamith Hareven's lovely novel of Jerusalem during the British Mandate, *City of Days,* where everything happens in time instead of space. And wonder out loud, from the Shrine of the Book to

Yad Vashem, about the hermetic cultishness and siege mentality we find even in the detective novels of Batya Gur, where a Psychoanalytic Institute and a Department of Literature both close ranks to hide their guilty secrets. We could look at poems by David Avidan, Nathan Alterman, and Natan Zach to see what's happened to Hebrew since Yehuda Halevi, Schlomo ibn Gabirol, and the Middle Ages. (According to Koestler, the Jabotinsky brownshirt who devised the first Hebrew crossword puzzle, "the real fun" only starts when the prophetic streak "cross-breeds with socialist sectarianism.") After which, maybe, we could get out of Mea Shearim, or even Jerusalem: To Tel Aviv, where they don't spend so much time hating one another (and the sight of women's knees). To Akko, and the underground Crusader city. To Haifa, and the tombs of the prophets. To Megiddo, where we will disappear down the cistern, like Aron into himself.

And dream our own past. We go into the desert to look at the Qumran caves. No more than Hebrew is Aramaic among my languages. So all I really know about the Dead Sea Scrolls is what I read next to the smudgy photographs in the newspapers, and what I remember years ago in Edmund Wilson. Thus I'm not competent to pronounce on the luridities of the new bestseller, *The Dead Sea Scrolls Deception,* except to say that, as rough as Oliver Stone was on the Warren Commission, Michael Baigent and Richard Leigh are even rougher on the coterie of Roman Catholic scholars who've been sitting on the scrolls since their discovery a half century ago.

But what if Baigent and Leigh are half right? The pen portraits in *Deception* of the "consensus" scholars and their academic enemies, the bureaucrats who were supposed to keep an eye on them in Israel, and the Vatican clerics with a vested interest in keeping the Gospels safe from revisionists, are a wonder of savage detail, as if we had strayed into an Iris Murdoch novel. (Would you believe Miles Copeland of the CIA? How about a California scholar who went to college with Thomas Pynchon and was taught there by Vladimir Nabokov?) And the reading of the archaeological, historical, analytic/textual evidence is always ingenious.

We are told that the coterie has suppressed texts that might embarrass the Vatican. That it has done its best to ruin the careers of independent scholars who challenged its working methods and its interpretations. That at least two of its members are on record as anti-Semites. That the scrolls belong to the first century A.D. instead of the pre-Christian era. That the authors of the scrolls weren't those sexless and pacifistic Essenes previously advertised, but rather the bloodthirsty Zealots who died at Masada. That Essenes, Zealots, and Nazarenes weren't separate sects at all, but more or less nicknames for different tendencies in one big Jewish nationalistic and messianic movement determined to overthrow the Roman occupation of Palestine. We are also told, most provocatively, that Paul himself may have been an informer, or an agent, of the Romans, promoting a new religion to subvert this revolutionary nationalism.

Well, now. I am reminded of the Khazars, about whom Milorad Pavič wrote a splendid novel a while back. There really were Khazars, of Turkish stock, between the Caucasus and the Volga, the Black Sea and the Caspian. From the seventh century to the tenth, they got in the way of the northern tribes of Bulgars, Magyars, Pechenegs, and Vikings nibbling at Byzantium; and they were also, in the south, hard on Arabs. About 750 A.D., the king, his court, and the military caste of these Khazars converted, inexplicably, to Judaism. Two hundred years and a Russian invasion later, they had vanished. Ransacking every passing reference to them—by the Arab geographer Muqaddasi and the Byzantine historian Constantine Porphyrogenitus; in dialogues in *Al Kuzari*, a theological tract by Halevi himself, the Jewish poet and philosopher of Moorish Spain; from Hebrew, Armenian, and Persian sources; and in meditations on these fragments by modern scholars such as Toynbee and the perplexed Hungarian Marxist Bartha—Arthur Koestler in *The Thirteenth Tribe* argued that the Khazars had disappeared into the Crimea, the Ukraine, Hungary, Poland, and Lithuania, where they turned into precisely those Eastern European Jews who suffered the Holocaust. So much, then, for "Semitism," and a Chosen People, and an ancestral homeland.

But *all* of this is Aroning: Megiddo and catacombs and citadels of David; the Jerusalem Star restaurant, full of Palestinian intellectuals, across the street from Ariel Sharon's house in the Arab quarter of the Old City; Masada, where the Zealots might have been better off hiking down the road to the Ein Gedi Spa for a mud pack, a sulfur rinse, and a Dead Sea float. It is possible on a single day to spend the afternoon at the Dome of the Rock, looking down; an evening hour at the Western Wall, looking up; to still have time for dinner in East Jerusalem and be back at the swimming pool at the King David before you hear a ram's horn.

Two religions are on top of each other, a third next door, archaeologists digging underneath, and what they've opened is a vein. Solomon built the First Temple, and Babylonians destroyed it. Herod built the Second; Romans did it dirt. The Wall is all that's left, propping up the plateau with the Mosque of Omar, built by Greek slaves. From the rock where the gold dome sits, the Prophet went to Heaven on a white horse. When the Crusaders came in the eleventh century, Muslims fled to the roof of the Dome, where they were slaughtered anyway. Inside the Dome, as if inside an ornate clock, under the golden mosaics and gaudy Ottoman tile work, there's something scary. Let your eyes go into an arcade, stare at a vine scroll. What it sees are the insignia of vanished empires, the breastplates, crows, and double-winged diadems of Byzantium and Sassanid. In stockingfeet, you get the creeps. The Dome is a trophy case: Look what Daddy brought home from his Holy War. They have been throwing rocks at the prophets in this desert for three thousand years. Only the Uzis and napalm are modern. A secular-humanist Israeli literature may have come of conscience and of age — David Grossman's Aron is everybody's wunderkind — but the Age of these politics is Bronze.

Amos Oz in the Desert

Not so long ago in London, Amos Oz told reporters that a reconciliation between Jews and Palestinians had to be Chekhovian, "with everybody a little disappointed," so that it wouldn't be Shakespearean, "with bodies littering the stage." Would you believe, instead, Megiddo? By bus bomb and assassination Ultras and Hamas got what they wanted, which was Bibi and Likud, meaning more settlers on the West Bank, more soldiers on the Golan Heights and more archaeologists and tourists tapeworming into the traumatized bowels of Al Aksa, while a lizardly Arafat bans books by Edward Said, and a rubber-bullet Olmert pretends to be the bandit prince Bar Kokhba, and the Pillsbury Doughboy in his Oval Office feels their pain. An earlier Amos prophesied a fire upon Judah, "and it shall devour the palaces of Jerusalem."

But Oz has been in the desert, hiding out from the reviews of *Fima* (1993), reconstruing marriage, children, and silence. In the dusty Negev new town Tel Kedar (pop. 9,000), an hour or so away from Beersheba and the daily papers, he has dreamed his way into the heads and hearts of Theo, a sixty-year-old semiretired civil engineer, and Noa, a forty-five-year-old teacher of literature. Theo, a tidy, gloomy insomniac, is so patient mixing a salad he might as well be painting it. Noa, a scatter of pages and ideas, is in such a rush she often fails to finish sentences, so worn out she falls into bed as if axed. Although they're not legally married, the relationship they've settled for is more intimate than most licensed monogamies—an almost hydraulic exchange of skeptical caution and heedless zeal; part pendulum and part crossruff. Although they are childless, Theo is as much Noa's father as her lover, and Noa, picking up stray children on the rainy highway, listening to Mahler's *Kindertotenlieder,* feeling guilty about her students, seems to mother half the Middle East. And although neither spends more than a minute thinking about, say, Arabs, Zionism, Judaism, or Jerusalem, their separate peace is about to tested.

One of Noa's dreamier students, the introverted Immanuel Orvieto, either falls or jumps to his death, perhaps because of drugs. When Immanuel's father, Avraham, either a military advisor or an arms dealer, arrives from Nigeria for the burial, he also proposes to bankroll, as a memorial, a clinic for adolescent drug users—if Noa, Immanuel's favorite teacher, agrees to do the scut work. Remorseful at having barely noticed Immanuel while he was alive, Noa flings herself into the project. With his connections, Theo could help. A long career of planning settlement areas, industrial zones, and leisure complexes has taught him how to deal with local and district councils, and from "the old days, when this country was nothing but sand dunes and fantasies," he even knows the mayor. But Theo, typically, is skeptical. He also knows Noa will resent his help. And so while the teacher plunges headlong into comical committee meetings, bureaucratic farce, archaeological memory digs and self-recrimination, the engineer makes salads, plays chess, listens to BBC news radio, and stares all night at the desert.

We shall presently try to imagine what he sees there, populating absences. But *Don't Call It Night* is a novel of domestic accommodation—almost a convalescence. From Tel Kedar, we can't see Hebron or Gaza, much less the Caracas where Theo and Noa met eight years ago. It's as if the fevers of eros and history had wasted them. In a town without a past, they are going through the motions. At least these motions—drinking iced tea or mulled wine, stopping at the Paris cinema or Entebbe bar, making rosebuds out of radishes—are reassuringly reciprocal. As they address us in alternating chapters (and Oz watches them watch each other), even the parentheses in their monologues are compensatory. Inside separate chambers, on either side of a hermetic seal, they mimic the same rotary wave. Theo longs for peace of mind. Noa lusts for significance. Eventually, he'll take a hand in her project. Predictably, she'll then develop doubts. (Why not an old people's home instead?) Finally, they discover their interdependence, which is also their consolation.

Meanwhile, we have met a town: Elijah, so-called because every five minutes in the post office queue he asks, "When's Elijah coming?" Blind Lupo, who apologizes to his own dog for kicking it. Muki, a lecherous investment consultant with sky-blue shoes. Avram, a falafel seller with a brand-new *shawarma* machine. Chuma, the militant vegetarian with "a particular hatred of potato crisps, mustard and stuffed intestines." Not to omit the newsagents, poets, bookbinders, garage mechanics, bank clerks, pharmacists, notaries, a Hungarian cantor, a Russian-emigré string quartet, the former weight-lifting champion of Lodz, and a piano tuner who's writing a book on *The Essence of Judaism.* As always in Oz, Israel teems with spinning types who kick against the cartoon bubbles limned around them. As always, there's a sort of moral blackmail to which the victims too eagerly submit. As always, there are missing mothers — Oz's own committed suicide when he was twelve — and thus a wounded emblematic child like Boaz in *Black Box,* with "the look of Jesus in a Scandinavian icon"; like Dimi in *Fima,* a "slightly cross-eyed albino child-philosopher"; like Immanuel in *Night,* seeming "to live inside a bubble of winter even in summer." And also as always there is his oddly *angry* lyricism. His physical world has an astonishing thickness of texture and scent. His feel for olives, lizards, candles, eucalyptus, marble, and moonlight is almost wanton. Yet this appreciation of surprise beauty is so masculine that it seems to resent its own esthetic shock, to want somehow to bite the face of grace.

> It is both a garrison state and a cultivated society, both Spartan and Athenian. It tries to do everything, to understand everything, to make provision for everything. All resources, all faculties are strained. . . . These people are actively, individually involved in universal history. I don't see how they can bear it. (Saul Bellow, *To Jerusalem and Back*)

What's missing — one of those absences on purpose — is politics. Or what Oz prefers to call "ethics." *Black Box* (1989) was consumed by West Bank settlements and Orthodox theocracy. Gideon, "tasting *schadenfreude* like expensive whisky, in small sips," has even written a book, *The Desperate Violence: A Study in Comparative Fanaticism.* In his opinion, we annihilate ourselves and will soon wipe out the species "precisely because of our 'higher longings,' because of the theological disease. Because of the burning need to be 'saved.' Because of an obsession with redemption. What is the obsession with redemption? Only a mask for a complete absence of the basic talent for life." *Fima* couldn't go to the movies without seeing Palestinians on a private sonar screen: "We're the Cossacks now, and the Arabs are the victims of the pogroms, yes, every day, every hour." Fima, the poet who works in an abortion clinic, "the Eugene Onegin of Kiryat Yovel," who would give away the whole of South America's magical realism, "with all its fireworks and cotton candy," for a single page of Chekhov — this tortured Fima explains:

> We must not become like the drunken Ukrainian carter who beat his horse to death when the beast stopped pulling his cart. Are the Arabs in the Territories our workhorses? What did you imagine, that they would go on hewing our wood and drawing our water forever and ever, amen? . . . Every Zambia and Gambia is an independent state nowadays, so why should the Arabs in the Territories continue come Hell or high water quietly scrubbing our shit-houses, sweeping our streets, washing dishes in our restaurants, wiping arses in our geriatric wards, and then saying thank you? How would you feel if the meanest Ukrainian anti-Semite planned a future like that for the Jews?

And that's just the recent fiction. For Oz in nonfiction like *In the Land of Israel* (1983), nationalism is mankind's curse: "Shall we aspire to rebuild the kingdom of David and Solomon? Shall we construct a Marxist paradise here? A Western society, a social-democratic welfare state? Or shall we create a model of the petite bourgeoisie with a little *Yiddishkeit?*" He'd be happier in a world "composed of dozens of civilizations, each developing in accordance with its own internal rhythm, all cross-pollinating . . ." Israel after the Six-Day War was "crude, smug and arrogant, power drunk, bursting with messianic rhetoric, ethnocentric, 'redemptionist,' apocalyptic — quite simply, inhuman. And un-Jewish. The Arab human beings under our dominion might never have been." And then this re-markable apostrophe:

> I study the elusive cunning of the Biblical charm of this landscape: and
> isn't all of this charm Arab, through and through? The lodge and the
> cucumber garden, the watchman's hut and the cisterns, the shade of
> the fig tree and the pale silver of the olive, the grape arbors and the
> flocks of sheep — these picturesque slopes that bewitched from afar
> the early Zionists like Yehuda Halevi and Abraham Mapu; these pri-
> meval glades that reduced the poet Bialik to tears and fired Tcherni-
> chowsky's imagination; the hypnotic shepherds who, from the very
> beginning of the return to Zion, captured the heart of Moshe Smilan-
> sky, who even called himself Hawaja Musa; the tinkle of the goats' bells
> which entwined, like magic webs, the hearts of the early Zionist set-
> tlers, who came from Russia thirsty for Arab garb and to speed on their
> horses toward this Arab Biblicality . . . the tales told around the
> campfires of the Palmach, the enchanted groves of Amos Kenan and
> the longed-for cisterns of Naomi Shemer, yearning for the bare-faced
> stony mountain, for merger into the bosom of these gentle, sleepy
> scapes so very far removed from shtetl alleyways, so very far from Yid-
> dish and the ghetto, right into the heart of this Oriental rock-strewn
> tenderness.

He is if anything unhappier in the collected broadsides in *The Slopes of Lebanon* (1987). The 1982 invasion of Lebanon—like "a timely investment in the stock market," like "the Empire Strikes Back"—enraged him. Not a pacifist, nor an admirer of the PLO, and equally disdainful of a secular left that "offers peace to the Israeli public as one part of a package that includes . . . the rights of nude sunbathers," he still favors a separate Palestinian state: "If only good and righteous people, with a 'clean record,' deserved self-determination, we would have to suspend, starting at midnight tonight, the sovereignty of three-quarters of the nations of the world." King Solomon, after all, gave away twenty cities to Hiram of Tyre, yet Solomon was not struck down, nor condemned by the prophets. Besides, "Hebron and Nablus will not be ours whether or not the proph-ets once walked there, whether or not the stones our ancestors liked to throw at the prophets still lie scattered there." So what if

Palestinians deceive us? "It will always be easier . . . to break the backbone of a tiny Palestinian state than to break the backbone of an eight-year-old Palestinian stone thrower."

At desperate issue on almost every page of *The Slopes of Lebanon* is Israel's soul and the Zionist ideal of a just society: "What have we come here to be?" If the logic of statecraft is that ends justify means, and the rule of thumb is that "it all depends," then "What began with the biblical words 'Zion shall be redeemed by the law' has come to 'Nobody's better than we are, so they should all shut up.'" He quotes Isaiah ("Your hands are covered with blood") and Jeremiah ("For they had eyes but they did not see"). "Veteran defeatists, both of them," Oz says: "Troublers of Israel. Self-hating Jews."

I suggest that some of this is what a sleepless Theo sees, staring at the desert. Never mind that "on the other side there is a forbidden valley containing secret installations." He's turned his back on more than Tel Kedar. He was asked himself to help plan Tel Kedar, back in the late sixties. By the light of a pressure lamp at the foot of a cliff, he sketched "rough preliminary ideas for a master plan that was intended to get away from the usual Israeli approach and create a compact desert town, sheltering itself in its own shade, inspired by photographs of Saharan townships in North Africa." For which he was ridiculed by his boss: "Same old Theo, carried away by his fantasies, it's brilliant, it's original, creative, the trouble is, as usual you've left one factor out of account: when all's said and done, Israelis want to live in the Israeli style. Desert or no desert. Just you tell me, Theo, who do you imagine suddenly wants to be transported back to North Africa? The Poles? The Romanians? Or the Moroccans? The Moroccans least of all. And just remember this, chum: this isn't going to be an artist's colony."

Theo's days as a senior planner in the Development Agency were obviously numbered, in spite of the British police stations and radar installations he'd once upon a time blown up in the Zionist cause. This great-grandchild of a Ukrainian gravedigger, with a couple of Herod's master-builder genes, would leave Israel as "a special advisor of regional planning"—to "develop" Veracruz, Sonora, and Tabasco; to redo Nicaragua after an earthquake; to wonder about atrophy, torpor, barrenness, and exile in Peru: "When he came across cruelty, corruption, barbarity or grinding poverty he passed no judgment . . . he had not come here to combat injustice but, as far as possible, to attain professional perfection and thereby perhaps, however minutely, to reduce disasters. Honor, the labyrinth and death were ever-present here, and life itself sometimes flared up like a festive firework display or a salvo of shots in the air: ruthless, spicy, noisy and cheap." But not for Theo until, in Venezuela, he met Noa—that Noa who comes home at night in one of two ways, either "setting up a row of electric lights in her path as though to illuminate the runway of her landing" or "as if she had flown into this room by mistake and now she's in such a panic she can't find the window. Which is open as it always has been."

And the Tel Kedar they made without Theo? It's hard to believe Elijah would come to such a place: Fifteen identical streets off Herzl Boulevard, with caged poinciana saplings wrapped in sackcloth against sandstorms; "a few eucalyptus trees and tamarisks, blighted by droughts and salty wind, hunched towards the east like fugitives turned to stone in mid-flight"; green street lamps and matching municipal benches; a solar panel on every roof, "as if the town were trying to appease the sun's blaze in its own language"; balconies shut up with cement, plaster blasted desert-gray; a chic northwest residential district "with projections, surrounds and arches, rounded windows and even weathercocks on gables, sighing for forests and meadows"; a commercial southeast of corrugated-iron huts, cement-block sheds, workshops, and junkyards; a billiard parlor for lottery tickets; a library, where only Noa seems to go; and a monument in memory of the fallen, with a cypress at each corner of the concrete column on which metallic letters read, THE BEAUTY OF ISRAEL IS SLAIN UPON THE HIGH PLAC S: "The penultimate letter is missing."

No wonder Theo's eyes are on the desert. As development

novels go, *Don't Call It Night* is up there with Norman Rush's *Mating*, and maybe Voltaire's *Candide*. And what Theo is probably looking for across the scrub and desolation, on slate slopes in the blue distance and dark scree, besides Arabs and meaning, is the Zionist dramaturge himself, a vanishing act like Shane.

> *I experienced strange sensations, I saw and heard my legend being born. The people are sentimental; the masses do not see clearly. A light fog is beginning to rise around me and it may perhaps become the cloud in which I shall walk.* (Theodor Herzl)

Before there was a Herzl Boulevard in Tel Kedar or anywhere else in Israel, there had to have been the godfather of Zionism — Theodor, the crackerjack journalist, mediocre playwright, "inveterate" misogynist, and manic depressive brought so vividly to life in Ernst Pawel's biography *The Labyrinth of Exile*. Worshipped by his mother, doted on by his father, innocent of Marx and Freud, "amazingly untouched by winds of change that revolutionized philosophy, literature and the state in his own generation," he loved Wagner, feared women, and foresaw the cattle cars and death camps. We can't understand him, says Pawel, without also understanding Prague, where he was born into ambivalence, and Vienna, with its "apocalyptic temper," and Paris too, where as a reporter he discovered anti-Semitism (the Dreyfus case) and anarchism ("the voluptuous pleasure of a great idea, and of martyrdom"). Pawel rereads his lame utopian novel, *Altneuland*; finds in his diaries those "idea splinters" that created the "vatic visionary"; sorts out the original plan (a mass conversion to Christianity!) from subsequent revisions proposing to settle the Diaspora anywhere from Argentina to Uganda; follows the argonaut to Paris, London, Rome, St. Petersburg, and Constantinople as he petitions popes, emperors, sultans, czars, and Rothschilds; and sits in on the assemblies where the playwright hit on an "alchemy of mass manipulation" that "successfully transmuted fantasy into power." Worn out at age forty-four, Herzl essentially killed himself for the cause. He was nonetheless, says Pawel, "the first Jewish leader in modern times." And what's more: "Thus far, the only one. Those who came after him were politicians. Still, Jewish politicians in a country of their own."

From Michael Berkowitz's enriching exploration of the rhetoric and imagery of *Zionist Culture and West European Jewry Before the First World War*, we get a broader picture of what Herzl and his brilliant and difficult fellow disputants wrought at Basel in spite of Martin Buber. Against all odds and despite a language question (Yiddish versus Hebrew), a built-in Talmudic hostility to pluralism, the deepest Pale of Settlement suspicions, and competing claims from revolutionary socialism, they composed an entire mythopoeic *Gesamtkunstwerk*. They composed this total theater out of European nationalism and German drinking songs; out of the idea of the Promised Land and a cult of male friendship in student dueling fraternities; out of paintings of the Wailing Wall and photographs of Palestinian flora; from selling books, trees, menorahs, kiddush cups, spice boxes, and Holy Arks—not to mention merchandising an iconography of Herzl himself, whose manly visage showed up on postage stamps, candy wrappers, canned milk, and packs of cigarettes. As if to schoolmarm this new macho image of an "orientalized" warrior Jew, on horseback with a rifle and Arab headdress, they brought back the matriarchs: Sarah, Rachel, Rebecca, Leah. It was agitation and it was propaganda, but it was also as thrilling as Impressionism. "First," said Herzl to Nahum Sokolow, "there has to be a home and peace for the Jews, then let them choose the culture they want. They will, of course, bring along with them many cultures, like bees who suck honey from different flowers and bring it all with them to one beehive; precisely this mixture will be far more interesting than one monotonous culture."

Just how interesting not even a playwright could have imagined, especially a playwright who somehow managed to forget there were Arabs already residing in this dreamscape, for whom Rachel's Tomb and David's Tower were as meaningless as

Herder's moonshine on folksy essence or a postcard from Vienna with the angel Zion wearing a Star of David as her halo, pointing from a shtetl in Eastern Europe to a harvest in sanctified Palestine. Even so, before peace and before home, the Zionists did create a culture with heroes, songs, symbols, and a flag with blue stripes borrowed boldly from the *talit*. Berkowitz is flabbergasted: "a strange nationalism of the twentieth century — in the face of more aggressive and exclusive ideologies — which proclaims that the community producing the finest books, the most sublime poetry, a comprehensive research university, and an advanced agricultural-experiment station would 'win' a country."

Oz recalls what it felt like in his childhood: summer evenings and neighborhood scholars in his parents' garden; Revisionists from Odessa, socialist Zionists from Bobruisk, scholars of mysticism and of deserts, interpreters of Maimonides, Hegel, Nietzsche, Marx, Lassalle, and Jabotinsky; "atheists, vegetarians, and other assorted world reformers, each with his own personal plan for the salvation of the People and the Reform of Humanity in one fell swoop. Everyone knew exactly what had to be done — and at once. . . . When the Hebrew State was born it must be such-and-such, and if not, there would be no point to it." But: "All this is finished here."

Some of this fizz just didn't travel, as those of us who grew up pretending to be Jewish cowboys slaughtering Arab Nazis have reason to know from a visit to Ben Yehuda's pedestrian mall in Jerusalem after our rented car has been stoned on the Sabbath. Cypress and honeysuckle, vineyards and olive groves, vipers and goats, chalk and salt — "Not 'the land of the hart,'" Oz has pleaded, "and not 'the divine city reunited,' as the clichés would have it, but simply the State of Israel. Not the 'Maccabeans reborn' that Herzl talked of, but a warm-hearted, hot-tempered Mediterranean people that is gradually learning, through great suffering and in a tumult of sound and fury, to find release both from the bloodcurdling nightmares of the past and from delusions of grandeur, both ancient and modern."

So many wars, and before and after each, the scavenging of the bonepickers.

This generation has created a new religion, the religion of history, a belief in the history of its people as a religious faith. . . . It would not be an exaggeration to say that they fought with verses from the Bible. Through archaeology these people discover their 'religious' values; in archaeology they find their religion, they learn that their forefathers were in this country 3,000 years ago. This is a value. By this they fought and by this they live. (Yigael Yadin)

This is what those Temple Mount tunnels are all about, besides a provocation and a real-estate expulsion scam. From Neil Asher Silberman's *A Prophet from Amongst You: The Life of Yigael Yadin,* we gather that for most of this century archaeology in Israel has been a Zionist dig, an identity-politics daydream of a glorious antiquity segregated into ethnic cultures with unchanging racial characteristics. Think of the Dead Sea Scrolls as a ticket of admission and a warrant. Not for nothing did Yadin's father spend his student days at the University of Berlin. Translating "The War of the Sons of Light Against the Sons of Darkness," he might as well have been reading a right-wing newspaper. And his soldier son improved on him; a veteran of so many battles, including Irgun versus Palmach, a Lawrence of anti-Arabia, he must have imagined himself a Bronze Age warlord, especially at Hazor, in whose rubble he deciphered a rousting of inconvenient Canaanites. Yadin loved it; what afflatus: To stand at Megiddo, where Solomon built a temple on the ruins of Tuthmose III. To burrow into the caves of Nahal Hever and find a basket of skulls left over from the bandit prince himself, Bar Kokhba. To glory in Masada—never again. From fallen columns, charred beams, headless statues, smashed pottery, shattered frescoes, ceramic fragments, bronze coins, goatskin bags, incense shovels, Roman tunics, and some Aramaic scribbled on papyrus, to intuit Eretz Israel—the Covenant as Deed in Perpetuity, handed down by archers, cavalry, charioteers, catapult stones, and a battering ram. Never mind dissenting archaeologists like Yohanan Aharoni, who counter-imagined a "gradual migration" of the Israelites into Canaan and a "social process" of assimilation instead of a turf war of gloryhounds with shofars for shillelaghs. Joshua was Yadin's kind of guy, a Little Big Horn in reverse.

Amazing that the ultra-Orthodox, for whom Mahmoud from East Jerusalem collects garbage and fixes sewers, should so much hate the bonepickers—"Death to the Hitlerite archaeologists!"—who shovel the same sand-dune fantasies. On the other hand, Oz has also talked to the settlers, who sound like a column by A. M. Rosenthal:

> As soon as we finish this phase, the violence phase, step right up, it'll be your turn to play your role. You can make us a civilization with humanistic values here. Do the brotherhood-in-man bit—Light unto the Nations—whatever you want—the morality of the Prophets. . . . Be my guest. That's the way it is, old buddy: first Joshua and Jephthah the Gileadite break ground, wipe out the memory of Amalek, and then maybe afterward it's time for the Prophet Isaiah and the wolf and the lamb and the leopard and the kid and that whole terrific zoo. But only provided that, even at the end of days, we'll be the wolf and all the gentiles around here will be the lamb. Just to be on the safe side.

Is it any wonder that Theo can't sleep? That he needs Noa, who insists on knowing, "And where are we meant to be shining, and by whom is our shining required"? So what if their love isn't epic theater or grand opera or a Song of Solomon? That the best they can hope for is more modest than messianic—an autumn sonata, some rock-strewn tenderness, and maybe "the basic talent for life"? *What have we come here to be?* Oz himself wants to be Chekhov. He can't be, of course. He is magnanimous enough, but not exactly gentle. Still, trying to be Chekhov in a century written by Dostoyevsky is a kind of heroism. *L'chayim!*

García Márquez, at War on Drugs

Except for the rooster, there is no magic in *News of a Kidnapping*, the new nonfiction by Gabriel García Márquez. There is shadow play, on the mediascapes of journalism and celebrity. And make-believe, on the part of a political class incapable of governing, and a drug cartel with its own diplomatic protocols, and "go-betweens" who wind up dead in the trunks of cars without license plates. But no-frills realism is otherwise the unrelenting mode of this account of the abduction and hostage-holding in 1990 and 1991 of ten prominent Colombians by Pablo Escobar as he negotiated the amenities of his surrender to such civil authority as everyone agreed to pretend still existed. This time, there will be no gathering up by God of Remedios the Beauty as she hangs the bedsheets out to dry—nor any deliverance by ice, mirrors, magnets, or windmills.

Missing as well is that other black art, ideology. García Márquez is sick at heart about a country capable of accustoming itself "to everything, good and bad, with a resiliency that may be the cruellest form courage can take." He seems to have been personally acquainted with many of Escobar's targets, and their influential families, and the politicians who issued wishful decrees, and the judges and editors and mayors under sentence of death, even the police and military for whom the narcoterrorists were not usefully to be distinguished from the ELN, FARC, or M-19 guerrillas. He improved this intimacy with interviews and had access not only to the diaries but also to the dreams of the kidnapped. "Their pain, their patience, and their rage," he says, "gave me the courage to persist in this autumnal task, the saddest and most difficult of my life."

This is not the place for a hemispheric macrohistory. If the reader needs background on the coffee-bean economies of countries like Colombia and the family elites that tweak them, it is readily available—from Harvard in *Coffee and Power: Revolution and the Rise of Democracy in Central America,* by Jeffrey M.

Paige; and from Princeton in *Open-Economy Politics: The Political Economy of the World Coffee Trade,* by Robert H. Bates. For what the rise of Escobar, the Ochoa brothers, the Rodriguez Orejuelas, and their Medellín and Cali cocaine cartels did to Colombia's economy and political culture, consult *The Heart That Bleeds: Latin America Now,* a collection of Alma Guillermoprieto's splendid *New Yorker* essays. By 1984, drug money had not only alarmed the upper classes by enabling "former punks and small-time hoods to buy property in the posh neighborhoods," but its investment in radio stations, travel agencies, soccer teams, drugstore chains, agriculture, and real estate amounted to 7 per cent of the gross national product. By 1989, Public Order Courts, fearful prosecutors, elite military units, and death-squad vigilantes were at war with the cartels, the cartels were at war with one another, left-wing guerrillas extorted a "war tax" on cartel-held cattle ranches, right-wing *narcoparamilitaires* gunned down politicians, bombs exploded in airports, restaurants, banks, telephone substations, cinemas, and even bullrings, and language itself metastasized: *los muchachos de las bandas* (gangbangers), *pistolocos* (crazy guns), *basuqueros* (addicts of coca paste), *punketos* (devoted to the Clash or the Sex Pistols), *desechables* (throwaway kids), *violentilógos* (the sociologists of the madness), and *sicariato* (the culture of hired assassins).

Escobar's August 18, 1989, hit on New Liberal presidential candidate Luis Carlos Galán was the last straw for outgoing president Virgilio Barco, who used his emergency powers to cosign an extradition treaty with the United States. (An earlier treaty in 1987 had been declared unconstitutional by Colombia's Supreme Court after another narcoterrorist killing spree. This time the court okayed it.) Barco's successor, César Gaviria, offered the cartels a carrot: Surrender, plead guilty to lesser charges, and reinvest the billions squirreled away abroad, and we promise the social security of a country-club prison sentence. Or the stick: A one-way ticket to the rest of your life in a Yanqui cell. Escobar, who had launched his criminal career by stealing gravestones from the Medellín cemetery, sanding them smooth, and reselling them to the freshly bereaved, sought to write himself a better deal by seizing hostages.

These were not exactly drive-by victims. They were variously negotiable, in currencies of local celebrity and blood relation. Besides their worldly class credentials — Maruja Pachón de Villamizar, director of FOCINE, the PR agency for Colombia's film industry; her sister-in-law, Beatriz Villamizar de Guerrero, press liaison for FOCINE; Diana Turbay, director of the *Cripton* TV news show and her crew of Azucena Liévano, Juan Vitta, Richard Becerra, and Orlando Acevedo; Hero Buss, a German reporter who'd tagged along with Diana on what they thought was a visit to the ELN guerrillas; Francisco Santos, the editor of *El Tiempo*; and Marina Montoya, a sixty-four-year-old former beauty queen who managed a Bogotá restaurant — they tended to be married to, or the mothers, daughters, sons, and siblings of, ex-presidents, publishing tycoons, TV personalities, ambassadors to Canada and Indonesia and UNESCO, clinical psychiatrists, and Kodak executives.

Thus the shadow play of family influence at exalted levels. Of easy access to inner sanctums, for promises that would not be kept to use intelligence agencies instead of rescue teams. Of secret visits to the clandestine headquarters of revolutionary armies, to be told they had nothing to do with the abductions. Of one relative producing an eight-part TV series on the psychology of hostages and another printing personal messages to the missing on his editorial page. Of an article in *El Tiempo* counseling against suicide on the very day Francisco has decided he has no other option. Of a scroll at the bottom of the TV news screen reminding an abductee to take her medicine. And of a campaign of film, theater, and soccer stars calling for release of the hostages: "Colombia Wants Them Back." No wonder Maruja begins to believe that "the glycerine tears of impossible loves" on the afternoon soaps are beaming coded notes to her.

And thus the make-believe that blue-blooded emeriti of previous regimes calling themselves "The Notables" can bargain in good faith behind the scenes with a phantom consortium of narco-lordlings calling themselves "The Extraditables," who, on their embossed stationery, communicate their nonnegotiable demands and denounce human-rights violations by the police while simultaneously paying a five-million-peso bounty per dead cop. That Escobar with his gold-plated bathroom basins, white grand pianos, and personal zoo should expect to be treated as a "political offender" and receive "the same treatment as the M-19 guerrillas, who had been pardoned and recognized as a political party." That clever lawyers could redefine the drug trade as "a collective, sui generis" offense somewhere on the ambiguous and "murky border between ordinary and political crimes." And that Pablo, upon his surrender, imagined that he could conduct business as usual, punishing enemies and plundering allies from his customized La Catedral prison with its computers, its prostitutes, and its Jacuzzi.

No wonder his former friends, calling themselves LOS PEPES ("Persecuted by Pablo Escobar") set fire to his prized Pontiac, which had once belonged to Al Capone.

Here's where I should explain that magical exception, the rooster. It crows throughout *News of a Kidnapping*, though never at dawn. Maruja and Beatriz are vexed in their captivity by its waywardness. Francisco, shackled elsewhere in Bogotá, is obsessed by this "demented" bird that "at first crowed at any hour, and as the months passed crowed at the same hour in different places: sometimes far away at three in the afternoon, other times next to his window at two in the morning." In García Márquez's own symbolic zoo, a rooster has a hard time competing with blue dogs, golden salamanders, cockatoos in clavichords, needle-threading bears, piano-toting mules, butterfly-eating alligators, blood-draining bats, cathedral-invading monkeys, leopards asleep on the velvet cushions of trains that fall off orchid-covered precipices, and sponges that make children cry in order to drink their tears . . . But his Colombia has gone crazy with violence and his rooster doesn't know the evil hour of night or day.

So make way for the unmagical realism of terror, which arrives, like the black Ford Falcons for the *desaparecidos* in Argentina, in a black Mercedes or a yellow cab, a Renault with a two-way radio or a Jeep with four-wheel drive. Which waves a 9-millimeter pistol or a mini-Uzi with a silencer. Which wears a ski mask, a sweatsuit, a Holy Infant medal, and a Brazilian wristband, or tropical wool suits and yellow silk ties and Italian loafers. Which plays dominoes, Parcheesi, and Nintendo when, between televised soccer matches, it isn't listening to Guns 'N' Roses, watching porn videos, anxiously rubbing alcohol over everything it might have left its prints on, or urinating in the washbasin and the shower drain. Whose names—Monk, Ant, Top, Shark, "Doctor," Gorilla—are ripped from comics. Whose brains, speed-freaked, crack-crazed, deep in Rohypnol tranquilizer dreams of cinematic mayhem, are off the claustrophobic wall; Mad Maxed and Thunderdomed.

Her most brutish captor, Barrabas, screams at Maruja: "You rich motherfuckers! Did you really think you'd run things forever?" This is the single semaphore of class hate in *News of a Kidnapping,* just as a fleeting reference to "the consuming countries" is all that's said about the international drug economy. To be sure, there are nicer guards than Barrabas, less inclined to sexual menace—schoolboys, almost. If the Medellín textile industry hadn't collapsed in the seventies, maybe they'd have jobs in a factory instead of roles in a splatter flick; wages instead of *basuco* in their sweatsuit pouches. As well as he knows the hostages brokered on this bloody stock exchange, García Márquez also knows the fatalistic street kids for whom a brief and gaudy arc from stolen goods to sudden death is better than long gray penury; for whom Pablo the bandit prince, with his pearl-handled pistol in a dainty ankle holster and his secret tunnel to a private dugout for the soccer matches, is both movie star and Robin Hood. But whose class is Maruja the enemy of?

She's screamed at after months of confinement in six square meters of unventilated room with two other hostages and a pair of *pistolocos,* where she must ask permission to sit, stretch, speak, smoke, or go to the toilet; where she must sleep under the shadow of a submachine gun in a single soiled bed with Beatriz, "their heads facing opposite directions like the fish in the zodiac"; where she is kicked in the head when she coughs and gagged if she snores. Hiding "inside herself like a snail in its shell," she survives 193 days of captivity, chronic cystitis, and malnutrition, not because of who she is or isn't—any more than Beatriz survives her panic, asphyxia, and gastric ulcer because she's a physical therapist; or Francisco survives his shackling to the bed bars because he's read Kundera; or Hero Buss survives because worse has already happened to him in Chile—but by arbitrary accident, a phase of the Escobar moon. They could have been Diana, whose selfless journalism had been entirely devoted to seeking peace. Diana is already dead when Maruja is screamed at, shot in the back by either trigger-happy thugs or careless cops. Equally dead is Marina: vain, flighty, and perhaps inconsequential in the grander mythomanias of sovereigns and assassins, but gallant as well, putting on makeup for her date with her killers, who, before they dump her body, will anyway cover her face with a hood:

> According to regulations . . . an anonymous corpse has to be buried with a serial number stamped on the torso, arms, and legs so that it can be identified even in case of dismemberment. It has to be enclosed in black plastic, the kind used for trash bags, and tied at the ankles and wrists with strong cord. The body of Marina Montoya . . . was naked and covered in mud, and had been tossed into the common grave without the identifying tattoos required by law.

There's your snapshot of the late twentieth century—a wish-you-were-here postcard from Pablo, Pol Pot, and the death camps; from Belfast, Beirut, Jakarta, and Jerusalem; from the secret police whose toothy grins glow in the dark at their pillbox slits; from that burning bush, "the lunatic of one idea," a Konstantinov, a Shining Path, the bomber of federal buildings and abortion clinics; from Torquemada, Robespierre, and the sky-writing kamikazes of Kingdom Come, Happy Valley, Laputa,

Zembla, Vheissu, and Dixie. Terror and counterterrorism—abduction, torture, rape, murder—all spin political excuses from their spidery bowels, but all are brain-smoking forms of crack. The cold, invariable, contemptuous purpose is to dominate, humilate, commodify, and dispossess; to create, as in the nightmares of Kafka and Beckett, environments entirely theoretical, mazes in which the rest of us are lab-rat matters of interpretation. With his alert sympathy, perfect awareness, and capacity to surprise, a great novelist reminds us that there is no redemption in contempt, nor any community. Colombia is what terror looks like. Maruja, Francisco, Diana, and Marina are what it feels like. García Márquez will restore to them their stolen autonomies of courage, memory, flair, and fear. They are ends, not means.

> *When you inflict punishment on someone who is not guilty, when you fill rooms with innocent victims, you begin to empty the world of meaning and erect a separate mental state, the mind consuming what's outside itself, replacing real things with plots and fictions. One fiction taking the world narrowly into itself, the other fiction pushing out toward the social order, trying to unfold into it. . . . This poet you've snatched. His detention drains the world of one more thimble of meaning.*
>
> (Don DeLillo, *Mao II*)

So eagerly awaited in 1991, so full of lunar images, canny notions, and clever talk, *Mao II* fogs off oddly at the end. Bill Grey is another of DeLillo's "men in small rooms," but this time a novelist. For twenty-three years he has worked on a book he refuses to publish because he has come to suspect that books in the West have lost their power. "Years ago," he says, "I used to think it was possible for a novelist to enter the inner life of the culture. Now bomb-makers and gunmen have taken that territory. They make raids on human consciousness. What writers used to do before we were all incorporated."

Bill says this to Brita, a European photographer who vanishes early on in the novel until she's needed again at the end to go to Beirut. Karen, a former Moonie who hangs around the Grey household for sex and television, also might have taken over as a heroine. She understands, from the TV frescoes, our rush to death among the believers in Mexico City and Teheran, the martyred in Tiananmen Square, the homeless in New York. But Karen is without volition; she needs crowds to believe *for* her; she's lost in the dusty light of "media catastrophe"—"the terror," we are told, "that came blowing through the fog." Implausibly, Bill will leave New England for London, Athens, and Beirut to seek the release of a young Swiss poet held hostage by a terrorist faction nobody's ever heard of. And it's not just terrorists who've taken over; it's also crowds, and images of those crowds, on television and in Pop Art, like silk-screen Warhols: a Maoist mass of victims, genocides. And so the isolation of the artist and the isolation of the hostage meet the twentieth-century mass mind and the twentieth-century collective death.

A grand theme, no question, and along the way we get some of the cerebral fireworks we've come to expect from our brainiest novelist, his cubist geometries and progressive jazz. But Bill Grey isn't up to the symbolic weight. A go-between and provocateur challenges him: "It's such a simple idea. Terrorize the innocent. The more heartless they are, the better we see their rage. And isn't it the novelist, Bill, who understands this rage, who knows in his soul what the terrorist thinks and feels? Through history it's the novelist who has felt affinity for the violent man who lives in the dark. Where are your sympathies? With the colonial police, the occupier, the rich landlord, the corrupt government, the militaristic state? Or with the terrorist?" To which the best Bill can muster in reply is this:

> The point of every closed state is now you know how to hide your dead. This is the setup. You predict many dead if your vision of the truth isn't realized. Then you kill them. Then you hide the fact of killing them and the bodies themselves. This is why the closed state was invented. And it begins with a single hostage, doesn't it? The hostage is the miniaturized form. The first tentative rehearsal for mass terror.

I believe these words. It's Bill on his way to Beirut I don't believe. Nor this novel, more willed than realized—a silk screen, a sculptured object, a nerveless brain. But most modern novels on the subject, seeking some sort of Vulcan mindmeld with the terrorist, wind up foggy. Wasn't it too easy for Mary McCarthy in *Cannibals and Missionaries*? For Paul Theroux, being almost bumptious about the IRA in *The Family Arsenal*? Did you for a minute believe John Le Carré's *The Little Drummer Girl*, much less the movie with Diane Keaton as a Mossad agent in Arab drag? Doris Lessing's *Good Terrorist* turned out to be part nanny and part practical nurse. The young Sephardic Israeli Uri, in David Grossman's *The Smile of the Lamb*, was all too willing to be a hostage for the Palestinian storyteller Khilmi. Heinrich Böll, trying in *The Safety Net* to save the high-culture caviar of liberalism from being gummed to death by red ants, gave us a German ruling class so full of bad faith it was just asking to get kidnapped, and a calmly murderous tribal cadre of terrorists who were the perfect children of that ruling class, as prideful and arrogant as their fathers. Alberto Moravia seemed to decide in *Time of Desecration* that, at least in Red Brigades Italy, the best explanation for political terrorism was sexual pathology — sodomizing late capitalism. Nadine Gordimer, as usual, was a lot more complicated in *Burger's Daughter* and *A Sport of Nature*, but her heroines never had to do the really dirty work.

The best novel I've read from the zone of dread is Alberto Manguel's *News from a Foreign Country Came* (1991). "People are responsible for their own deaths," says Antoine Berence, a French military officer retired to the shores of a lake in Quebec after years of shadowy service in Algeria and Argentina. In his library, stared down on by a copperplate Dürer engraving of a knight-errant and the Devil, he reads Camus, quotes Dante, and feels very much misunderstood. There are things he can't quite say to his ten-year-old daughter, Ana:

> He wanted to tell her that we have all been measured in different ways for different lengths, that we are all made of time, like grass or sundials or water. He wanted her to think of . . . the visible shapes of time, growth and decay, rivers, insects, the clusters of lantana flowers whose

stems she liked to suck . . . even the slowly shifting constellations in
a darkness that was also dying.

A child will drown in the lake in Quebec. Earlier, in Buenos
Aires, another child drowned in a bucket of water in a police
station. Earlier still, there was a sea monster, fished up dead on a
dock in Algiers. At the end of the novel, a third child looks up
from the bottom of a silent sea, watched by phosphorous faces;
she is drowning in history instead of water. And for every image
of drowning, there's an image of burning—caterpillars, when
their tree web is set on fire; a madwoman and a holy man consumed to ash by their knowledge of God; a body in a flaming bed
after the Latin Americans have come to Quebec with their
bomb. Nor are these paired images the only correspondences.
To counterpoise the copperplate knight: Our Lady of Africa,
peach-colored in the Algerian sunset. To compete with Brahms,
a screaming. When figures move with watery silence through
white-tiled rooms, are we in a monastery or a torture chamber?
News from a Foreign Country Came insists that we imagine
someone who resorts to torture to preserve "cleared space" and
"necessary order," a "still center" and the "last intimate and perfect point" of western culture, against chaos and destruction;
who thinks of torture as a "cleansing," and of himself as "puri-
fied" by his "aspiration and responsibility"; who teaches his
methods to other policemen everywhere, a system so "detached" and so "meticulous" that "it verges on boredom, like
the slow rotation of a planet"—and who advises his "students":

> And all this time you must tell yourself: I am not a part of this foreign
> country, this alien body, this other suffering. It is he, the patient, who
> has brought this on himself. . . . No one ever drowns. People
> choose to stop living. Drowning is a suspension of the will.

Leave it to García Márquez to abandon this writerly intellec-
tualizing of "the violent man who lives in the dark," reverse the
obscenely Fanonized raincoat of the shadow cadres, and see the
dispossession of the innocent through their own wild eyes.

Maybe, as in Jacobo Timerman's *Prisoner Without a Name, Cell Without a Number,* nonfiction is the best discipline because you can't make the mind of a torturer or terrorist as interesting as your own, can't furnish it with Dante's *Inferno,* Masaccio's Christ, Bluebeard's Castle, Gramsci's prison notes, or Guevara's prescription pad. Moreover, by choosing to focus on narcoterrorism rather than, say, Sendero Luminoso, you finesse those embarrassing left-right questions, not to mention getting to skip over the fabulous derangements of Gonzalo Thought, and not having to decide in Peru who's worse, Túpac Amaru or Fujimori. Let your readers do this worrying. The word "kidnap" may be of recent, seventeenth-century origin — "nabbing" children, selling them to sea captains for transport to colonial plantations — but the activity's older than recorded history. At least since Cadmus married Harmony, abduction and rape were not only what gods did constantly to mortals, but also the principal form of East-West cultural exchange in the ancient world: with Europa, Io, Medea, and the Argonauts; Helen stolen first by Theseus and later by Paris of Troy; Ariadne in Argos and Naxos; Persephone in hell. Slavery was kidnapping's ugliest form, until the cattle cars and the death camps and the "disappeared." The forcible dislocation and relocation of entire peoples is one variation — according to the 1997 *Human Rights Watch World Report,* political violence displaced over 750,000 Colombians in the last decade — as are reservations and refugee camps. But our century is especially rich in spin-offs, in skyjackings and embassy seizures, Lindbergh babies and Bobby Franks, Aldo Moros and a Patty Hearst. Stalin kidnapped Isaac Babel and Osip Mandelstam.

That's one way to think about this book. But there's another. With Pablo safely dead and Medellín's cartel in disarray, *Cali's* cartel bought the next president of Colombia, Ernesto Samper, and went into heroin production in the Andes — to meet the changing market in the United States and Western Europe. Let's look at one of those "consuming countries."

It's a funny war when the "enemy" is entitled to due process of law and a fair trial. By the way, I'm in favor of due process. But that kind of slows things down. (William Bennett)

See the Great Moralizer, fresh from the $700-a-week therapeutic funny farm to which he'd resorted to kick a two-packs-daily cancerstick habit, cracking his sunflower seeds, wadding his nicotine gum, blowing out smog from the holes in his head, before he decides instead to blame Hollywood and Geraldo for our shortfall from virtue. Bill Bennett didn't start the War on Drugs. He just happened to be one in a long line of loony legionnaires — starting with Richard Nixon and John Mitchell and not perhaps ending with George Bush, Ed Meese, and Bill Casey—whose "zero tolerance" of poor people, black people, and young people would eventually come to include a disdain as well for that fussy inconvenience, the Bill of Rights.

There is no better briefing on this evil burlesque than Dan Baum's richly anecdotal, statistics-saturated, and more than occasionally sarcastic aria of indignant muckraking, *Smoke and Mirrors: The War on Drugs and the Politics of Failure*. It's as if Lincoln Steffens and Jonathan Swift had teamed up for a miniseries featuring every pol who ever exploited the class and culture wars; every cop ever impatient with those legal niceties that distinguish this country from, say, Myanmar; every ninja narc eager to break down doors and bust up heads and confiscate a yacht; every prurient sleuth needing a license to rummage in our garbage, our mail, our bedrooms, and even our bowels; and every star of a TV cop show for whom presumptions of innocence are such a narrative-clogging drag. They got what they wanted. And we got prisons.

First of all, there never was a drug epidemic when the Nixon Justice Department declared its dirty little war. More Americans, 1,824, died falling down stairs in 1969 than perished from every illegal drug combined, and twice as many choked to death on food. As many died from gun accidents in 1971; ten times more committed suicide. Not to mention a 1972 body count of

33,000 cirrhosed livers and 55,000 highway accidents, most of them alcohol-related, and not even to think about cigarettes, which in 1989, when Bill Bennett was trying to kick his habit, killed 395,000, wheras cocaine killed 3,618—which is fewer than expired from anterior horn cell disease. Nobody dies from smoking pot. Nor is there any evidence that it's a "gateway" drug to stronger stuff. Nor are there any reliable figures on how much crime is addiction-related. And if it weren't criminal to toke up, there wouldn't be eleven million "regular" (monthly) users of illegal drugs in the United States; there would be two million, about 350,000 of them cokeheads.

But declaring war on drugs was Nixon's way of retreating from LBJ's War on Poverty. By 1982, the Reaganaut abandonment was full-throttle: budgeting for child nutrition, down 34 percent; urban development action grants, down 35; education block grants, down 38; school milk programs, down 78; energy conservation, 83. By the end of Reagan's second term, spending on prisons and police had increased 600 percent and even local county governments lavished $2 billion more each year on criminal justice than on schools—astonishing, since counties don't pay for imprisonment but finance virtually all K–12 education. Our prison population doubled, and the proportion of those inside for drugs rose from one in fifteen to one in three, 85 percent of them for mere possession, not for dealing.

And this skewed priority is far from the worst of the Drug War's residue. The Constitution has been battered. Step by angry and depressing step, Baum takes us through these manifold abuses, most approved by a Supreme Court still pretending to be strict-constructionist: "Loose" warrants, a weakened Miranda, and wiretaps on traditionally privileged conversations with doctors, lawyers, and clergy. Forfeiture proceedings that allow prosecutors to confiscate the homes and bank accounts of purported potheads without due process, just compensation, or even a conviction—a license to loot for bounty-hunting cops. RICO prosecutions that send college kids to prison for conspiring to introduce two people later caught peddling drugs. Legalized no-knocks and preventive detention. Warrantless searches of cars at roadblocks and of schoolchildren's lockers. Random urine tests of federal employees, American soldiers, and workers in "sensitive" positions like the transportation industry and pro football. Permission to open suitcases and first-class mail on the say-so of a barking dog. "Courier profiles" that target Latinos and Nigerians. Forced defecation, into airport wastebaskets, by anybody remotely resembling such a profile. The end of "exclusionary rules" on evidence gathered by heretofore illegal searches and seizures, based on anonymous tips or a hunch. Revoking passports of U.S. citizens caught with as much as a joint. Kicking first-time possession offenders *and their families* out of public housing and canceling all federal benefits, grants, student loans, mortgages. Unleashing on dope fiends and other pedestrians, despite the Posse Comitatus Act of 1878, the military, the Coast Guard, and our own homegrown *narcoparamilitaires,* the CIA. Shall I go on? Baum does, indefatigably.

From Baum, we learn more than we want to about G. Gordon Liddy and Operation Intercept; Nelson Rockefeller and life imprisonment without parole; heroin addiction in Vietnam and how to make it worse; bribing Turkey to stop growing opium; total war on defense attorneys, paraquat, and synthetic THC; Ross Perot as Texas drug czar; an invasion of Humboldt County in California by black helicopters right out of Pynchon's *Vineland*; the "crack baby" fraud; Procter & Gamble's purchase of exclusive rights to Nancy Reagan's "Just Say No" slogan; and flamboyant DEA raids on criminal florists selling the sort of indoor gardening equipment that can be used to grow either pot or orchids—which florists dared to advertise, next to the bongs and roach clips, in magazines like *High Times.* More than a million Americans in 1990 were arrested, 264,000 for pot possession, as if nobody had told them marijuana makes you impotent or gay, depending.

Are you surprised to learn that, with the help of Operation Hammer, the LAPD managed at one time or another by the end of the last decade to arrest three quarters of all young black men in Los Angeles? That Operation Clean Sweep, a warrantless "inspection" search of the Chicago housing projects, found not only some drugs and associated paraphernalia, but also forty thousand people who happened *all* to be of color? That, between 1985 and 1987, the percentage of drug-trafficking defendants nationwide who also just happened to be African-American was *99*? That perhaps the huge discrepancy in sentences for dealing crack versus dealing powder cocaine can be accounted for by the fact that 90 percent of crack dealers are black, retailing small hits, while dealers in powder tend to be white wholesalers? That one out of every four young black men is in prison, on parole, or on probation? That even as fifteen hundred people a week went to jail in the first six months of 1994, there were more drugs than ever before on the streets? That in this country capable, like Colombia, of accustoming itself "to everything, good and bad" or even paranormal so long as it's fat-free, the average number of jailbirds per prison guard is three, whereas the number of pupils per public-school teacher is thirty? That, as the Rand Corporation noted in May, 1997, spending $1 million on long mandatory prison sentences reduced cocaine consumption by 29 pounds a year, while that same $1 million used to treat heavy users would cut consumption 220 pounds? That what Bill Clinton purposes to do to these cartels is freeze their assets off?

I am reminded of a passage in *The Autumn of the Patriarch,* when the wretched children, who were "disappeared" because they made the mistake of picking a winning lottery number, are discovered and released, and even the thuggish Caligula experiences a qualm:

> In spite of it all, he did not measure the true depth of the abyss until he saw the children like cattle in a slaughterhouse in the inner courtyard of the harbor fort, he saw them come out of the dungeons like a stampede of goats blinded by the brilliance of the sun after so many months of nocturnal terror, they were confused in the light, there were so many at the same time that he didn't see them as two thousand separate chil-

dren but as a huge shapeless animal that was giving off an impersonal stench of sun-baked skin and making a noise of deep waters and its multiple nature saved it from destruction, because it was impossible to do away with such a quantity of life without leaving a trace of horror that would travel around the world.

So, too, in our Drug Wars, are the Fourth, Fifth, and Eighth Amendments *desaparecidos*. And thus, as well, contemptibly, has our black American manhood been kidnapped

Eduardo Galeano
Walks Some Words

In a Latin America rampant with Magical Realists, Eduardo Galeano calls himself a Magical Marxist—"one half reason, one half passion, a third half mystery"—which may explain why, in *Walking Words,* after the affair of a white rose, a sprig of coriander, and a police truncheon, José is convicted of a "violation of the right of property (the father's over his daughter and the dead man's over his widow), disturbing the peace, and attempted priesticide." And why Calamity Jane leaves South Dakota for a Comayagua brothel where, with a magic lasso, she ropes her very own archangel. And why in Haiti anyone telling a story before dark is disgraced: "The mountain throws a stone at his head, his mother walks on all fours." And why a cowboy who turns himself into a jaguar finds it afterward impossible to "disenjag." If Jesus on His Second Coming is not a happy camper ("They want me to jump without an umbrella. . . . A pancake from God"), it's even worse for the bandit Fermino. While Fermino's soul goes straight to heaven,

> On earth his corpse was split in two. The body was thrown to the vultures and the head to the scientists. . . . Their analysis revealed a psychopathic personality evidenced by certain bulges in the skull characteristic of cold-blooded assassins from the mountains of obscure countries. [His] criminal destiny was also apparent from one ear that was nine millimeters shorter than the other, and from the pointed head and oversized jaws with large eyeteeth that continued chewing after he was dead.

Whimsy with a sting: This Magical Marxist began his vagabond life as a newspaperman, in Montevideo and again in Buenos Aires, always leaving town a step before a dictatorship got him. On that road, he became a historian. His *Memory of Fire* trilogy is famously anecdotal and juxtapositional, a rollercoaster and Ferris wheel. (Imagine an account of our century that leaps in a single bound from Superman to the Bay of Pigs, while keeping one eye on General Trujillo as he reviews the troops at West Point with an ivory fan, another eye on Carmen Miranda dancing for the King of Belgium with a banana, and a third on Pancho Villa reading the *Arabian Nights*.) Late in the 1980s, however, after completing *Century of the Wind*, Galeano turned to something different—still political, still literary, still anthropological, but a lot more personal.

In *The Book of Embraces* (1991), we heard about his thinning hair, his heart attack, and his wife, Helena, for whom at night "a line formed of dreams wishing to be dreamed, but it was not possible to dream them all." We got gossip about such buddies as Pablo Neruda, Julio Cortázar, and Gabriel García Márquez. And, as if Latin American boom-boom had for a night cohabited with Pascal and Lichtenberg, there were eavesdroppings, aphorisms, minitexts, and footnotes on friendship, courage, muscle, wind, theology, art, silence, a snowy beach in Catalonia, and the culture of terror. "There is a division of labor in the ranks of the powerful," Galeano explained; "The army, paramilitary organizations, and hired assassins concern themselves with social contradictions and the class struggle. Civilians are responsible for speeches." And: "In the final analysis, it doesn't bother anyone very much that politics be democratic so long as the economy is not." And: "We are all mortal, until the first kiss and the second glass of wine." He also collected graffiti. On a Bogotá wall: "Proletarians of all lands, unite!" (And, scrawled underneath in another hand: "final notice.") Or, in Montevideo: "Assist the police. Torture yourself."

Walking Words is an anthology of stories about "ghouls and fools," derived from the urban and rural folklore of the Americas, with "windows" between chapters for the stray paradox and sneaky afflatus, and woodcut illustrations, like sarcophagus rubbings, by the Brazilian *cordel* artist José Francisco Borges: a kind of commonplace book of mysterious transcendence. But it could also be thought of as a line of dreams wishing to be dreamed by Helena. Besides Jesus and Calamity Jane, shoemakers, coachmen, fishermen, wine-sellers, coffee-grinders, and socialist-realist poets dream about tango dancers, soccer stars, and Moon People; frogs with feathers and parrots "born from grief"; Saint George on a Yamaha motorcycle, warlocks on seahorses with vests of burning fat, and a Virgin at sea so busy resuscitating the drowned that "she didn't have time for bad luck on dry land." Often these dreamers feel awful, as if "dirty water rains inside me." Or like a tabloid headline: "KILLED MOTHER WITHOUT GOOD CAUSE." A cure for the blues will not come cheap: "Candido charged for his miracles in advance. He was no cheap saint. 'What do they want?' he'd grumble. 'A favor from God for the price of a banana?'"

Yet always, somehow, there is levitation: "Memory eats the dead. The vulture, too. Just like memory, the vulture flies." Besides: "We come from an egg much smaller than the head of a pin, and we live on a rock that spins around a dwarf star into which it will someday crash. But we're made of light, as well as carbon and oxygen and shit and death and so much else." Finally, wonderfully: "The Church says: *The body is a sin.* Science says: *The body is a machine.* Advertising says: *The body is a business.* The body says: *I am a fiesta.*" It's oddly Rabelaisian, with a Kurtness of Vonnegut—as if magic tricks and peasant cunning were still capable of subverting the greedhead warlocks and the banal surfeit and oppressive patterning of the admass media/consumer grid. One dreams so, like Helena. I am reminded of a passage from his *Book of Embraces.* In Peru, Galeano drew a picture of a pig on a little boy's hand. Suddenly,

> I was surrounded by a throng of little boys demanding at the top of their lungs that I draw animals on their little hands cracked by dirt and cold, their skin of burnt leather: one wanted a condor and one a snake, others preferred little parrots and owls, and some asked for a ghost or a dragon. Then, in the middle of this racket, a little waif who barely cleared a yard off the ground showed me a watch drawn in black ink on his wrist. "An uncle of mine who lives in Lima sent it to me," he said. "And does it keep good time?" I asked him. "It's a little slow," he admitted.

So we are all, a little slow, but in spite of the odds . . . a fiesta.

Epilogue

Happy Bastille Day!

Observe the twitchy green-eyed only child, a year younger than his century: a seventeen-year-old *lycée* dropout, gorged on Nietzsche, Spengler, and Dostoyevsky. A twenty-year-old chain-smoking pistol-packing Paris dandy, with moleskin gloves and a cape like Baudelaire's. A twenty-two-year-old Dada-disdaining dealer in pornographic books and speculator on the stock exchange, who lost his wife's shirt in a Mexican silver mine investment and promptly vamoosed for Southeast Asia. In Cambodia, in 1923, he stole basreliefs from a Khmer temple and stood trial in Phnom Penh. In Saigon, in 1924, he edited an anticolonialist newspaper till French authorities shut it down. In between, he *may* have helped organize the Young Annam League, a precursor to the Vietminh, but probably not. He certainly never met the Comintern agent Borodin. The closest he got to the Chinese revolution was Hong Kong in 1925 during a general strike. And yet in 1933—after five warm-up books, two of them surreal whimsies; after a preface to *Lady Chatterley's Lover* in lieu of a biography of Edgar Allan Poe; after digging up "Greco-Buddhist" potsherds in the Afghan outback and squatting with Sufi sages under a pomegranate tree in a miniature garden in exotic Isfahan—this thirty-two-year-old magazine-editing, art-collecting, hemp-smoking German Expressionist cinéaste used that Chinese revolution to think out loud, in a novel of genius, about how to die with dignity in the absence of God, having acted meaningfully on behalf of others.

André Malraux was a sketch. Hearing, in January 1928, that Trotsky had been banished by Stalin to Siberia, he proposed a literary commando force to bail him out. It was as harebrained as his plan in 1971 to lead an expeditionary force to fight for Bangladesh. (On the other hand he *did* muster an international air squadron to drop Republican bombs on Franco.) Nor was Trotsky grateful. When he finally got around on Prinkipo to reading *The Conquerors,* he accused Malraux of "excesses of individualism," "esthetic caprice," and "condescending irony" toward the Chinese masses. Which didn't deter André from bearding Leon in his next exilic den, at a seaside villa in Saint-Palais, where, with a revolver between them like a paperweight, they discussed Pasternak, movies, and death. After which, if we believe André, Leon would commend *Man's Fate* to his own New York publisher while its author left for the Arctic Circle to collect icy local color for a never-written novel about the insurrectionary petroleum workers of Baku—and to marvel at seagulls eating rainbows.

But we can't believe André. He lied a lot. Many of us have flown in planes over Africa. We have not, however, done so in a two-seater, to spot what we insist is the lost city of the Queen of Sheba, nor made an emergency landing at Obock, in northeast Somaliland, where they gave us a glass of Pernod and a live gazelle. (And did you know that Buddha spoke to the gazelles?) Many of us have been to Russia. We did not, however, say we met Stalin at Gorky's summer dacha. Nor, even if we had, would we have chatted with Uncle Joe about Laurel and Hardy. (Thinking he'd dropped his passport, André looked under the table to see "Stalin, Molotov and the rest of them trying to twist their fingers like Stan Laurel.") Many of us have also been to Kyoto, and admired Takanobu's *Portrait of Taira no Shigemori.* But not with a portentous Japanese friend to explain: "You want to be *in* the painting, whereas we want to be outside it. European painting has always wanted to catch the butterflies, eat the flowers, and sleep with the dancers."

All this, mind you, *before* the Spanish Civil War, during which he wrote another novel, made his only film, and annoyed Hemingway. (Being Malraux, he fought the battle of Madrid from the birthplace of Cervantes.) *Before* the fall of France, after which "Colonel Berger" joined the Resistance, wrote *The Walnut Trees of Altenburg,* abandoned a monograph on Lawrence of Arabia, twice escaped his German captors and decided, without telling anyone why, that Communists were now the bad guys. (Being Malraux, he says he also faced a mock execution, just like Dostoyevsky. And, needing a place to stash his weapons, he found a lovely cave, with paintings of giant aurochs and swimming stags, and it was of course Lascaux.) *Before*, famously, de Gaulle, who, after some pillow talk about Marx, Michelet, Clausewitz, Diderot, and Catherine the Great, summons him to service in two postwar cabinets. Upon which accession to power, wearing a chartreuse camel's hair topcoat in the rumble seat of a raven-black chauffeur-driven Simca limousine, the double-breasted Minister of Culture declares: "Adventure only exists now at the level of governments." He will write no more fiction, unless we count his autobiographies.

Those autobiographies — the confabulating *Anti-Memoirs,* the pleiadic *Felled Oaks,* and the little evasions, *Picasso's Mask* and *Lazarus,* attached to the big ones like tassels to a Hide-A-Bed — are especially suspect. Where he might have cleared up questions of fact, he quotes from his fiction. Instead of intimate, we get oracular. Not a word on his first wife, Clara, who made such fun of him in five volumes of *her* memoirs. His sons died before him. So did their mother, Josette. His father gassed himself. His grandfather split his skull with an ax. Looking back on the rainbow arc of a long career, from swashbuckler to bureaucrat, from red flag to the Cross of Lorraine, he averts his eyes with a signature wince: "I once wrote: 'What do I care about what matters only to me?' Egoism only tends to make us prefer ourselves, with a muddled vehemence." His latest biographer, Curtis Cate, calls this dreamy indifference to homely truths "Cubistic." It is also vanity inverted. Malraux knew we'd have to deduce him from the holes in his alibi. "Modern man," he told his doctor in *Lazarus,* "has been fashioned on the basis of exemplary stereotypes: saint, chevalier, caballero, gentleman, bolshevik . . ." Existential before Sartre, Absurd before Camus, Structuralist before Lévi-Strauss, he *styled* himself, even as history appeared to mimic him. He wrote *The Mad Realm* (1922) before he had left France, much less seen Persia; *The Conquerors* (1928) before he made it to Canton; *Days of Wrath* (1936) before either arrest by the Nazis; *Man's Hope* (1938) before a bell tolled Papa. From Goya, Piranesi, de Sade, and Gothic novels he imagined prison, torture, and terror before the century franchised them. Maybe he was thinking of himself when he said of Saint-Just: "He wanted to live inside history as holy men inside their faith, to be confounded with the Republic as saints lose themselves in God."

It is impossible to write a dull biography of Malraux, and, like Jean Lacouture and Axel Madsen, Curtis Cate hasn't. But his feeble idea of literary criticism is to quote from old reviews, so you'd never guess that *Man's Fate* is a masterpiece, *Man's Hope* isn't, and *Paper Moons* is silly. It's not even clear his grand theme was fraternity, which is the meaning of the great scene in *Man's Fate* when Katov gives up his cyanide to Kyo to face the locomotive's fire alone. Kassner in *Days of Wrath* is saved by a stranger's self-sacrifice. The best pages in *Man's Hope* describe a "human chain" in the Descent to Linares. *The Walnut Trees of Altenburg* snaps out of its somnambulism to report on Bulgako in World War I, after the Germans release poison gas on their Russian enemy, are then appalled by what they've done, and converge in an "assault of pity" to bear the bodies out of a chaotic forest "in which stricken and dead swarmed like brothers under the blood-stained greatcoats gesticulating in the wind." He summed up in *Lazarus*: "I have come to the conclusion that the enigma of cruelty is no more tantalizing than that of the simplest act of heroism or love." Besides: "Fellowship is often as powerful as death itself." By then, of course, he had found fraternity everywhere *except* in revolution: in masks and masterworks and crucifixions. In art, rather than in radical politics, he honed his hedge against death. Fetishism replaced history as his symbolic compost. Instead of the class struggle, Great Men. Instead of social justice, individual genius. Instead of barricades and burning zones, a "Museum Without Walls" into which he disappeared, like Old Gisors into opium. Picasso told him: "The cat eats the bird; Picasso eats the cat; painting eats Picasso." The century ate Malraux.

*   *   *

And now I must make my own confession. This rummaging in the laundry hampers of dead French writers seemed like a good idea for Bastille Day. After talking about André and fraternity, I'd talk about André and *glory*. Isn't the temptation to be glorious more French than cheese, an affliction as much of left as right, what sociobiologists call a "culturgen"? Don't they all, with sword, pen, and penis, long for a tomb like Napoleon's, a sarcophagus of imperial pink porphyry under a Baroque dome, quasi-Egyptian? And don't the rest of us, agnostics about reality itself, enjoy making fun of the ink they spill on the altars of their histrionic self-importance — Sartre doping himself up on corydane to kill God, trying to explain to factory workers "the true intersubjectivity of the proletariat," quacking like a Donald Duck? Camus, having first removed the free pair of shoes he received each year from the government because his *pied noir* father had died for France, swinging from Gide's trapeze? Simone Weil starving herself to death in solidarity with the Resistance? In this scheme, which I now abandon, trolling for glory would prove to be contagious even for the Belgian-born Georges Simenon, who complained when Camus won the Nobel Prize: "Do you believe that asshole got it and not me?" Only the Dublin-born Samuel Beckett, who fled from Stockholm as if from a "catastrophe," seems to have been immune to such Prometheus Envy, a *force de frappe.*

But then I read a June 23, 1997, editorial, bumptious even for *The New Republic,* sneering at the French. What had the French done to *The New Republic*? "In the grand tradition that produced the reigns of Robespierre, Napoleon and Vichy," the French had voted socialist. Imagine the radical impudence. First, they want jobs; then they want pensions. "Obtuse and suicidal," said *The Neo Republican.* Some of us are anxious to forget where we came from (an older Republic) so as not to think about who we have become (glad rags on a Beltway hanger, sperm deposits in a Bundesbank). It's as if Beckett had delivered on a promise made in 1936:

My next work shall be on rice paper wound around a spool, with a perforated line every six inches. . . . The length of each chapter will be carefully calculated to suit with the average free motion. And with every copy a free sample of some laxative to promote sales. The Beckett Bowel Books, Jesus in farto. Issued in imperishable tissue. Thistle-down end papers. All edges disinfected. 1000 wipes of clean fun. Also in Braille for anal pruritics. All Sturm and no Drang.

But scruples about social and economic justice that were upon a time the normal respiration of informed intelligence are now in disrepute. Neocons everywhere have concluded that the French Revolution was itself a terrible idea, dreamed up by disgruntled aristocrats, egged on by what Simon Schama, in *Citizens,* calls the "polemical incontinence" of hack writers and bad actors who had read too much Rousseau and succumbed to Romanticism, "with its addiction to the Absolute and the Ideal; its fondness for the vertiginous and the macabre; its concept of political energy as, above all, electrical; its obsession with the heart; its preference for passion over reason, for virtue over peace." In Schama's opinion, despite a corrupt court, an absentee king, incompetent ministries, suspended *parlements,* a huge foreign debt, a domestic recession unto bread riots, and a tax system of unimaginable inequity, Louis XVI's *ancien régime* was well on its way to becoming a modern capitalist state. All it needed was better middle-management. What it got, instead, was a revolutionary calendar with a month for wine and a month for mist, weeks for hazelnuts and roses, festival days for heroic deeds and brilliant opinions, and hearts of martyrs in agate urns. Masonic eyes and the *Marseillaise*! Isis and pornography! Truffles and a guillotine! Beware of poetry and the passions; the head you off may be your own.

I'm in favor of writers and actors. I long for an agate urn. When I can't even get Barbara Ehrenreich or Marshall Berman on their answering machines, I'm nostalgic for a culture where literary intellectuals went out in public without Leon Wieseltier's permission, gathered in cafés to write books, read newspapers, and send up indignations like Montgolfier balloons;

where Voltaire made religious toleration and the French criminal code his personal business after Jean Calas was broken on a wheel; where Zola made Dreyfus *his* business, and Gide, the Congo, and Sartre, Algeria. "The writer has a place in his age," said Sartre. "Each word has an echo, as does each silence."

Moreover, I like to be reminded that once there were writers for whom the convulsions of our time were a revelation, an insult or a wound, instead of a thesis topic cross-linked in a Nexis search to syndicate a rant. I am not one of those prurient readers who seek in every biography of an intellectual the score marks of his waffling on the twentieth-century grid; for whom each bygone text is an autopsy of Gods That Failed, an I-Told-You-So rather than a first draft scribbled in blood on a bandage; who consult Arthur Koestler, Victor Serge, Gustav Regler, and Manes Sperber solely as litmus tests; who are incapable of imagining backward except to finger sores, and seem never with a shiver to appreciate nobility of sentiment, heroic action, or genuine regret. From comfort zones like the cable chat shows, these Chicken Littles, whose bravest deed has been to deplore affirmative action, presume they would have had Lenin's number before the Finland Station and Trotsky's before Kronstadt, and dare now to snipe at the safely dead, whose body of work they ate like mushrooms when they were young enough to be better people. As Beckett observed of Proust and time: "We are not merely more weary because of yesterday, we are other."

Anyway isn't it nifty to know that pubescent André liked to whistle arias from Massenet's *Manon*, that blue-eyed Sam hated Bach and wanted to be a pilot, that altar boy Georges was a whiz at marbles and anti-Semitic? And a comfort to hear that, grown up to young manhood, Malraux, when he wasn't comparing Browning automatics with Picasso, and Simenon, when he wasn't sleeping with ten thousand women (two minutes each!), and Beckett, when he wasn't sitting still for both games of a Mets doubleheader on his only visit to New York, all went in Paris at the same time to the same movies, plays, concerts, exhibits, and apothecaries, all drank dangerously too much, and all were reviewed, in *Nouvelle Revue Française,* by Jean Paulhan? And a caution to learn that, as brave as Malraux and Beckett both were during the Occupation, joining the Resistance, Simenon was more craven than Picasso, with fewer friends to betray; that while André recovered from his wounds and Sam built his hospital for the Red Cross, the creator of Maigret was selling off his movie rights to Nazi filmmakers and hiding out for ten years in America from accusations that he had been a collaborator?

I am chided for my taste for publicity, as though God Himself had no need of his church bells! (Simenon)

The story, doubtless apocryphal, goes that Alfred Hitchcock once telephoned: "Hello, may I please speak to Mr. Simenon?" "One moment, please. . . . I'm sorry, he's just started a novel." "That's all right, I'll wait."

He was not a nice man, maybe because his mother seems never to have kissed the boy, or taken him on her lap, and always loved his brother best. His father, who sold insurance, couldn't get a policy on his own life because of poor health, and died with assets of three hundred francs. Even before this death, mom took in boarders, some of whom were Russian Jews who made Georges read Gogol. He quit school and the Catholic Church simultaneously, preferring women and sin. After brief military service, guarding a stable of cavalry horses, he caught on as a cub reporter at the right-wing Liége *Gazette,* soon achieved his own column, and fell in with the local bohemian set, of which he made merciless fun in his first published novel, at age eighteen, while also writing a series of articles based on the *Protocols of the Elders of Zion*: "The Jewish octopus thus extends its tentacles into all classes of society and into all spheres, where its influence is still felt. And so it will be until the world finally decides to react. Unless by then it is too late."

After three years at the *Gazette* he was off to Paris as a dogsbody and ghostwriter for various Action Française types. He married Regine so as not to have to prepare his own meals and clean his own apartment. The best advice he got at *Le Matin* was from Colette (!), who told him to rid his prose of all the "litera-ture" (adverbs). Between 1924 and 1931, he published 190 pulpy "novels for secretaries" under seventeen pseudonyms, with titles like *Secret of the Llamas* and *The Panther Sulks*. While he spent each day churning out his eighty pages per, you'd find him at night in flat cap and knickerbockers at the Boeuf sur le Toit with Maurice Chevalier and Coco Chanel, about which time he also had a love affair with Josephine Baker and her "famous butt."

He's still remembered for something he didn't do in 1927. Though he'd signed a contract to write a novel for *Paris-Matin* in a single week, in full view of the public in a glass cage at the Moulin Rouge—hadn't Molière written *Le Bourgeois Gentil-homme* in one month, on command? And Victor Hugo *Bug-Jargal* in two weeks? And Voltaire *Candide* in a single night?—ridicule dissuaded him. He got himself a boat instead and sailed all the way to Finnish Lapland, typing up a tempest, which may be when, in 1928, he first imagined Maigret, the cop who seeks "to understand and not to judge." Berlin, Africa, Tahiti, Gal-apagos, enormous sums of money, and many defamations of character followed, which meant Saville Row suits, silk shirts, designer fedoras, Delage sports cars, Medoc wines, supper at Maxim's, and the friendly interest of André Gide, whom he first met in 1935, and whose homosexuality filled him with contempt, but who woozily announced in 1939: "I consider Simenon . . . the greatest and most authentic novelist we have in French literature today."

Although I've read all of his Maigrets, some of them several times by accident, I am not an admirer of Simenon's "hard" or "destiny" novels, of which there were so many, hundreds, that his biographer, Pierre Assouline, has organized his criticism in thematic clumps, like "key events," "leitmotif," "obsessional re-turn," and "incantatory formula." James M. Cain, his closest American analogue and an altogether more agreeble human be-ing, did it better. The *Intimate Memoirs* were embarrassing and the late-life tape-recorded *Dictées* so pinheaded and inconsequential that it's no wonder Helen Wolff declined to publish them. But here's something odd. He seems seldom to have had a kind word to say about any other living writer. There is little evidence he read them. While Malraux read practically everybody and published many of them, and Beckett professed enthusiasm for everything from *Nausea* to Agatha Christie to *Catcher in the Rye,* Simenon spent his adult years watching TV, visiting brothels, and talking about sex to Henry Miller and Federico Fellini, except when Charlie Chaplin dropped in to use the swimming pool at the Swiss estate with the dollar sign flaunted like a logo on its seigneurial gate.

Maybe the ex-husband deserved his ex-wife's savage memoir, *The Golden Phallus.* Not even Simenon, however, deserves what happened to him as a father. After calling him on the phone and asking him to tell her that he loved her, his daughter, Marie-Jo, shot herself to death.

Nothing is funnier than unhappiness. (Samuel Beckett, *Endgame*)

Not only was Beckett born ("under the table," he said) with a bad case of the blues, but he also grew up weird. This happens to writers who must first invent themselves, and then their readers. I remember when *Godot* opened in Boston in 1958. Their business done, the actors stayed on stage inviting our questions. Dumbstruck, we hadn't any. What a disappointment we must have been to the playwright. But having grown up morose in a Dublin suburb, he was an acrobat of disappointment. Dierdre Bair and James Knowlson both agree that he smoked too much, hit the Irish whiskey hard, found it difficult to sleep, suffered a nervous breakdown and years of therapy and was susceptible, especially in situations of emotional stress, to boils, cysts, and pleurisy. Not to mention emphysema and Parkinson's. He also had trouble with his eyes, his teeth, his feet, and his mother. As he explained in *The Unnamable*: "I'm looking for my mother to kill her, I should have thought of that a bit earlier, before being born." On the other hand, till the end of his life, he held in his head an image of little Sam walking the hills with his father:

Hand in hand with equal plod they go. In the free hands — no. Free
empty hands. Back turned both bowed with equal plod they go. The
child hand raised to reach the holding hand. Hold the old holding
hand. Hold and be held. Plod on and never recede. Slowly with never
a pause plod on and never recede. Backs turned. Both bowed. Joined
by held holding hands. Plod on as one. One shade. Another shade.

I'm as suspicious as you are of writers and their mothers. But
Sam's mother, puritanical and possessive, seems to have been
why he left Dublin for Paris. Knowlson, an old friend and
founder of the Beckett Archive, with privileged access to diaries
and notebooks and a number of wonderfully interesting things
to say about the influences of painting and music on the novels
and plays, is less given to Freudulence than Bair was. But Sam
himself was obsessively interested in the psychoanalytic. (He
called Freud's biographer "Erogenous Jones.") And it's hard
not to read *Malone Dies* and *The Unnamable* as attempts to rid
himself of mother May. They didn't work. As Bair suggests,
only a "womb fixation" can possibly explain his stuffing of so
many people into mounds (*Happy Days*), urns (*Play*), and trash
cans (*Endgame*).

If I had the use of my body I would throw it out of the window.
So said Malone, dying. But Sam used his as well to swim, golf,
tennis, cricket, and crack up motorcycles. If as a lad he liked
Schopenhauer (gloom), Sam Johnson (scrofula), Dante, and
Céline, he was also partial to Gilbert and Sullivan, Charlie
Chaplin, and, like Stalin and Malraux, Laurel and Hardy. If, in
London, he was a failure at literary journalism (Cyril Connolly
told him to get an honest job); if, in Paris, he was an errand boy
for James Joyce (and an obsession of his daughter's); if *Murphy*
was turned down by forty-two publishers (he kept a list); and if,
after chewing his way to the end of the tether of language, all the
way down to squeak, he'd still call his stories "miseries," nevertheless: Nancy Cunard believed in his genius and paid for it.
Peggy Guggenheim went to bed with him and called him "Ob-
lomov." Duchamp was a buddy; his book on chess inspired

Endgame. And he did last long enough to win a Nobel, unlike Nabokov, Borges, Calvino, or, of course, Simenon.

Do you believe in the life to come? Mine was always that. See him, after the death of his father, flying a kite, reading a horoscope, and visiting a loony bin. See him, in Germany in 1936, drinking beer, eating bananas, contemplating Otto Dix, afraid of heights and appalled by Nazis. See him, his "face like an Aztec eagle," marrying the momlike Suzanne, getting hit by a truck and stabbed by a pimp, translating de Sade, hurting the feelings of Nathalie Sarraute, narrowly escaping death when his Resistance cell was compromised — "merely cursing, under my breath, God and man, under my breath, and the wet Saturday afternoon of my conception." He is impatient with Wagner and Mahler: "Less is more." He spends his money on political prisoners. (As Havel wrote to him: "You are not one of those who give themselves away in small change.") When he dreams, it's of Joyce, who is dying "and being carried at arms length like a quarter of beef." He declares the theme of his life and work to be: "To and fro in shadow, from outer shadow to inner shadow. To and fro, between unattainable self and unattainable non-self."

I used to like to think of Beckett so drunk one night with Giacometti in the Dôme that they trapped themselves in a revolving door and whirled round and round, just like modernism. Now I am struck, not only by his decency and courage, but also by his "Hold and be held." He suffered death more slowly than any other great writer I can think of, and made of it an eerie music. This is heroic and maybe even glorious, like *Man's Fate.* So what happened to Bastille Day? It turns out that *I* want to be glorious, too — like Malraux, to drop bombs on Franco and command tanks in the Resistance even though he'd never learned to drive or fly; like jailbird Havel, to write a new social contract on the stage of the Magic Lantern theater in velvet Prague; like Byron, to die at Missalonghi for a greater cause than tenure, lecture fees, or the approval of the editors of *The New Republic*; to eat the flowers and sleep with the dancers, in a revolutionary month of mists.